SUN TZU
IN SPACE

SUN TZU IN SPACE

WHAT INTERNATIONAL RELATIONS, HISTORY, AND SCIENCE FICTION TEACH US ABOUT OUR FUTURE

GREGORY D. MILLER

NAVAL INSTITUTE PRESS
Annapolis, Maryland

Naval Institute Press
291 Wood Road
Annapolis, MD 21402

© 2023 by Gregory D. Miller

All rights reserved. No part of this book may be reproduced or utilized in any form or by any means, electronic or mechanical, including photocopying and recording, or by any information storage and retrieval system, without permission in writing from the publisher.

ISBN: 978-1-68247-845-5 (hardcover)
ISBN: 978-1-68247-846-2 (ebook)

Library of Congress Cataloging-in-Publication Data is available.

♾ Print editions meet the requirements of ANSI/NISO z39.48–1992 (Permanence of Paper). Printed in the United States of America.

31 30 29 28 27 26 25 24 23   9 8 7 6 5 4 3 2 1
First printing

*  *

TO KELCIE, JAY, BROOKE, TREY, AND SILAS.

YOU WILL LEAD THE FUTURE GENERATIONS OF HUMANITY,

YOU MAKE ME PROUD, AND I CANNOT WAIT TO SEE

WHERE LIFE TAKES YOU.

* ✸ *

CONTENTS

	List of Tables	viii
	Acknowledgments	ix
	INTRODUCTION	1
CHAPTER 1	HEGEMONY: THE EAGLE LANDS AGAIN	15
CHAPTER 2	THE BALANCE OF POWER: PLANETARY PARTNERSHIPS	51
CHAPTER 3	PAX TERRA: A FEDERATION OF STATES	89
CHAPTER 4	HOSTILE TAKEOVER: BIRTH OF THE MULTIPLANETARY CORPORATIONS	131
CHAPTER 5	MARX ON MARS: SOCIAL REVOLUTION IN SPACE	168
CHAPTER 6	VENUS RISING: A FEMINIST FUTURE	209
CHAPTER 7	AN ARTIFICIAL FUTURE: THE PROMISE AND PERILS OF SINGULARITY	248
	CONCLUSION	284
	Notes	301
	Bibliography	329
	Index	353

TABLES

1.1	EVALUATING THE HEGEMONIC SYSTEM	44
2.1	EVALUATING THE BALANCE OF POWER SYSTEM	81
3.1	EVALUATING THE FEDERATION SYSTEM	125
4.1	EVALUATING THE CORPORATE SYSTEM	163
5.1	EVALUATING THE MARXIST SYSTEM	203
6.1	EVALUATING THE FEMINIST SYSTEM	243
7.1	EVALUATING TWO AI FUTURES	280
C.1	FINAL ASSESSMENTS OF ALL SCENARIOS	294
C.2	SCENARIO RANKINGS	296

ACKNOWLEDGMENTS

One of my earliest childhood recollections was seeing *Star Wars* in the theater at age four. That movie, especially that opening scene, made a huge impression on me, and I still remember how I felt staring up at the screen while the star destroyer passed overhead. Forty-five years of life (especially my time spent in graduate school and then in academia) made me pessimistic about humanity's future. Studying wars, military alliances, and terrorism for more than two decades often had me questioning the possibility of cooperation between states, groups, or even people. A more recent professional focus on space as well as time spent rekindling my affection for science fiction has renewed my optimism and sense of awe about our future. This book is, at least partly, an attempt to affirm that there is hope for our future. That hope may lie in human nature, in technology, in corporations, or in an international organization that unites all of humanity. But regardless of the source, I believe our children and grandchildren will do what previous generations talked about but have been unable to do: to venture out into the solar system and live beyond Earth. I hope that this work contributes to that future in some small way.

Like most books, this one is the product of several helpful and generous people. I want to thank Adam Kane at Naval Institute Press for embracing the idea when I pitched it to him and for pushing me to pursue it. I thank Glenn Griffith, also at Naval Institute Press, for shepherding the book through the publication process. Thank you as well to the reviewers who provided thoughtful comments on an earlier draft and helped make the final product better, and to Lisa Yambrick for her edits making the prose more readable and logical. Any remaining errors or mistakes are my own (though I will blame them on this old, glitchy laptop).

The idea for this book came to me while I was a professor at the Joint Advanced Warfighting School (JAWS) in Norfolk, Virginia. It is impossible to express how valuable it was to work with such scholars as Bryon Greenwald and Keith Dickson for my first job in professional military education. We spent countless hours debating the nature of man and the definition of war and coming up with ideas for research projects, including one that became this book. Thank you both for your friendship and mentorship.

I also thank my current employer, the Air Command and Staff College (ACSC), in Montgomery, Alabama. The school, my supervisors, and my colleagues created an environment in which scholarship is important and valued—but usually not taken overly seriously. The views expressed in this book are mine alone and do not reflect the policies or opinions of Air University, the Department of Defense, or the U.S. government.

I am so honored to be able to teach some of our country's finest military officers and federal employees, as well as some fantastic international officers. I learn something from you every time I step in the classroom, and I hope that I have given you some piece of knowledge or information that helps you succeed. Thank you for what you do in the service of your country and for challenging me to never stop learning.

For incredibly helpful feedback and encouragement on the earliest drafts of my first few chapters, I thank Mike Pavelec. Mike is a friend, an ally, and, for most of the past decade, a colleague (first at JAWS and now at ACSC). He is an incredible instructor and scholar, but his friendship is most valuable when we simply sit around and throw ideas at each other (or debate the best album of all time, and I am sticking with "Weird Al" Yankovic *In 3-D*).

Finally, I thank my family for the support and love they provided throughout the writing and editing process. To my wife, Mandy, in particular, even though we see the world through different lenses (and have very different taste in music and movies), you are everything I need to balance me personally and professionally. I thank you for being a wonderful mother, wife, and friend. Although I dedicated this book to our children (and grandchild), I dedicate my life to you . . . as long as you keep watching science fiction with me—or at least put up with me watching it.

INTRODUCTION

> Before the engagement, one who determines in the
> ancestral temple that he will be victorious has found that
> the majority of factors are in his favor.
> —SUN TZU, *The Art of War*[1]

We have reached the point in history at which human exploration, colonization, and exploitation of space will soon be a reality. More importantly, humanity's future will be tied to our ability to expand beyond Earth, first into, and eventually beyond, other parts of the solar system. Exploration is a primary human driver, but our long-term survival also requires that we not "keep all our eggs on one planet." Even an outpost on the moon, while mitigating some risk, would not provide the resources necessary for sustaining a growing human population, which might not be able to survive without external support and aid. Mars could become self-sustaining at some point, but that would likely require new technology and at least some minimal level of cooperation between states. This premise is the starting point for this book: humanity is in space and is at least trying to develop permanent, sustained outposts on other solar bodies. This could occur in several ways, and each chapter offers analysis and discussion of a different possible future.

This book draws on our current understanding of international relations (IR) theory, history, and science fiction to identify plausible paths forward as humans venture into space. Each chapter begins with a scenario derived initially from IR scholarship, draws on history to identify the likely trajectories as well as the pros and cons of each scenario, and then identifies the steps humanity must take now to either realize or prevent each outcome. Each chapter also uses science fiction—books, television shows, and films—to illustrate how these different futures might look.

The rest of this introduction more thoroughly acquaints readers with the premise and purpose of the book, summarizes the main worldviews in IR, discusses how history and science fiction add detail to the scenarios, and then briefly highlights the different approaches in each chapter.

This book was born of my fondness for the academic disciplines of IR and history, as well as my affection for science fiction. Several recent scholarly books connect IR to popular science fiction and fantasy culture phenomena including *Harry Potter*, *Battlestar Galactica*, zombies, *Star Wars*, and *Game of Thrones*.[2] This book is intended to appeal to a similar readership, but it has a slightly different purpose. Its goal is not simply to make IR theory and history more accessible to the public or to science fiction fans, but also to use the links between those academic disciplines and science fiction to discuss and analyze seven possible futures involving human exploration of the solar system. The broader goal of the book is to identify the best strategies to pursue now to aim for the future that will be most advantageous to humanity—or at a minimum, to get us thinking about the ways in which we can draw upon our past and present to shape our possible future.

The seven scenarios presented in this book, each of which is written as a future history, use worldviews or schools of thought in IR as their starting points. These perspectives provide different lenses through which IR scholars seek to explain and understand the behavior of states in the international system. These same lenses are the starting points to develop each of the seven scenarios for humanity's potential in space. In addition, because the scenarios arise from IR theories and concepts, and because many of those theories emerge out of historical analysis, there are clear linkages between the scenarios and real events in military and diplomatic history. Several such historical examples in each chapter provide a discussion of lessons and implications for humanity moving forward.

To add to the richness of the narrative, I tie these scenarios, which occur in space in the future, to classical works in science fiction as well as some of the more contemporary stories. The depth of the science fiction literature allows for significant comparisons with IR and history and helps clarify what the future scenarios might look like, how actors might behave, and what the pros and cons of each possible system would be for all of humanity. Essentially, this book melds my academic and personal interests to suggest a path forward as humanity reaches for the stars—or, more accurately in the short term, for the closest planets orbiting our star.

This book relies on a few basic assumptions. The first is that humanity will expand into space in the relatively near future. A future Earth in which humans are still bound to the planet will have its own possible scenarios, similar in many ways to the ones presented here but even more heavily connected to the past and affected by continued resource scarcity (which could be alleviated as humanity expands into the solar system).

I also assume that while history never completely repeats itself, we can identify general patterns in the behavior of humans and states, and that the lessons we draw from history, if understood properly, can help us avoid some of the mistakes of the past, even when applied to a future in space. Thus, it is not enough to simply derive future scenarios from IR; we also need to examine historical parallels to identify the pros and cons of each scenario and determine how to minimize the negative results or costs.

Finally, I assume away aliens or any kind of extraterrestrial involvement in this future, which would pose its own challenges and generate somewhat different scenarios. Some of the science fiction I reference does include extraterrestrial elements, but the seven scenarios focus on humanity exclusively. The central question is: How can humanity expand into space in a way that is productive and profitable, without being destructive to either ourselves or our environments?

EVALUATING THE SCENARIOS

One of the biggest challenges in developing a scenario for each chapter was determining the outcome of events as positive, negative, or some mix of the two. One concern was to avoid writing the scenarios to achieve desired outcomes and therefore advocate for certain choices moving forward. The counter is simply that the scenarios are the best representation I could make of each worldview and its theories. I wrote each scenario after completing the IR and historical sections of that chapter so that the greatest influence on the scenarios would be the historical analogies and IR theories themselves. The result is, I believe, an accurate—or at least plausible—scenario that is consistent with each worldview.

The common thread woven through each chapter is Sun Tzu's classic work, *The Art of War*. The relationship between the seven scenarios and Sun Tzu is related to the maxim in the epigraph: that wars are won by the side that has the best information, that is better prepared, and that avoids wars they cannot win. The goal of this book is to minimize catastrophic choices so that humanity can achieve a future that benefits the most people. This book does not present any scenario as inherently good or bad, although readers' worldviews will color their perceptions of the relative advantages and disadvantages and thus determine their preferred scenario. My standard for evaluation of each scenario is that humanity should actively pursue whichever future will provide the greatest good for the least cost in four areas: reducing the likelihood of major war (war that fundamentally alters the number of great powers or causes a dramatic shift in the balance of power); promoting human space exploration; advancing science and technology (S&T); and improving human standards of living (SoL).

These four goals have their origins in the enduring interests, or national security pillars, laid out in several recent U.S. National Security Strategies (NSSs): security, prosperity, values, and international order.[3] While these interests appear as national goals in the NSS, they apply here in a more universal sense, to all of humanity, to help judge the preferred future. They are not perfect parallels, but they provide standards by which we can evaluate each scenario.

If we take security as the survival of humanity, rather than simply the survival of a country, then space exploration is the most important step for ensuring the continued and long-term existence of human beings. Prosperity for many in the future will depend on improvements in S&T, including advances in artificial intelligence, robotics, and human enhancement. Values, or principles, are the foundation for improving human SoL, because without those improvements, it will be increasingly difficult for people to pursue life, liberty, and happiness. The types of advances included here are those that would reduce poverty, hunger, illness, and the like, not just for one population or class of people, but for all humans. The comparison does not suggest that equality of wealth or power will be the result, but rather that the scenario leads most people to be better off than they otherwise would be. Finally, I interpret international order, or stability, as minimizing major wars between the primary political actors of the time, whether they continue to be nation-states or other actors such as multinational corporations or entire planets. There should be no expectation that we will eliminate political violence from humanity, whether that violence takes the form of war, revolution, terrorism, or something else. As Sun Tzu suggests in the very first line of *The Art of War*, "Warfare is the greatest affair of state, the basis of life and death, the Way [Tao] to survival or extinction."[4] But decreasing its frequency, or at least its destructiveness, especially between the most powerful actors, benefits humanity.

There is obviously some overlap between these measures of success, but they are valid goals independent of one another. For instance, if enhanced S&T helps reduce poverty, hunger, and illness, better SoL could be the result. But one can also imagine a focus on great advances in S&T coming at the expense of some portions of the population. Likewise, S&T could facilitate space exploration, but advances in SoL resulting from S&T could also lull humanity into believing exploration is unnecessary or too risky. Therefore, each of these four goals is evaluated independently for the seven scenarios, and I intend to treat each scenario as equally plausible and capable of producing both benefits and costs.

INTERNATIONAL RELATIONS AS A GUIDE

IR scholars produced a great deal of work over the past century on a variety of actors and activities in the international political system. We still cannot predict how states or people will behave, but we are more capable than ever of identifying and explaining trends in behavior ranging from the declaration of wars to the formation of alliances to the development of international laws and norms. Randall Schweller suggests that IR theories will begin to lose some of their explanatory power because the international system, like all closed systems, will tend to move toward entropy and fragmentation, meaning disorder, chaos, and unpredictability.[5] While his logic is sound and somewhat disturbing, the bright side is that Schweller fails to account for the long term, in which international politics no longer applies just to Earth-bound actors. Even if we accept his argument for the moment, if we want to rescue IR theory, then the closed system needs to be opened. The very point of this book is to suggest that a significantly more open system is not far in the future. Even more importantly, this book highlights how IR theory will continue to be useful for understanding and explaining the behavior of political actors.

Background for each of the chapters draws on some of the most widely used and cited worldviews, theories, and concepts from IR scholarship. A worldview, sometimes referred to as a paradigm or school of thought, is a philosophy or conception of how the world works and why actors generally behave the way they do. Scholars within a worldview accept common assumptions about the nature of the international system and the behavior of units within that system. Worldviews are sometimes incorrectly equated with theories, but theories reside within and under worldviews. The theories that fall under each school of thought rely on the core assumptions of that worldview. Theories are generally testable, whereas the worldviews from which scholars derive theories are philosophical beliefs about reality, nature, and truth rather than testable predictions of behavior. For example, theories within the realist worldview include balance of power, the security dilemma, and offense-defense theory, all of which are addressed in chapters 1 and 2.

The three main worldviews that occupy much of the IR literature are realism, liberalism, and constructivism. This book also addresses Marxism (which has diminished in influence but is not gone), and feminism (which is increasingly influential throughout the social sciences). These five IR worldviews provide the foundation for the seven scenarios. Both realism and liberalism support two different scenarios, partly because of the richness of theories and concepts that comprise those worldviews, but also because important divisions exist within the realist and liberalist worldviews to the point that it would be flawed to treat them as homogenous, relegated to a single scenario.[6]

For example, realists frequently disagree on key elements of state behavior. One such disagreement led to a split into what came to be called offensive realism and defensive realism, and that divide forms the basis for chapters 1 and 2, respectively. Two critical distinctions between these variants, which are fundamentally about how states behave in the international system, have implications for the two scenarios. One difference has to do with whether states seek power or simply security. The other is the degree of agency people and states have over their behavior, meaning whether they control their decisions or are compelled to act in certain ways because of factors in the international system or the state itself. The two chapters on realism dive into these distinctions in greater detail.[7]

Likewise, there is no single liberalist IR worldview. There are three primary strands, two of which I address in this book. One, often referred to as republican liberalism, focuses on the importance of government type and inspired the development of democratic peace theory. This theory suggests that democratic states do not go to war with each other, the implication being that when more states are democratic, the overall likelihood of wars is reduced. Because this book does not address government type in a significant way, I omit this strand of liberalism. Instead, this book focuses on the variants of liberalism that emphasize the role of international organizations and economic interdependence. Scenario three is based on neoliberal institutionalism, a strand of liberalism that examines the role of organizations in promoting cooperation between states. Scenario four draws from commercial liberalism, which focuses on the benefits of trade and economic exchanges between actors, particularly as a means of restraining motivations for war. For example, interdependence theory suggests that wars become less likely as states grow mutually dependent upon each other.

The other three worldviews that provide the basis for my scenarios are Marxism, feminism, and constructivism. Marxism was a popular alternative to realism and liberalism during the Cold War. The label somewhat fell out of favor, but Marxist theories still exist, and scholars use them to explain certain types of international behavior.[8] The main element of Marxism used in this book (in scenario five) has to do with class divisions, both within states and across the international system.

Early Marxists viewed politics as a conflict between the working class and the capitalists who owned most of the wealth in a society. IR scholars apply that same concept to divide the world into core and periphery states, sometimes referred to as North and South or developed and developing. The underlying theme of most Marxist scholarship is the exploitation of the many by the few, whether it be workers and owners in a factory, client states and superpowers, or colonists on other solar bodies and citizens of Earth.

Feminism and constructivism are different from realism and liberalism in that they are more difficult to measure and test and provide few generalizable theories to explain state behavior. They are, however, useful lenses for explaining and describing behavior from nontraditional points of view. Feminism encompasses a variety of works that apply different perspectives to international politics. Many feminist scholars examine the roles of both men and women, contributing a gendered perspective that mainstream IR theory historically lacked. Other feminist scholars focus on how IR perpetuates the masculine perspective, so that even when women are in power, they are judged and evaluated using masculine qualities. Scenario six is derived from feminism and focuses on an extreme future in which women—for biological and practical reasons—are the main actors in a future spacefaring society. In other words, the scenario not only exemplifies the agency of women but also uses an extreme case where men have almost no role to play.

In much the same way, scenario seven is derived from constructivism and takes away at least some human agency and gives it to an artificial intelligence (AI). Constructivism focuses less on the role of human nature or the characteristics of the system than either realists or liberalists would suggest. Instead, it is about the interaction of the many actors in the system, through which identities are created, altered, or destroyed. These identities simultaneously help to construct the society in which the actors reside. Though constructivism is often considered a competing or alternate theory to realism and liberalism, constructivists, like feminists, can be as pessimistic about cooperation as realists or as optimistic about it as liberalists. While realists and liberalists tend to focus on material factors such as wealth and military power, constructivists tend to focus on factors of influence that are more difficult to measure, such as culture, identity, norms of behavior, and even language. This worldview closely aligns with the scenario regarding AI in the role of understanding the literatures on post-human IR and technological agency (though taking the human element out of decision-making poses an interesting question for many IR scholars, not just constructivists).

HISTORICAL ILLUSTRATIONS

In addition to drawing on IR worldviews and theories to develop the seven scenarios, each chapter discusses historical cases to support and illustrate the patterns of behavior that would exist should that scenario mirror our past. This is accomplished in three different ways. First, I use several historical anecdotes when they help illustrate key points in my discussion of IR theory. Historians often accuse political scientists of doing poor history or of cherry-picking historical cases to fit their theories.[9] The purpose of these historical examples is not to support or prove a theory but simply to highlight how the theory might play out in the future based on examples from the past.

Second, each chapter contains more detailed case studies that closely parallel the scenario. These histories illustrate how the scenario might come about, how states will likely behave under those conditions, some of the advantages and disadvantages of the scenario, and some ways that the scenario might end or be disrupted (for good or for bad). These offer more detail than the anecdotes and often provided a foundation for the scenarios themselves. What they are not intended to do is impart new historical evidence or overturn conventional wisdom about a case.

Finally, I draw lessons from Sun Tzu's *The Art of War* for at least some of the main actors in each scenario. Sun Tzu's observations tie the chapters together, but they also introduce some tactical and operational discussions to a book that is otherwise largely strategic and philosophical. Although his central principles, themes, and tenets appear to be common sense today, they are still critical approaches to understanding war and politics, and they will continue to be valid in the future. Each chapter discusses one or more of these principles and their applicability to that specific scenario. Some of the links to Sun Tzu are admittedly tenuous, and a couple are intended to be humorous, considering the different historical eras and translations. In other words, the use of Sun Tzu, though often helpful, should not be taken literally in every case.

In addition, those familiar with history will recognize that many of the fictional scenarios that begin each chapter appear to mirror real-life events. This is intentional, to show how often the present does seem to mirror the past. At the same time, there are differences in the scenarios that distinguish them from history. Not only are different actors included but also events are altered and timelines are changed, both to allow for creative license in the scenarios and to illustrate that even while history appears to repeat itself, it is never an exact replica of what came before. Historical analogies are valuable for understanding a problem and identifying possible solutions, but no two events are perfectly identical, and the lessons we derive must always be tempered by time and circumstances.[10]

SCIENCE FICTION AS A MODEL

A great deal of science fiction related to humanity's future is set in space, and many of the scenarios in this book mirror, and in some cases borrow from, at least parts of storylines from classic books, television, and films in the science fiction genre. The film *2001: A Space Odyssey*, for instance, clearly shows a multinational space station but also shows separate U.S. and Soviet bases on the moon, illustrating cooperation in certain areas and competition in others. *Dune*, although not centered in our solar system, portrays houses pitted against each other, much like nobles in early modern Europe, as well as an emperor who rules over all of them and a corporation that controls space travel. As such, elements of *Dune* play a role in several scenarios.

Exploring science fiction is also a valuable way to tie together our past, present, and future because many of the best works of science fiction take a historical or contemporary problem and place it in a different time or place. This allows us to see how changing even one variable can make those problems better or worse. Joe Haldeman's *Forever War*, for example, clearly draws on Haldeman's experiences in Vietnam—not only the time lost in war, but also the fact that soldiers no longer recognize, or fit into, the society to which they return. The book's ultimate criticism of war is of the inability of two sides to communicate and avoid war in the first place.

To clarify these connections between IR, history, and science fiction, I discuss a handful of examples of literature, television, and film that parallel, or in some way tie to, the scenario presented in each chapter. This is not intended to be an all-inclusive exploration of science fiction and its links to IR theory; nor should references to any works be taken as a recommendation. This exercise is meant to provide a representative sample of the genre and to facilitate understanding of IR for those who are interested in science fiction. There are several wonderful works of science fiction that I omit, but I include the stories and films with which I am most familiar, that closely fit within the broader purpose of the book, or that provide useful parallels to the seven scenarios.[11]

OUTLINE OF THE BOOK

> The dinosaurs became extinct because they didn't have a space program. And if we become extinct because we don't have a space program, it'll serve us right!
> —LARRY NIVEN[12]

The seven scenarios presented in the chapters that follow are not predictions, because there are so many possible variations within each future (some of which I discuss in the chapters). Instead, they are plausible systems that would define the behavior of actors in a future where humanity is in space. None of these scenarios are to be taken exclusively, nor are they an exhaustive list of possibilities but rather are archetypes based on the behavior of states on Earth, both now and in our past.

The first four scenarios are derived from realism and liberalism, the two primary rationalist and positivist approaches to international relations. Rationalist simply means that the theories within these two schools of thought assume all actors in the international system will make logical choices according to their goals and preferences and within any constraints they face. They are positivist in that they believe there is a knowable, objective truth that can be determined through observation and empirical assessment and then understood through reason and logic. For positivists, there are general laws of behavior that allow for the possibility of prediction. For political scientists, that means the methods of science apply to the study of international politics.

Scenario one examines the situation in which a single state becomes the dominant actor in the solar system. The scenario builds off one variant of realism, offensive realism, and focuses on the rise and fall of a potential circumsolar hegemon. It examines several concepts that make up the realist worldview and inform the scenario, identifies historical cases of hegemonic and imperial powers, discusses examples of hegemonic empires in science fiction, and then provides both analysis and recommendations for the emergence of this type of system.

Scenario two is also derived from realism, but from the defensive realism variant. In this scenario, rather than having a single dominant power, the solar system sees competition and rivalry between multiple powerful states. The resulting balance of power has its own historical parallels, as well as several examples from science fiction, that provide lessons learned and lessons to be applied to a future that, for the moment, appears likely based on current trends.

The next two scenarios draw upon liberalism, which is the worldview that most closely competes with realism for primacy in IR theory. In scenario three, states work with one another in an organization, the goal of which is to promote increased cooperation between actors. The development of historical international institutions parallels this notion of a federation of states, in which actors agree to give up some national sovereignty in exchange for the benefits of cooperation. Similar examples are also evident in a variety of science fiction storylines, most notably *Star Trek*.

Scenario four focuses on another variant of liberalism, highlighting the importance of economic linkages in preventing actors from engaging in war against one another. This scenario deviates from the first three scenarios in that it emphasizes the role of corporations as nonstate economic actors with the ability to establish their own control of the solar system, separate from the sovereignty of states. Although no clear-cut historical parallels exist, there are examples of multinational corporations becoming powerful and at least attempting to compete with states for control. There is no shortage of science fiction in which corporations are the primary actors, and some of these stories help identify ways to implement such a scenario if it is deemed most likely to advance human development.

The last three scenarios come from what are often referred to as critical theories or reflectivist approaches.[13] Although there is some variation, these approaches are generally post-positivist, meaning there is no objective truth; every actor has a subjective view of the world and reality. As a result, the attempt to develop laws of behavior is futile. These approaches are often more descriptive and normative, meaning they seek to understand choices without the need to generalize decisions to other actors or situations, and they tend to make arguments about what actors ought to do, rather than focus simply on what they did or will do. There are many diverse alternatives to realism and liberalism, but the most common ones discussed in this book are Marxism, feminism, and constructivism.

Scenario five builds off the less common, but still influential, Marxist school of thought. The scenario starts from the point of social divide and class conflict and eventually considers the possibility of revolution to overthrow inhabitants of other bodies in the solar system because of perceived exploitation. IR concepts discussed in this chapter include the notions of core and periphery as well as *dependencia* theory. Several works of science fiction examine themes of exploitation of colonists by a core planet and the conditions that lead to revolt.

Scenario six relies on a feminist interpretation of IR for building a scenario in which women make up the primary inhabitants of the solar system off of Earth. Although theoretically drawing from a worldview that identifies different feminist and gendered perspectives on the behavior of actors in international politics, this scenario suggests that women are both more physically durable than men in the environs of space and use fewer resources than them, making circumsolar bases more efficient when they are inhabited exclusively, or at least predominantly, by women. The scenario explores some of the implications of this future, especially in comparison to the previous five scenarios. Just as no corporation has ever wrested control from a state, as occurs in scenario four, there are no historical examples of women taking over politics. There are cases of female leaders, so those examples provide some insight into what a feminist future in space might look like. Of course, past female leaders had to play the game according to the existing rules and were judged by, and compared to, their male counterparts. There are plenty of works of feminist science fiction, some of which explore futures where women are not just considered, but play a dominant role, so this is less an original idea than one that needs to be explored for its benefits and challenges to humanity's future.

Scenario seven borrows some elements of constructivism, as well as a common science fiction trope to posit a future in which AI takes much of the decision-making away from humanity. This can be viewed either positively or negatively, but it provides some interesting questions for discussion and debate regarding how humans should develop machines in the future. The connection here with IR is that the scenario poses a challenge, in some ways, to the constructivist notion that every individual has the ability to deconstruct the existing system and to change the world and reality. In a world dominated by AI, this scenario questions whether that perspective is valid and whether the influences of machine learning and superintelligence challenge the ability of humans to shape their identity and their future.

The conclusion summarizes the scenarios and compares the pros and cons from each against what I offer as the four overriding purposes of human involvement in space—minimizing war given its increasingly destructive character, expanding human life beyond Earth, enhancing science and technology, and improving human standards of living. Each of the seven scenarios is weighed against these four goals and compared with one another to identify the scenario that seems to provide the greatest benefits. I then offer some final thoughts on how we should proceed toward that scenario.

CHAPTER 1

HEGEMONY
THE EAGLE LANDS AGAIN

Now when the army of a hegemon or true king attacks a great state, their masses are unable to assemble. When it applies its awesomeness to the enemy, their alliances cannot be sustained. For this reason it does not contend with any alliances under Heaven.
—SUN TZU, *The Art of War*

In 2035 the National Aeronautics and Space Administration (NASA) established the first permanent human colony on the lunar surface. The United States spent nearly two decades expanding its influence over the solar system, subsequently developing colonies on Mars, on Ceres in the asteroid belt between Mars and Jupiter, and then on the Jovian moons Europa and Callisto. These bases, and others that followed, helped the United States establish and expand its circumsolar empire. On each solar system body that was habitable by humans or workable by machines, the United States claimed the most valuable territory, controlled the bulk of the resources and materials on those bodies, and doubled down on its technological advantage to deliver more of its citizens to each colony than all the other spacefaring states combined.[1] The United States also used its military advantages, many of which were born of its space program, to limit the activities of the other states. For instance, it set quotas on the number of people allowed to migrate to the moon and elsewhere, ostensibly to protect the various ecosystems. But such policies were more about preserving U.S. power and influence over the colonies, as well as expanding its relative power over other states.

These activities gave the United States virtual control of the solar system by 2055, which it used to create organizations to which all spacefaring states would belong and the rules that all states would follow. These institutions set the terms of everything having to do with space, including colonization, resource extraction, and navigation. Despite being instrumental in creating the rules, the United States ignored those rules when following them did not suit its national interests. This practice contributed to growing resentment among some of the other states, which saw the hypocrisy of the United States serving its own interests while U.S. power compelled them to follow the rules of the system.

For more than two decades, the solar system prospered, and most states benefited from U.S. hegemony. The stability was unlike anything in the history of Earth and led to high levels of both peace and prosperity for most of the solar system. But by 2065 attitudes noticeably changed. Other governments on Earth began to challenge U.S. control of the solar system. They first began to cooperate with one another on commercial and diplomatic matters, as a means of countering U.S. control over those domains. These agreements eventually turned to military alliances that started on Earth but spread into space and directly challenged U.S. military supremacy. There were several skirmishes and low-level conflicts during those years. Some involved minor actors on the margins, some involved U.S. attempts to protect stability, and some involved U.S. action to punish those who challenged the rules or threatened the system. For example, the United States intervened when Japan and Korea nearly went to war on their neighboring bases on the moon, and it maintained a significant military presence there as a peacekeeper to prevent the two sides from escalating the tension in the future.

Likewise, many of the circumsolar bases under U.S. control began to resent being exploited by an Earth government whose colonial interests were subordinate to its national interests. For instance, terraforming on Mars was a priority for those living on the planet, but from the U.S. point of view it was unnecessary; wealth spent on it detracted from resources the United States needed elsewhere. Relations between holders of these different interests, and the ensuing conflicts they created, became especially tense as new generations who grew up knowing only life off of

Earth began taking leadership roles on their worlds. Many felt they were being robbed of wealth that was rightfully theirs, with no discernable benefits in return. Ceres, for instance, was forced to export most of its mineral resources to Earth and did not like the United States dictating the terms of trade, or controlling, from such great distances, the way in which the Ceresian people lived to service Earth.

The United States also faced increasing opposition from nonstate actors, including some violent groups. Some of these represented the interests of other states or planets that saw various forms of violence as their only real means to counter overwhelming U.S. power. For others, violence was a way to get attention for their cause, whether it be achieving independence for a group of people, advocating for a particular political ideology, or bringing awareness to the destruction of a planet's environment and ecosystem. Other violent actors simply opposed U.S. power or wanted the United States to follow more of its own rules. Vandalism, sabotage, kidnappings, and even murder grew in frequency as more colonies opposed U.S. rule. Attacks targeted authorities sent to govern the populations and security forces that supposedly were there to keep the peace but that the government often used to put down protests. From the U.S. perspective, each of its territories created more vulnerability from both external and internal challenges.

The United States also struggled to remain economically dominant. Despite positioning itself for the greatest opportunity to exploit resources across the solar system, it increasingly had to protect its claims from external actors, take care of ever-growing populations, and contend with the rising costs of empire. Initially, the value of the extracted resources and the benefits of system stability offset these costs. But the balance of benefits and costs shifted with each new challenge to U.S. hegemony.

U.S. power was visibly in decline relative to that of several competitors and rivals, but the most significant threat to the status quo came from the growing power and influence of China. For years, China and the United States were friendly competitors in space, with both actors benefitting from the status quo. Over time, though, the Chinese grew tired of being treated as a second-class power in the solar system and began to emphasize in public statements those ways in which it was disadvantaged by the system. For example, China had minimal access to some of the most resource-rich regions of Mars because the United States tightly controlled those areas.

On the U.S. side, any Chinese activities that appeared to challenge the status quo were perceived as threatening to U.S. survival. It was difficult for many in the United States to understand why the Chinese would want access to those valuable regions on Mars other than to weaken U.S. influence on the planet. Many in the United States also had trouble imagining a solar system where China was the most powerful state. Even though it might not be that different from the status quo, the fear of what a powerful China would do to the United States and its interests compelled U.S. leaders to view all Chinese activities, statements, and interests through the lens of insecurity. Ultimately, the United States began to contemplate war with China to prevent a more significant transfer of power. Rather than deterring China from expanding its influence, this rhetoric made it feel even more threatened and less secure, in turn prompting a greater Chinese military build-up and more aggressive behavior. Thus, fear of the unknown created a self-fulfilling prophecy. Lacking what it felt was adequate access to Martian territory, the Chinese government began placing increasing numbers of crewed spacecraft in orbit around Mars, ostensibly for monitoring the progress of terraforming, a pretense viewed with suspicion by the United States.

As states and colonies picked sides, some allying with the United States and others supporting the rising challenger, war began. Nobody now remembers how it started—whether the United States struck at China first or China made the initial move. The official story from the Chinese government is that the United States attacked a peaceful Chinese colony ship heading to Mars. U.S. officials claim the Chinese ship was bringing in more colonists than were permitted by quotas, and they intended to take part in insurrections on Martian bases, during which several U.S. colonists were killed. A third story, often advanced by those outside of either government, is that the discovery of a new resource in the Chinese sector threatened to overturn the delicate balance of power between the United States and China. U.S. attempts to expand its footprint on the planet and gain control over the new resource, through military action if necessary, led the Chinese to strike preemptively in 2070.

Regardless of who was responsible or what precipitated the war, the result was system-wide warfare on a scale that humans had never before seen. The most destructive violence occurred in space rather than on Earth (despite national differences, those people still inhabiting Earth felt they had more in common with each other than they did with those living elsewhere). There was no clear winner, but once all sides agreed to end the war in 2075, it was apparent that the United States was no longer a hegemon. What emerged from the war was a tenuous balance of power between several dominant states, held by a loose agreement to avoid another war. The United States did not disappear and remains a player in circumsolar politics, but it no longer has the same influence it once did, and it lost several colonies to other states. The institutions and organizations that the United States created continue to promote cooperation and stability but are being slowly altered by the changing balance of power and the interests of the other emerging great powers.

In the end, part of what defeated U.S. hegemony was the lack of a vision and strategy. Most of its activities seemed to be conducted for the sake of amassing more power and wealth, with little thought about its vision of the solar system in the future. In other words, defending the status quo became a priority, regardless of what that status quo looked like, whom it benefited, or what it cost to preserve. Fear of a different system—or, more broadly, the fear of change and the unknown—also brought about conflict between major powers that might otherwise have been avoided.

The main assumption undergirding this scenario, derived primarily from the offensive realist worldview, is that a single state will have a monopoly on the use of power in space. This hegemon can create and enforce the rules of the system, provide for the collective good, and bring stability, at least for a period of time. In this scenario, the hegemon is a state-run government. There is, of course, the possibility of states losing sovereignty and influence and the hegemon being a corporation. Since realists assume states are the primary actors in international relations (IR) and that other actors, including corporations, are merely extensions or instruments of the state, the focus of scenario one is on the hegemon being a state—in this case, the United States, as an extension of the American century. But the hegemon could just as easily be a superpower China or some other country, such as India or Japan, that has developed a revolutionary new technology that pushes it to become the central power in the solar system.

Several possible variations exist within this scenario based on the character of the hegemon. A hegemon could be benevolent and impose order and stability on the system to benefit all actors. The hegemon could also be purely self-interested (or even malevolent) and simply want to control and dominate everything and be willing to do anything to achieve that goal. Obviously, states focus on their own interests and are never purely benevolent or malevolent in the realist worldview. Regardless of how the state views itself, the way in which other actors behave will depend on how they perceive the hegemon. Despite this important variation and the effect it might have on the behavior of other actors, even a hegemon with benevolent intentions will often be perceived as self-interested; thus, other actors, both on Earth and elsewhere in the solar system, will eventually challenge its authority and control.

Many realists believe that systems will resort to a balance, so if one state becomes too powerful, others will put aside their own interests and cooperate with each other to oppose it. Examples of this include the coalition of European powers that allied against Napoleonic France, and the alliance between the United States, United Kingdom, and Soviet Union to fight Nazi Germany in World War II. Sometimes this cooperation occurs before a rising challenger becomes too powerful, but it can also happen after a state establishes itself as the dominant actor. A state might emerge from a major systemic disruption as a hegemon and therefore avoid being balanced against for a time, much like the United States after the Cold War. But that does not prevent future decline. The point is that all empires are challenged and eventually fall. There is no reason to expect a scenario involving circumsolar hegemony to be any different. The biggest variations would simply be the actors involved and the length of time a hegemon retains its power.

Before discussing some historical examples of hegemons as well as some hegemonic actors in science fiction, we must first discuss some of the core concepts and theories within the realist worldview, focusing primarily on those that helped inform this scenario. This chapter centers on the core assumptions of realism (especially those connected to offensive realism) and on three theories that relate to the rise and fall of powerful states—hegemonic stability theory, balance of power theory, and power transition theory—and then discusses realist views of imperialism and the concepts of preventive and preemptive war.

REALISM

> Beyond a critical point within a finite space, freedom diminishes as numbers increase. . . . The human question is not how many can possibly survive within the system, but what kind of existence is possible for those who do survive.
> —FRANK HERBERT, *Dune*[2]

Realism has been the dominant IR worldview since the end of World War II. While its primacy has waned, it still largely sets the standard against which other worldviews are measured. It also provides some of the best explanations for conflictual behavior in international politics, ranging from the initiation of wars to the formation of alliances as a balance against rising powers. But realism is not monolithic; there are disagreements within realism, which can lead to theories of state behavior that contradict one another.

Realism also has several flaws. For instance, realism struggles to account for state behavior as a product of factors internal to the state rather than in response to the actions of other states. Variables such as the type of government and economy, the role of the military, and the ethnic make-up of a population can all contribute to a state's behavior. Realism does not easily explain long-term cooperation for purposes other than balancing power or threat. Realism also has trouble explaining change, especially sudden change, in international politics.

Core Realist Assumptions

Several assumptions make up a worldview, and realism is no different. Realists see states as the primary actors in IR. This does not mean that other actors (international organizations and nonstate actors) do not exist or that they are not important—merely that states are the *most* important actors, in that their behavior has the greatest influence on other actors and on the international system. Other common realist assumptions are that the international system exists in a state of anarchy; that states are unitary, rational actors; that states are self-interested and behave in ways that benefit themselves, such that long-term cooperation between states is unlikely; and that war is always a possibility, so states must prepare for it.

One of the defining features of international politics for many scholars—not just realists—is that the international system exists in a state of anarchy; there is no central governing authority to make and enforce the rules. That does not mean rules do not exist or that there is a perpetual state of chaos, simply that without some form of government to oversee the system, the states themselves are required to create and then enforce whatever rules might exist. For realists, this condition limits the extent to which states will trust each other. Other scholars accept the presence of anarchy but believe it has different, potentially less negative consequences for cooperation. Anarchy is not a variable that gives rise to war or peace. The factors that bring about war are often at the national level or are the product of individual decisions. But anarchy is a persistent condition in international politics, and its existence creates the ever-present possibility of war, for which states must always prepare or else risk their survival.

Realists assume that states are not only the main actors in IR, but also that they are unitary and rational. Unitary means that realists treat each state as an individual actor. It does not mean that the entire population of a state is unanimous in its support of the government or a policy. Rather, in analyzing the behavior of states, realists care little for the internal factors or variations that may exist within a state. As a result, realists often refer to states as black boxes, within which nothing of relevance exists for explaining behavior, or as billiard balls, in which all actors behave according to external forces rather than internal factors.

Being rational means that states can identify their interests and pursue those courses of action that provide the best chances of achieving those interests for the lowest cost. Realists accept that events can get in the way of the unitary, rational actor assumption; sometimes bureaucracies take on a life of their own, and even individuals can influence state behavior. But realists believe that states generally behave as if they are rational, which is a useful assumption for explaining general trends in behavior rather than attempting to predict specific choices.

Because of both anarchy and the rational actor assumption, realists see international politics as a self-help system, where states look out for their own interests. That is not to say that states will never cooperate, but collaboration is temporary and is only likely if the cooperating states perceive that they will gain some benefit. As soon as the benefits cease to exist or become outweighed by the costs, cooperation will end. Moreover, realists generally believe that politics is conflictual and a zero-sum game, meaning one actor can only gain at the expense of another. This type of thinking, when practiced by decision-makers, stymies attempts to cooperate. For realists, it explains both the lack of long-term trust as well as the possibility of war. If there is no central authority, and if states pursue their own selfish interests, then war is always a possibility for which states must prepare, because they cannot count on others, or on international law, to prevent it. This environment itself may sometimes lead to tension or even war, but the cost of a state not being able to defend itself is its survival, which leads most states to prepare for worst-case scenarios.

Realists also believe that states generally view survival as the most important goal, although a source of tension among realists involves disagreement over how states can best ensure their survival. Classical and offensive realists tend to believe that states will seek to maximize power as the best way to survive, so they expand when they can. If given the opportunity, states will pursue empires that protect and perpetuate their power. Defensive realists, on the other hand, believe states value security over power, the implication being that states will only expand when they must for their security. States may even retract or reduce their power if necessary for their security.

An obvious problem with these realist assumptions is that they do not always hold true.[3] States within the North Atlantic Treaty Organization

(NATO) continue to cooperate on multiple issues even after seventy years, and some states, such as Costa Rica and Panama, abolished their standing military forces, at least partly in the belief that their neighbors pose no threat to their survival or that there are states that would defend them if necessary. While these assumptions do not hold true all the time, realists contend that they describe how actors tend to behave in international politics. If generally valid, then there is no reason to believe states would behave any differently in space.

Having discussed some of the main realist assumptions, I now turn to some key realist theories and concepts for identifying the plausibility of a hegemonic scenario. This first scenario draws heavily on what is called hegemonic stability theory and is based on the theorized benefits of a single state playing a dominant role in the international system.

Hegemony and Hegemonic Stability Theory

Hegemony, also sometimes referred to as a unipolar structure, exists when one actor possesses enough power to dominate an entire system. Typically, this involves not just military power, but also economic, diplomatic, and even cultural power. Realists tend to focus on the measurable aspects of power that are typically referred to as hard power—such as military and economic strength—versus soft power. But a true hegemon will be dominant in several significant ways and across the globe.

There is some debate over whether a hegemon must project global power or if there are regional hegemons. Regional hegemony is more common because dominance in just one region is a lower bar to clear than global dominance. It also is a less accurate parallel to a state that controls the solar system, so the focus here needs to be on true global hegemons. Only a few historical examples fit this description. The most common examples, and the ones discussed in the historical section below, are the Roman and British Empires.

Realists also disagree over whether hegemony leads to greater stability or more competition. In the scenario at the start of this chapter, the initial benefits of a hegemonic power are clear to most of the actors, but this still eventually leads to attempts to overturn the status quo of dominance by a single state. Later in the chapter, I will address how the pursuit of hegemony can lead to "balancing behavior." In the rest of this section, I focus on the hypothesized benefits of a hegemon based on hegemonic stability theory (HST).

The basis of HST is the collective action problem, one example of which is the tragedy of the commons. The collective action problem exists whenever there are public goods that would benefit large groups of people but that are so expensive that no one actor is willing or able to pay for them. Common examples are police, fire departments, parks, and national defense. When a government is functioning, it can solve the collective action problem by coercion, such as through the collection of taxes from the population, which it then uses to provide those public goods. A state can punish anyone who fails to contribute with fines or imprisonment, but that ability assumes a functioning government. In international politics, because of anarchy and the lack of a central authority to impose and enforce the rules, it is difficult for public goods, such as peace and stability, to emerge, much less to endure for any significant length of time.

Advocates of HST suggest that when a single actor is willing and able to provide for the collective good, that actor's behavior will generate stability that benefits the system and most actors within it.[4] An actor that can dominate the system eventually takes on the attributes of a central authority. Effectively, the hegemon, by being the dominant actor, can create and enforce rules, mitigating the negative effects of anarchy.

Hegemonic stability theory is not a strictly realist concept, and it draws on economics for its logic. What most offensive realists accept from the theory is the notion that all states at least strive to become the dominant actor. As such, the possibility of a hegemon, or a unipolar system, developing in space is consistent with offensive realist assumptions about state interests and the pursuit of power to ensure state survival.

But this theory creates a bit of a dilemma for realists. As offensive realists suggest, states desire power and will pursue empire if given the opportunity. At the same time, if states are self-interested, why would a hegemon pay the high cost of providing public goods that benefit others? The main argument in support of HST is that the hegemon has an interest in maintaining the status quo because it benefits from the existing system more than any other actor does and probably more than it would benefit from some other type of system. If it became the most powerful actor because of the existing system, or because it created the existing system, then it has an incentive to preserve that status quo for as long as possible. In specific terms, if the hegemon has the largest economy and trade market, it benefits from keeping lines of commerce open, even if it must do so through costly military power, and even if others benefit from its activities. Hegemons also tend to create regimes—rules, institutions, and organizations—that help perpetuate and preserve the status quo and ensure the hegemon's dominance. More importantly, these regimes continue to enforce the rules of the system even after the hegemon starts to decline.[5]

Balancing Theories

Another theoretical problem for this scenario is that while HST suggests that the existence of a hegemon will solve the collective action problem and create stability, many realists believe the pursuit of empire leads other states to engage in balancing behavior. Defensive realists believe that when one state pursues power or begins to become more powerful, other states will ally against it to prevent hegemony. So, for some realists, hegemony is unlikely, and even if a hegemon emerges, its dominance is likely to be short-lived.[6]

Surprisingly, John Mearsheimer, the father of offensive realism, refers to the "stopping power of water" to justify his skepticism over the possibility of global hegemons rising. For him, geography prevents states from conquering over great distances or easily conquering island states. He suggests states will generally be content with regional hegemony. Yet this notion is contrary to the basic assumption of offensive realists that states desire power and is more about capabilities than a desire for power—his argument says nothing about states with the ability to conquer over water being restrained from seeking power. And does this concept of stopping power apply to the space domain? Fewer states are able to project power into space than can project power over water, but would the "stopping power of space" prevent the rise of a true hegemon the way Mearsheimer suggests of water? Or would it limit competition, and thus provide even more opportunities for hegemony to those few states that can make the first journeys into the solar system, with fewer states having the ability to properly balance that hegemon?

Likewise, just as control of the seas provided an advantage to some states (one that the British exploited as part of their empire), control of space will provide even greater advantages if a country can obtain it. Alfred Thayer Mahan wrote, "Communications dominate war; broadly considered, they are the most important single element in strategy, political or military.... The power, therefore, to insure these communications to one's self, and to interrupt them for an adversary, affects the very rest of a nation's vigor."[7] Not only will control of space influence future communications and commerce the way maritime control once did, but it will likewise affect the outcome of future wars in ways we can only imagine. And because of the importance of space, wars are likely to occur as states attempt to control it or attempt to prevent other states from doing so.

In this one hypothetical scenario, where the United States maintains its power and pursues full control of the solar system, defensive realists would expect other spacefaring states to cooperate with one another to prevent the United States from really developing an empire in space. Once a hegemon exists, offsetting its power is more difficult, so states will attempt to prevent each other from getting to that point. Balance of power theory here serves as a foil or counter to the notion that the existence of a hegemon will create long-lasting stability in the solar system. While Napoleon attempted to create hegemony, coalitions of other European states cut short his empire and reign—one of the best historical examples of states balancing to prevent the acquisition of power by one state. Likewise, the United States and United Kingdom allied with the communist Soviet Union to balance against German power in World War II.

What is unclear, and where realists also disagree, is the extent to which states have agency over their balancing behavior. Defensive realists see balancing as a natural, almost automatic, reaction to shifts in power, so that even a benevolent hegemon will face challenges from other states. Offensive realists, though, see balancing more as a choice and are more inclined to accept that states might align with a hegemon rather than balance against it.[8] This type of alliance choice, called bandwagoning, is discussed more in chapter 2.

Theories of Imperialism

Theories about imperialism come in a variety of shades. Some focus on how empires arise, some emphasize how empires behave (and how states act when confronted with an empire), and still others examine how and why empires eventually decline. There is an important distinction between an empire and a hegemon.[9] In some ways, a hegemon is the most extreme form of empire. While multiple empires can exist at the same time, and there are several examples of that in history, there can be only one global hegemon. So while hegemons and empires are not the same, theories of imperialism should also be able to explain hegemons, especially if we stick with the realist lens.

The traditional view, typified by the Roman Empire, is that empires arise through military conquest. But within the past two centuries, the definition expanded to also include economic control of large pieces of territory and populations. Many theories about imperialism fall within the Marxist school of thought, which emphasizes class divisions and social conflict and tends to blame imperialism on capitalist economic systems, especially under competition. If true, then a hegemonic scenario should be much more likely if the dominant power is driven by a desire for market control rather than ideology or politics of any kind. Such theories, which say a great deal about the rise and fall of empires, are scrutinized in chapter 5, which examines a Marxist future.

Other theories of imperialism are still relevant here because this scenario posits a state becoming an empire, and that drive for dominance must begin somewhere. There are realists, such as Hans Morgenthau, who believe imperialism is simply a result of states pursuing their best interests, which usually involve accumulating as much power as possible, and thus creating the possibility of an empire.[10] For Hannah Arendt, imperialism was less about colonization or empire building and more about expansion for the sake of expansion.[11] This view fits well with the offensive realist perspective of states seeking power as both a means and an end. Others see imperialism as a way to secure the status quo within a state—expanding markets and pushing external social conflicts outside the state's borders, but also bringing aspects of the more advanced society to those lesser developed countries, often based on assumptions of cultural superiority. Examples of this thinking can be found in works of fiction by Rudyard Kipling and in Benjamin Disraeli's policies to expand British influence.[12] Imperial Japan took a similar view of its need to conquer Asia.

For all these reasons, if states remain the dominant actor in space (rather than corporations or other nonstate actors), there is every reason for offensive realists to believe states will continue seeking to accumulate as much power and wealth as possible. Just as control of the oceans and commerce fed the British Empire, so too the actor that controls space commerce will emerge as a circumsolar hegemon.

One problem with hegemony is that it is costly to maintain an empire, and there is no reason to believe that would be any different in space. As a state gains power, it constantly feels insecure and must expend resources to protect its expanding territory. As its territory grows, the cost of securing the borders increases, as does the feeling of insecurity. The result, as Paul Kennedy suggests, is imperial overstretch, in which the hegemon eventually collapses under the weight of its commitments. For Kennedy, at some point empires become so powerful that they begin to feel insecure—they take on so much territory and so many responsibilities that they are unable to maintain the security of the full empire while remaining prosperous, and thus they feel even less secure.[13]

During the well-known and often-cited Melian Dialogue in Thucydides' *History of the Peloponnesian War*, the Athenians justify their conquest of the island of Melos using this logic that empires must continue to expand or lose security. "As well as extending our empire, we should gain in security by annexing you," the Athenian envoy says to the Melians, while justifying the impending invasion.[14] The Melians posed no direct threat to Athens, but because the borders of the Athenian Empire stretched to Melos, taking the island became necessary for securing those expanded borders. This certainly fits the empires Kennedy discussed in his work and may explain the United States today.

Jeremy Black provides two main challenges to Kennedy's theory. First, he critiques the concept of imperial overstretch on the grounds that for it to exist, there must be a perfect level of imperial stretch, where power, security, and wealth are all maximized. Since one never knows where the tipping point is until after the empire declines, Black suggests it is not a particularly helpful concept for policymakers or theorists. Second, he criticizes the focus on a single factor—economic commitments—as a cause for imperial decline. Black contends that every era is different and that more important than the financial obligations of the empire is the willingness of other states to recognize and tolerate the empire.[15] If true, then a hegemon that others perceive as benevolent should receive more support than one perceived to be either self-interested or malevolent.

Regardless of these critiques, this notion of empires perpetually needing to increase power out of fear of a loss of security has implications for space. Any hegemonic aspirant will likely follow the same trajectory of creating dominance, setting up institutions, and eventually feeling that it must continue to expand. Doing so lays the groundwork for its own demise, either through the formation of balancing coalitions or through its own inability to keep up with the cost of empire. Given the expansive nature of space, this feeling of imperial insecurity is likely to be a dominant feature of any hegemonic future.

One of the biggest differences between traditional views of imperialism and the type of hegemony discussed in scenario one is the presence of people in the expanding territories. Empires of the past faced local inhabitants and often threatened local customs, rules, and institutions. In space, none of the new territories have inhabitants—at least as far as we know—so critiques of imperialism for spreading culture and superiority are significantly less relevant, at least until new generations of populations are born and grow up in the various parts of the solar system.[16]

Preventive vs. Preemptive Actions and Power Transition Theory
The final element of realism discussed in this chapter is the distinction between preventive and preemptive actions (strikes or wars). These are not realist concepts, strictly speaking, but they represent an important divide between realism and liberalism and refer to actions that a hegemon must be willing to take if it expects to preserve its power.[17]

These concepts are frequently confused or used synonymously, but the distinction is critical when discussing the potential pros and cons of a hegemonic system. Preemptive actions are those that are taken in self-defense, against impending threat. One of the most widely cited examples of preemptive action was the Israeli attack on Egypt and Syria on 5 June 1967, kicking off the Six-Day War. Israel's attack was in response to both Egyptian demands that United Nations peacekeeping troops leave the Sinai and to troops from several Arab states amassing near the Israeli border. Today, international law and norms generally accept the need for states to engage in preemptive strikes, when they do so for self-defense (consistent with Article 51 of the United Nations Charter, which allows states to defend themselves either individually or collectively). The problem has to do with definitions and perception, because one state's preemptive response to a perceived impending threat is another state's illegal, preventive action.

Preventive acts are those directed against a potential adversary or future threat. The Peloponnesian War is a good example of a preventive action, considering Sparta made war on Athens out of fear of the future that accompanied Athens' rising power. The Israeli strike against Iraq's Osirik nuclear facility on 7 June 1981, in which Israel attacked a target out of fear of a potential nuclear-armed Iraq in the future, is another example. More recently, the 2003 U.S. invasion of Iraq qualifies as a preventive war, over the perceived threat of Iraqi weapons of mass destruction.[18] Preventive action is generally more difficult to defend or justify than preemptive action in terms of international law and just war principles, as well as with respect to public opinion.

One of the flaws in a hegemonic strategy—one where a state actively pursues, and then seeks to preserve, its status as the dominant actor—is that it may require preventive war to fend off challenges to the system that it creates. According to HST, the most stable system is one in which there is a clear, dominant power, and there is an obvious hierarchy between the hegemon and the weaker powers. The challenge is maintaining that system and preserving the status quo in a way that does not financially strain the hegemon or overturn international rules to the point of compelling other states to balance against the hegemon. In addition, if a hegemon benefits from the stability that it produces and defends the status quo, the hegemon must be willing to use military force to maintain its status as the dominant actor.[19] It cannot allow a rising challenger to threaten the status quo, or the system would become unstable. As a result, wars against rising challengers can occur and in the future are likely to be even deadlier than the historical examples of wars between hegemons and rising challengers (e.g., the Napoleonic Wars, World Wars I and II). While preventive actions may be perceived as necessary for the hegemon to preserve its dominance, willingness to take preventive actions can perpetuate fears of the hegemon's hostile intent and expedite calls to balance against the status quo, and therefore increase the rapidity with which the hegemon declines.

Another problem is that not everyone will be happy with the system created by a hegemon. Not everyone will benefit from the system, and even states that do benefit may eventually resent being viewed as or treated like lesser powers. In 1906 Austria-Hungary's leaders resented the tone of a telegram they received from their German allies, who thanked them for their support at the recent Algeciras conference, indicating they were always loyal followers of Germany. The Austro-Hungarians took the message as an affront to their state's status as a great power, and this so-called "seconding telegram" strained relations between the two states. Although Austria-Hungary did not switch sides or balance against Germany, language and perception of prestige can influence relations between states.

Power transition theory illustrates one specific way in which the system might change with the declining power of the hegemon. The theory suggests that one common cause of war is when a status quo power is in decline and faces a rising challenger. Both states have reasons to initiate war for control of the system. The declining hegemon has an interest in waging preventive war to preserve the status quo and will do so before it can really be challenged. Rising challengers initiate war to alter the status quo but occasionally miscalculate their power and fail to unseat the hegemon, because they either strike too early or appear to pose enough of a threat to the system that other states support the hegemon to preserve the status quo.

Before World War I, rising German power—and an increased desire to be treated as a great power—directly challenged British dominance, especially at sea and in East Africa. The British response to the German naval build-up led to a naval arms race and eventually war. The naval arms race was only one of several contributing factors to Germany and England fighting against each other during World War I, but it was one of the most significant sources of tension between the two states, despite the presence of many common interests prior to the war.[20]

Having provided the hegemonic scenario and discussed some of the realist theories and concepts that contributed to the development of that scenario, I turn now to historical examples of hegemonic systems that parallel the scenario presented in this chapter. Although examples of historical empires abound, I focus on cases of hegemons and explain the difference between the two in more detail.

HEGEMONIC HISTORY

> Alexander wept when he heard Anaxarchus discourse about an infinite number of worlds, and when his friends inquired what ailed him, "Is it not worth of tears," he said, "that, when the number of worlds is infinite, we have not yet become lords of a single one?"
>
> —PLUTARCH, "On Tranquility of Mind," *Moralia*[21]

There is no agreement on which historical examples of powerful states constitute a hegemon since no consensus exists on how to define power or measure systemic dominance. States sometimes included on lists of hegemons are China during the Spring and Autumn periods (770–480 BCE), Portugal (1494–1580), The Netherlands (1580–1688), and Habsburg Spain (1516–1700). Critiques of viewing these states as hegemons involve regional application of power (rather than global), the fact that some of the dates of hegemony overlap (precluding the existence of one dominant power), or domination in only one or two fields, such as banking or trade. Other states had hegemonic potential based on their capabilities but did not act like a hegemon or seek dominance. Two examples are Germany under Otto von Bismarck and the United States before World War II.[22]

Many suggest that the United States was a hegemon in the decade following the Cold War. By some measures of power, it was the most powerful state even during the Cold War. I do not examine the U.S. case in detail here, because while we know what brought about its rise as a superpower and then a hegemon, we can only speculate about the factors that may or may not contribute to its decline. There are, however, some hegemons about which most experts agree. Two commonly referenced examples are Imperial Rome (27 BCE–AD 180) and the British Empire (1688–1914).

Studying the rise and fall of these two hegemons can inform us about some characteristics of a future hegemonic scenario. The purpose is to help future actors identify how best to avoid the pitfalls of the past, to profit from stability, or to influence the system (either to protect it or to overthrow it). Empires sometimes arise through military conquest and the acquisition of territory (like the Achaemenid Empire, or First Persian Empire, from 550 to 330 BCE). Other imperial origins include the development of new technology providing a significant advantage (like the stirrup provided to the Mongols in the thirteenth century), the use of political sabotage and religious conversion (like the Maurya Empire in India, from 322 to 180 BCE), or control of a domain (such as the oceans) giving one state (the Dutch Empire) an influx of wealth. Each of these factors is present in the scenario regarding the rise of a circumsolar hegemon because the state that develops a new technology, or that can control commerce and movement in the domain, will have a major advantage in controlling the solar system as well as other domains.

Rome provides an excellent distinction between empire and hegemon, because one could argue Rome was already a hegemon while it was a republic but began losing its hegemony long before the collapse of the empire. While the Roman Empire lasted from 27 BCE to AD 476, Roman hegemony began closer to 31 BCE, with the Final War of the Roman Republic, in which Octavian defeated Marc Antony and Cleopatra. Rome was probably hegemonic in capabilities much earlier than that but suffered from so much internal instability it could not act like a hegemon. On the other hand, Rome's hegemony was largely gone by AD 180 upon the death of Marcus Aurelius, the last of the "Five Good Emperors," even though the empire persisted for nearly three hundred more years in one form or another.

There is no single explanation for either the rise or fall of the Roman Empire. Conquest through military superiority was certainly a critical factor in its rise, as is true with many empires. It also came about because of technological innovation, particularly involving military organization and tactics. But other factors contributed as well, all of which highlight why the Roman Empire endured for as long as it did but also eventually fell.[23]

Rome's policies of extending Roman citizenship to its conquered people meant not only a larger pool of recruits for war, but also a greater sense of belonging for those conquered people. At least that was the theory. Together with military conquest was economic development. Roads facilitated trade and military movement, coins encouraged more economic interaction and easier ways to pay soldiers, and slaves (often obtained through conquest) made possible the growth of large farms, and these allowed owners to focus on producing high-value crops. At the same time, innovation in areas such as sanitation allowed the city of Rome, and the whole empire, to support larger populations than would have otherwise been possible. Finally, we cannot ignore the relative weakness of other actors in the region, giving Rome a relatively free hand.

Even when the Roman Empire was at the height of its power, at a time often referred to as the Pax Romana, it engaged in a series of violent military campaigns,[24] so it may be more accurate to think of it as the "Stability of Rome" rather than the "Peace of Rome." That is consistent with most realist views of hegemony—the hegemon's goal is preserving the stability of the system rather than preventing war, and stability sometimes requires war against those who would challenge the status quo.

There are also several theories about the fall of the Roman Empire. Rome reached its peak of territorial control in AD 117. It persisted for three and a half more centuries, suggesting that there was no single cause of its demise but rather a variety of factors. Beyond the deaths of the "Good Emperors" by AD 180, plagues created high mortality rates, making defense of frontiers more difficult. Neighbors grew in power, both internally and through alliances to challenge Roman hegemony. The weakening of internal political institutions and the rise of Christianity as a threat to the power of the state are also frequently cited factors. In addition, many of the conquered people never fully embraced the empire, and this contributed to its decline. James Stephen, for example, suggests that "Gaul ceased to be a nation without becoming, in sentiment or in spirit, an integral member of the empire." He goes on to suggest this is why Gaul "fell an early prey to her German invaders."[25] The empire itself divided and united multiple times.

Still another factor is the role of personal ambition. Julius Caesar's desire for power was a threat to others, and this led to his assassination (44 BCE) and the ensuing establishment of the Roman Empire under Augustus (27 BCE–AD 14). Yet once he established the empire, personal ambition became the norm, especially for leaders such as Caligula (37–41), Nero (54–68), and Otho (January–April 69). In the end, Rome's rise and fall, like that of most empires, was the product of several factors, many of which can be seen in the scenario at the start of this chapter, as well as in the British case.

The first British Empire began to take shape as early as 1583, but it was one of several empires operating colonies around the world and should not be considered hegemonic at that point. By 1688 the British and Dutch allied against Louis XIV's France, resulting in a stronger colonial England. The Nine Years' War (1688–97) weakened Europe's continental powers and signaled the beginning of British hegemony. This hegemony spanned two centuries, interrupted by a brief period (1776–1815) in which the loss of its North American colonies and the rise of Napoleonic France challenged its dominance.[26]

The first period of British hegemony (1688–1776) is defined by British dominance in textiles and command of the seas, and was less about central governmental control of expansion. Much of the first Industrial Revolution (1760–1840) took place in Britain and provided significant advantages to civilians and the military. One could argue that war contributed to the rise of the Industrial Revolution in England, as increases in mobility from the steam engine and advances in firepower from dynamite and the breech-loading rifle changed the character of war. The telegraph and electric generator were other advances that were not directly military but contributed to spreading British power.

Great Britain emerged again as a dominant power after the defeat of France in the Napoleonic Wars. What followed was the second period of British hegemony: nearly a century of commercial and naval might, in which British economic power opened global markets. Like Rome, the British Empire benefitted from technological innovations that precipitated both military and economic success. Railways and fast steamships, among other factors, contributed to the expansion and protection of the empire. The British also believed that the empire would bring trade, governance, and technology to those who were otherwise backward. Thus, the empire viewed itself as less about conquest and more about enlightening and improving mankind. For example, in 1807 the British banished the slave trade in the empire, in a complete reversal of the policies of the 1700s.

We also cannot ignore the role of the British East India Company, which was one of the first multinational corporations. It often acted independently of the British government, collecting taxes and raising its own armed forces, which operated alongside the British navy in several campaigns. The company also helped spread British culture. It was even given an exception to the Slave Trade Act. While the act abolished the slave trade in the empire, it did not apply to territories administered by the East India Company.

Even though the British Empire's economic interests went together with its naval power, as in Rome, the cost of preserving the system eventually grew beyond what the hegemon could sustain. That, combined with the need to respond to rising challengers in the late 1800s—including Germany, but also France and Russia—eventually took its toll on the British ability to retain dominance. Naval laws, for example, required the British navy to be larger than the next two largest navies. With Germany intent on building the world's second largest navy, with both France and Russia expanding their fleets, and with the introduction of new technology such as the dreadnought battleship, British resources were strained, creating greater tension between the powers.

Although World War I was costly in terms of lives lost and money spent, it paled in comparison to the devastation of World War II to both England's economy and its infrastructure. The war completed the decline of British hegemony. The United States emerged as the financial center of the world and the only state with atomic weapons. It used this position as the new world leader to set up institutions and rules for the system, including the United Nations, NATO, and the Bretton Woods economic agreement. This peaceful transition highlights how changes to the system may occur between actors who are not belligerents against each other. War still helped precipitate systemic change, but the transfer of power occurred between allies—England and the United States—largely without conflict because the United States did very little to alter the system from that which benefited it and England. The main difference is that the United States took the lead on promoting trade and commerce and protecting the sea lines of communication, as well as protecting Western democracies from the growing threat of communism.

The most obvious lesson from history about hegemons is that their reign is not permanent. It may last for a couple of centuries, but eventually all empires fall. The few hegemons that existed met similar fates because of rising challengers, the cost of maintaining the status quo, and internal divisions of one kind or another.

Some contend that the United States faces the same danger of decline, and for many of the same reasons. While analysts question the duration of U.S. hegemony—whether it already passed or will continue for some time—this is not a question for this book. The point is that similar challenges to those facing past empires are likely to be present against any spacefaring hegemon in the future. Even if the United States develops a new technology that allows the American Century to continue, eventually its solar empire will decline for one or more of the same reasons.

HEGEMONS IN SCIENCE FICTION

> In the last millennium of the Empire, the monotonously numerous revolts made Emperor after Emperor conscious of this [the empire's vulnerability to conquest], and Imperial policy became little more than the protection of Trantor's jugular vein.
> —ISAAC ASIMOV, *The Foundation*[27]

A dominant government attempting to control all aspects of the universe is a common setting in science fiction. Some of the best illustrations of this are Isaac Asimov's *Foundation* trilogy, Frank Herbert's *Dune*, and the *Star Wars* films.[28] In some cases, the empire or hegemon simply provides the environment in which characters operate; in others, it is the primary antagonist controlling everything, oppressing the weaker actors, or employing the main characters.

Asimov's *Foundation* was first published as a series of short stories in 1951 and later expanded into a series. The first book begins with the Empire already on the verge of collapse, yet only a handful of Psychohistorians are aware of this looming future.[29] Though the Empire never fully dies off, it goes through a period of decline—what Asimov calls darkness, where a central authority no longer exists to govern the millions of planets that make up the Empire. This leads to a sort of chaos, with worlds battling each other to gain power and fill the vacuum left by the Empire's decline. That is mostly background for Asimov's main story but is a relevant parallel with the scenario above. *Foundation* then follows the Encyclopedists, who believe they can create a book of knowledge that will shorten the time of chaos between the demise of the existing empire and the rise of the next.[30]

Asimov based his Galactic Empire on Rome.[31] Asimov's Empire arose because of the development of a new technology—hyperspace travel. But over time, the drive for innovation disappears, and the Empire's focus is simply to sustain itself. This loss of innovation, which leads to stagnation, parallels the Dark Ages in Europe. As they did in Rome, civil war and revolts weaken Asimov's Empire, as do power struggles on the periphery of its territory with those it would govern but who prefer to remain independent.

Hari Seldon, one of the leading Psychohistorians, has a plan for reducing the duration of the darkness between the old Empire and the next one to rise. Initially, this plan appears to be a gathering of experts on a distant planet to write an encyclopedia of humanity's knowledge and history, information that would otherwise be lost to the darkness (not unlike the Great Library at Alexandria). Without revealing too much from the plot of the book, one finds over the course of the story that Seldon's plan is somewhat different from the one he offered the Empire but is ultimately still about reducing the length of time in darkness.

In Herbert's *Dune*, although there are Houses (royal families) that control each planet and that compete with one another, each House owes allegiance to the Padishah Emperor, much like the feudal system of early modern Europe. According to *Dune* and later books in the series, the empire came about after the Butlerian Jihad, a war to defeat a race of intelligent machines. The result of this revolt against machines was a ban against any computers or artificial intelligence. As the Reverend Mother tells Paul Atreides: "Once men turned their thinking over to machines in the hope that this would set them free. But that only permitted other men with machines to enslave them."[32] In a parallel with scenario one and Asimov's *Foundation*, this ban leads to stagnation in innovation and technology, which allows for the eventual demise of the Empire.

On the planet Arrakis, where much of *Dune* takes place, are religious settlements of Fremen, wanderers from Terra who follow a hybrid religion of Zen Buddhism and Sunni Islam, who made Arrakis their home. Just as some suggest that Christianity hastened the fall of the Roman Empire, the Fremens' willingness to engage in self-sacrifice while following Paul Atreides contributes to weakening the Empire. The books depict the Empire's eventual collapse, in this case because Paul gains control of the most valuable resource in the universe and uses it (along with marriage to the emperor's daughter) to gain control. This alone does not destroy the Empire but begins its decline. Even though Paul becomes the new Emperor, the future set in motion by his actions (arguably even earlier by his mother's decision to give birth to a boy instead of a girl) leads to the collapse of the Empire and an ensuing famine.

One significant difference between *Dune* and other science fiction with an empire or hegemon is the involvement of a nonstate actor. While the empire controls system politics, the Spacing Guild controls both banking and interstellar travel. The Spacing Guild is heavily dependent on the spice melange as an ingredient for interstellar travel, and that is only available on one planet—Arrakis (Dune). This makes the Guild heavily reliant on one of the most significant challengers to the throne. In other words, even a hegemon can be made vulnerable if its primary competitors become dependent on each other in a way that their cooperation can lead to the weakening of the hegemon. The Spacing Guild mirrors the British East India Company in many ways. So, despite being separate from the empire, one can still imagine a government ruling politics in space even as one of its private economic actors maintains dominion over commerce and finance.

While this role of a commercial entity is not seen in Asimov's trilogy, *Foundation*'s focus on science and technology essentially allows it to take over these duties from the stagnant empire, at least within its small corner of the universe. It controls nuclear power when other worlds have forgotten how to generate it and so is able to use technology for protection and as a bargaining chip for other needed resources. In contrast, *Dune*'s Spacing Guild, like many empires in history and in fiction, was prone to a lack of innovation: "The Guild navigators, gifted with limited prescience, had made the fatal decision: they'd chosen always the clear, safe course that leads ever downward into stagnation."[33] In other words, empires in both of these stories fall because of challenges from inside and outside, as well as the lack of scientific and technological innovation.

On film, one of the most archetypal examples of a dominant government is the Galactic Empire in the *Star Wars* saga.[34] Released in 1977, *Star Wars* takes place in an unnamed galaxy at an unnamed time in the past and focuses on two sides: an Empire and a rebellion. The movie was originally followed by two sequels—*The Empire Strikes Back* and *Return of the Jedi*—and spawned a prequel trilogy, a sequel trilogy, several spin-off films, and numerous books and television series. Although there are several parallels to scenario one in other parts of the *Star Wars* collection, the closest comparisons are with the original film trilogy, and that is the primary focus here.

This Empire was once a republic, like Rome, and turned imperial because of claimed threats and instability to the system, as well as personal ambitions. Regardless of the nature of the government, the pursuit of dominance by one entity, seeking to crush all opposition, is the defining feature of this story and how it relates to scenario one. This Empire is also portrayed as evil and menacing, so that audiences are invited to root for the rebels. But according to realists, even a benevolent empire will invite balancing behavior from other actors, which could include violent opposition, either by other states or by nonstate actors, as in the case of a rebellion.

The Rebel Alliance draws the Empire into a prolonged conflict. Despite the Empire's numerical and technological superiority, it is vulnerable to deception and sabotage and is often caught off guard by the weaker opponent. Much of the fighting mixes conventional forces with what we would call today asymmetric warfare. The Empire, embodied by the Emperor (a figure one hears about but does not see until *Return of the Jedi*), appears to focus almost entirely on the acquisition of power for its own sake, and the presence of a rebellion is a threat to that power. The mysticism of the Force also parallels the Roman case, as the Jedi pose a threat to the Empire, much as Christianity challenged the primacy of the Roman leaders and the devoted Fremen threatened the Empire in *Dune*. The Jedi were even once part of the Empire and change sides only once the Emperor's evil intentions become clear—unfortunately, only after it is too late for many of the Jedi order.

By the end of the original trilogy, the Emperor and Empire fall, eventually defeated through a combination of military action and deception, as well as the rise of a mystical figure who rallies opposing forces to defeat the more powerful army. The parallel between Luke Skywalker and Paul Atreides is both stark and informative in its representation of weak actors defeating stronger forces. One can also easily imagine that years of fighting the rebellion left the Empire financially burdened.

ANALYSIS

> If you expose the army to a prolonged campaign,
> the state's resources will be inadequate.
> —SUN TZU, *The Art of War*

Based on IR, history, and science fiction, it certainly seems plausible that a single state could emerge and dominate, at least during the initial period of humanity's future in space. It could also be a corporation or some supranational entity that consumes states and takes on the role of a hegemon. But realists (supported by history) tell us that even when companies are innovative and powerful, and even when states agree to belong to organizations or subscribe to a concert intended to prevent future wars, state interests eventually emerge as the primary motivating factor.

There are a variety of sources of conflict in realist thought, but one of the most common for offensive realists has to do with resource scarcity. Resources may be defined as material goods, such as oil, but can also include populations, territory, and even security itself. According to realists, states are more likely to have conflict when they compete with one another over scarce resources. Either one state has the resources and others want them, or nobody owns them and states compete for them. The former is a distinct possibility in a hegemonic future where states expand to unexplored worlds and seek control of valuable resources. The hegemon, by definition having most of the power and resources, may engage in violence to protect its status, while others might engage in violence to get what the hegemon has.

Realists also see politics as a zero-sum game, where one actor's gain is a loss for someone else (or everyone else). Realists have a difficult time accepting that states can cooperate for their mutual benefits over the long term. States can and do cooperate when they face a common threat, but eventually, other states will view even a benevolent hegemon as having dominance only at their expense. They will ally to balance against the state, but that cooperation will only last as long as necessary to restore the balance of power.

Many realist explanations of war apply to states, regardless of whether they are hegemons, simple great powers, or minor powers. The theory that most applies to hegemons as a source of conflict is the theory of hegemonic war, a variant of power transition theory, in which rising challengers and declining hegemons are likely to go to war over control of the system. This, then, points to two likely sources of conflict in this future. First is the development of a new technology that allows a new state to challenge for control of the system. Second is imperial overstretch, where the hegemon begins to decline because of the financial cost of maintaining its dominance. The first case will likely lead a rising challenger to initiate war to alter the status quo. The second will lead the hegemon to engage in preventive war to preserve the status quo.

Perhaps the biggest variation in this scenario is unclear because it would depend on how the dominant state slides into its hegemonic position. If it becomes dominant simply because it was the first to arrive at various points in the solar system, then a variety of actors will challenge that dominance. This is like the competition for colonies among European powers in the nineteenth and twentieth centuries, or a *Dune*-like scenario where a single valuable resource or location becomes a source of rivalry and competition. If dominance comes about because of a technology that is relatively easy to copy or counter once it is made public, that too increases the likelihood that a hegemonic system is short-lived as

TABLE 1.1. **EVALUATING THE HEGEMONIC SYSTEM**

MEASURES OF EVALUATION	SHORT-TERM (DURING HEGEMONY)	LONG-TERM (AS THE HEGEMON DECLINES)
Minimizing war	Mixed	No
Human expansion	Yes	Yes
Enhancing science and technology	Yes	Depends on nature of power transition
Improving standards of living	Depends on nature of hegemon	Depends on nature of hegemon

more competitors challenge for leadership or to at least balance power. In contrast, a dominance created by an advanced technology that is difficult to reverse-engineer and to counter might extend the duration of one actor's hegemonic rule, or at least prolong the time in which states are willing to cooperate with the hegemon.

If we evaluate the likely effect of this scenario on the four key elements of success discussed in the introductory chapter—minimizing major war, expanding humanity beyond Earth, enhancing science and technology, and improving human standards of living—we find somewhat mixed results in a hegemonic future (see table 1.1). Short-term results are positive for at least two of the four factors and possibly all four, depending on the nature of the hegemon and whether any of the wars to preserve the system escalate into systemic wars. Over the long term, the successes disappear, humanity enters a period of scientific stagnation, and, in a worst-case future, even human expansion into space is halted.

We expect a hegemonic system to minimize threats to the status quo, not necessarily to prevent wars. A true hegemon must be willing to wage war to maintain its position and may engage in preventive wars to do so. Similarly, even a benevolent hegemon may not prevent small wars from occurring at the sub-systemic level. As actors grow weary of the status quo, states and nonstate actors begin to challenge the hegemon, and the resulting wars could be catastrophic for humanity. So, minimizing war is a mixed result because the simple existence of a hegemon would reduce the likelihood of major wars in the short term. But it could increase the likelihood of smaller wars, either initiated by the hegemon, or simply allowed to occur because they do not pose a threat to the hegemon's reign or to the status quo. In the long term, even systemic wars can occur, either because of the hegemon's decline or as a contributing factor if challengers are able to weaken the hegemon.

The presence of a hegemon, especially as laid out in this scenario, leads to the expansion of humanity beyond Earth. In fact, that expansion into space is likely to be one primary driver of the hegemon's rise to power, so the two are linked inextricably. Even after the hegemon declines, assuming war does not wipe out humanity, there will already be a significant human presence throughout the solar system that even a major war is unlikely to reverse. In the worst case, one could imagine expanding no farther, but at least humanity would inhabit more than a single planet.

Science and technology will flourish under the hegemonic system, at least for a time. Because the hegemon will initially benefit from technological advances, it will be eager to fund new and innovative research. As its economic struggles to maintain the system grow, research will decline, S&T education will become less important, and innovation will stagnate, at least within the hegemon. Unless another actor is immediately willing and allowed to step in and play the dominant role in S&T research, human advances will halt in parallel with the Dark Ages or Asimov's period of darkness between Empires. Whether long-term research thrives in other corners of the solar system will depend largely on the nature of the challenge to the status quo. If the transition of power is relatively peaceful, such as that between the United Kingdom and the United States after World War II, then the continued stability will reinvigorate science. If, on the other hand, power changes hands because of systemic war, humanity will likely enter a period of innovation darkness.

The benefits of hegemony to human standards of living will also be mixed and will depend heavily on the interests and nature of the hegemon. A benevolent hegemon will use its resources to promote welfare and provide for the people of its own state and colonies as well as others (at least to the extent it can do so), though this noblesse oblige will diminish as the hegemon's power and wealth decline. A malevolent hegemon, on the other hand, might look out for the interests of its own people but be indifferent to the suffering of others, whether because of war, disease, or hunger. And as with S&T, the longer-term benefits of this system, even under a benevolent hegemon, will depend on the nature of the power transition and the type of system that emerges. In the worst case, the malevolent hegemon will only care for the elites in its country, leaving even its own people to suffer.

Compared to the other scenarios, hegemony may not be in the best interest of humanity, especially in the long run. This scenario ranks in the middle of the pack, so it is far from the worst option of the considered scenarios. If hegemony emerges and plays out like this scenario, then once the hegemon begins to decline, the most important thing will be managing the transition in a way that avoids catastrophic war and innovative stagnation. War will continue to be possible, but if the declining power and rising challenger can avoid war, this type of system can still produce positive results for most of its inhabitants. But that may depend on whether the system that emerges contains a new hegemon or leads to a balance of power as highlighted in scenario two.

Cooperation in this future would largely take three forms. First would be cooperation through control and coercion, meaning the hegemon would compel other states to cooperate to preserve system stability. If the hegemon behaves like the United States after World War II, it will develop laws, rules, and norms that govern state behavior in the solar system—whether it follows those guidelines itself or not. The United States helped create the Comprehensive Nuclear Test Ban Treaty, the Moon Treaty, and the Rome Statute that led to the International Criminal Court, and then chose not to ratify any of them. It often enforces the Law of the Sea without itself being a signatory. It is easy to imagine a hegemonic space power imposing rules on others while reserving for itself greater freedom and flexibility to make self-interested decisions.

States might also cooperate with the dominant power to avoid being conquered or to share the spoils of hegemony, much as Benito Mussolini's Italy sought to do with Nazi Germany, or how Western Europe bandwagoned with the United States after World War II.

The third form of cooperation is the states that ally against the hegemon to revise the status quo. If the hegemon is out for self-interest at the expense of others, as a victorious Nazi empire would have been, we can imagine a great deal of conflict, with numerous actors allying against the hegemon to bring about a better status quo, much like the European coalitions that fought against Napoleonic France. This balancing is a common form of cooperative behavior when states face a dominant power, and realists would expect similar activities in a solar system dominated by one actor. Eventually, these challenges from other actors would take their toll on the hegemon and contribute to imperial overstretch.

The Sun Tzu quote that opened this chapter does not just refer to a hegemon, though that is obviously a useful link to the scenario and ensuing discussion. But we must put Sun Tzu's statement in context. One interpretation is that a hegemon referred to a ruler whose power made allies unnecessary. If true, then Sun Tzu suggests that a hegemon will be able to defeat even an alliance of foes. While this might be true in the beginning, he also offers a glimpse into why that does not hold true over a long period, especially when the hegemon must continually engage in war.

In chapter 2 of *The Art of War*, Sun Tzu focuses on the dangers associated with prolonged fighting. He suggests a preference for avoiding war and achieving victory without resorting to military action, but if one must wage war, it should be done quickly and decisively to avoid the costs associated with long conflicts. He suggests that "a victory that is long in coming will blunt their [the army's] weapons and dampen their ardor."[35] Even an effective military campaign will result in significant costs if it lasts too long, and it can reduce the state's ability to protect itself or wage additional wars. There is also a financial cost to prolonged wars. Thus, prolonged wars negatively affect both the finances of the state and the spirit of the military, not to mention the willingness of the people to support the state.

History suggests that at least part of the reason hegemons decline is they have a difficult time following this advice. The tendency is to engage in numerous campaigns, usually justified as preserving the empire or system stability, but that often result in personnel and financial losses and eventual loss of power and public support. German tribes defeated the Romans, the American colonists beat the British, the Nazis—even in defeat—inflicted enough cost on the British to weaken the empire, and the Afghan Mujahedeen beat the Soviet Union. What do these historical cases have in common, and what can they tell us about how to deal with an empire in the future? For one thing, the victors were all weaker actors who helped contribute to the weakening of an empire through prolonged campaigns.

An additional cost of prolonged campaigns that Sun Tzu does not address is the potential loss of allies or supporters from other parts of the system. Whether those states realign and support the other side or simply stop supporting the hegemon, the loss of supporters at home and allies in the war can have a deleterious effect on the morale of the people, the outcome of the war, and ultimately the security of the state.

Despite Sun Tzu's advice about avoiding prolonged conflicts, he offers no specific advice on how to do so. Kublai Khan of the Mongols supported small states and opposed the formation of large states, believing that only wars against other large states would be prolonged.[36] T. E. Lawrence wanted to provide limitations on destruction even in small wars and counterinsurgencies to prevent prolonged campaigns.[37] He suggested using advanced technology and a focus on indirect approaches rather than masses of force to cause the most devastation to the enemy. If we take some of Sun Tzu's other lessons, discussed in later chapters, he does provide some hints about this. You must know whether you can win quickly or not, which requires understanding yourself and your enemy. If you cannot, engage in deception, diplomacy, or some other form of warfare (as some might suggest China and Russia are doing today), or avoid war altogether. Only use force in cases where you expect to win, but also have clear objectives so you avoid those prolonged fights that drain your resources and strain your population.

While hegemons tend to suffer from this principle, those opposing the hegemon can use it to their advantage. Those who are already weaker will lose relatively less in a prolonged war, so drawing the hegemon into extended campaigns can help bring about the opportunity to challenge the status quo. As history shows, it is not particularly difficult to draw a larger state into a prolonged war, so we need not spend much time on advising future weak actors. The key is to merely let the hegemon do what hegemons always seem to do. Henry Kissinger famously wrote of U.S. involvement in the Vietnam War that "we lost sight of one of the cardinal maxims of guerrilla war: the guerrilla wins if he does not lose. The conventional army loses if it does not win. The North Vietnamese used their main forces the way a bullfighter uses his cape—to keep us lunging in areas of marginal political importance."[38]

The hegemon must remember these lessons and not get drawn into conflicts that will be prolonged or that are of minimal value to either the hegemon or the system, relative to the cost. On the other hand, the nonhegemonic actors must strive to draw the hegemon into these very conflicts if the goal is to bring down the system, or at least bring it into more of a balance.

SUMMARY

> The fall of Empire, gentlemen, is a massive thing, however, and not easily fought. It is dictated by a rising bureaucracy, a receding initiative, a freezing of caste, a damming of curiosity—a hundred other factors. It has been going on, as I have said, for centuries, and it is too majestic and massive a movement to stop.
>
> —ISAAC ASIMOV, *Foundation*

Realists are pessimistic about the possibility of long-term cooperation, and their assumption that actors are generally selfish is likely to remain valid even as humanity enters the age of space habitation. At the same time, realists expect states to cooperate when balancing against power, and that type of cooperation is likely in a future that involves a hegemon in space.

Several potential benefits emerge from a hegemonic scenario. At least for a short time, we could expect stability and an enforcement of rules, mitigating some of the negative effects of anarchy. The hegemon will spur technological advances that benefit everyone, and markets will thrive under the protection of the hegemon. But given the history of empires eventually crumbling under the cost of maintenance and the threat of rising challengers, the most likely outcome of a solar system dominated by a single government would eventually be war and change.

Empires do not last. They become overextended or they compel others to balance, eventually leading to the downfall of the hegemon and the establishment of a new bipolar or multipolar system.[39] The downside to this inevitability is that it often involves a major systemic-level war to alter the system fully. On a solar level, this could be catastrophic for humankind, depending on the nature of the weaponry available at the time a revisionist actor challenges the hegemon.

In addition, the decline of the hegemon would not necessarily be a positive outcome. If hegemonic stability theory is valid, then the emerging bipolar or multipolar world that would replace the unipolar system could be less stable and more conflictual. Even if a concert formed briefly between the major powers, history suggests that it would not last and would be replaced by a return to great power rivalry.

To avoid this scenario, whichever state is first to colonize the moon or a planet must recognize that it faces a decision where a drive for short-term hegemony can have negative consequences, whereas cooperation can mitigate some of the costs and risks discussed in this chapter. It can use its temporary advantage to set up a system that benefits itself, perhaps at the expense of others, or it can create a system of rules and order that benefits all states.

Building on the nature of hegemons to tend toward decline, chapter 2 continues this discussion of realism by focusing on a future where there is not a single dominant actor but rather several relatively equal actors competing for control. This next scenario could emerge if multiple states compete from the beginning of the first lunar colonies with relatively equal technology. It could also become the new status quo after a hegemon falls and relinquishes control over the system to other actors.

CHAPTER 2

THE BALANCE OF POWER
PLANETARY PARTNERSHIPS

> Thus the highest realization of warfare is to attack the enemy's plans; next is to attack their alliances.
> —SUN TZU, *The Art of War*

In 2030 the United States and China arrived on the moon within two months of each other to establish permanent human bases. Like the rush to gain land in the American West, the two states quickly sought to expand their territory, and this prompted other countries to rush to space in the hopes of establishing their own outposts. The Europeans (mostly the French and Germans) established their own base two years later, as did the Russians one year after that. The Indians, Japanese, and Koreans joined resources in 2035 to get to the moon (North and South Korea having combined their space programs in 2030) but, upon landing, went their separate ways, establishing their own small outposts.

There was initially a great deal of cooperation between the colonies, as the dangers from space and the lunar environment provided common threats to everyone, regardless of nationality or level of patriotism. In addition, because most of the first settlers were scientists and engineers, they saw collaboration across state lines as natural and unthreatening to national interests. However, as the lunar bases grew, as newfound resources came under the control of certain bases to the exclusion of others, and as nationalist sentiments resurfaced with each new ship of colonists arriving from Earth, the different colonies distanced themselves from one another.

In 2040 the four entities with the most advanced space programs—the United States, China, Europe, and Russia—began to expand beyond the moon to other parts of the solar system. All four received support from the smaller powers, but even some of these less powerful states competed for control of asteroids, which they could exploit for resources or use as strategic bases against each other. The larger states started colonies on several solar bodies, developing a mutual acceptance of a kind of sphere of influence that each state had over certain portions of the solar system. These spheres of influence quickly devolved into the colonies taking on a great deal of autonomy, but under the control of the main sponsor. For instance, although all the major powers had colonies on Mars by 2047, the planet nominally fell under Russian influence, partly as a function of the greater resources available to the Russian colony, but also because Russia parked several military assets in orbit around the Red Planet, effectively claiming it until someone was willing to risk challenging Russian control. China focused most of its attention on the Outer Belts, including the protoplanets Ceres and Vesta.[1] Europe concentrated on the Jovian moon, Europa, mostly for the symmetry of the name.

Key pieces of territory for the solar system, beyond the planetary bodies and moons, were the Lagrangian points.[2] The international community placed an international space station on the earth-moon L_4 Lagrangian point to facilitate colonization and manufacturing. While other states quickly expanded from their lunar colonies to other planets, the United States focused its efforts on construction of a space station at the earth-sun L_4 Lagrangian point to facilitate space travel as well as surveillance of the system. This initially put the United States behind the other states in terms of gaining resources until the United States shifted its focus to Saturn's moons.

There was very little human exploration at this point. Other than Mars and Ceres, which became inhabited colonies, states automated most of these bases with the intent of extracting resources and acting as resupply bases for further exploration. Other locations were largely up for grabs, including bodies in the Kuiper Belt and the other moons of Jupiter (Callisto and Ganymede). Competition for these solar bodies became so fierce that states nearly went to war over portions of the solar system often for little reason other than preventing others from possessing them.

The system was initially stable, but as states competed for resources, and as certain colonies became incredibly wealthy from resources discovered on the planets and therefore valuable to their sponsoring nation, competition led to rivalry and eventually to conflict. Technological competition was particularly tense between Russia and China, and while this contributed to faster expansion into the outer solar system, it also increased the possibility of war between the states. An increase in Russian military personnel on the moon and in orbit around Mars threatened the sovereignty of other colonies there. Likewise, China's increased military presence in the Outer Belt sent a message to all actors about Chinese interests and intentions. By 2048 sponsoring states began to restrict trade, which initially flowed freely between the colonies, to prevent each other from gaining any kind of advantage from the exchanges.

Formal military alliances began to develop, not only between other spacefaring nations, but also with the colonies. Several members of the European Union and India aligned with Russia, although Europe also signed a nonaggression treaty with the United States. The Korean, Indian, and Japanese governments formed an entente centered around their lunar bases.[3] Most of these alliances started as trade agreements that benefitted some states to the exclusion of others. Over time, some morphed into defense pacts and promises to support one another in the event of war. Despite their defensive purposes, states believed that other alliances were intended to exploit weaknesses or vulnerabilities. In fact, while everyone was aware that these partnerships were forming, few of them made the terms of their agreements public, increasing distrust between them. Those alliances that were public were so vague that everyone believed there had to be secret annexes that were more hostile. The United States tried to remain unaligned because it had interests in promoting peaceful trade throughout the solar system, but it was also fearful of being isolated without an ally. Thus, it pursued a mutual agreement with China, essentially promising to protect the ability of all states to trade with the Outer Belt even while accepting a Chinese sphere of influence there.

In 2050 the moon and Outer Belt skirmished as proxies for India and China. At issue was lunar access to resources in the Outer Belt, but that was merely an indirect way for India and China to use their colonies to take aim at one another. Inhabitants of the Indian base on the moon demanded greater access to Ceres, both for its resources and as a central location to other parts of the solar system. As part of the Outer Belt, and perhaps emboldened by its agreement with the United States, China felt it had the right to control access to Ceres and was unwilling to back down to India. The Europeans and the United States intervened, calling for a conference to resolve the dispute. All the spacefaring states attended this Ceres conference and agreed that the Outer Belt was autonomous and free for use by all states and colonies, but they also recognized that China enjoyed a special relationship with the Outer Belt. This was a source of tension between India and the other states, as only Russia supported India at the conference (many suspect Russia of pushing India into the crisis).

Although nobody wanted war, the competition over resources and colonies increased, and the value of those resources fueled feelings of both insecurity and optimism. Science and technological innovation focused on the militarization of space, and especially the ability to defend colonies. States believed that their new technologies gave advantages to whomever struck first, so every state planned for war until it became a self-fulfilling prophecy that seemingly nobody could avoid.

The war was the result of several factors, but the trigger seemed to be the killing of a Martian diplomat in 2057, which Mars and Russia blamed on the Outer Belt and indirectly on the Chinese government. In response to the death of its diplomat, Mars issued an ultimatum to the Outer Belt. There is evidence that Russia emboldened its colonial sphere to challenge the Outer Belt, believing that China would back down but that Russia and Mars would have the initial advantage if war resulted. The ultimatum called for the Outer Belt to bring to trial all participants in the plot, to cease support for groups stirring up discord on Mars, and to allow Martian police access to Ceres to assist in the investigation. The Outer Belt accepted nearly all the terms of the ultimatum except for one. They would not agree to allow Mars to send law enforcement personnel, which would have amounted to China ceding its controlling interest in Ceres. The result of this decision was war.

The rivalry manifested itself on Earth in many ways, including by some small-scale battles between Russia and China. But most of the fighting took place between the Outer Belt and Mars. The United States, Japan, and Korea allied with China. Despite an alliance with Russia, Europe remained neutral because of its nonaggression pact with the United States and concerns over the war spreading more widely on Earth. India, despite its history of tension with China and its alliance with Russia, tried to stay out of the fray as much as possible. Most of the lunar colonies gave their support to the Outer Belt to prevent Martian expansion and, combined with the entente, led India to fear that too much direct involvement would lead to a loss of its influence on the moon. So, most of India's support was behind-the-scenes financial aid and intelligence while trying to minimize the direct involvement of its lunar colonies.

The war ended in 2060, when Russia and Mars, facing a much larger alliance of rivals, recognized they were simply outgunned and outmanned. Several Martian colonies experienced upheaval and changes in leadership that caused them to sue for peace separate from Russia. This left Russia virtually alone, so it agreed to sign an armistice ending the war.

The international community assigned to Russia the bulk of the blame for the war and stripped it of its possessions in the solar system, though it retained its space travel capabilities to provide aid and technological assistance to Russian citizens in various parts of the solar system. Mars was made an unaligned planet, not in the sphere of any one state. The victorious states—China, Japan, the United States, and Korea—divided Russia's colonies on Mars and on other planets. Although on the winning side of the war, China suffered tremendous losses and struggled to maintain control over the Outer Belt. Europe and Japan emerged stronger after the war and gained prominence not only on Earth but also in other parts of the solar system. Japan consolidated power on Mars and absorbed some of the previous Indian colonies on the moon and on Mars, as well as some Russian colonies. Europe profited heavily from its noninvolvement in the war, particularly given the distance of its Europa colony from much of the fighting. This led to competition between Japan and Europe for control of the solar system, mostly along philosophical lines. While Japan approached the system from a standpoint of technology and modernization, intent on terraforming every world to make it habitable by humans as quickly as possible, Europe took a more conservationist stance, wanting both to protect the environment as much as possible and to maximize what humanity could learn from scientific study of the planets.

While the cost of the war reduced the number of states that could compete in the solar system, it did not reduce competition between the states that retained their circumsolar possessions. After the war, there were attempts to create a solar league to prevent future wars between the various nations and colonies. Members agreed to bring all conflicts before the league rather than resort to violence to resolve disputes. Members also agreed that they would come together to stop any wars, even against a fellow member, if necessary. Few states were convinced of the utility of the agreement, at least partly because some of the great powers were not members. The league did not invite Russia to join as punishment for its involvement in provoking the war between Mars and the Outer Belt. Japan opted not to join, and India, though initially a member of the league, left after four years. As a result, those Earth nations that retained their space colonies after the war eventually began competing with one another again, because the main sources of conflict between them—competition for valuable resources and increased vulnerability through new military technologies and their accompanying arms races—remained unresolved by the war and its aftermath.

This second scenario is one where multiple states compete with one another for greater levels of control over the solar system. Many of the concepts used in this scenario will be familiar to students of the pre–World War I era, but they are also prominent elements of defensive realism. Notable features of this multipolar system are the role that alliances play and the effect of technology on the willingness of states to go to war, especially if it favors the offense.

A great deal of variety is possible in any balance of power scenario, depending on how many spacefaring states exist. I could, for instance, have modeled the scenario on the Cold War bipolar system with two primary actors competing against one another, but that would have been too similar to the ending of scenario one. This scenario treats states as the primary actors that balanced each other, with those colonies inhabiting the solar bodies as secondary actors. One could also imagine a scenario where the populations of the moon, Mars, and the Outer Belt balance against the power of a single state or even a unified Earth. That variation also would have been too similar to scenario one and to the storyline in *The Expanse* (discussed below). The point is that even with two chapters based on realism, too many possible variations exist to account for all realist scenarios. The two presented in these first two chapters are plausible based on realist ideas and current politics.

REALISM CONTINUED

> It's the problem with politics. Your enemies
> are often your allies. And vice versa.
>
> —JAMES S. A. COREY, *Leviathan Wakes*

The sections below expand on the discussion of realism from chapter 1 and highlight differences between offensive and defensive realists. They also start to bring in economics and discuss some of the other variants of realism. A defensive realist is much less likely than other realists to embrace the hegemonic scenario discussed in the previous chapter. The expansion of one state's power will generally threaten other states, which will in turn attempt to increase their power. The history of international politics suggests that when hegemons emerge, they will not last for very long. More importantly, defensive realists see security as more desirable to states than power. As a result, states should be less likely to pursue hegemony, especially if doing so reduces their security and makes them more vulnerable, either because of imperial overstretch or because of the coalitions that form to balance against a potential hegemon.[4]

Defensive Realism

Defensive realists differ most from offensive realists in their view of a state's ultimate objectives and its willingness to seek an empire.[5] Whereas offensive realists see states as pursuing power and expanding whenever they can, even to the point of pursuing an empire, defensive realists contend that states prefer to pursue security, which means they only expand when they believe they have to. This also means states will reduce their power, or retract, if they believe doing so will increase their security. The Soviet decision to give up its empire to ensure the survival and security of Russia is difficult to explain from the offensive realist point of view, but retrenchment does happen and is more consistent with the defensive realist perspective of states prioritizing security over power.[6]

Through the defensive realist lens, states are significantly less likely to pursue empire, understanding that doing so can create insecurity in other states that are likely to balance growing power by building up their capabilities, forming alliances, or both. Recognizing that the pursuit of power can create insecurity in other states provides defensive realists with one of their primary theories to explain conflict in the international system: the security dilemma. Other key defensive realist concepts are the offense-defense theory and the balancing behavior of states.

The security dilemma theory, sometimes called the spiral model of conflict, says that because no state ever truly knows the intentions of other states in an anarchic international system, states must always prepare for the possibility of war. As states build up their military capabilities, even for purely defensive reasons, other states will interpret that build-up as aggressive and will increase their power in response. This can result in a cycle of escalation that leads to arms races or even wars.[7]

The dilemma that this theory raises is that even if two states have peaceful intentions and only increase their capabilities to enhance their security, they could end up in a war that neither of them wants. One state's increase in power still threatens its neighbors, who in turn are compelled to increase their capabilities because they do not know the intentions of their neighbor. As a result, all states feel less secure than before and again seek to enhance their capabilities, resulting in a spiral of conflict.

In the scenario that begins this chapter, the arms race between Russia and China illustrates this concept. A historical example of the spiral of conflict is the naval race that emerged between England and Germany prior to World War I. The Germans feared the British navy's ability to impose a blockade on Germany in the event of war and so pursued a naval build-up—the Tirpitz Plan, or Risk Fleet—that would not directly challenge British naval superiority but would prevent a blockade. The problem was that this German naval expansion threatened the domain that was most critical for the British, who then felt compelled to increase their naval construction—they were in fact obligated by law to do so.[8] This arms race is one of the many causes of tension between England and Germany that precipitated the outbreak of war in 1914.[9]

The effects of this theory are strongest when states compete in various domains, such as trade or establishing colonies. Resource scarcity can also exacerbate the security dilemma, as states assume their competition for resources will inevitably lead to conflict. If increasing power decreases the security of others, who feel less secure when their neighbors build up capabilities, then the security dilemma suggests that states can enhance their security by posing less of a threat to their neighbors, which they may be able to do by reducing their military power. Despite being a logical extension of the theory, given the anarchy of international politics, it is difficult to convince states, especially their domestic population, that they can increase their security by reducing their military capabilities.

The security dilemma is also related to deterrence.[10] For a state to issue a credible deterrent threat, it must have at least enough capabilities to impose costs on the target should it engage in an unwanted act. The problem is that focusing on capabilities to deter can enhance the security dilemma. The trick is knowing when a state has enough power to deter but not so much that it compels its rivals to build up their own capabilities and escalate tension. Unfortunately, leaders cannot know how much until either deterrence fails or states are trapped in a spiral of conflict.

In addition to requiring the capabilities to impose cost, deterrence also requires some level of credibility. The deterrent threat must be believable, and the threat to use force must be plausible as well. This means states that want to deter must have a willingness to use their military in the event a threat fails to deter.[11] States can take actions that enhance their credibility, such as positioning forces in a way that strengthens their commitment, or leaders can make statements that commit them to a certain path. But these measures can also precipitate a security dilemma, or even the war they intended to avoid, if taken too aggressively.

These are policy challenges for which there are no clear answers. Many defensive realists believe there is often a lack of agency involved in these situations, meaning states can find themselves at war with no real choice or intent behind that decision. In a sense, security dilemmas are automatic and remove rational decision-making from the equation. Neoclassical realists disagree with this notion, preferring to believe states have more choice or agency about decisions to go to war, even if internal political forces sometimes compel the state into action.[12]

The offense-defense balance is another defensive realist theory that attempts to explain the likelihood and character of war by examining whether it is easier to engage in offensive operations or to defend. When it is relatively easier to engage in offense than defense, the theory suggests that wars will be quick and decisive, and as a result wars become more likely (as security dilemmas increase, alliances become activated more quickly, and states fear the loss of a war from not acting fast enough). In contrast, when defense has the advantage, wars will be long, drawn-out affairs, both costly and painful to states, but they will be less likely. States are less likely to overreact to everything that happens, and premade alliances become less critical so that diplomatic solutions are easier to achieve. The implication, then, is that when defense has the advantage, the international system is less prone to wars.[13]

A criticism of the theory is that it is often difficult to assess the balance, since the offensive or defensive character of a weapon is generally ambiguous and depends on how a state plans to use it. When states introduced the tank in World War I, they primarily used it in a defensive manner. This did not change the balance until the Germans used their tanks offensively in World War II. More critical for the theory is that there is disagreement over how to measure the offense-defense balance.[14] One short-hand approach is that mobility contributes to offense while firepower contributes to defense. However, this approach is problematic in many ways. Trains, for instance, contribute to mobility but are not necessarily useful for attacks because they depend on the existence of train tracks, which retreating forces can destroy more easily than advancing forces can repair or build new tracks.

Another problem with this theory is that policymakers rarely know in the present whether defense or offense has the advantage, so they often act based on perceptions, which may be incorrect. Prior to World War I, most leaders believed offense had the advantage to the extent that whichever state attacked first would win the war.[15] The real defensive character of war at the time led to trench warfare and millions of fatalities over five years. In this case, perception mattered more than reality for determining the likelihood of war, but the reality determined the character of the war.

It appears that offense currently has the advantage in space since it is easier to target space capabilities than it is to defend them. But history tells us this balance routinely shifts. When offense has the advantage, states rely on it to develop their war plans, but they also seek defensive counters, which we see in contemporary discussions of the need for resiliency in satellite systems.[16] There is no way to know where the balance will fall in the future. It will depend on the types of new technologies that arise and, more importantly, how actors use those advances on the battlefield.

Balancing is a realist concept that is related to the concept of system polarity (discussed below). The idea is that states will ally with one another to prevent any one state from becoming too powerful.[17] There are, of course, multiple variations of balancing, because not everyone agrees with Kenneth Waltz's theory that states will balance against power. Other realists argue that states balance against threats[18] or that they balance according to their interests in either preserving or altering the status quo.[19]

Balancing can also be either internal or external. External balancing involves the formation of alliances to check the power or growth of another state or group of states. Sometimes, though, states will balance internally by building up their military capabilities. They may do this because they cannot find any willing and reliable allies, or they do not want to entrust their security to others and would rather retain more autonomy by enhancing their own capabilities. Both internal and external balancing can lead to security dilemmas. In one of the best examples, shortly after the creation of NATO to defend Western Europe, the Soviet Union responded with the creation of the Warsaw Pact to help it control its buffer zone in Eastern Europe. Similarly, after the formation of both the Franco-Russian alliance and the Triple Alliance in the late nineteenth century, the British feared being isolated, so they first considered joining the Triple Alliance but did not trust Germany. They did form an alliance with Japan, which balanced Russia's power in Asia but not so much in Europe. Then, as Germany became more belligerent, the British joined France and then Russia, forming the Triple Entente.[20]

As with the security dilemma, realists disagree about whether balancing is a decision by leaders or simply a natural function of the international political system (with little human agency). Defensive realists are more comfortable with balancing being a force that compels states to act, whereas other realists are less accepting of the lack of human agency and prefer to think of balancing behavior as something leaders choose to engage in or choose to avoid. To support this notion of national leaders having agency to choose, history shows us that states do not always balance against power, threats, or interests. Sometimes they ally *with* the most powerful or most threatening states, either to avoid being conquered or to share in the spoils of victory. And sometimes states choose to remain neutral, attempting to distance themselves from conflict because they are unwilling to get involved, they lack the capabilities to get involved, or they lack the support of other states.

Whether states balance or not depends less on the distribution of power than on whether they view the rising state as a threat. U.S. *power* after World War II did not push Western European states to balance against it. Instead, they allied with the United States, or balanced against the *threat* from the Soviet Union. Likewise, when the Cold War ended and the United States emerged as the lone superpower, at least initially, states allied with the United States rather than balance against it, especially those states that were previously part of the Soviet sphere of influence. For almost three decades after the end of the Cold War, we started to see some balancing behavior, though it was more often diplomatic and economic forms of balancing rather than the traditional form of military balancing. More recently, the expansion of China's military capabilities and Russia's use of hybrid warfare both point to a renewal of military balancing. The question is whether they are balancing against U.S. interests, against the United States as a perceived threat, or against U.S. power. Or are they even balancing against the United States at all? One could argue their focus is more regional and is only about the United States because the United States still sees itself as a hegemon playing a role in every region.

It is common to view alliances as a means for states to enhance their power. But states ally for a variety of reasons—not just aggregating capabilities against a common adversary. States may ally to try to influence each other's behavior in three different ways, collectively known as a managing alliance.[21] *Tethering* alliances are an attempt to reduce animosity between two adversaries. Examples include the 1996 defense agreement between Israel and Turkey and the more classic 1939 Nazi-Soviet Nonaggression Pact. There may be ulterior motives, such as forestalling a conflict until better prepared for war, or these may be genuine attempts to reduce the likelihood of war. *Binding* alliances involve smaller states allying to try to have more influence over larger powers (e.g., many of the NATO states). These often look like bandwagoning, the difference being these are attempts to influence an ally's decisions rather than simply profiting. Finally, *blocking* alliances are intended to prevent two states from allying with each other. An example of a blocking alliance, or what is sometimes referred to as a wedge strategy, is the Triple Alliance of Germany, Austria-Hungary, and Italy before World War I. Neither side felt Italy was critical for winning a war, and Austria-Hungary did not trust Italy to be a reliable ally, even having a war plan for an invasion of Italy. Nevertheless, Germany wanted to keep Italy in the alliance because that was better than the alternative of Italy allying with England and France, which would give them greater access to the Mediterranean and increase Austria-Hungary's vulnerability.

Another aspect of the security dilemma is related to alliances, in which states fear both being abandoned by their ally and being entrapped or dragged into an unwanted conflict.[22] States forming alliances face this dilemma because a tighter alliance with more specific requirements decreases the likelihood of being abandoned by an ally but also increases the likelihood of entrapment. In contrast, looser agreements, with few specific requirements, can reduce fears of entrapment but subsequently increase fears of abandonment. The amount of fear also depends on the state's reliability as an ally. Being unreliable increases fears in partner states that they will be abandoned. At the same time, being reliable can embolden an ally, which increases the chances of being dragged into an unwanted war.[23]

System Polarity and Power Distribution

A balance of power system is determined, at least in part, by the number of great powers that are active in the system. Great powers are states whose behavior influences other powerful states as well as the system, and who could compete to become a hegemon. The nature of the balance of power is that as one state begins to become too powerful, other states will ally against it to prevent it from becoming a hegemon. But there are differences of opinion over which type of system polarity is most effective at preventing systemic wars.

A bipolar system is one where there are two main great powers, sometimes referred to as superpowers. There may be other major powers, as well as minor powers, all of whom will typically ally with one of the two superpowers, creating a world that is split into two opposing camps. Bipolar systems often highlight fundamental differences between the political or economic systems or the ideologies of the two sides. Some scholars suggest these are the most stable systems because there is little uncertainty—the great powers know who their allies and adversaries are—and because the competition is based on ideological differences, there is little likelihood of states switching sides.[24] This lowers fear of abandonment and reduces tension. Proponents admit bipolar systems may lead to arms races but generally view them as less likely to bring about system changing wars; thus, they are stable.

A multipolar system is one with three or more great powers and is notable for their willingness to shift allegiances as one state becomes too powerful or attempts to upset the status quo. Some scholars believe that the greater levels of uncertainty associated with this type of system create more stability in terms of states not wanting to upset the status quo.[25] States will avoid trying to become too powerful and losing their allies to balancing behavior. Those who favor bipolar systems, by contrast, argue that this uncertainty leads to greater concerns over insecurity, which result in expanding military capabilities and the formation of alliances. Eventually, this heightened distrust and fear of abandonment can lead to security dilemmas and possibly wars.[26]

Multipolar systems, regardless of the number of great powers, tend to bipolarize through the formation of alliances, especially as leaders perceive a growing likelihood of war. States will find themselves picking sides, and even neutral states find themselves isolated and either must pick a side or deal with the consequences. One example of this is the alliance system before World War I. Until 1900 the British preferred a policy of "splendid isolation" in which they refrained from permanent alliances. By 1901, however, the British felt such a policy would lead to vulnerability, so they formed an alliance with Japan. By 1904 the British joined an entente with France, which they extended to include Russia by 1907, solidifying the European great powers into two rival camps. Another example of a multipolar system forming two camps is the Axis and Allied Powers in World War II.

Some scholars even challenge the idea that system polarity affects state behavior, suggesting instead that the concentration of power is a more important factor.[27] In other words, there is variation even within system polarities. One can imagine a bipolar system with two superpowers and several other great powers (as was the case during the Cold War). But one can also imagine a bipolar system completely dominated by two superpowers and no other great powers. Levels of stability and the behavior of states will vary, even across these seemingly similar systems.

Relative Gains

One of the biggest differences between realists and liberalists (discussed in chapters 3 and 4) is their view of relative versus absolute gains. For realists, states are primarily concerned with their gains or losses in relation to other actors.[28] Trade disputes are a good example of this mentality. States are generally better off economically if they trade freely with one another. But if one state begins to benefit more than the others because of the free trade, other states are more likely to impose barriers to trade, which can lead to retaliation and possibly trade wars. As a result, everyone ends up worse off.[29]

The arms race during the Cold War is another illustration of this mindset. Even if the United States had enough nuclear weapons to wipe out the Soviet Union, and even if the nuclear triad made those weapons incredibly secure from an attempted first strike, any increase in Soviet weapons had to be matched.[30] Part of the motivation was fear of the Soviets gaining a first-strike advantage, but most of it had to do with this relative gains mindset.

Once humanity is in space, there will be numerous opportunities to choose between gaining more either in absolute terms or in relation to other actors. For critics of realism, the tendency to see the world through the relative gains lens helps explain why the realist view of IR is so inherently conflictual. On the other hand, as liberalists suggest, when actors view gains in absolute terms (relative only to their own past, and not to the present or future of other actors), cooperation becomes easier to explain and to achieve. The problem with this, realists suggest, is that the security of states—their survival—is a zero-sum game, in which one actor's gains are another actor's loss. This mentality is not simply an assumption of the worldview but for realists is a policy necessity because too much is at stake to assume other states have peaceful intentions or that allies will always provide support.

Another illustration of relative gains thinking for realists is economic policy based on mercantilism, which emphasizes self-interest and nationalism. An understanding of how realists, liberalists, and Marxists view trade and broader economic policies will help explain some of the choices that actors make in each scenario.

Mercantilism

Mercantilism, or economic nationalism, is the economic system most closely associated with realism. It was the dominant school of economic thought from the fifteenth through the late eighteenth century, when economists such as Adam Smith began to argue for a free trade system. Much like realism, the primary driver of mercantilist states is self-interest and relative gains, and since wealth is necessary for power, economics must serve political goals. The basic premise of mercantilism is that states benefit when they sell more products than they purchase—the idea being that when a state's currency remains within the country, there are more options for transforming that wealth into military power, whether by developing new weapons, hiring mercenary armies, or building larger national militaries. In contrast, when a state purchases foreign products, its currency leaves the country, allowing other states to increase their wealth and thus potentially their military power. This concept was prevalent when states conducted trade using gold and silver. Even today, though, when trade no longer relies on precious metals, states often revert to mercantilist policies out of concern for trade partners gaining too much relative wealth and becoming potential rivals or to ensure control of certain strategic industries.

This trade system is problematic, especially when a significant number of actors use mercantilist policies, and it is surpassed by the economic benefits of free trade (discussed in chapter 4). Mercantilists view that trade as a zero-sum game, but other economists argue that free trade makes everyone better off. Liberal economists point out that hoarding money gives it less value, defeating the purpose of holding onto it. But states often resort to mercantilist-type systems, or at least impose barriers to free trade, when they feel vulnerable to their trade partners, when they worry a trade partner benefits more from trade, or when there are security concerns (maybe unrelated to the trade partner) that require immediate access to wealth.

Mercantilist policies are still common among small countries or states trying to develop a new industry that would otherwise be unable to compete on the global market. Alexander Hamilton, one of the founding fathers of the United States, advocated mercantilist policies, at least until the nation's infant industries could compete on the global market.[31] These kinds of policies grew more popular between the two world wars, because many blamed the global trade system for contributing to World War I. During the Great Depression, governments spent a lot of money, devalued their currency, and imposed barriers to trade. The result was a reduction in global trade, which led most states to fall even further into economic decline.

Much of what goes on today under the umbrella of a free trade system is various forms of protectionism, strategic trade, or economic interventionism. A common feature of mercantilism is a high tariff on imports, to increase the cost of, and therefore reduce demand for, foreign goods. More frequently, states use nontariff barriers to trade (such as quotas, licenses, and environmental standards) to get around agreements that prohibit high tariffs, but all of those methods hinder the free flow of goods.[32]

Mercantilism does not have a strong record as a successful economic policy. States that tried it recently have not done as well as states that opened their economies to free trade. This forces domestic industries to become more competitive rather than being creatively lazy because the government protects them from external competition.

Other Variants of Realism

Scenarios one and two relied heavily on offensive and defensive realism; however, there are other variants of realism that are perhaps less academically and politically influential but that could become more applicable in the future. I do not discuss classical realism in these first two chapters for a couple of reasons. For one thing, many of the concepts that emerge from classical realism are evident in the discussions of offensive and defensive realism, so a section on classical realism would be repetitive. In addition, the focus on human nature of classical realists, like Niccolò Machiavelli and Hans Morgenthau,[33] was more about national policy than international politics, so it is less applicable to the purpose of this book.

Neoclassical realism is the most recent scholarly competitor to both offensive and defensive realism. Scholars in this camp generally attempt to do two things. First, they wish to return to some of the focus on human nature that was part of classical realism but was lost in the neorealist focus on great powers and the international system. Second, they embrace some of the critiques of realism, especially by liberalists. Neoclassical realists are more likely to incorporate domestic politics and international institutions into their explanations of state behavior.[34] They still focus generally on conflictual behavior between states but criticize the lack of agency in many defensive realist theories. Instead, they agree with liberalists that certain government types and international organizations can reduce conflict, but concerns over self-interest, national survival, and domestic politics still contribute to what are ultimately relative gains choices.

Other forms of realism are variously referred to as ethical realism, moral realism, pragmatic realism, or principled realism. These concepts have been around but most recently were highlighted in the 2017 National Security Strategy.[35] At best, these are foreign policy approaches rather than international relations schools of thought, and they lack the testable hypotheses of other variants. At worst, they are slogans that poll better in surveys of citizens, rather than basing policy choices entirely on self-interest.

HISTORY OF BALANCING

> If Hitler invaded hell I would make at least a favourable reference to the devil in the House of Commons.
> —WINSTON CHURCHILL, 1941

Given that balancing can refer to both bipolar and multipolar systems, numerous historical examples are available. My choice is to focus on one of each type, Europe during the multipolar pre–World War I era, which resulted in major power war, and the bipolar Cold War, which saw numerous small wars and conflicts but no major power war. That one of my cases led to war and the other did not should not be interpreted as one system being more stable than the other or my advocacy of one system over the other. They are merely two examples of different balance of power systems. These time periods are useful illustrations of the systems and were both valuable in developing the scenario at the beginning of this chapter. Both eras also end with a dramatic shock to the system: one with World War II and the rise of a new superpower, the other with the retrenchment of a former superpower and the emergence of a hegemon.

More relevant to the topic of balance of power, both historical cases show different ways alliances can operate and the effects they can have on state behavior and the system as a whole. While scholars often portray multipolar Europe before World War I as having inflexible alliances, the truly inflexible alliances of the Cold War did not result in war the same way. The two cases also provide different technological dimensions, with one at the infancy of airpower and the other spanning the nuclear age.

There are several historical examples of multipolar systems, but one of the most frequently cited is Europe's great power system before World War I. From 1866 until the outbreak of war in 1914, several major powers balanced one another through both temporary and longer-term alliances. Of course, a state's status as a great power depends on one's measure of power, but undisputed great powers at the time included the United Kingdom, Germany, France, and Russia. Other major powers included Austria-Hungary, Italy, Japan, the Ottoman Empire, and the United States. But not all major powers are the same. Russia's defeat in the Russo-Japanese War (1904–5) propelled Japan into the ranks of the great powers, while both the Austro-Hungarian and Ottoman Empires grew increasingly weak due to internal division and instability. The United States was a great power—the strongest power by some measures—but rarely acted like one prior to World War I. Geographic distance from Europe, not wanting to get involved in power politics, and preoccupation with the Western Hemisphere all precluded U.S. involvement in European affairs.

Significant rivalries existed between the great powers—England and France, France and Germany, Germany and Russia, and Russia and Austria-Hungary. Despite that—and perhaps because of it—the great powers also formed alliances, such as the Triple Alliance (1882) between Germany, Italy, and Austria-Hungary, the Franco-Russian Alliance (1891), the Anglo-Japanese Alliance (1902), the Anglo-French Entente (1904), and eventually the Triple Entente (1907). Each of these formed either in response to a growing rival or as a counter to an existing alliance.

Scholars often classify this alliance system before World War I as tight and inflexible, unlike a balance of power system, in which states should be able to shift alliances to prevent any one actor from growing too powerful. But this inflexibility only existed in the few years before the war. Going back to the early eighteenth century, the British played the role of kingmaker, effectively balancing against whichever continental power became too strong. England and France allied against Spain

(1716). Spain, in turn, allied with Austria (1725). By 1731, with England and France split, England allied with Austria, and Spain and France allied again. When, in 1756, Austria withdrew from its alliance with England to ally with France, the British allied with Prussia to balance power on the continent.

During the Napoleonic Wars, Europe's great powers allied with each other multiple times to counter the growing power of France. From 1792 to 1815, seven different coalitions formed to confront France, though the level of cohesion between allies varied from one coalition to the next. Great Britain was involved in all seven coalitions to some extent, allying with Austria, Prussia, and Russia, as well as other smaller European states. That was the nature of multipolar Europe prior to the twentieth century, but a series of events between 1901 and 1914 made the alliances seem tighter and less flexible (though states still feared abandonment by their allies).

By 1900, with the Concert of Europe falling apart and Europe's great powers forming alliances, the British felt it was necessary to abandon "splendid isolation" and form an alliance rather than be left alone and vulnerable to attack. They initially considered an alliance with Germany, seeing the combined forces of France and Russia as the greatest threat. When that alliance did not materialize,[36] they allied with Japan (1901). As the German threat grew from a combination of a naval build-up and aggressive behavior toward China and French colonies in Africa, the British formed an alliance with France (1904). The Anglo-French Entente, or Entente Cordiale, which became the Triple Entente when Russia joined (1907), gave the impression that Europe was divided into two opposing camps. Prior to World War I, events such as the Boer War, Fashoda Crisis, Russo-Japanese War, two Moroccan crises, and the Balkan wars all contributed to a growing sense of mistrust in Europe, with respect to the hostility of rivals as well as the reliability of allies.[37]

Until the development of the Triple Entente, there were still concerns that alliance commitments could shift. France consistently worried about Russia realigning with Germany and Austria-Hungary, reviving the League of the Three Emperors (1873–80). Similarly, Germany was concerned that Italy would realign with France and England. The fact that Italy initially declared neutrality in the war and then switched sides (1915) shows that the alliances were not as tight as often claimed.

The existence of a multipolar balance of power system did not prevent major power war from occurring. Too many factors contributed to World War I to single out a primary driver. In the context of the alliance system, the alliances themselves did not cause war, but their secretive nature contributed to the mistrust and insecurity that played a major role in its outbreak. When the terms of an alliance are secret but other states know the alliance exists, the assumption is those secret terms involve hostile intent. If even the existence of an alliance is kept secret, it may not increase insecurity, but neither can it contribute to deterring war.

Another factor contributing to World War I was the lack of U.S. balancing. Despite its distance from Europe, a major power's unwillingness to commit to either side affected decision-making and prevented the balance of power from operating effectively. We cannot say that a quadruple entente with the United States would have deterred war, but it might have given Germany and Austria-Hungary pause before declaring war. What this case shows is that while a multipolar balance of power system can be stable in terms of preventing systemic change, it can also devolve into major power wars if states are unwilling or unable to balance or if there is too much insecurity.

Another balance of power system was the bipolar Cold War between the United States and the Soviet Union. The United States was supported by other democratic free-trade states, primarily in Western Europe, while the Soviet Union's sphere of influence included other communist states with largely state-run economies. Most states felt compelled to join one of the two camps. Though some states tried to remain neutral or to play the superpowers off one another, such attempts rarely worked for long.

Although one can trace the beginnings of the Cold War to the strained Allied relationship in World War II or further back to the Russian Revolution during World War I, the immediate aftermath of World War II was a brief unipolar moment for the United States The United States was the only belligerent to not suffer battles on its territory, and it emerged from the war in a better economic condition than before the war and as the world's leading economic power. It was the only state with atomic capabilities, at least for a brief time (the first Soviet atomic test was not until 1949), and it led the establishment of the United Nations and the Bretton Woods economic agreement.

In 1946, Winston Churchill gave his "Iron Curtain" speech, suggesting the world was already divided between East and West.[38] Over the next decade, a series of events intensified the Cold War, including the Berlin blockade (1948–49), the establishment of NATO (1949) and the ensuing Warsaw Pact (1955), the Soviet development of nuclear weapons (1954), and the launch of the Sputnik satellite indicating a working intercontinental ballistic missile (1957). Over four decades, this competition influenced nearly all of world politics in some manner. Even local and regional issues took on global implications if one of the superpowers became involved.[39]

Competition came in the form of arms races and space races, proxy wars, and attempts to gain allies from the handful of neutral or unaligned states that existed. The United States alone formed numerous alliances during the Cold War, some of which were bilateral with another country (e.g., with Japan, South Korea, and the Philippines). Other alliances were multilateral, including the failed Southeast Asia Treaty Organization and Central Treaty Organization as well as the still-active Australia, New Zealand, United States Security Treaty and NATO. All of these were intended to balance the Soviet threat. Unlike the pre–World War I alliances, the allies made the terms of these agreements public, though both sides undoubtedly assumed there were secret annexes and passages.

Wars between superpower proxies or with superpower involvement occurred in Korea, Vietnam, Angola, and Afghanistan, among other places, but these never threatened to alter the stability of the system. Fears of realignment were low, but it did occur on occasion—most notably when France withdrew from NATO's integrated military command in 1966 and when the United States opened relations with China in 1972. But these are examples of alliances weakening because of changing domestic and international conditions. There was never any real concern of France realigning with the Soviet Union because they subscribed to different political and economic philosophies. Likewise,

China abandoning communism was unrealistic in 1972, even if it did open relations with the West.

Despite the view of some scholars that the Cold War's bipolar system was stable—either because of the structure or because of nuclear weapons[40]—there were times when the two superpowers neared the brink of war. The closest they came by some estimations was the Cuban Missile Crisis (16–28 October 1961). Yet other events could also have escalated to superpower war. In 1983 the Soviet Union detected a U.S. missile launch, an event that normally would have called for a full-scale retaliation. One Soviet officer, who (correctly) believed the warnings of a U.S. launch were errors and chose not to advise his superiors, may have prevented war. That the two powers did not escalate to war at any point leads some to extol the virtues of the bipolar system or the strength of the nuclear deterrent. Others view it as dumb luck.[41]

Several factors contributed to the end of the Cold War and collapse of the Soviet empire. The weak Soviet economy, attempts to compete with the United States technologically, and the quagmire of military action in Afghanistan (in which the United States supported the local militias to counter Soviet power) all contributed to the Soviet demise. Regardless of the reasons or the various steps that led to the opening of Eastern Europe and the break-up of the Soviet Union, what emerged was a unipolar system with the United States as the only global power. The willingness of the Russians to give up empire, rather than fight to keep it, is a challenge for offensive realists and helped give rise to constructivist thinking in IR (discussed in chapter 7). It is more consistent with defensive realist views of states assigning more value to security than power, because the Soviet leadership, most of whom were Russian, calculated that the best way to secure a stable Russian future was to stop holding on to an artificial empire at the expense of Russian interests and security.

The examples of a bipolar balance of power in this chapter also show what happens when such a system breaks down. In the case of the Cold War, the fall of one superpower meant that the remaining superpower became, at least for a time, a hegemon. In other words, one outcome of the decline of a balance of power can be the emergence of an actor who is significantly more powerful than any other actors. Such a scenario, especially according to realists, is often short-lived and leads to balancing behavior by other actors, with the balance of power eventually restored (though it may involve different actors the next time around). It was also more likely, given the way the Cold War ended without superpower war. A war between the United States and the Soviet Union might have ended the bipolar system but is unlikely to have created a hegemon out of either state given the likely level of cost and destruction involved in such a war.

BALANCES OF POWER IN SCIENCE FICTION

> The time was coming that Mars wasn't going to ignore them anymore. And when Mars took action, it wouldn't matter if Earth followed suit. It would be the first real war in the Belt.
> —JAMES S. A. COREY, *Leviathan Wakes*

Balances of power are less common in science fiction than are the types of hegemonic systems discussed in scenario one. Stories with multipolar systems often portray humans competing with alien races rather than against each other. I avoid using those works because I want the focus to be on human interaction. One exception is Ted Chiang's "Story of Your Life," a short story that was made into the film *Arrival*. Although it features aliens who come to Earth, it also portrays competition between states, all of whom are trying to figure out the aliens' language and therefore their motive. But like most movies involving aliens coming to Earth, the population of Earth ends up cooperating, either to defeat the threat or, as in Chiang's story, to become a more advanced species. More frequently in stories of alien threats, like *Starship Troopers*, *Ender's Game*, and *Forever War*, the nations of Earth come together to collectively tackle the alien threat, either in a distant system or at home (in a classic example of balancing threat, such as in *Independence Day*). Stories involving human competition for control of our own solar system are less common.

One book that does show competition between Earth and the moon is Robert Heinlein's *The Moon Is a Harsh Mistress*. This story is about a lunar base that started as an Earth penal colony and eventually demands its independence and recognition among the states of Earth. Strictly speaking, this situation fits the balance of power system, but rather than bipolarity, the moon is more like a colony that breaks away. It is also heavily dependent on an artificial intelligence, so I save further discussion of this book for my examination of Marxism and the exploitation of weak actors (chapter 5), as well as my focus on artificial intelligence and constructivism (chapter 7).

James S. A. Corey's *Leviathan Wakes* is the first book in *The Expanse* series (also a television series).[42] It is a recent but useful example of a balance of power system in science fiction. In this case, a single United Nations government controls Earth. Early in the series, Earth and Mars form a bipolar system after Mars declares its independence. As the series progresses, those who live in the outer planets and asteroids—known as Belters—form a tripolar system, with numerous corporations and non-state actors also influencing the system and each other. This tripolarity emerges partly because Earth and Mars focus their attention on one another, much as China arose out of the Cold War competition between the United States and the Soviet Union. But the Belters also gain a new technology and leadership that provide them the cohesion to be a major player.

Some scholars suggest that the behavior of states in a tripolar system is different from those in other types of multipolar systems (i.e., with four or more great powers) and that tripolar systems are less stable than other types of multipolar systems. The interwar period is sometimes considered a historical example of tripolarity.[43] Perhaps the most famous example comes from George Orwell's *1984*. Three superstates—Oceania, Eurasia, and Eastasia—experience constant war between two of the states, but the belligerents frequently change and history books are altered to avoid any mention of an alliance with the state against which it is currently fighting. As the main character, Winston, writes, "It was only four years since Oceania had been at war with Eastasia and in alliance with Eurasia. But that was merely a piece of furtive knowledge. . . . Officially the change of partners had never happened. Oceania was at war with Eurasia: therefore Oceania had always been at war with Eurasia."[44]

Even *Dune* addresses the dangers of tripolarity. As Paul's mother states, "We've a three-point civilization: the Imperial Household balanced against the Federated Great Houses of the Landsraad, and between them, the Guild with its damnable monopoly on interstellar transport. In politics, the tripod is the most unstable of all structures."[45] So the tripolar *Expanse* system might be different from one with more than three primary actors, but we can still glean some interesting parallels between Corey's fictional future and historical cases of multipolarity.

One seemingly common feature of all nonhegemonic systems is the assumption that states in other alliances are closer to each other than they are. The Belters, for example, see the inner planets of Earth and Mars as uniform in their goals and opposition to the Outer Belt, whereas those from Earth and Mars give little thought to the Belters and see each other as the primary threat—so much so that they build up their military capabilities in the event of a clash with one another. This mirrors the behavior of states in the multipolar pre–World War I era as well as in the Cold War. Even when states considered their alliances tight, they still worried about the reliability of their allies, while generally assuming rival alliances were strong and cohesive.

Greg Bear's *Moving Mars* is an interesting story that has some fantastical elements but also contains much that relates to balance of power and defensive realism. The story follows Casseia Mujamdar from her college days of protesting Mars's new unified government to her involvement in helping to establish a unified government on Mars. Earth still has nation-states, but four main economic alliances conduct most of the planet's business and politics: "The fiction of separate nations and government control was maintained, but increasingly, political decisions were made on the basis of economic benefit not national pride."[46]

Humans have settled most of the solar system, but the story takes place almost entirely on Mars, with only passing mentions of the moon or the Outer Belt. There is a linked economy between Earth, Mars, and the moon, known as the Triple, and a single currency. The moon is largely subservient to Earth, while Mars is more independent, operated initially by a system of Binding Multiples (BMs), which are a type of hybrid between extended families and corporations. The backstory is that the first settlers organized into these groups or families, and each one specialized in one aspect of Martian life. For example, the Mujamdar BM, to which the main character initially belongs, is a banking BM.

Earth is initially supportive of a unified Mars, if that statist government takes power away from the BMs and gives Earth more influence. That statist government is deposed through a combination of its own corruption and fear by the people of Mars that Earth would control the government. As the book continues, Mars becomes more unified, but not in the manner desired by Earth. A Federated Republic is formed, with an interim government until elections can be held. The main character, having changed BMs through marriage, then becomes the vice president of the planet.

Most of the BMs support a Federated Republic, though there are some who oppose it and remain outside the new government. Earth also is opposed to Martian autonomy and especially to an independent Mars that Earth cannot control. As the main character offers, "I think Earth has some greater plan, and autonomy of any part of the Triple stands in their way. Eventually, they'll want to tame and control Mars as they've already done with the Moon. And then they'll work on the Belters, the asteroids and space settlements . . . bring us all into the fold, until their central authority controls all the resources of the Solar System."[47] In other words, Earth is seeking hegemony, and, as defensive realists would suggest, that leads to balancing. In this case, the BMs form an alliance against a more powerful and threatening entity, even as a few BMs choose to bandwagon with Earth instead (or they are balancing against the BMs that would gain power under a unified Martian government).

The story also illustrates several aspects of offense-defense theory and the security dilemma. Martian scientists invent a new technology that can move huge masses, including a planet, across great distances. This is immediately recognized as a possible weapon, and the Martians in power realize how much of a threat this poses to Earth. This new technology is clearly an offensive weapon for which there is no defense. And while there is some possibility of a type of mutually assured destruction, a rogue faction on Earth authorizes a drone attack before the technology is finished on Mars. This is halted briefly when Mars exhibits its ability to destroy Earth, but Earth launches a second attack once it has its own device (essentially daring the Martians to retaliate and kill millions on Earth). As predicted by the theory, offensive capabilities exacerbate the security dilemma and lead to offensive action out of fear.

After Earth's first attack, there is even an ultimatum given to Mars, not unlike that from Austria-Hungary to Serbia after the assassination of Archduke Franz Ferdinand on 28 June 1914. The terms of the ultimatum require surveillance by Earth and regular visits by inspection teams.[48] Mars refuses and provides a display of its new technology, essentially threatening Earth with destruction and forcing the attack to be halted. While this show of force serves its purpose and stops the attack, it compels Earth's scientists to redouble their efforts to develop their own version of the new technology: "We all know what's going to happen now. . . . They [Earthlings] have the resources in people and machines and laboratories, to duplicate your discoveries. . . . And as soon as they can do what we can do, it's just a matter of time before somebody strikes somebody else."[49] As expected, Earth's development of a comparable technology forces the new Martian government to take drastic steps to avoid being destroyed.

Moving Mars is now a quarter-century old, and Greg Bear wrote it before computers were commonplace. Because of that, some of the discussions of technology appear a bit quaint. At the same time, the primary technology is a largely unbelievable invention that drives the plot and gives the book its title. Despite that, and the requirement that readers suspend some belief, the themes of the book are true to defensive realist views of politics and illustrate many of the concepts and theories discussed in this chapter.

Science fiction in which humans created an empire in space or came together as a united Earth are much more common than stories involving a balance of power between political entities. That does not mean balances are unlikely, especially since they are the most common system in human history. Perhaps it is not an interesting backdrop for stories of the future because it is so prominent in our history. But we know it breeds high levels of competition, and forms of cooperation rarely last for long before they break down into system-changing wars.

ANALYSIS

> Thus one who does not know the plans of the feudal lords cannot prepare alliances beforehand.
> —SUN TZU, *The Art of War*

Some of the main sources of conflict for defensive realists, which we see in the scenario and in history, are misunderstanding, misperception, and accidents. Resource scarcity, zero-sum thinking, and simply the nature of humans are all common explanations of conflict for most realists. But defensive realists also see conflict as a function of factors and conditions beyond the control of leaders. The security dilemma, offense-defense balance, and the concept of system polarity all take agency out of the hands of leaders, suggesting war is more a function of systemic factors. This is one reason neoclassical realists challenge many elements of defensive realist thinking.

Major potential variations in this scenario have to do with the number of great powers and the polarity of the system. Different scholars view bipolar and multipolar systems differently, and it would be impossible to capture all these variations in a single scenario. All realists believe humans are inherently self-interested, and this translates into whatever type of polity they govern and whatever type of system is in operation. Whether it is the city-state, nation-state, empire, nonstate actor, multinational corporation, or international organization, all realists see self-interest as the primary motivation for an actor's choices. Defensive realists, though, suggest that this need for self-interest often takes agency out of the hands of leaders and puts them in positions where they are compelled to go to war even if that is not anyone's intention.

Based on IR, history, and science fiction, it is plausible that several actors could establish some type of balance of power in space. These actors could be states, colonies of Earth, nonstate actors, or some combination of the above. As in scenario one, this defensive realist–based scenario finds mixed results when used to analyze the four primary standards of evaluation (see table 2.1). Although realists are generally pessimistic about certain aspects of politics, like the self-interested nature of states and the lack of long-term cooperation, there are some benefits to either a hegemonic or a balance of power system. While the systems are agnostic about the standard of living of the people—since that depends more on the nature of the state than the nature of the system—both systems would do a decent job of preventing short-term systemic wars and of driving innovation and the human exploration of space. This means that security and exploration technology will thrive, and much of this will spill over into the civilian sector. What it does not guarantee is that the populations of Earth or its colonies will have enough food, shelter, and other necessities to survive, much less flourish.

Short-term results are positive for at least two of the factors, including human exploration and enhancing S&T. In the case of S&T, the nature of the balance of power system will drive innovation, especially in the military and security realms, though there is often spillover into the civilian world. This competition is not universally positive because it can lead to rising tension, arms races, and even war. Analyzed independently, competition does tend to drive innovation in science and technology in both the short term and the long run.

Just as the European powers expanded throughout the world, establishing colonies in the Americas, Africa, and Asia, so too will multipolar competition drive human expansion out into the solar system. While this competition can increase the likelihood of war, concerns about security could either increase expansion to provide buffer zones or stymie expansion as states divert their finite resources into their militaries. From a

TABLE 2.1. **EVALUATING THE BALANCE OF POWER SYSTEM**

MEASURES OF EVALUATION	SHORT-TERM (DURING BALANCING)	LONG-TERM (AS BALANCE DETERIORATES)
Minimizing war	Mixed (minimizes systemic wars)	No
Human expansion	Yes	Yes
Enhancing S&T	Yes (mostly military)	Yes (mostly military)
Improving SoL	Depends on nature of balance (internal or external) and the nature of the actors	Mixed (some states but not others)

strictly defensive realist perspective, states will not expand simply for the sake of power, but they will still compete for strategically valuable parts of the solar system. Human expansion should continue regardless of the security environment, restrained only by technological capabilities and the distance between worlds.

A balance of power system should minimize systemic war if one accepts the central tenets of realism, but history provides little evidence of long-term stability regardless of the polarity of the system. Balances will fail because some states choose not to balance—either remaining neutral or allying with a rising power—while others may not have the ability to balance internally or externally. In systems with a neutral state willing to act as kingmaker and shift alliances to keep the balance, as the British did before the 1900s or as Bismarck did while he managed German foreign policy, then the system can prevent wars for a time. But history shows all multipolar and bipolar systems eventually succumb to system-changing wars or some other event that shocks the system. While these systems can minimize systemic wars in the short term, they will not prevent wars between small states, nor will they prevent great power war in the long term.

Depending on the nature of the main actors and on the level of tension between the powers, standards of living could rise or fall. If the states place heavy emphasis on security, then standards of living will not rise as quickly as if the states focus on nonmilitary development. Comparing the United States to the Soviet Union during the Cold War provides a glimpse of this variation. Even within the United States, there was a constant struggle between national security balanced with the other interests of the American people. Over the longer term, if the system remains in place (meaning competition still drives policy decisions), it is unlikely all states will be concerned about their population's welfare. Only some populations will see significant improvement in this area.

In addition, states that balance externally by forming alliances should generally have more resources to spend on populations than states that balance internally. Internal balancing requires spending on defense rather than on the country. The challenge of external balancing is being dependent on another state for at least some part of one's own security. States that are fearful of abandonment should be more inclined to balance internally rather than risk entrusting their security to another actor.

Cooperation in balance of power systems occurs, but, according to realists, it is temporary and focuses entirely on self-interest. Once cooperation ceases to be beneficial, actors will go their own way. For example, realists accept that cooperation occurs when states face common threats but argue that it tends to decline as the threat diminishes. The United States and England allying with the Soviet Union during World War II typifies this. These temporary alliances are not necessarily bad and can contribute to a functioning and stable balance of power system more than tight, inflexible alliances can. But these systems also tend to fall apart.

When the Cold War ended, many realists expected NATO to fold, since its main reason for existence no longer posed a threat to Europe. The Western states formed NATO to deter Soviet aggression into Western Europe, but they also designed the alliance to keep Germany from threatening its neighbors again and to keep the United States engaged in Europe (to "keep the Russians out, the Americans in, and the Germans down"[50]). It was about not only cooperating against a common threat and aggregating capabilities, but also managing the foreign policy behavior of its members. As a result, the disappearance of the threat, which typically causes an alliance to fall apart, had no such effect on NATO.

NATO's other purposes, combined with fifty years of institutionalization, meant the alliance gained its own interests and continued to operate beyond the Soviet threat. Realists counter by arguing that NATO's members, especially the United States, still believe it provides more benefits than costs, and so they remain tied to one another.[51] However, if any shift occurs in national interests or in the operations of the alliance, we could see states withdrawing from it.

One of the biggest differences between realists and liberalists relates to their view of international organizations. Chapter 3 addresses this in more detail, but realists see international organizations as tools of the powerful states. States set them up to help pursue their national interests and will remain involved as long as they fulfill that need. In contrast, liberalists believe institutions can promote cooperation between states and restrain their self-interested behavior. For liberalists, international institutions can even prevent wars. Realists counter this by arguing that institutions do not prevent wars—they emerge after wars end, once the new hierarchy of powers is established, to promote the interests of the victors. The League of Nations emerged after World War I, the United Nations and Bretton Woods economic agreement both arose after World War II, and the World Trade Organization developed after the end of the Cold War. All these institutions did promote some degree of cooperation, but only after the new great powers determined the type of cooperation they desired.

In multipolar systems, as with any type of system, states will also cooperate even with a current threat if they see an opportunity to profit off an alliance. Realists see this type of bandwagoning when states join what appears to be the winning side of a war, but it can happen during times of peace as well. Such behavior goes against the logic of the balance of power but is a consistent element of historical multipolar systems. A less cooperative form of bandwagoning is when states capitulate to avoid being invaded and occupied by a more powerful state. This is less about cooperation and more about surrendering to avoid defeat.[52]

One other form of cooperation that can emerge in a multipolar system, most frequently after a war has been fought, is a concert. This is an agreement, sometimes informal, between the great powers, that they will refrain from settling their differences with violence. Like most of international politics, though, concerts tend to be short-lived forms of cooperation. One of the most famous examples of this was the Concert of Europe, put in place after the Napoleonic Wars (1815) and lasting until the revolutions of 1848, and then renewed under the leadership of German chancellor Otto von Bismarck from 1871 until the outbreak of World War I in 1914. A concert does not mean there will not be wars, just that the great powers agree not to go to war with each other. Chapter 3 explores many of these organizations as well as the concept of a concert.

The Sun Tzu quotes in this chapter enhance our discussion of alliances. This is intentional given the focus of defensive realism on balancing power and the various reasons states form alliances. The quote that begins this chapter talks about the importance of weakening an adversary's alliances, second only to weakening his plans (or in other interpretations, his strategies). This is consistent with Sun Tzu's general advice on only fighting wars that can be won quickly and winning even before the war begins. Sun Tzu suggests going after a rival's allies, driving a wedge between them, and perhaps fighting against a lone actor rather than a coalition of adversaries or possibly even bringing them over to your side.

The corollary to this advice, though less developed by Sun Tzu, is that a state must ensure its alliance is strong before entering into war. Allies have different levels of reliability and different capabilities, and the effective leader will leverage an ally's strengths and mitigate their own weaknesses, either internally or with other allies. This relates to the alliance security dilemma discussed above, because a strong alliance will be one with minimal fears of both abandonment and entrapment, while a smart leader will use those fears to drive a wedge between rival alliances. It also means preserving one's reliability as an ally, to prevent partners from being siphoned off by a potential rival.

The quote at the beginning of this section also highlights the role of alliances, but it advises that one should know the adversary's intentions to pursue the best allies for that situation. This is an important message that is discussed too infrequently in both politics and academics. Not all allies are right for each operation or war. Understanding the other side's strengths and weaknesses, and having the ability to find allies that will help take advantage of those weaknesses, is a key to success in the event that one must fight. The coalition against Iraq in 1991, for example, excluded Israel. Although its location and capabilities were valuable from a military point of view, its involvement might have prevented many Arab states from joining against Saddam Hussein and weakened the overall coalition.

A good ally will have some offensive capabilities if it is expected to fight. The British and French promised to defend Poland from Nazi Germany but had few offensive capabilities.[53] Thus, when Germany invaded, there was little the British or French could do. While the United States is geographically distant from Europe, the stopping power of water forced the United States to develop offensive air and maritime capabilities if it hoped to influence World War II. These capabilities then gave the United States the ability to project power globally during the Cold War, making it a capable ally.

Being a good ally, though, is not just about capabilities. Good allies are reliable; they are willing to support a partner when attacked and to avoid dragging their allies into unwanted conflicts. While allies are important and can be critical to winning, they can also bring about unwanted war—as the United States nearly did during the Cuban Missile Crisis and did with several of its allies in Iraq in 2003. One concern over U.S. security guarantees to Taiwan is the possibility that the agreement would drag the United States into war with China. More recently, as China builds up its military capabilities and shows a greater willingness to flex its muscles regionally, Taiwan's growing concern is whether the United States will honor its commitment and support Taiwan in a war against China.

Another passage from Sun Tzu, referencing focus terrain, is not directly about allies, but one can interpret it in a way that is valuable for alliance politics. Sun Tzu writes, "Land of the feudal lords surrounded on three sides such that whoever arrives first will gain the masses of All under Heaven is 'focal terrain.' "[54] He is referring to territory that allows access to other great powers and thus is incredibly valuable for both offense and defense. In his translation of *The Art of War*, Samuel Griffith claims that "All under Heaven" is a reference to the empire,[55] suggesting that whoever controls that focal terrain will receive offers of friendship from the empire. One must think of key allies as a form of focal terrain. Not only will they be courted by all sides, but it is important to understand their value, in terms of logistics, offensive, and defensive capabilities in the event of war. A future interpretation might be about the importance of the Lagrangian points between Earth, the moon, and the sun. This focal terrain in space provides potentially valuable access to the solar system and therefore the ability to control the system. It is likely to breed competition for access to it, and those who control it—or who can prevent others from controlling it—will have an advantage.[56] It also gives a broader meaning to "All under Heaven."

SUMMARY

> Earth has always hated Mars. . . . When I was in the navy,
> we ran projections for this. Battle plans if Earth and Mars
> ever really got into it. Earth loses. Unless they hit first, hit hard,
> and don't let up, Earth just plain loses.
> —JAMES S. A. COREY, *Leviathan Wakes*

Balances of power can be incredibly stable systems that create innovation and prevent war. The problem is that they do not endure. The international system is dynamic, which means state power rises and falls, and states sometimes are unable or unwilling to balance against growing powers or increasing threats. In such circumstances, the historical tendency has been toward major war.

Multipolar systems are difficult to avoid and are common in international politics because they arrive through a natural division of power in the system. Attempts to avoid a balance of power system may be fruitless, but we could focus on how to avoid some of the worst elements—although some may be impossible to counter, especially from the defensive realist point of view. If one accepts the realist view of human nature, and especially the defensive realist explanation of conflict arising from misperception and misunderstanding, then an obvious resolution is for states to be more open and honest. However, states have too many incentives to provide false information about both their capabilities and their interests. Similarly, if states care most about security, then they could act to reduce the security dilemma by reducing their capabilities, but this is problematic in an anarchic world. Finally, if wars are less likely in a defense-dominant world, then states could reduce tension by always developing defensive weapons. The problem is that most weapons can be either offensive or defensive, and a state's intentions are not known until it uses the weapon in war.

Up to this point, this book has used realist notions to explore two possible scenarios of humanity's future in space. The rest of the book examines other worldviews, many of which are critical of aspects of realism. This does not necessarily mean they are more attractive as future scenarios, but they do offer different lenses on our future. One of the concepts introduced in this chapter was that of a concert, an informal agreement between states to avoid war. While alliances represent one form of international organization, most of them are limited in scope, membership, and duration, serving only the short-term interests of their members. We also discussed NATO as one long-term example of cooperation. Broadening the concept of alliances and introducing more formal versions of a concert, chapter 3 examines the liberalist worldview, with a particular focus on the role of international organizations and international law and the opportunities for cooperation between states in space.

CHAPTER 3

PAX TERRA
A FEDERATION OF STATES

> One who excels at employing the military cultivates
> the Tao and preserves the laws.
> —SUN TZU, *The Art of War*

World War III (2033–35) nearly devastated Earth, but as often happens after incredibly destructive wars, the great powers banded together, either in the name of cooperation or out of sheer exhaustion, to prevent another destructive war between them. The war led to significant military innovation and several new ways for humans to kill each other, but it stunted technology in other areas, such as energy creation and space exploration. After the war, the remaining powers led a global cooperative effort to expand into space and start a new civilization away from the destruction inflicted on Earth. In the beginning, states continued to exist, power disparities continued to influence state choices, and there was no interest in creating an all-powerful world government. But states did give up more of their sovereignty to the United Nations (UN) in exchange for the hope that cooperation would lead to greater human advancement in space. Eventually, the success of that cooperation spread exponentially until the great powers finally realized they were all better off in cooperation than in competition, and thus began the era of the newly created United Nations Federation (UNF).

Stepping back, we must examine the lead-up to the war to understand the course of events that gave rise to the UNF. The war began between China and Russia over resources in Siberia, but that was just the first spark before tensions spread globally. The Russians were either unwilling or unable to extract resources in the harsh terrain. China gradually increased the population of loyal Chinese citizens in Siberia over the course of decades until ethnic Chinese living there outnumbered Russians by two to one. For more than a decade before the war, China played the United States and Russia against each other but was generally on good terms with Russia. In exchange for favorable terms of trade and badly needed development loans, the Russians turned a blind eye to the growing influence of Chinese citizens in the easternmost parts of Russia.

By 2030 the Chinese economy was the largest in the world, surpassing that of both the European Union and the United States, but the needs of the Chinese population continued to outpace the ability of the Chinese economy to provide for it. The solution that the Chinese believed offered the least resistance was to take the resources in Siberia. Chinese propaganda labeled it "taking back," in reference to the 1860 Convention of Peking. This was known in China as the Unequal Treaty, which forced the less powerful China to give concessions to the more powerful England (which received Hong Kong), France (land was returned to and protection was promised for Christian missionaries), and Russia (which received the territory China referred to as Outer Manchuria). Only after China struck the first blow did it appear that this had been part of its plan for at least a decade, and it was just biding its time until the conditions were favorable to act.

The irony is that China adopted the same initial tactics that Russia used to seize territory in Abkhazia, Georgia, and Ukraine in the early part of the century. The Chinese handed out passports to sympathizers in the area, manufactured an emergency, and then moved the military in to "protect Chinese citizens." The military forces initially had no Chinese markings on their uniforms and took up defensive positions in the largest towns before the Russians figured out what was happening. By that point, the only way to reverse Chinese gains would have been with nuclear weapons against the occupying forces. Russia was reluctant to take that step, at least in the beginning, because of the deaths it would cause among Russians in the area, as well as the fear of Chinese nuclear escalation in response.

The United States and Europe tried to stay out of the war, but neither belligerent made that easy. In trying to blockade Russian naval activity in Asia, Chinese forces routinely violated the sovereign airspace and maritime territory of U.S. allies. The Russians, realizing the Chinese outmatched them in the east, opted to focus their attention on the west. Some suggest this was an effort by the government to divert the Russian people's attention from losing the east and focus on making potentially more visible gains in the west. But this decision resulted in a two-front war for Russia. Russian incursions and cyberattacks into the Baltics challenged NATO cohesion. When several NATO members failed to support an Article V vote to support those states, the alliance began to fall apart. Most of the newer members, who joined the alliance after the Cold War, withdrew from both NATO and the European Union and more closely linked their economies with that of Russia to avoid risking the loss of their territory.

NATO continued to exist, but its membership reverted to just twelve of the original members plus Poland, until it too was conquered by Russia. Belgium, trying to remain neutral, expelled all remaining NATO ministers from the country, so the organization moved its headquarters to London. Eventually, NATO meetings became a simple partnership between the U.S. and British joint staffs.

The United States and England were already leaning toward supporting China because of Russian aggression into Europe and because the U.S. economy was much more closely linked to China than to Russia. They officially joined the war on the Chinese side after Russian ships fired on British ships patrolling the Mediterranean to enforce the Montreux Convention.[1] France and Germany chose not to fight in the war, but the Germans provided material support to Russia, based on their need for Russian energy, while the French sided with China but only through the provision of monetary aid. Poland held out for as long as it could with U.S. support, and the Baltic states struggled for a time with support from Sweden. But eventually they all signed either a neutrality pact or a defense agreement with Russia. Other European states tried to stay out of the fray as much as possible, though cyberattacks from both Russia and China—mostly in the form of disinformation campaigns—even targeted neutral states.

In the United Nations Security Council (UNSC), Russia offered a resolution condemning Chinese actions and calling for a UN force to expel China from Russian territory. China vetoed the resolution. The United Kingdom, France, and the United States authored a similar resolution condemning Russian activities in Europe, which Russia vetoed. This impasse reminded all the permanent members of the futility of the UN in its existing format, and operations of the UNSC were suspended. The General Assembly remained open as a place for multilateral negotiations and discussion, but almost all other units in the UN closed down. The Secretary General also resigned, creating uncertainty for the organization's role in future international politics.

South America and the Middle East were divided over allegiance to Russia and China. Several Russians allies, such as Cuba, Venezuela, and Syria, supported their long-time sponsor. Others with stronger economic ties to China opposed Russia and its allies, and this, combined with long-time regional rivalries, led to several battles being fought in both regions. Africa and North America were the only continents to escape significant violence on their territory, though both the United States and Canada suffered from significant cyberattacks by Russian-sponsored hackers.

Once it appeared Siberia was lost, and because of fears the Chinese might next direct their attention farther west, perhaps even threatening Moscow, Russia decided to launch a portion of its nuclear weapons at Chinese forces in Siberia. It was a last desperate act of a government trying to avoid total defeat. Russia only used part of its nuclear arsenal, hoping that keeping some in reserve would deter China from retaliating. It did not work. The Chinese retaliation likewise used only part of its arsenal, and none of the other states "went nuclear." China did express concern to the United States and England about how India would react to Chinese retaliation. The British relayed a message to the Chinese that India would not react, as India was concerned about potential escalation with Pakistan and was unwilling to challenge an alliance that included England and the United States. Though relatively limited compared to what was possible, the nuclear exchange killed millions of people, sickened thousands more with radiation poisoning, and affected global weather patterns. It also prevented China from extracting Siberia's resources safely and efficiently, which was likely part of the Russian calculation. Russia's first use of nuclear weapons lost it any international allies it had that were not already under Russian control. Russia could have launched its remaining arsenal at China or even at the United States, but those few decision-makers in Moscow who survived the Chinese strike made the choice to stand down their nuclear forces, though they were not yet willing to admit defeat. The fighting continued at the conventional level for about a year but did not go nuclear again.

After the war, the great powers decided to cooperate to prevent future wars.[2] While China was the victor, the war largely destroyed the People's Liberation Army, and, as after World War II, the United States remained as the great power that suffered the fewest losses and emerged economically stronger than the other powers. The result was a de facto rejuvenation of American hegemony. But everyone, including the United States, was tired of power politics. A proposal was made for a new version of the UN, one that was more representative and more powerful and thus able to enforce its rules. The UNF was created to fit the new reality of the world. Russia was removed from the UNSC and replaced with India, South Africa, and Brazil, providing each continent with a permanent representative. These seven permanent members did not each have a veto, but any two permanent members could vote down each resolution. The number of nonpermanent members decreased from ten to eight to keep the total number of UNSC members at fifteen. More important than structural changes was that the victors all agreed to work together to prevent wars but also to rebuild Russia and those parts of Eastern Europe affected by the war. There were hard feelings toward China for starting the war but more animosity toward Russia for escalating to nuclear weapons.

The primary emphasis was for states to work together to rebuild Earth and to cooperate more in the future. The new UN was redesigned to be more of a federation in which states agreed to give up more autonomy in the hope that they could create more stability. Agreements included completely eliminating trade barriers and granting more power to the International Criminal Court (ICC), including a promise from the great powers to enforce rulings. One of the UNF's first actions was the elimination (but not the destruction) of all nuclear weapons. This federation of states converted the world's remaining intercontinental ballistic missiles (ICBMs) into rockets capable of traveling to the moon and Mars. The collective governments selected their best scientists and engineers, as well as other individuals with critical skills for a burgeoning civilization, to develop and inhabit the first colonies away from Earth.

From the beginning, the newly formed UNF set the conditions for the settlers on the moon and Mars to put aside their national interests and collaborate for the sake of the colonies and all of humanity. To avoid nationalism, each colony was a mix of nations, races, and religions, and no one state had purview over a colony. The UNF had to approve every mission, and the UNF body had to ratify every new rule passed by the colonies.

Although the UNF often faced division and disagreement on colonial matters, national differences quickly disappeared, replaced by a focus on the greater common good, dealing with common threats to survival. This allowed the federation to focus its efforts on continuing expansion in the solar system, as well as rebuilding the human population on Earth. Over the decades that followed, that initial cooperation built upon itself and grew. By 2060 humanity was spread throughout the solar system, further strengthening cooperation on Earth. Eventually, the unification of all states into a world community became a reality. This is not to suggest that conflicts never occurred or that nationalism did not occasionally reappear, but most people recognized the degree to which cooperation in space provided benefits for all of humanity, and the desire to build upon that led to greater levels of cooperation.

This third scenario involves the establishment of a federation of states, which eventually governs one planet (the way Earth is ruled in the *Expanse* series discussed in chapter 2). States are still the primary actors, as they are in the first two scenarios, but they cooperate not solely for self-interest but to promote their mutual interests in science, technology, and space exploration, as well as to reduce the likelihood of future conflicts and wars.

The benefit of several states working together to cooperate in space exploration is that they share the cost as well as the risk, lowering both the price and the chance of failure. They would also have to share the rewards, but resource scarcity is less likely to be a problem in the future—at least in the beginning of human space exploration—so the temptation for cheating will be minimal. This allows states to focus on absolute economic and technological gains rather than gains relative to an adversary or rival.

A realist will read this scenario and view it as implausible and unrealistic. I discuss below how a realist would finish this scenario, but I wanted each scenario to be true to the IR worldview from which it originates. It would be overly biased to start a scenario from the liberalist point of view and conclude it according to realism. This ending is intended to be consistent with the liberalist school of thought, however impossible or fanciful a reader might consider it.

While realists accept that cooperation exists in international politics, it occurs only for as long as states benefit from the cooperation. Realists (particularly neoclassical realists) also accept that institutions can shape some of the behavior of states, but they are more frequently created by, and serve as the tools of, the major powers. For realists, states do not cooperate because they are members of an organization; institutions may facilitate cooperation to a point, but if states cooperate, it is because of their short-term interests.[3]

Realists are perfectly comfortable with the idea of a concert emerging out of war, as an attempt by victors to prevent another challenge to the status quo. Concerts might even persist for a while if the major powers see the mutual benefits. In the above scenario, for example, that benefit involves space exploration that is cheaper and more effective as a collaborative effort.

Realists also do not generally believe that institutions prevent war. Instead, the end of war allows for cooperation between states to arise, as dictated by the victors of the war. The League of Nations grew out of World War I; the victors of World War II created the UN, placing themselves as the five permanent members of the UNSC; and the

World Trade Organization (WTO) formed after the end of the Cold War, as more states embraced free trade. Likewise, any future world war, assuming there are survivors, would likely lead to the creation of new institutions, whether formal organizations, regimes of behavior, or international laws. These would be created by the victors, which in this scenario would be China, the United States, and the United Kingdom, as well as several other smaller states. This grouping would likely not make dramatic changes to the existing institutions, though we must assume that China would already have begun implementing its vision for international institutions long before the war began, and some of those would survive the war.

Realists would also disagree with many elements of this scenario. For one thing, the major powers are unlikely to give up their ICBMs, even after a destructive war. They might be even less likely to do so after a war in which states used those weapons. One exception might be if states developed a replacement for nuclear weapons that enhanced state security or power. A parallel is the U.S. and Soviet willingness to sign the Strategic Arms Limitations Talks agreement (1972), which limited the number of nuclear missiles in both arsenals, even as the United States developed the ability to place multiple warheads on a single missile (the Soviets had similar technology by 1975). Therefore, the agreement was mostly symbolic because this cap on missile numbers had little effect on the total number of warheads.

Realists would also expect national interest to conflict with the collective good at some point in the scenario, defeating the cooperation. While liberalists believe states will give up sovereignty for the benefits of cooperation, and that cooperation can breed greater levels of cooperation, the realist rejoinder is that it only takes one self-interested actor willing to take advantage of the others to end all cooperation. In addition, because of their emphasis on relative gains, realists expect the benefits of cooperation to be shared unequally, which can lead to vulnerabilities. If one state benefits less than others do, or less than it thinks it would without cooperation, that potential inequality can breed distrust and eventually weaken relations.

Therefore, the realist version of this scenario would have some state, at some point, decide that cooperation is no longer in its interest, which would lead that state to take advantage of the others and bring the whole federation down. Loss of cooperation could even happen through stupidity or miscalculation, from a defensive realist mindset, but the result would still be the decline of cooperation. It might happen on Earth if one state realizes it would have an advantage if it defected from the cooperative model. Or it could happen elsewhere in the solar system, as one or more colonies preferred to be on their own rather than controlled by an organization made up of states on Earth.

LIBERALISM

> The 1,143-year-long war had begun on false pretenses and only because the two races were unable to communicate. Once they could talk, the first question was, "Why did you start this thing?" and the answer was, "Me?"
>
> —JOE HALDEMAN, *The Forever War*

One way classical liberalism differs from realism is in its view of human nature. Whereas realists adopt a Hobbesian view, believing that humans are self-interested and are only restrained by a strong government, liberalists believe human nature is inherently good and is only corrupted by a loss of freedom—commonly associated with too restrictive of a government. Domestically, liberalists advocate for small governments and minimal interference in the economy and other aspects of people's lives. In international politics, they generally focus on ways to limit the effects of anarchy by promoting greater levels of cooperation between states.

Just as the realist worldview has multiple variations, such as offensive and defensive realism, there are several variants of the liberalist worldview, though much of it comes from the writings of Immanuel Kant. In *Perpetual Peace*, Kant offers a three-part prescription, now referred to as the Kantian triad, for the international community to avoid wars in the future. According to Kant, as more states exhibit each of these three elements, the likelihood of war will decrease. First, states should embrace republicanism, because such systems give power to the people, and the people generally oppose wars because they are the ones who suffer during war. Second, there should be a federation of states whose members renounce war. Third, individuals should be free to travel and do business anywhere in the world.[4] Although Kant argued all three of these elements are necessary, liberalist scholars part ways on which leg of the Kantian triad is the most important for promoting cooperation between states.

One of these variants, sometimes called republican liberalism, focuses primarily on the nature of governments and led to development of the democratic peace theory. This theory, which some scholars claim is the closest thing we have to a law in international relations, suggests that representative democracies do not go to war with one another.[5] There is no consensus explanation for this separate peace between representative states, and not everyone is convinced of the theory's validity. In any event, because this variant of liberalism focuses on the internal politics of a state, it is less applicable to the topic of this book. Instead, scenarios three and four highlight the other two variants of liberalism.

The second variant of liberalism, and the one most closely associated with the scenario above, is often referred to as neoliberal institutionalism. Scholars within this branch of liberalism focus on the nature of international organizations, regimes, and international law and contend that these institutions can reduce the effects of anarchy and increase the likelihood of cooperation between states. President Woodrow Wilson is often identified as the modern embodiment of this branch of liberalism because of his efforts to establish the League of Nations after World War I. As a result, neoliberal institutionalism draws heavily from the Wilsonian idealism of the early twentieth century.[6]

The third variant is commercial liberalism, which focuses on the nature of state economic systems and on the degree of economic interaction between states. Although Kant's argument was for universal hospitality, meaning "the right of a stranger not to be treated as an enemy when he arrives in the land of another," that has morphed into a focus on the connections between states. A main tenet of this branch of liberalism is interdependence theory, which suggests that as states increase their mutual dependence, they reduce the likelihood of war between them.[7] This interdependence is commonly measured as levels of trade but can refer to other linkages, such as joint membership in international organizations, student exchanges, and foreign direct investment.

The rest of this chapter discusses the core assumptions of liberalism as a whole, then transitions to focus on neoliberal institutionalism (scenario four will examine commercial liberalism).

Core Liberalist Assumptions

Despite their internal differences, all liberalists share some common assumptions. In fact, the modern liberalist worldview starts with some of the same assumptions as realism. Liberalists accept that the international system exists in a state of anarchy, that states are the primary actors in international politics, and that states have a primary interest in survival. However, each assumption has a different meaning and more positive implications when viewed through the optimistic lens of liberalism. Whereas realists view these as reasons states have difficulty cooperating, liberalists contend that states can cooperate despite these challenges.

Liberalists accept that the international system exists in a state of anarchy, but they believe certain factors reduce the effects of anarchy and increase the likelihood of long-term cooperation between states. Some of these factors are internal to the state, such as its type of government or economic system or civilian control of the military. Variants of liberalism suggest that democracies and states with free market economies are less likely to go to war with one another. Other factors have to do with common interests between states making cooperation more beneficial. For example, states that are members of the same international organizations are more likely to share common interests that make cooperation more likely. Their joint membership also creates opportunities for communication and conflict resolution. Likewise, states with high trade volumes are less likely to go to war because of the economic cost of cutting that trade. In other words, while liberalists accept that anarchy exists, they do not see it as a condition that makes self-help behavior necessary for states. Instead, states with common government types, economic interests, or security interests can achieve long-term cooperation despite anarchy. Liberalists acknowledge that anarchy makes cooperation more difficult than if a world government provided order, especially if one or more states adopt realist policies, but it does not make cooperation impossible.

Even long-term cooperation that does not always satisfy the short-term interests of states is possible.[8]

States are the primary actors in the international system, but liberalists also pay careful attention to other actors. These include actors operating above the state level, such as international organizations like the WTO and supranational organizations like the European Union; nongovernmental organizations, such as aid groups and human rights advocates; and multinational corporations, such as Toyota and Walmart. The system also includes actors engaged in illicit activities, such as transnational criminal organizations and violent extremist organizations.

Liberalists are also less inclined to view states as rational and unitary. They focus more than realists on the actors influencing state decision-making and affecting levels of competition and cooperation between states. This may be the military as an organization or simply the key advisors who have the greatest influence on a state's leaders. Several scholars discuss the fact that militaries tend to favor offensive doctrines, so states tend to be more offensive-minded when militaries have a great deal of influence over their governments, whereas strong civilian control of the military tends to produce more defensive policies. This supports the notion that democracies are unlikely to go to war with one another, since most democracies (almost by definition) have strong civilian control of government. Such concepts are not inconsistent with realism but are often overlooked by those who view states as a black box or billiard balls. These ideas about the importance of internal factors are also largely about foreign policy rather than international politics, so they do not receive much attention here.

Although liberalists accept that security is a critical self-interest for states, they ascribe at least equal importance to prosperity, not at the expense of security but often in conjunction with it. Whereas realists see wealth as a means to ensure power or security, liberalists are much more inclined to view security as a means to attain wealth. One consequence of this is that liberalists often advocate for free trade economic policies. Such policies create wealth for all involved parties, and states with high trade levels may be less likely to go to war against one another because of the wealth they would forfeit. For realists, wealth can translate into power, as illustrated by China's willingness to convert some of its economic growth into greater military capabilities. While liberalists extoll the mutual benefits of cooperation as being both wealth and security, realists view the wealth of an adversary as a source of its potential military power and therefore one's own insecurity. Similarly, states that possesses wealth without the military power to protect it risk being conquered.

Where liberalists differ the most from realists is not just in the level of cooperation or the chance of cooperation, but in the reason for cooperation. Even neoclassical realists, who see value in international institutions, believe states only cooperate when it is in their interest to do so. As a result, when that interest wanes, or when the state no longer benefits from cooperation, it will cease to cooperate. In contrast, liberalists suggest that states sometimes cooperate for the sake of cooperation. That may not happen among rivals who do not trust each other, but for states that are already on friendly terms, cooperation can have a value all on its own. Liberalists also subscribe to the writings of Adam Smith, who suggested that in a free market, actors pursuing their own interests will, without their knowledge or intent, benefit the market as a whole. So, even liberalists who acknowledge the self-interested nature of states are inclined to see the possibility of economic cooperation if it creates wealth for all involved.

Absolute Gains

Another significant difference between realists and liberalists is based on their views of gains. Whereas realists concern themselves with relative gains, as discussed in the previous chapter, liberalists are more concerned with absolute gains—focusing on choices that provide the greatest good for the least cost, regardless of how much others benefit from that choice.[9] For realists, states can convert wealth into military power, so free trade that benefits one state over another, or interdependence in which one state is more dependent on the other, creates vulnerabilities for a state. While liberalists accept that states can convert wealth into military power, most subscribe to the idea that greater interdependence reduces the likelihood of war. That influence is even greater when states have higher levels of wealth, because then at least one cost of war—the revenue no longer gained from trade—will restrain states from resorting to violence.

A reasonable middle ground between the realist and liberalist schools of thought on this topic is that relative gains matter in some situations, while absolute gains matter in others. Relative gains might matter more in the security domain than in other areas, such as economics and scientific exchange, that are less about national survival. Likewise, relative gains might matter for adversaries and rivals, while allies and partners can allow themselves to be more concerned with absolute gains. If true, then cooperation is more difficult on matters of security and when dealing with adversaries, whereas cooperation is more likely on nonsecurity matters and when dealing with existing allies. A true realist would not even accept absolute gains for an ally, because today's ally can become tomorrow's adversary. Nevertheless, most would view an ally's gains differently from the gains of a rival or a neutral state, which is one reason the United States accepted British and French nuclear weapons but opposes proliferation in Iran and North Korea.

Since the focus of republican liberalism is on domestic political systems, it has less relevance to this project than the other variants of liberalism. Nonetheless, there are some concepts from that variation that are useful for understanding other parts of liberalism. One is the idea of a social contract, put forward by Jean-Jacques Rousseau. In a social contract, the people form an agreement of sorts with their government in which they give up some of their freedom in exchange for the government providing order, from which everyone benefits.[10] This contract is not permanent, and if at any point the government no longer serves the interests of the people, they can demand a change. The American colonists made this very argument in justifying the revolt against England, as the Declaration of Independence states: "Governments are instituted among Men, deriving their just powers from the consent of the governed,—That whenever any Form of Government becomes destructive of these ends, it is the Right of the People to alter or to abolish it, and to institute new Government." This is applicable to international politics in that a similar type of social contract occurs between international institutions and their member states.

Whatever one's view, the pertinent point for this scenario is that a federated system requires states to fully embrace absolute gains, at least on the issues that require cooperation, where they work together for the good of the community—sometimes perhaps even at the expense of an individual state's short-term interests. Every international organization requires states to give up some of their sovereignty. That is why realists view organizations with such pessimism, but even realists acknowledge that states are willing to give up sovereignty when their survival is at stake or when they believe that the benefits outweigh the risks. In a federation, states will have to give up sovereignty for the sake of the federation itself, but through this international version of the social contract, cooperation can grow in other areas.

Having discussed the core assumptions of liberalism, the next step is to discuss some of the key concepts, theories, and actors that neoliberal institutionalists suggest promote cooperation between states. This is just one branch of liberalism, emphasizing the importance of international institutions for promoting cooperation between states. But it is also an important view to understand because there are several institutions that already attempt to promote greater cooperation with respect to space.

International Institutions

Neoliberal institutionalism focuses on the importance of international institutions, which include regimes, different types of international organizations—intergovernmental organizations (IGOs) and nongovernmental organizations (NGOs)—as well as international laws and norms. This section focuses on regimes, IGOs, and international law (because those play the biggest role in this scenario) and discusses the prisoner's dilemma game. I address NGOs in chapter 4 and discuss international norms along with constructivism in chapter 7. This chapter also examines two important elements of international organizations as they relate to the security realm—cooperative security and collective defense. Although those are similar concepts, there are important differences that make collective defense more likely from the realist point of view but make collective security ideal for liberalists to achieve long-term cooperation.

According to Stephen Krasner, regimes are "implicit or explicit principles, norms, rules and decision-making procedures around which actors' expectations converge in a given area of international relations."[11] These are patterns of behavior that typically fall short of having the formalized structure or charter of an international organization, but most members of the international system, or at least most great powers, must agree to abide by the same rules of behavior for a regime to form and persevere.[12]

Regimes form when there is a need for states to cooperate over a particular issue. For realists, states form regimes, like all international institutions, to enhance their influence on the international system, and so they primarily serve the interests of the great powers.[13] As a result, regimes are most effective when power is concentrated in the hands of a small number of great powers, or perhaps with a hegemon that is willing and able to create and then enforce regimes. Liberalists believe regimes, like many international institutions, increase cooperation between states by enhancing transparency, thereby helping states reward good behavior and impose costs on poor behavior. They generally recognize that there must be at least acquiescence by, if not approval of, the great powers for a regime to take hold, but for liberalists, regimes influence state behavior, even under multipolar systems.[14]

Today, for example, there are regimes regarding Antarctic exploration, nuclear nonproliferation, trade, and arms control, to name a few. The regime involving Antarctic exploration is largely a function of the 1959 Antarctic Treaty, the purpose of which was to prevent conflict over issues of sovereignty. That treaty expanded into what is often referred to as the Antarctic Treaty System and includes the original treaty, conventions on conservation, a scientific committee, and a minerals regime to address potential exploitation of the region's resources. Among the provisions of these elements are the prohibition against militarization of the region, freedom of scientific investigation, and international cooperation. One challenge for this regime will be surviving China's rise in power. Both China and Russia show interest in exploiting the Antarctic, so it will be interesting to observe the extent to which this regime survives and continues to restrain the interests of major powers as the character of the international system shifts.

One way regimes can endure over time is that they can become formalized in an international organization. The WTO grew out of the free trade regime and the multilateral trade negotiations called the General Agreement on Tariffs and Trade. The Bretton Woods international economic system that emerged after World War II is another example of a regime intended to strengthen the principles of free trade and to support monetary policy and economic development, though it too led to the expansion of international organizations, such as the World Bank and the International Monetary Fund.

Another example is the nuclear nonproliferation regime, which is formalized in a treaty and in the UN-based International Atomic Energy Agency. It is in the interest of the great powers who already possess nuclear weapons to prevent other states from obtaining them, so they generally accept and work within the rules of that regime. At the same time, states are also interested in profiting from the sale of nuclear energy materials and facilities. There is a short step between that and facilitating nuclear weapons development in allied countries, both to help states enhance their security and to balance against their rivals. Therefore, while this regime exists and may constrain some states, there are also significant challenges to it.

Regimes can change, either before or after formalization, and this change can be in either a positive or a negative direction, depending on relations between the great powers. They are strained currently, so some of the regimes that formed and promoted cooperation under bipolarity and then hegemony may come under fire with an increasingly multipolar international system. One example is the arms control regime that developed during the Cold War and proliferated during the early years of the post–Cold War but may now be moving in a different direction. Agreements between the United States and the Soviet Union over ballistic missile defense and intermediate-range nuclear forces are already defunct, suggesting that this regime already morphed.

Intergovernmental organizations are often created by treaty, formal agreement, or formalization of a regime, and they are then responsible for coordinating behavior between states. IGOs often have some type of physical presence, like a headquarters, or at least conduct regular meetings between their members. They may have limited membership, which can be based on a geographic region or a common interest, or they may allow global membership (though that does not mean all states will join). Examples of IGOs with limited membership include NATO, the European Union (EU), and the Organization of Petroleum Exporting Countries (OPEC).

The UN is an IGO with global membership, as most states have representation at the UN. Even some nonstate actors are involved, such as the EU, which holds permanent observer status and has enhanced participation rights. Palestine is another nonmember with observer status. Another example of an IGO with global membership is the WTO, which has 164 members, including the EU, and 23 actors with observer status, most of whom are in the process of becoming members. Only twelve states currently express no interest in joining. Several other IGOs also have observer status at the WTO, including the UN, the International Monetary Fund, the World Bank, and the Andean Community.

IGOs exist either for a specific purpose or to tackle a wide variety of issues. OPEC's mission is to coordinate the production and export of oil by its members, to provide them with the greatest profit possible from their oil sales. A general purpose IGO is the EU, which started as a trade and customs union and later expanded to address and coordinate issues such as immigration, law, and foreign policy. It is also considered a supranational organization because decisions by the EU are binding on members in those areas where the states agreed to give up autonomy in favor of cooperation. For example, the EU can pass legislation—not as a function of decisions made between states, but arising organically from the organization. The broader an IGO's mandate, the more sovereignty its members typically give up, but they also potentially benefit from cooperation across a broader range of topics. Likewise, organizations with more members potentially dilute benefits but also allow greater opportunities for cooperation, even outside the scope of the IGO.

Realists and liberalists disagree on the role that organizations play and the extent to which the rules of IGOs bind states. Realists see organizations as a product of short-term cooperation, being tools of the great powers and serving their national interests. While that can grow into long-term cooperation, it will cease to be influential once the organization no longer benefits the members. For liberalists, on the other hand, organizations can restrain state behavior and potentially promote long-term cooperation by reining in national interests or making cooperation an interest in itself.

Realists and liberalists also disagree on the durability of international organizations. If an IGO only serves the interests of its members, then realists believe the organization will fall apart when those interests no longer exist. Liberalists suggest organizations can be more durable. Organizations often become self-interested, and so they take on a life of their own and will search for ways to continue to exist even when their original purpose is gone. It is also costly to create an organization, in both time and resources, and that investment will continue to fuel their existence even if they no longer provide significant benefits for states.[15] Many realists believed that NATO would cease to exist once the Cold War ended and its original purpose—defending Europe from the Soviet Union—was no longer necessary.[16] The fact that NATO still exists, and has expanded both its membership and its mission, challenges this view of organizations, at least for that one case. NATO also illustrates how an organization can alter itself over time. Not only did NATO expand its membership and mission set, but also most liberalists now see NATO as more than just a military alliance because of its durability and the benefits it provides to its members even outside the security realm.

Liberalists contend that international organizations promote cooperation between states in several ways. Specifically, they increase the importance of reputation, the likelihood states will interact in the future, opportunities for communication, and the benefits of cooperation and the costs for failing to cooperate. One of the best ways to illustrate how IGOs promote cooperation is with the prisoner's dilemma (PD) game.[17]

Realists frequently cite the PD as an accurate model of international politics, and the game should be familiar to anyone who has watched police or legal dramas.[18] The background story is about two prisoners who are arrested for a minor crime but whom authorities believe are responsible for a more significant offense. They are held separately so they cannot communicate directly with one another, and each is offered a deal: whoever confesses to the major crime will get a shorter sentence, while the other person will serve all the time. Making this offer to each prisoner creates four possible outcomes, since each prisoner can either confess to the crime or keep quiet.

While the two prisoners have a mutual incentive to keep quiet (cooperate), each is individually concerned that if they keep quiet while the other person talks, then they will receive the longer sentence (referred to as the sucker's payoff). Because neither prisoner wants the longer sentence, they both end up confessing (defecting) and receiving the worst possible combined outcome. To break down the choices, no matter what prisoner two does, prisoner one is better off confessing. If prisoner two cooperates by keeping quiet, the optimal choice for prisoner one is to confess (defect) and go free rather than serve one year in prison. If prisoner two confesses, prisoner one's best choice is still to defect and receive a shorter sentence (eight years) than would otherwise be the case (ten years). If we assume both prisoners are rational and understand these outcomes, both will choose to defect, and in doing so will serve longer sentences than if they had kept quiet.

Illustrations of this game exist throughout international politics. If states sign an arms control agreement, they are mutually better off if they adhere to it, but each is individually better off if they cheat on the deal and defect. If one state defects, the other state is vulnerable, so the result is often mutual defection. Similar decisions exist for abiding by peace agreements, or any time states have mutual interests in cooperating but fear the consequences of cooperating if the other side defects.

For realists, the PD fits international politics because it illustrates the lack of trust that exists between states and the difficulty of cooperating under anarchy. While liberalists accept that the PD often parallels international politics, they offer numerous ways to promote cooperation between the prisoners, and international organizations provide similar benefits to their members. For instance, the basic PD assumes no prior history or future interactions, but if the prisoners have a history of working together and keeping quiet under arrest, they are more likely to do so the next time. Even if the prisoners are unable to communicate, a historical record helps reputations form that can increase the chances for cooperation. Likewise, international organizations enhance the importance of state reputations, or what one might call the shadow of the past. Because international organizations endure, they provide a record of states that honored their past agreements related to the mission of the organization. This record of a reputation allows states to know more about the actors with whom they are dealing and allows trust to grow more easily.

Another means of promoting cooperation is by increasing the shadow of the future, through expectations of repeated interactions. If the prisoners expect to see each other again or work together again, the likelihood they will both be quiet increases. Actors who are unlikely to cooperate if they know they will only interact one time are more likely to cooperate when they know they will have future contacts, especially if such contact allows retaliation or punishment for defection. Organizations enhance this shadow of the future by increasing the likelihood states will interact again, especially when combined with the opportunity to retaliate or punish bad behavior. For many, this explains the success of the WTO, even in its ability to impose costs on its member states for violating their trade agreements.

If the prisoners are allowed to communicate with one another—say, through a third party such as a lawyer who can inform each of them the other is keeping quiet—the chances of mutual cooperation increase. States that are members of international organizations have more interactions with one another than would otherwise be the case. This interaction promotes greater levels of cooperation because it allows states to negotiate and deal with tension in a more productive way than using military force. In many ways, this is an interdependence argument that focuses more on organizational membership than trade levels. But it also suggests that communication enhances the likelihood of cooperation. For example, NATO offers its members a forum to discuss a wide range of topics, sometimes even outside the military realm. Greater interaction also increases opportunities to catch cheating. The WTO produces annual reports on its members' trade practices, which provide useful information that facilitates greater cooperation by identifying and calling attention to uncooperative behavior.

Finally, one can change the payoffs of the choices to make cooperation more agreeable and defection more painful. If both prisoners are members of an organized crime family, then even if they had not worked together before, they know that keeping quiet, even if they go to jail, comes with additional rewards; being a rat and defecting leads to harsher costs that likely outweigh the benefits of going free. By altering the payoffs, we change the game from a PD to something more cooperative. International organizations can impose costs on member states for failing to honor their agreements and can reward those members who do. The WTO, for example, can facilitate the punishment of member states who violate their free trade agreements with other members. States remain a part of the WTO because of the broader benefits it provides, and they are willing to accept WTO decisions because they understand that the overall benefits of membership outweigh the costs of one ruling. The WTO's ability to punish bad behavior may even act as a deterrent, preventing states from violating their trade agreements in the first place.

For liberalists, each of these influences on the PD increases cooperation and is a benefit of an international organization. Just by being members, states increase past and future interactions, making history more valuable. The organization itself provides more opportunities for communication and in some cases can alter the payoffs so states have incentives to cooperate and disincentives to defect.

One other benefit of international institutions is that once they are created, they tend to endure even beyond the balance of power that created them. Realists use this to support their argument that institutions are simply state tools to perpetuate the status quo. For liberalists, it means cooperation can endure through institutions, long after the status quo changes. In either case, states tend not to destroy international institutions that already exist, though they may be altered to adjust to changes in the status quo (I explore this further in the discussions of the UN and NATO below).

Another type of international institution is international law. Whereas national laws are written by a central authority and enforced by that government, international law comes from tradition and agreements between states and relies on the states for enforcement, even in cases where international organizations exist to monitor adherence to the laws.[19] For example, when Iraq violated the UN charter by invading Kuwait in 1990, it was breaking international law, but the UN had to rely on its members to enforce the law and rectify the situation. The main realist criticism of international law is similar to the critique of organizations—under anarchy, if international law is enforced by the states, then enforcement is contingent upon the ability and willingness of states to enforce it. Like all international institutions, international law may be more influential under a hegemonic system, at least to the extent that the hegemon is willing to enforce it (which was the case in

1990). Under bipolar and multipolar systems, international law is only enforced to the extent the great powers agree to do so or allow others to do so.

Much of international law is codified in treaties between states, either operating independently or as part of an organization. One principle of international law is that ratified treaties must be observed. Realists will highlight how frequently treaties are broken or ignored, while liberalists will point to examples of treaties that are honored despite the cost to the states. Liberalists also emphasize the importance of reciprocity. States obey international law because they want other states to follow suit. This is true if states are satisfied with the status quo or there is a hegemon to enforce the rules. When there are challengers to the status quo, reciprocity is less likely to induce adherence to the law.

Yet for operating in an anarchic system, international law has considerable influence on the behavior of states. There are a number of important international laws that liberalists suggest constrain states in ways that otherwise would not be the case. Some of the most prominent examples of international law include the law of war, human rights, and respecting the rights of diplomats. Many such laws are written under the auspices of the UN, usually to address a common problem. One example of law written by the UN is the Convention on the Law of the Seas (UNCLOS). There is also a set of laws that govern the behavior of states in space and are of particular interest to this project.[20]

UNCLOS provides a good example of the realist view that states, or at least the great powers, will not embrace international law when it does not serve their interests. In practice, the United States accepts and complies with most of the terms of UNCLOS and frequently enforces its provisions, such as asserting freedom of navigation and challenging excessive maritime claims. Yet the United States refuses to ratify the treaty. The treaty was drafted in 1982, and the United States initially opposed it because of its approach to deep seabed resources beyond national jurisdiction. No U.S. president signed it until Bill Clinton did so in 1994, after significant revisions addressed some of the United States' concerns. Even then, the Senate was not satisfied enough to ratify it. In 2004 the George W. Bush administration requested Senate ratification of UNCLOS, but the United States remains a non-party to the agreement, mostly based on vague claims that it would impinge too greatly on U.S. sovereignty.

International law and international organizations intersect in several places. One example is the World Court, a branch of the UN formally called the International Court of Justice. A more recent example is the establishment of the ICC, an organization designed to enforce international law regarding human rights violations and crimes against humanity, when national courts are unable or unwilling to try such cases. The ICC is another example of an international institution that the United States did not join. The United States helped write the Rome Treaty that set up the ICC, the purpose of which is to prosecute war crimes—a goal that the United States wholly supports. But the United States refused to ratify the treaty and join the ICC out of concern that the court would pursue U.S. military personnel for performing their job under orders of the commander in chief. The United States not only refrained from joining the ICC but also passed the American Service-Members' Protection Act of 2002, giving presidents the authority to use military force to free American citizens in ICC custody. The United States also signed bilateral "Article 98 agreements" with 102 states (46 of whom are ICC members) to ensure those states would not detain U.S. citizens at the request of an organization to which the United States does not belong.

As China gains power, it too begins to resist international laws set up either during the Cold War or by the hegemonic United States. A 2016 decision by the Hague Tribunal ruled against China's construction of islands in the South China Sea. China ignored that ruling, especially considering there are few real consequences for doing so. So far, the United States and others are reluctant to challenge China on this point, and this illustrates the weakness of international law, especially when rulings go against the interests of one of the great powers. When one state ignores international institutions, a precedent is set for future powers to do the same, which defeats the purpose of setting up that institution in the first place.

Collective Defense and Collective Security
The distinction between collective security and collective defense is complicated, at least partly because the terms are often used incorrectly and

sometimes interchangeably,[21] but also because international law equates collective security with a different term, collective self-defense (based on Article 51 of the UN Charter). The difference between the terms is important because while liberalists often focus on the promise of collective security, realists doubt its practicality but do see value in collective defense.[22] Collective defense organizations, like alliances, often identify a clear external threat, sometimes even naming the state against which the agreement is directed. In contrast, collective security addresses a broader range of potential threats and therefore does not always reflect the interests of the great powers.

Collective defense is an agreement in which states pledge to defend one another if any one of them is threatened. Such agreements may be a part of a formal organization or an alliance, but it need not be an alliance and can be a more informal type of agreement. An example of a less formal collective security arrangement is the Concert of Europe that formed after the Napoleonic Wars. Informal collective defense sometimes looks like collective security. For example, the Concert of Europe appears to be collective security because of the promise of the great powers to avoid war, but the concert said little about preventing great powers from attacking small states. Despite the concert, Prussia waged three wars in less than a decade and unified Germany. Under collective security, the other great powers would have allied against Prussia, to protect the rights of Denmark, Austria, and France. Because the intent of the concert was only to avoid great power war, it was an example of collective defense.

There are several regional organizations that are intended to promote collective defense, including the Organization of American States (OAS) and the African Union (AU). While the OAS contains a great power (the United States), the AU does not, yet there are still power disparities in the AU, and both organizations contain members that may be less committed to stopping aggression. Although the EU is neither a collective security nor a collective defense organization, there are calls to develop a collective defense component, providing for a European approach to security issues without having to rely on the United States and NATO.

NATO is an example of a more formal collective defense organization, but it also illustrates how an organization can transform over time. When NATO engaged in operations outside of its membership (for example, in Bosnia and Kosovo, and against piracy off the coast of Africa), it appeared to be transforming itself from collective defense to collective security—not just defending its members from attack but also protecting the rights of nonmember states and non-state actors. Its emphasis is still on the protection of its member states, evidence by its minimal response to Russian actions in Georgia and Ukraine, neither of which were members of the alliance. But it is at least willing to consider broader protections.

Collective security typically refers to actions involving a larger region, or even the globe, and may be part of a formal institution or ad hoc cooperation between states to protect the interests of another state. Article 51 of the UN Charter authorizes collective self-defense, in which if any one country is attacked, other countries have the right to use force against the aggressor in a type of group enforcement action. The League of Nations after World War I was an attempt at a collective security agreement, but it fell short because of a lack of great power involvement and acceptance of the organization.

A. F. K. Organski suggested five assumptions behind collective security theory: member states can identify an aggressor in an armed conflict; all members are equally committed to stop aggression; all members have equal freedom of action against the aggressor; the collective power will be greater than the power of any one aggressor; and the collective power of the members will deter or, if necessary, defeat any aggressor.[23] These are basically conditions necessary for collective security to be effective. The same assumptions do not necessarily apply to collective defense.

For Arnold Wolfers, collective defense was no different than an alliance, where members pursue self-interest.[24] Collective security, however, requires states to act according to legal principle rather than national interest, and they cannot remain neutral even if acting goes against their interest. For liberalists, collective security should be better able to protect peace because more power is thrown at an aggressor. Realists suggest it is hard enough to rely on states to honor their alliance commitments and is even less likely that states will risk war when it does not serve their interests.

There are times when the concept of collective security is effective, even without a formal organization in place. In 1990–91, Iraq's invasion of Kuwait brought together thirty-nine states and, more importantly, most of the great powers to remove Iraqi forces from Kuwait. Realists suggest this was possible because of the unipolar world and U.S. leadership of that coalition of states or the common threat many states faced from Iraq gaining more power in the Middle East or controlling more oil. Liberalists point out the importance of international rules of sovereignty and territorial integrity that brought the states together for a common purpose, as well as the quick decision by the UNSC to authorize the use of force. The next section discusses one collective security organization (the UN) and a collective defense organization (NATO) but first examines the Concert of Europe as an example of a security regime.

HISTORY OF INTERNATIONAL INSTITUTIONS

> We fully realize today that victory in war requires a mighty united effort. Certainly, victory in peace calls for, and must receive, an equal effort. Man has learned long ago, that it is impossible to live unto himself. This same basic principle applies today to nations. We were not isolated during the war. We dare not now become isolated in peace.
>
> —HARRY TRUMAN, *address to the United Nations Conference, San Francisco, 25 April 1945*

The three historical examples of cooperative institutions discussed here represent different aspects of international cooperation and liberalism. The Concert of Europe was an international regime between the great powers, which was essentially an informal promise not to wage war.[25] The UN and NATO are formal organizations, both of which formed after World War II. While the UN has global membership and deals with a variety of topics, NATO has limited membership and focuses on security issues.

There are other examples of effective international institutions, such as the WTO and the Antarctic regime, that promote cooperation and influence state behavior. But while realists contend that cooperation is easier on nonsecurity matters, the cases below suggest how cooperation can form even in the security realm. These are more difficult tests of liberalism yet still show that cooperation is possible, even without a common threat. These three cases were also important for developing the scenario in this chapter.

A concert is a particular type of regime formed by all the great powers of an era. It provides a forum for negotiating and limiting the exercise of power. In this case, it refers to a series of congresses, or meetings, that collectively institutionalized the Concert of Europe. There is some controversy over use of the term concert because it is not well-defined, and by most definitions, only one has occurred in history. The Concert of Europe may be a unique case of great power cooperation, but it is still informative based on its origins and effectiveness.

The Concert of Europe was an informal agreement between the great powers after the Napoleonic Wars. The concert itself set up this separate class of states we often refer to as the great powers. These actors have the potential to influence international politics the most, so they need to be part of any regime that might successfully prevent war. The great powers of the time agreed that no territory would change hands unless accepted by all the great powers, and they intended to hold periodic meetings to provide consultation and dispute resolution. Given the historical context, the concert privileged conservative governments, almost biasing cooperation against liberal revolutionary movements. This was later formalized in the League of the Three Emperors between Germany, Russia, and Austria-Hungary, lasting from 1873 to 1880. While the concert promoted stability in Europe for almost one hundred years, this bias toward conservative governments caused problems as liberal ideas, like republicanism and self-determination, spread across Europe, challenged the status quo, and weakened several of the great powers.

There is some debate over the real value of the concert. For some, it contributed to a century of relative peace in Europe and illustrates how cooperation can exist between the great powers, even after destructive wars. Others contend it simply allowed the great powers to build up their military capabilities in preparation for the next wars. There are also disagreements over when it fell apart. The concert was officially over by 1914, when World War I broke out, splitting the great powers into two belligerent camps and altering the international system. But it began to unravel with the war between Denmark and the combined Austrian and Prussian forces in 1864, resulting in Denmark giving up territory. This was followed by the war between Austria and Prussia in 1866. German states joined both sides, and the resulting Prussian victory meant it became the protector of German interests and a powerful actor in Europe. Prussia's victory over France in 1871 earned it more territory and led to the unification of Germany, with the Prussian king as the new kaiser.

While realists highlight the wars that occurred, the shifts in power, and the concert's eventual demise over issues of security and trust, for liberalists, the Concert of Europe restrained the power politics impulses of the great powers for nearly one hundred years. This was not an attempt at either collective security or defense but was rather a forum in which communication prevented war between the great powers, at least for a time.

Fifty states signed the UN Charter in 1945.[26] The UN borrowed much from the failed League of Nations while attempting to address some of its shortcomings. Unlike the League of Nations, the UN did not exclude any states from its membership, although the only states invited to the initial conference were those that declared war on Germany and Japan. It also took some time for certain states to join: Italy did not join until 1955, Japan not until 1956, and East and West Germany not until 1973. Because the five victors of World War II helped create it, they all embraced the value of membership.

Several components make up the larger institution of the UN. The UNSC is perhaps the most important of these, given its focus on security issues and the permanent member status and veto held by the five victors of World War II: China, France, Russia (formerly the Soviet Union), the United Kingdom, and the United States. They set up the UN to institutionalize their influence and interests, although the Cold War often divided the UNSC.

In addition, several specialized agencies and programs focus on topics of interest to the UN's members, and they often have limited membership. The UN High Commissioner for Refugees, created in 1950 to help

Europeans who lost their homes in World War II, continues to assist refugees worldwide. States, as well as private donors and foundations, provide the staff and resources.[27] The International Monetary Fund and World Bank determine membership and voting weight according to the amount of money each country gives to the agency.

The UN is intended to provide collective security for all its members. This is difficult in practice because any authorization for military action requires approval by the UNSC. This means nine of the fifteen members (the five permanent members [P5] and ten nonpermanent members) must agree that aggression occurred and that the UN needs to act, and all permanent members must refrain from vetoing military action. This makes action difficult to approve and coordinate, and action is nearly impossible against any of the great powers.[28]

The UN has done several positive things, from establishing a Universal Declaration of Human Rights in 1948 to conducting peacekeeping operations. While critics often disparage the UN for being slow to act and not doing enough in certain cases (such as preventing genocide in Rwanda) or only acting when in the interest of the great powers, there is undeniably more cooperation between states on these types of issues than would exist in the absence of the UN.[29]

The UN has grown as new states formed and joined the organization (currently at 193 members), and it has taken on some new missions, but it has largely the same objective as when it formed. It continues to perpetuate the post–World War II system in that World War II victors are still the only states with a veto on the UNSC. While all five are still important states, one could argue that the current make-up of the UNSC no longer represents the balance of power in world politics. While there are several calls for reform, they would need the approval of the P5, which is unlikely because any changes would dilute the influence of those states and because specific national interests will oppose approval of almost any new permanent members. China opposes Japan and India because of national rivalries and historical tension, and several states oppose Germany because Europe is already overrepresented on the UNSC, with three of the five permanent members and up to three of the ten nonpermanent members at any given time. This desire to control the organization highlights the role self-interest still plays even in a large and influential IGO like the UN, providing a mixture of support to both realist and liberalist schools of thought on international organizations.

NATO was formed in 1949 when representatives from twelve states signed the North Atlantic Treaty (also known as the Washington Treaty), promising to defend one another in the event of an attack against any of the members. The treaty did not specifically identify the Soviet Union as the target of the alliance, but there was no question that the treaty's primary purpose was to deter the Soviet Union and to defend Europe in the event deterrence failed.

Beyond deterrence and defense, NATO was also intended to keep Germany from remilitarizing and threatening its neighbors and to ensure the United States remained engaged in Europe, rather than withdraw back across the Atlantic Ocean. It also promoted nonmilitary cooperation among its members. Article II states, "The Parties . . . will seek to eliminate conflict in their international economic policies and will encourage economic collaboration between any or all of them." It is this nonmilitary mission that many suggest makes NATO a unique military alliance and that perhaps contributed to its success in promoting cooperation among its members even beyond the security domain.

NATO was established as a collective defense organization because of Article V of the North Atlantic Treaty, which states that an attack on any member of NATO will be considered an attack on all members. This language was an attempt to strengthen the commitment of the members in light of overwhelming Soviet capabilities, but it was never invoked during the Cold War. Its first use was after the 9/11 terrorist attacks by al-Qa'ida against the United States. In response, NATO contributed air support to bolster U.S. security and contributed forces to the military operation against the Taliban in Afghanistan, accused of providing a safe haven to al-Qa'ida members and leadership. In 2007 Russian cyberattacks against NATO member Estonia could have again triggered Article V, but the organization opted not to vote on whether the cyber operations constituted an attack on NATO. The lack of a vote was largely out of concern that a failed vote would weaken the organization's credibility and embolden Russia to do more, while a successful vote might lead to a war between NATO and Russia. Critics of the organization saw this lack of vote as a sign that "old NATO" was unwilling to challenge Russia to protect the newer members and that this signal emboldened Russian president Vladimir Putin to become more aggressive toward Eastern Europe. NATO did set up a cyber defense center of excellence in Estonia as a response, and there is evidence that this action improved member state cooperation, at least in the cyber domain.

After the Cold War, there was debate over the future of NATO. Many realists expected the organization to wither, since the primary purpose for its existence—deterring the Soviet threat—ceased to exist.[30] Instead, the organization adapted to the new security environment, taking on new members and new missions even outside of Europe. These included counterpiracy operations off Africa, enforcing a no-fly zone in Libya, and earthquake relief in Pakistan. NATO also provided security training in Iraq and Afghanistan, maintained a presence in Kosovo, conducted surveillance and counterterrorism operations in the Mediterranean Sea, and provided sea and airlift capabilities for African Union peacekeeping missions.

Liberalists point to NATO as an example of an international organization that evolved over time—from an alliance to an organization and now to a community of states in which war between them is almost unthinkable. The addition of new members expanded that community, and the acceptance of new missions expanded the organization's influence beyond the North Atlantic region.[31] Four states joined NATO during the Cold War: Greece and Turkey (1952) to reinforce NATO's southern flank; Germany (1955) when its status as an occupied country ended; and Spain (1982) after the death of Francisco Franco and the 1981 military coup. Since the end of the Cold War, fourteen more states have joined NATO, including three former Soviet republics (Estonia, Latvia, and Lithuania).

One of the ways NATO influenced states was to have requirements for joining the organization, which included making political reform toward representative government and economic reform toward free markets; ensuring civilian control of the military; resolving territorial disputes with neighbors; and reforming the military toward compatibility with NATO forces. The fact that so many European states wanted to join meant they were willing to make these change for the added security and other benefits of membership. Through this process, states became politically more open and militarily more capable faster than would have been the case without NATO pushing for the change or being viewed as beneficial to these states' interests.

FEDERATIONS IN SCIENCE FICTION

> Citizenship is an attitude, a state of mind, an emotional conviction that the whole is greater than the part . . . and that the part should be humbly proud to sacrifice itself that the whole may live.
>
> —ROBERT HEINLEIN, *Starship Troopers*

The United Federation of Planets from the *Star Trek* universe, represented operationally by Starfleet, is perhaps one of the best-known federations in science fiction. It united not only Earth but also other humanoid civilizations under a single banner. That does not mean it was wholly hegemonic, as the Federation did face opposition (Klingons, Romulans, Borg, etc.), but as far as humans were concerned, the Federation of Planets was the central authority and existed because of cooperation between people rather than conquest by a single state.

Given the timing of the original television series, it seems clear that the Federation represented NATO and that the original antagonists, the Klingons, were an allegory for the Soviet Union.[32] But what does science fiction tell us about the society that would flow from such a federation? The Federation is governed by a constitution and is intended to assure mutual protection to all member planets. It started with 5 founding member planets and eventually expanded to more than 150 members.[33] While the Federation in *Star Trek* appears to have a post-wealth economy and to embrace equality and diversity, it is not clear how realistic such a society could be.[34]

This Federation did not prevent wars; many of the *Star Trek* story lines involve conflict with one alien race or another. But the Federation did two things that are consistent with liberalist thought. First, it helped prevent war among its members. That does not mean there was never conflict or tension—only that it did not rise to the level of war. Second, it was welcoming to potential new members who wanted to share in the benefits of cooperation.

For realists, the only way to achieve this type of central authority for the whole Earth would be if we faced a common threat, either from Earth itself or from some external force. This could be an alien menace (a common theme in science fiction), an approaching meteor that threatens human extinction, or, as with the scenario above, a result of exhaustion and devastation. Absent those common dangers, realists see national self-interest getting in the way of long-term global cooperation.

Several science fiction novels portray a united Earth because an alien species is threatening humanity. Rarely is the threat of the aliens the impetus for world government, but this threat to humanity is a common element of books involving a united Earth of any kind. Four classic books fall within this genre and have many similarities but also some striking differences.

Joe Haldeman's *Forever War* involves people coming together in a United Nations Exploratory Force (UNEF) because of the threat from an alien race that attacked human colonists.[35] The UN is not a major player in the book, other than being responsible for the training and equipping of the UNEF. However, it is a constant presence despite the centuries that pass for the main character, William Mandella, due to time dilation during his space travels from one battle to another.

There are two versions of the book, the biggest difference being the description of the earth to which Mandella returns after completing his first tour of duty. In the 1974 version, Mandella finds Earth run by the UN; there is little room for people, but it is generally a pleasant place—just a different Earth from the one he remembered. His mother dies because she is unable to convince the government she deserves health care, and that prompts his return to service. In the original version (which was not published until 1991), when Mandella returns to Earth, he finds it nasty and dangerous. Bandits violently kill his girlfriend's parents, which compels them both to rejoin the UNEF.

In Robert Heinlein's *Starship Troopers*, humanity has formed the Terran Federation.[36] Like Haldeman, Heinlein portrays the soldiers as well-equipped elite units of mobile infantry. They do not necessarily have the high IQ required of the UNEF soldiers in *Forever War* but are nonetheless highly skilled. One difference between the two books is that the soldiers in Haldeman's UN are drafted because of their intellect, whereas the volunteers in *Starship Troopers* primarily join to gain the rewards of citizenship: "Under our system every voter and officeholder is a man who has demonstrated through voluntary and difficult service that he places the welfare of the group ahead of personal advantage."[37] Both books portray men and women serving alongside one another.

While Haldeman takes a more negative position toward the military and war, Heinlein presents a more positive image of military service. The endings of the books also portray very different attitudes about humanity's future. Both imply that wars began because of a lack of communication. But Heinlein's book ends with yet another attack, while Haldeman's book closes with the birth of a child and the end of hostilities once the two sides finally communicate with each other and discover neither side wanted war.

John Scalzi's *Old Man's War* is a bit different in that the protagonist fights for the Colonial Defense Force (CDF), a somewhat mysterious organization that has limited contact with Earth itself other than recruiting but that is autonomous in its role of defending human colonies throughout the universe. While the CDF does not unite the nations of Earth in the same way as the UNEF or Terran Federation, it does represent a type of institution that brings humans together to address a common threat.

Another example of humans coming together to defeat an alien threat is Orson Scott Card's *Ender's Game*, which follows a boy through tactical and strategic training in preparation for an attack on an alien species' home planet.[38] While the nature of Earth politics is never particularly clear, there is plenty of evidence of states still being important and even at odds with one another. There are specific references to the United States, when an officer claims, "Americans are quite apt at playing stupid when they choose to."[39] There are also references to Russia and to the Warsaw Pact.[40]

Yet several lines in the book suggest humanity is united, at least in its military preparation to defeat the alien threat that already attacked Earth. The schools are clearly multicultural. There are several references to an international fleet,[41] the teaching of Standard language,[42] and the power shared between the political leader of Earth (the Hegemon), the head of solar system defense (the Stratego), and the commander of the international fleet (the Polemarch).⁴³ Along these lines, Ender is told, "It isn't the world at stake, Ender. Just us. Just humankind," and "Humanity does not ask us to be happy. It merely asks us to be brilliant on its behalf."⁴⁴ Although there is an attempted coup toward the end of the book, one is left with the impression that it fails at least partly because of the additional unity created by Ender's actions.

In addition to the similarities of humans coming together to fight against a common threat, *Ender's Game* also shares the theme of war resulting from a lack of communication. In trying to explain why humans are at war with the bugs, Colonel Graff offers his opinion being the lack of ability to communicate with the bugs, and Ender replies, "So the whole war is because we can't talk to each other."⁴⁵ Then after destroying the alien home world, the remaining queen is able to communicate with Ender: " 'If only we could have talked to you,' the hive-queen said in Ender's words. . . . 'Instead we killed each other.' "⁴⁶

ANALYSIS

> Subjugating the enemy's army without fighting
> is the true pinnacle of excellence.
>
> —SUN TZU, *The Art of War*

Sun Tzu talks about putting your state in such an overwhelmingly advantageous position that the adversary backs down without resorting to war, saving all sides the cost of conflict. At its heart, a collective security agreement is intended to do just that—to deter potential aggressors through the threat of overwhelming cooperation by all members of the organization. Unfortunately, history suggests that this level of cooperation only emerges after incredibly destructive wars. But if we understand what is necessary for cooperation to work and compare this scenario's pros and cons with those of the other scenarios, it is apparent that the best option is to pursue some type of cooperative exploration of space without war being necessary. If one takes a purely liberalist approach, there are positive outcomes from a federation across all four measures (see table 3.1).

A federation will reduce the likelihood of war. This is one of its intended purposes. Unlike a concert, it does reduce the chances of great

TABLE 3.1. **EVALUATING THE FEDERATION SYSTEM**

MEASURES OF EVALUATION	SHORT-TERM	LONG-TERM	LONG-TERM (REALIST VERSION)
Minimizing war	Yes	Yes	No
Human expansion	Yes	Yes	Yes
Enhancing S&T	Yes	Yes	Depends on nature of challenger
Improving SoL	Depends on nature of federation	Depends on nature of federation	Depends on nature of federation

power war, but because of the collective security approach it should also minimize the frequency and duration of all types of wars. It is also unlikely that long-term results would be any different, at least from the liberalist point of view.

Whether human standards of living improve will depend on the nature of the federation. A less formal federation built more like a concert is still just a collection of states, so the SoL for humanity will depend on the interest of each state in addressing the needs of its population. In contrast, a federation that is significantly stronger and centralized, to the point that it can pool resources, means that a focus on human security and human rights will be a priority. At a minimum, a federation will not detract from human standards of living.

As for human expansion and S&T, both measures are likely to improve simply through the sharing of ideas and costs that occurs between members of the federation, regardless of the type of federation that forms. The competition between states that sometimes drives technological innovation will not be as prevalent in a federation. But the benefits of cooperation and cost-sharing will outweigh any possible lull in innovation.

Because realists are unlikely to accept the liberalist view that drives this scenario, table 3.1 includes an additional column to illustrate how realists would interpret the long-term success of a federation. Even if we take a realist approach and contend that no concert lasts forever and that most institutions are challenged when power shifts occur, whatever federation forms will be eventually challenged and weakened and perhaps even destroyed or replaced. Even if that is true, the measures of success are still higher than in most of the other scenarios, simply because of the early cooperation brought about by the federation. For a realist, a federation will not prevent war in the long term, but human expansion would have already occurred by the time the federation falls and would likely continue, even if it is on a more national level. The degree to which SoL rises would still depend on the nature of the federation that forms. And S&T could still grow, but the types of advances would depend on the nature of the challengers. If the challenge to the status quo is military, states will strive to protect themselves and focus on military technology, reducing other types of S&T and negatively affecting SoL. If the challenge is more economic, both S&T and SoL could still rise because of the benefits bred by competition.

The two main goals of a federation of actors are to promote cooperation between members, thereby reducing the likelihood of conflict, and to reduce external threats through collective security. As a result, there are few sources of tension that cannot theoretically be resolved peacefully through the federation itself. That, at least, is the view of federations through a purely liberalist lens. For realists, the source of conflict in this system is the vulnerability states feel that corresponds with their loss of sovereignty and higher dependence on other states for security, as well as the possibility that states will not view their self-interests as being served by the collective. In such circumstances, states may withdraw from the federation and may even challenge its influence on the international system. It only takes one strong actor to upset a federation or concert, and realists argue this is always a possibility. In this respect, the greatest potential sources of conflict will come from within the federation itself.

It is also important to recognize, especially looking through the realist lens, that cooperation is not guaranteed simply because an institution exists. The League of Nations (1920–46) intended to provide a forum for resolving disputes but failed to do so. Even agreements that involve the great powers do not assure cooperation. The three Washington Naval Conference treaties (1921–22) attempted to limit military capabilities, and the Kellogg-Briand Pact (1928) renounced war as an instrument of policy. Yet none of these prevented the world's powers from fighting World War II less than two decades later.

The point of this system is to maximize cooperation, and membership in the federation is a critical source of cooperation. That does not mean cooperation is guaranteed, because it is still elusive under anarchy. From the liberalist point of view, cooperation is more likely to occur because of the ways in which international organizations help states solve the collective action problem. They help identify good and bad behavior and then can help reward or punish such behavior. Likewise, even though most regimes, organizations, and international laws lack means of enforcement, they still constrain states and improve the likelihood of, and opportunities for, cooperation between states. The strength of the neoliberal institutionalist approach is starting with the same realist assumptions yet highlighting the ways that even self-interested actors under anarchy can cooperate and have their choices influenced by international institutions.

Sun Tzu's focus on war and warfare suggests he was a realist, so it is difficult to link his thoughts or maxims to non-realist concepts such as cooperation and international institutions. Yet his emphasis on winning wars without having to fight is consistent with the liberalist view of institutions contributing to an international system where all states can benefit without having to resort to the use of military force.

An alternative translation of the Sun Tzu epigraph is: "To subdue the enemy without fighting is the acme of skill."[47] The most common interpretation of this passage is a reference to deception or to having a strategy that is so effective it compels an adversary to back down even before fighting. It is an admitted stretch to apply these ideas to an international organization, especially since Sun Tzu was not an internationalist and saw one purpose of the state being to wage war. But what if the anarchy that makes war so prevalent for realists was mitigated by an international institution? Would Sun Tzu have opposed such cooperation if it provided benefits to the state without all the costs and risks of war? If the acme of skill is winning without fighting, that can be interpreted in several ways. Sun Tzu contends that war is unnecessary and to be avoided if an adversary can be beaten using nonmilitary means, such as politics or deception. A broader interpretation of beating an enemy without resorting to the use of the military is by bringing rivals into an organization that promotes cooperation and constrains behavior.

Although Sun Tzu does not specifically talk about international organizations, law, or regimes, he does discuss the importance of allies as one way of avoiding war by convincing an enemy to back down before fighting. As such, he would not likely oppose any type of institution that provided benefits to the state without having to resort to war or an agreement that provided collective security to help states avoid war.

The closest Sun Tzu comes to discussing international institutions is when he writes, "The laws [for military organization and discipline] encompass organization and regulations, the Tao of command, and the management of logistics."[48] In the language of the day, Sun Tzu is talking about doctrine and the rules of commanding a military force. Yet the terminology suggests some similarities with the types of laws that neoliberal institutionalists indicate are useful at promoting cooperation in the international system. Just as militaries need rules and strong leadership to function, and just as Hobbes argues that man's self-interested behavior can be checked by a strong central government, so too are states more cooperative when there are rules governing their behavior and creating opportunities to cooperate and ways of enforcing the rules. For realists, anarchy leads to self-interested behavior and a lack of trust. For liberalists, anarchy is simply a challenge for cooperation, but institutions and rules can help mitigate some of the effects of anarchy, whether in an army or in the international community.

The key is to learn the lessons of history in devising the organization. While it is critical to have buy-in from all the great powers, that alone is insufficient for success. Too many members can dilute an organization's decision-making abilities, but too few can make it less relevant. One also must have an organization that states want to join because of the benefits it provides to its members. A starting point might be an organization of all states having certain capabilities in space but that is open to those who will achieve that level of know-how. Once they join, new members will earn a share of the launch contracts as well as a percentage of the profits from any resources discovered. This will drive cooperation among members to share costs and risk, as well as rewards, while also promoting innovation among the emerging space powers.

It is also clear that while general purpose organizations can be useful as a forum for negotiations, those that are specific are sometimes able to operate more efficiently. Therefore, if one wants an organization for space exploration, that should be its focus. Flexible organizations that can adapt to change are also more likely to remain relevant. This means that while the initial effort may be about putting a permanent colony on the moon and Mars, the charter should leave open the possibility of further expansion of both membership and mission.

SUMMARY

> The prejudices people feel about each other disappear when they get to know each other.
> —JAMES T. KIRK, *Star Trek*

Realists might challenge the outcome of the scenario in this chapter, but if we are to stay true to liberalist views of human nature and international politics, we must allow for the possibility that states can cooperate and that their tendencies to distrust and fight can be reined in by international institutions such as regimes, organizations, and laws. One general view held by liberalists is that greater levels of interaction between states lead to greater cooperation and a lower likelihood of war. The interaction could be trade, mutual membership in organizations, scientific exchanges, or a variety of other forms of contact. The point, illustrated by *Forever War* and *Ender's Game* and evident in the *Star Trek* epigraph, is that hatred and anxiety are more likely to grow when there is no contact, whereas interaction and communication help fight those tendencies and can breed cooperation instead of conflict. If one accepts this point of view, then it is not too great of a leap to believe that cooperation in space can grow, and that can even lead states to cooperate in other arenas.

Even if one prefers to stay true to the realist school of thought, concerts and alliances do form, so cooperation is possible, if only in the short term and only for self-interested reasons. Realists also admit that cooperation is more likely in non-security areas. While space has the potential to affect security, cooperation that could get humanity into space need only be in the areas of S&T and perhaps economics. We also see, through institutions such as NATO, that cooperation in one area can expand to other areas. As a result, even realists, if they accept the premises that they already conceded, must admit the possibility of cooperation in space and that even short-term cooperation can be beneficial to humanity in several ways. If we begin to focus on this now, perhaps it will not require a system-changing war to bring this type of cooperation to fruition.

The challenge is that so much of space is tied to security, from the rocket technology itself to the use of space for intelligence to the fear of weapons in space having terrestrial effects. Yet there is precedent for space cooperation. After NASA's cancellation of the shuttle program, the United States was dependent on Russian launch capabilities to provide crews for the International Space Station. This cooperation persisted between the states even during times of tension in other areas.[49] Although the growth of commercial space launch is already making that cooperation unnecessary, it still offers a potential framework for future cooperation in space between the great powers. On the other hand, the United States prohibits any type of space cooperation with China over the fear of stolen technology. This thinking, while logical from a realist perspective, only drives the great powers further away from one another.

CHAPTER 4

HOSTILE TAKEOVER
BIRTH OF THE MULTIPLANETARY CORPORATIONS

> When the Three Armies are already confused and doubtful, the danger of the feudal lords [taking advantage of the situation] arises.
> —SUN TZU, *The Art of War*

The growth of multinational corporations (MNCs) began to weaken state sovereignty as early as the 1990s, but the process became more pronounced on a solar scale once the U.S. company SpaceX established its first base on Mars in 2040. The first humans to walk on another planet arrived not because of the efforts of a state government or even collaboration between partner states, but because of the drive of a commercial entity to achieve something nobody had before—and, more importantly for investors, with the promise that it would generate considerable profit. SpaceX and other early commercial actors in space became the first multiplanetary corporations (MPCs) and, through contractors and subsidiaries, managed nearly every aspect of their colonies, including population control, importing critical resources such as food, and establishing trade routes to transport valuable resources between colonies throughout the solar system.

Corporations did not initially control the solar system. The United States landed a crewed spacecraft on the moon in 2030 for the first time in sixty years with the intent of establishing a lunar colony. This was expected to facilitate travel to Mars and eventually elsewhere in the solar system. But the effort to return to the moon led to cost overruns, accusations of waste and corruption, and multiple congressional hearings, until the United States decided to cancel any further crewed space operations, including the planned missions to Mars. The U.S. economy continued to decline relative to other powers, and Americans were unwilling to pay the cost to put a few people on Mars. Congress even forced NASA to sell off its infrastructure on the moon to SpaceX, and at that point, the United States ceded its place in the solar system to other states and to private companies willing to pay the cost and take the risk to move humanity farther into space. NASA continued to launch and operate satellites for monitoring weather and climate as well as for deep space imagery. But NASA and the United States were officially out of the business of crewed spaceflight. That decision, while saving the U.S. economy in the short run, proved disastrous for the United States and several other governments in the long run.

Other corporations followed SpaceX's lead, establishing their own bases in search of profit from either the development of space tourism or the acquisition of valuable resources. Some began in a nationalist fashion, with corporations recruiting crewmembers only from their home country and promoting that country's culture within their colony. A Chinese company, OneSpace, was initially under direct guidance from, acting almost as a front for, China's Xi Party (an elite group within the Chinese Communist Party) and the China National Space Administration. Its first flights were crewed almost entirely by members of China's ruling party. Even SpaceX's first crews were predominantly American. Over time, however, competition between companies for the most qualified crewmembers, regardless of their nationality, weakened political boundaries as corporate loyalties grew to compete with national loyalty. Over time, corporate cultures replaced national cultures, and eventually conflict emerged between the most powerful corporations. Initially, tension over competition for crewmembers and contracts manifested in simple cases of espionage and corporate theft. That escalated to competition for resources on other planets and moons, which led to sabotage and attempted assassinations against corporate and colonial leaders. Eventually, it turned into piracy and then all-out corporate warfare.

Early in the 2040s and 2050s some states (like China, India, and Japan) could compete with the MPCs for influence because those governments had larger budgets and existing space agencies that gave them a head start. Lunar colonies, for example, remained largely under the control of the Earth governments that established them, except for the U.S. lunar colony under SpaceX control. But inefficiency and bureaucracy in administering space flight, research and development, and procurement significantly handicapped those governments, especially compared to the more efficient operations of the private corporations. Eventually, other states made the same decision as the United States, with some retaining only their lunar colonies and others getting out of the space business altogether. As corporations grew profitable from their activities in space, corporate power overtook that of the nation-state, and it was the MPCs that directed and oversaw the future of human colonization of the solar system.

By 2060, although states were still relevant political actors even on Earth, they ceased to be as influential as they had been or as influential as the first six corporations that established colonies in the solar system. States had virtually no influence off Earth. Most colonists maintained an Earth government citizenship but paid taxes to the corporation that ran their colony, and few people ever returned to Earth (over time, doing so would have been physically difficult). As a result, the corporations themselves wrote the rules that governed colonial operations and enforced them within their spheres of influence, and they only occasionally negotiated common rules for MPC interactions.

Each colony had a different system of government and different rules, depending on the main corporation overseeing the colony's daily activities. The SpaceX colony on Mars was led by scientists and engineers and operated on a highly meritocratic system, with the leads of each science team serving on the colony's governing board. The OneSpace colony on Mars was much more hierarchical. It was led initially by a member of the People's Liberation Army who was also a distant relative of Xi, and succession occurred by compromise between corporate interests and the wishes of the ruling party on the colony. There remained some loyalty to the Chinese Communist Party, though more people felt direct loyalty to OneSpace for providing their livelihood and their security. Over time, as fewer members of the colony rising to positions of leadership were old enough to have been members of the Communist Party in China, primary loyalties shifted from China to the colony itself. The corporation still technically answered to China but had significant autonomy in its off-Earth activities, which was necessary for it to compete efficiently with its corporate rivals.

A still different model was the colony run by Arianespace, a former partner of the European Space Agency that got its start launching satellites and then expanded to space exploration and colonization because of significant financial backing from several European states. It ran its Mars colony in a more democratic way than most of the other corporations. Each part of the colony had a representative on the governing body, which made most of the major decisions on behalf of the company in the absence of direct guidance.

In addition to SpaceX, OneSpace, and Arianespace, the other three original corporations with Mars colonies (known collectively as the Big Six) were Blue Origin, another U.S.-based company that also collaborated with the British-based Virgin Galactic; Bell-ANTRIX, a collaborative effort of eight Indian firms; and Interstellar, a company based in Japan. Later entrants into the space colony market that controlled significant portions of the solar market included SpaceIL, an Israeli company; Al Yah Space, a company representing several Arab states; and Airvantis, a company based in Brazil.

While these colonies were largely independent from Earth decision-makers, they traded with each other and supported one another in emergencies. The MPCs had several rules, or regimes, governing their activities and those of the colonies, some of which grew out of previous space law, like the Outer Space Treaty. For example, all the companies agreed that any emergencies in space would be answered by the nearest ship or colony, regardless of corporate ownership. There were also trade agreements between some colonies. While there were no rules against tariffs, or trade taxes, on most products, there were certain goods—those critical for colony survival, like food and water—that were prohibited from being taxed.

Although corporations ran the colonies, they hired professional diplomats and legal experts to negotiate trade deals, boundary disputes, mineral rights, and the like. As on Earth, these officials were to be given respect and protection by colonies and corporations, even if they represented a rival during periods of tension. Companies often hired diplomats and lawyers from different countries, just as they hired the best crews regardless of nationality. National ties were quickly dropped in favor of the actor paying the diplomat's salary and ensuring the provision of food, water, and oxygen. This created common situations where diplomats from the same country might represent the interests of different corporations.

Corporate alliances did not begin forming until the MPCs controlled colonies in other parts of the solar system. Rather than SpaceX-Mars trading only with SpaceXEuropa,[1] it was more efficient and more profitable for multiple colonies to trade with one another. As a result, a SpaceX transport from Mars to Io might take goods to the SpaceX and Arianespace colonies on Io. These trade partnerships became more formalized over time and eventually started to address other issues, such as mutual defense. Some of these trade relationships formed between colonies that were geographically close to one another simply to reduce the cost and time of transport. Others formed between colonies that shared similar types of governance; while it was relatively simple for colonies run by scientists to interact with each other, it proved more challenging for a scientist-run colony to cooperate with a colony run by a military officer. Ultimately, most trade blocs formed through personal relationships, either between colony or corporate leaders. Trade blocs also brought more profit to the corporations with the ability to move the most goods by using larger ships or making more frequent trips. This demand led the corporations to exert a great deal of effort and money on researching new technologies, particularly in the areas of ship construction and propulsion.

From the beginning, corporations employed security forces, who were usually hired to ensure the safety of the colonists and enforce the laws of the colony when necessary. Some colonies had a sort of judicial system with courts and judges. Others gave the power to punish violations of the rules to the head of the colony or the deputy. The nature of the security forces also depended on the type of corporation and colony. Some corporations directly hired retired military and law enforcement from their home country on Earth. Others contracted with security firms, which may have been from their home country or serving an international clientele. Still other corporations saw the opportunity to expand their services further and created their own security firms under their corporate umbrella. Likewise, compensation varied, with some security personnel paid directly for the service, while others received corporate shares as compensation—in some cases even receiving promises of colonial leadership positions—in exchange for providing service to the company or its colonies.

As trade between planets became a more lucrative business, space piracy also grew. Some of the offenders were private groups eking out a living by raiding shipments and then selling the stolen products on the black market. Others were more like privateers, employed by corporations to cut into the profits of their competitors. From the beginning, there were regular acts of espionage, sabotage, and cyberattacks between corporate rivals. This alone caused the MPCs and their colonies to employ larger security forces and more cyber security experts. But piracy of goods, especially under the direction of other corporations, was a growing threat. Corporations hired ever-larger security forces to protect their shipments, some traveling on the cargo ships, some on their own escort ships designed to patrol trade routes and keep open the space lines of communication. Some corporations went a step further and developed fleets of armed spacecraft that, though intended to defend against pirates, could also target the spacecraft of other corporations.

This combination of trade unions creating rival blocs of actors and companies hiring larger numbers of security forces and arming their ships almost ensured that conflict would arise. What became known as the First Cartel War (in a pessimistic assertion that of course there would be more than one) started in 2067, when a privateer loosely connected to Blue Origin hijacked a ship transporting goods from Mars to Europa on behalf of Interstellar, a relatively young MPC. Normally, after taking the shipments, pirates would allow the ship and crew to go free. Occasionally, the pirates not working for a company would hold the ship for ransom, but there was rarely harm inflicted on any of the crew. In this case, after stealing the cargo, the pirates destroyed the ship and killed the entire crew, including a son of Interstellar's chief executive officer (CEO), who was simply being transported to Europa to help with some local trade deals. The CEO declared war on Blue Origin for hiring the pirates. He also called in all the favors he had with other corporations (SpaceX and Bell-ANTRIX) to side with him in the war. This led Blue Origin to do the same with its closest partner companies (ArianeSpace and Airvantis). Smaller companies were forced to pick sides. The result was a two-year war between the two camps of corporate alliances.

Earth states largely stayed out of the war, though some were willing to sell technology and resources to both sides. After two years, neither side achieved much except reducing trade and revenue for all the involved corporations. Security companies profited, as did ship manufacturers, and the fighting was largely relegated to space, with only one instance of a colony being occupied by the security forces of another corporation. The United Nations negotiated a peace treaty between the two sides, and all the belligerents agreed to the terms because they were anxious to renew their economic activities.

Unfortunately, since the treaty failed to resolve the tension that initially led to the war, less than a year later the corporations were back to the use of espionage, sabotage, and cyberattacks; it was only a matter of time before war would break out again. Each year, some of the corporations would lose power, particularly if they were hit hard by piracy or suffered costly emergencies at a colony. Others would gain wealth, usually through the discovery of new mineral deposits or new technological innovations. But each of these discoveries and inventions often generated more tension between the corporations.

This scenario involves a significant shift away from one of the assumptions of the first three scenarios—that states would remain the primary actors in the solar system. Instead, this scenario explores the possibility that corporations will take over from states as the primary actors, although the scenario suggests they will operate much as states do. Variations of this scenario could evolve in ways similar to any of the first three scenarios but with companies in place of countries. One can imagine a monopoly in which one company acts like the hegemon from scenario one, establishing colonies based on an innovative technological advance and then proceeding to make and enforce the rules that ensure its continued dominance of the solar system. Alternatively, a balance of power might form like in scenario two, but companies would compete for markets and power. Finally, like the federation in scenario three, a conglomeration of companies having an interest in space habitation and exploration might work together to achieve a stable system that is prosperous for all.

Another likely continuation of the scenario is a hybrid of outcomes, in which corporations become regional hegemons over certain colonies or even entire planets but compete for greater levels of influence in the solar system. This competition, though unlikely to lead to war in the short term, will breed rivalries that could compel companies to form alliances and might morph into violent competition.

Although this chapter is intended as a discussion of commercial liberalism, it is also important to have at least one scenario that examines how the rise of corporations would look. If one accepts that corporations will act like states, then our IR theories will continue to be useful for explaining the causes of conflict and the challenges of cooperation. Although this chapter may appear to contradict the assertion that I wanted each scenario to be true to the assumptions and ideas of that worldview, in fact it is consistent with the commercial liberalist view of how actors will behave when they have few connections to restrain their aggressive tendencies. One could argue that this scenario ends on a highly realist note, with war between alliances formed by the primary actors. However, the intent was to highlight the consequences of a lack of interdependence and of representative governments, both in the colonies and typified by the corporations themselves. As a result, while the outcome may appear realist, it is consistent with liberalist expectations of a system having few binding international institutions, minimal interdependence across trade blocs, and few representative governments.

The link between commercial liberalism and the loss of state sovereignty to multinational corporations is not perfect, but it is not inconsistent with a liberalist view of the future where wars between states are less likely because of the high levels of trade between them. That does not preclude the possibility of war between other actors, such as corporations. History provides several examples of corporations becoming powerful and not necessarily preventing conflict. On the contrary, in many historical cases corporations become a militarized arm of their host government. While the most critical opponents of corporate influence are often Marxists, which I discuss in chapter 5, the above scenario is also consistent with realist thinking—or at least would be if realists paid more attention to nonstate actors.

LIBERALISM CONTINUED

> They [the Rich] are led by an invisible hand to make nearly the same distribution of the necessaries of life, which would have been made, had the earth been divided into equal portions among all its inhabitants, and thus without intending it, without knowing it, advance the interest of the society, and afford means to the multiplication of the species.
> —ADAM SMITH, *An Inquiry into the Nature and Causes of the Wealth of Nations*[2]

Chapter 3 discussed an important strand of liberalist thought based on neoliberal institutionalist views about the importance of international institutions such as regimes, organizations, and law. This chapter focuses on a different strand of liberalism in international relations that highlights the importance of economics, both for preventing conflict and for improving global conditions. This section discusses several aspects of this commercial liberalism. It also examines the theory of interdependence, highlights some of the main nonstate actors in international politics, discusses how interdependence might negatively affect the influence of states in the future, and then explores some other variants of liberalism.

Classical liberalists like Thomas Jefferson and Adam Smith believed that society was better off when there was minimal government interference in society and the economy. This translates into international politics because when trade is allowed to move freely between states with little government interference (through tariffs, quotas, or other barriers to trade), wars between states will be less likely and the international system will be more stable. While the scenario above focuses on the rise of corporations, this notion of all-powerful corporations is only one possible consequence of a truly global free market. Liberalists might offer that a global free trade regime would just as easily lead to a federation of states cooperating for space exploration (as in scenario three). But as free trade has grown and globalization has increased, corporations have become increasingly wealthy and more powerful. There is debate over whether that means a loss of state sovereignty, and the future could involve a mix of state and corporate actors in space, but as the rest of this chapter suggests, it is not clear how that would be more conducive to cooperation.

Liberal Economics

Chapter 2 briefly discussed mercantilism, highlighting its connection to realism as well as some of its problems. Whereas mercantilism has several similarities with realism because of the focus on self-interest, free trade economics is connected to liberalism because both focus on absolute gains—making everyone better off through the free exchange of goods.[3] The point of a free trade system is that states agree to reduce barriers to trade and allow the markets to operate without constraints or government intervention. This rarely exists perfectly, as states usually impose some type of restriction on trade, subsidize certain products or companies that they want to be competitive in the market, or protect certain industries to enhance their level of competitiveness in both domestic and global markets or to ensure the availability of key strategic resources.

According to liberalists, a system that is generally more open and freer of restrictions will promote cooperation between states and reduce the likelihood of war. Perhaps more importantly, liberal economics suggests that free trade creates wealth, and while wealth creation is never equal (there are always relative winners and losers), everyone will benefit in some way from the increased growth of the global economy and refrain from activities (such as war) that would stunt that growth and endanger the production of wealth.

Liberalist scholars would likely suggest a trade regime in space similar to the ideal free trade system proposed on Earth. Regardless of who owns a certain territory or resources, the more that actors allow goods to flow freely, the more that space will benefit more people. Because trade is conducted by corporations and individuals, free trade systems are beneficial to the companies and to consumers but may produce less revenue for the state (depending on corporate tax rates), since the lack of tariffs means fewer taxes on imports. This type of system can also create challenges for workers as industries constantly move to areas with cheaper labor and lower standards. As a result, there is often domestic political pressure for states to interfere in the free trade system. This interconnection between free trade desires and state interventions to promote a healthy social community is sometimes referred to as embedded liberalism.[4]

Competition can also breed distrust, which can compel states to impose trade barriers out of fear that other actors will benefit more from trade and will use that additional wealth to increase their military power. This looks more like relative gains thinking than the absolute gains mentality we typically see from liberalist theories. In addition, as corporations grow wealthier and more influential, they often put pressure on their home and host countries to pass laws that benefit them and hurt competitors, further reducing the benefits of the free market.

Interdependence Theory

An important part of the commercial liberalist worldview, though broader than just economics, is interdependence theory. This theory suggests that as states become more mutually dependent on each other, the likelihood of war between them will decrease.[5] Scholars most frequently measure this variable using trade levels, but we can measure it in other ways, such as common membership in international organizations, education or scientific exchanges, or foreign direct investment.[6] The rationale is that the more dependent two states are on each other, the greater the cost of going to war and severing those ties. War becomes less likely when states have an interest in avoiding wars and preserving the benefits of their partnership. In contrast, states with no connections to one another lose little if they go to war, so there are fewer restraints on them from acting aggressively toward each other.

The United States put this theory into practice when President Bill Clinton increased trade with China to reduce tension between the two countries. In 1998 he supported giving China permanent most favored nation status and supported its accession into the World Trade Organization,[7] knowing that such actions might increase Chinese wealth and, therefore, its potential military power. Clinton believed that greater trade connections would increase China's middle class, which would put pressure on the government to open up politically. It also would make Chinese and U.S. economic growth so interdependent that neither state would risk going to war with each other in the future.

Although interdependence theory is a key element of commercial liberalism, there are several criticisms of it. Both realists and Marxists challenge the theory's assumption that all parties to trade will benefit.[8] For Marxists, unequal trade means that more advanced states will benefit from exploitation of developing states (chapter 5 discusses the Marxist *dependencia* theory). Realists equate interdependence with vulnerability. One party is always more dependent on the other, and these differing levels of dependence create more tension rather than less. Some scholars even suggest that higher interdependence increases the likelihood of war, rather than decrease it, and often cite World War I as an example.[9]

Other criticisms of the theory target its underlying assumptions, one of which is that states sever their ties in war. Because corporations trade, not states, it is not clear companies stop trading even when their home states are at war. This is even less likely when dealing with MNCs, which can trade from multiple locations. Certain types of wars may hinder certain types of trade but could increase others. A second assumption is that the actors who suffer in war have the influence to prevent wars. Even if companies lose trade revenue because of war, it may be false to assume these companies have the power to prevent their state from going to war. If neither assumption is valid, then the theory's logic is flawed. Yet as the histories in this chapter show, there are companies that were able to drag their home states into war, so if some of them have the power to do that, perhaps some have the power to prevent war.

Nonstate Actors

Chapter 3 discussed intergovernmental organizations in some detail because of the emphasis that neoliberal institutionalists place on those actors. But IGOs are not the only nonstate actors that operate in the international system or that we could expect to operate in space. Realists pay little attention to nonstate actors because they do not typically have the power to affect states or the international system. Realists acknowledge their existence but rarely consider their influence as anything more than tangential. Even neoclassical realists, who accept the relevance of IGOs, generally ignore other types of nonstate actors. One exception to this was after the September 11 attacks, when some realists began to pay attention to terrorist groups. Perhaps the U.S. reaction to the attacks convinced realists that these groups can even influence great powers, or perhaps it was the significant research funds thrown at terrorism scholarship after 9/11. Either way, that is only one exception to the realist focus on states.

Liberalists, on the other hand, view nonstate actors as important players in international politics and often highlight the ways in which they can influence and even alter state behavior. There are multinational corporations, as we see in the above scenario, but there are also nongovernmental organizations, transnational criminal organizations (TCOs), and violent extremist organizations (VEOs).

In broadest terms, NGOs include several different types of nonstate actors (discussed below). More commonly, they are narrowly defined as organizations that are independent of states and provide a variety of services and functions. NGOs are usually nonprofit entities, sometimes run by volunteers, that focus on specific issues, including but not limited to human rights, public policy, education, and health care. Some are active within the borders of a single country, but many have international activities. The UN even awards some of these international NGOs observer status at certain functions and meetings. Religious groups are also considered a type of NGO; they often have members in several countries, and some view missionary work as an important part of their beliefs. Through these, they often have influence across national boundaries.

NGOs in the United States may lobby members of Congress to support their activities, and several do receive funding from the U.S.

government. For example, more than one-third of U.S. global health aid is funneled through NGOs, which implement those programs. This is often done through the Department of State and the U.S. Agency for International Development.[10] Some NGOs may also have charitable status in many of their home and host states.

One well-known NGO is Doctors Without Borders, which provides medical services to people in need, especially in conflict areas. Many who provide services do so voluntarily, and the organization earned the Nobel Peace Prize in 1999. CARE International focuses on ending poverty and social injustice, often emphasizing the rights of women and children. Amnesty International tackles issues related to human rights through research, mobilization, and advocacy. Some, like UNICEF, are created by IGOs, in this case to be a part of the UN system. It focuses on the needs of women and children in developing countries.

Although the literature on NGOs is growing, they remain underrepresented in IR theory because realists pay little attention to them, so they are exclusively studied by liberalists and constructivists.[11] Even if NGOs are not able to alter state behavior or the international system, they play an important role in helping individuals or even whole communities to overcome disasters, some of which are naturally occurring, while others are created or perpetuated by the states. Therefore, it is problematic to omit such actors from a discussion of international politics, and they will likely operate in space, at least in some capacity. In fact, if corporations focus on profit as this scenario suggests, NGOs may play an even larger role in the future, replacing some of the human security activities traditionally performed by states.

A multinational corporation is a company that controls the production of goods or services in more than one country. According to *Black's Law Dictionary*, to qualify as an MNC, a corporation must receive at least 25 percent of its revenue from operations outside of its home country.[12] In many ways, these actors are the pinnacle of liberal economics, because they transcend state borders, focus on generating wealth through the free market, and may be able to restrain state impulses for war.[13] Yet they are also criticized for their early links to aiding colonialism and more recently to their business practices of ignoring environmental standards and human rights in pursuit of greater revenue. Some lack close ties to any country, while others can advance the culture and interests of their home country, sometime even altering the interests of their host countries. While consumers often benefit from lower prices and greater variety, the losers from the rise of MNCs are often workers. In 2019 nine of the top ten companies in the Forbes Global 2000 ranking were based in either the United States or China, the tenth being a Dutch oil company, Royal Dutch Shell. Also, seven of the ten are in the banking and financial services sector.[14]

There is a strong connection between the rise of MNCs and globalization, which combine to decrease the power of the state and perhaps its sovereignty.[15] There is, of course, debate over the implications of so many large MNCs and their trend of continued growth in both wealth and numbers. Some suggest this rise of MNC wealth and power heralds the transformation of the global economic system and that states will cease to be the most important actors in international politics, at least in the international economy. The counter is that while states have the power to wage war and the ability to disrupt corporations by nationalizing them, breaking them up, or creating competitors, MNCs will only have power as long as states allow them to have it. For now, MNCs benefit their home country in several ways, and even the ability to influence state decisions does not threaten the state enough to outweigh the benefits. It will be interesting to watch how MNCs change if China does surpass the United States as the largest economy and if more Chinese firms enter the Global 2000 ranking, especially in conjunction with the relative decline of several U.S. firms.

TCOs operate across state borders, pursuing economic gain through illicit activities such as narcotics and human trafficking, arms sales, and cyber crime.[16] These groups are often violent and benefit from economic globalization just as the MNCs do. As a result, they challenge not only free markets and the open nature of democracies, but possibly also states themselves, usually in some of the countries with the weakest governing institutions. This type of nonstate actor is represented in the scenario by the space pirates who steal shipments of goods and operate on the black market. We would also expect cyber crimes to remain a danger to corporations and colonies in space, perhaps posing a greater threat than they do today. States or their proxies carry out some cyberattacks and hackers are responsible for other attacks, but some are the work of criminal organizations that use it for identification theft or to steal intellectual property to sell on the black market. States support some of the space pirates in the scenario, while corporations sponsor others, but because they are privateers motivated by wealth rather than a political loyalty or cause, they would also qualify as TCOs.

VEO is a broad term to include groups that engage in violence of some form, usually for political or ideological reasons. These can include terrorist groups of all varieties (religious, racist, separatist, etc.) as well as guerrilla groups. VEOs sometimes begin as legitimate political groups that either are shut out of the political process or become impatient waiting for change through peaceful means. In the *Expanse* books and TV series, the Outer Planets Alliance (OPA) is a network of the outer bodies of the solar system. Prior to that, it was a labor union that morphed into a terrorist group using violence to pursue the interests of the Belt inhabitants.

In the early stages of colonization, individuals on the bases will have been evaluated and screened and are unlikely to engage in organized violence for political reasons. But as the colonies grow and incorporate larger populations, the chances for individuals to become disaffected or radicalized will increase. Likewise, as companies become violent competitors, in addition to hiring privateers, they may also sponsor certain groups to wreak havoc on their competitor's interests, which could lead to assassination attempts or acts of terrorism against colonies. At the same time, while some VEOs are international, others are domestic, and future corporations may suffer from internal violence resulting from too little freedom, too much freedom, harsh working conditions, or an ideology that arises in a colony and challenges the company's status quo.

The most significant distinction between VEOs and TCOs is the political motive of the former. International efforts are made to address both types of groups, but most efforts occur at the national level. We should not be surprised by the possibility of political violence on other planets. There is some concern about partnerships between TCOs and VEOs, although the extent to which the two types of groups have overlapping interests is debated.[17] Because TCOs are driven by profit and VEOs by a political goal, trust is usually lacking between the two actors, and an organization may be more inclined to transform itself, if necessary, rather than cooperate with another type of group. An example of such a transformation is the Revolutionary Armed Forces of Colombia entering the drug trade after losing Soviet backing and essentially taking over part of the business rather than cooperate with the drug cartels.

Sovereignty Lost
Over the past few decades, scholars have written a great deal about the loss of state sovereignty and power.[18] Realists believe that state sovereignty has been a fundamental guiding principle of international politics since the Peace of Westphalia inaugurated the ascent of the modern nation-state. Prior to 1648, the primary political actors were feudal principalities moderated by religion and religious actors like the Catholic pope. Looking back to ancient Greece, the city-state was the primary political actor. Therefore, if states have not always been sovereign, there is no reason to assume that state sovereignty will endure forever.

Certain indications also suggest that the power of the state is declining. The principle of Responsibility to Protect is increasingly challenging the preeminence of state sovereignty, suggesting that what a state does to its own people is no longer simply a matter for its internal politics. Instead, there is a growing sense that states have not just the right, but perhaps an obligation, to protect all human life, even if that requires intervention into another country.[19]

State sovereignty may also be in decline in part because of economic globalization. As trade, travel, and communication become more global, national borders may grow less important. Sovereignty is also in decline because of the growing number of international organizations, nongovernment organizations, and other nonstate actors like terrorist groups and criminal organizations. These trends show the positive and negative aspects of globalization. Likewise, any loss of state sovereignty is likely to include both positive and negative consequences.

Although several scholars agree that state sovereignty is in decline, there is much less agreement regarding the implications of that trend. Samuel Huntington argued that the decline of state sovereignty meant that cultural identities would replace state identities and that future conflicts would be in those regions where civilizations compete for territory, rather than between nation-states.[20] Others point to the willingness of states to open barriers to trade to create trade regions, as well as the European states' willingness to give up sovereignty to a larger supranational entity in the EU. They suggest the future will continue to see the consolidation of states into larger political and economic blocs. Still others suggest that even if state sovereignty declines, the state will remain the primary actor in international politics. Whatever the reason for the decline of sovereignty or the consequences of that decline, at least one possibility for the future is the rise of the multiplanetary corporation—hence the role that MPCs play in this chapter's scenario.

While some might see the replacement of state sovereignty with that of corporate sovereignty as a challenge for IR theory, if corporations become the primary political actors, they will start to act like modern-day nation-states. As a result, many of the theories that apply to today's states will still apply to tomorrow's corporations. A shift in the primary polity does not require dramatic changes in how we understand human nature or the behavior of self-interested actors.

Additional Variants of Liberalism

In chapters 3 and 4, two of the main variations of liberalist IR thought are discussed. Chapter 3 focused on neoliberal institutionalism and highlighted the importance of international organizations. Chapter 4 focuses on commercial liberalism and explores the importance of trade, as well as the rise of the megacorporation. A third variant of liberalism that is not discussed much in this book is republican liberalism, or the notion that a state's type of government will influence its behavior. The most significant theory to come out of this worldview is the democratic peace theory, which some suggest is the closest thing IR scholars have to a law.[21] It is derived from Kant's assertion that representative states are more peaceful than other states because the people have a say in government policy and are less inclined to support war. The modern theory suggests that democracies, though not inherently more peaceful than other types of states, will not go to war with each other.[22]

Although there is compelling evidence to support this theory, there is no agreed-upon explanation for why it might be true, and realists provide several counterarguments. For the limited time democracies have been around, they have faced common adversaries in monarchs, fascists, communists, and Islamic extremists, so democratic states have had an interest in avoiding wars between themselves because they faced common threats that tie them more closely together. There is also evidence that promoting democracy may be a poor policy choice because new democracies are incredibly unstable and violent, suggesting that only stable, mature democracies avoid war with each other.[23]

If one accepts the democratic peace theory, then one might argue democratic regimes should also be good for reducing the likelihood of war in space. While republican liberalism is not directly related to this book because it focuses more on the internal characteristics of a state, it does suggest that democratic colonies might be better suited to keeping peace, though many liberalists would contend that peace also requires international institutions and free trade. One also must wonder how democratic peace theory will play out in space if colonies choose to adopt nondemocratic forms of government, either if corporations control them, because they are treated like property of an Earth state, or if they are governed independently by scientific meritocracy or through a military commander. Colonies run by corporations with a democratic home state will not necessarily be democratic themselves. They will likely operate in accordance with the corporation's governance structures, which are usually quite hierarchical. There may be a board and shareholders who have a say in certain activities, but holders of these positions are usually determined by wealth and influence and are not typically representative of the population. They also tend to care more about revenue and profit than they do the interests of the people. As a result, there are many reasons we should not be optimistic about a future run by corporations, especially if governments continue to decline in power, but particularly those corporate colonies that are unrepresentative of their residents.

HISTORY OF CORPORATE POWER

> I hope we shall ... crush in it's [sic] birth the aristocracy of our monied corporations which dare already to challenge our government to a trial of strength, and to bid defiance to the laws of their country.
> —THOMAS JEFFERSON, *letter to George Logan, 12 November 1816*

Although there are no historical examples of corporations overpowering their home state, there are several cases of wealthy individuals and companies influencing governments. There are also cases of the power and behavior of large multinational corporations testing state sovereignty. Some obvious examples of these types of nonstate actors are the Medici family, the British and Dutch East India Companies, and the United Fruit Company.

The examples below are intended as historical illustrations of the power that corporations have had, sometimes acting as an arm of the government, and sometimes even competing with governments. In none of these cases did corporate power foretell the decline of the nation-state, so we must make a bit of a leap to get to corporations running our lives. But a key difference between the past and today is the growing number of multinational corporations, many of which are wealthier and more influential than most of the countries in the world. Current trends suggest that corporations will continue to amass both wealth and power. According to a Global Justice Now analysis of states and companies, 69 of the top 100 economic entities and 157 of the top 200 economic entities are corporations.[24] This means that many companies are already more powerful than all except the wealthiest thirty states. And there is reason to believe these trends will continue into space, with companies like SpaceX leading the way for the U.S. government, and with other governments growing increasingly reliant on private launch companies.

Even if corporate sovereignty does not replace state sovereignty, if corporations continue to gain power the two sets of loyalties will at least conflict, especially for any colonists living off Earth, physically separated from the governments of Earth but connected to whatever entity provides employment and secures the provisions that are necessary to sustain life. Add to that the potential for loyalty to a colony or an entire planet that is not Earth, and states might have little to do but manage their own domestic affairs. The intent of the cases below is not to provide an in-depth analysis of each economic entity, but instead to highlight some critical ways these actors exhibited political power and influence and to compare how they acquired that power with how they lost it.

The Medici family's power came about primarily through the wealth the family gained through its commercial ventures prior to holding political positions. Few members of the family held official political positions, but even those who did not wield formal political power were still leaders in the city of Florence, and in Europe more generally, because of their wealth and influence.[25]

The House of Medici came to power in Florence in the 1200s primarily because of its trade and banking successes, and the next several centuries saw the repeated rise and fall of Medici influence. The family produced four popes and helped put Florence at the center of Renaissance art. The bank, created in 1397 by Giovanni de' Medici, lasted nearly one hundred years and contributed to the political power the family acquired. The bank operated throughout Europe and helped spur several banking innovations, such as holding companies and double entry bookkeeping.

The family's influence began to wane for the first time before the 1400s when Salvestro de' Medici was forced into exile. Another branch of the Medici family then took up the mantle and began the dynasty, first with Cosimo de' Medici (Cosimo the Elder). Cosimo was already influential in Florence, but by 1420 he began to serve as an ambassador of the city to places like Milan and Bologna and to Pope Martin V. In 1433 a more powerful family exiled him from Florence, but he was welcomed in other parts of Europe, and he used his business interests to expand his wealth and influence. He was recalled from exile the following year and began his unofficial rule of Florence.

As an uncrowned monarch until his death in 1464, Pope Pius II once described Cosimo's influence: "Political questions are settled at his house. . . . The man he chooses holds office. . . . He it is who decides peace and war and controls the laws. . . . He is King in everything but name."[26] Cosimo's son, Piero the Gouty, and his grandson, Lorenzo the Magnificent, further promoted the arts, pushing Florence to become the center of the Renaissance.

Giuliano de' Medici, Piero the Gouty's second son (and younger brother to Lorenzo the Magnificent) was killed by the Pazzi family at an Easter church service in 1478.[27] The Pazzi were a rival banking family, backed by the Catholic church to wrest political control away from the Medici in Florence. Lorenzo escaped the assassination attempt and was protected by the people of Florence, who killed many of the conspirators, including the archbishop of Pisa. This attack led to a war between Florence and Pope Sixtus.

The war was financially costly for the Medici and for Florence. By 1494, because of the war and lack of business acumen from the individual Medici ruling at the time, the bank closed all its branches and nearly went bankrupt. Despite the loss of the bank, the family still had a great deal of wealth, which it continued to pour into the arts and politics. In addition, several Medici enemies were killed, which solidified the support of the people of Florence for the Medici family.

In another example of declining influence, Lorenzo the Magnificent's son, Piero the Unfortunate, accepted a peace treaty with France that was perceived unfavorably, and he was forced into exile in 1494 after only two years in power. His younger brother Giovanni (a cardinal and future pope) helped the family return to Florence in 1512, leading to the peak of the family's influence in Europe. Piero the Unfortunate's son, Lorenzo II, took power in Florence from 1516 until 1519. Lorenzo II's daughter, Catherine, became queen of France after marrying King Henry II in 1547. Three of her sons would lead France, continuing the influence of the family not only in Italy but also spreading it to other parts of Europe. Another Medici daughter, Marie, married Henry IV in 1600, making her queen of France. Her son would be Louis XIII, king of France from 1610 to 1643.

By 1720 the Medici line of rulers had become much less effective, and the dynasty ended in 1737 with the death of the last Medici, who had no male heirs. This case is not so much an example of a company challenging the sovereignty of the state, but of wealth allowing one family to exert more political influence than would have otherwise been the case. The same can be said about the wealthiest companies.

The British East India Company (EIC) was formed in 1600 by royal charter to trade in the Indian Ocean and became the first true MNC.[28] It eventually controlled large parts of the Indian subcontinent, colonized parts of Southeast Asia, and led its parent country into war with China. By 1607 the company was already building its own ships. But the EIC was more than just an MNC. Around 1670, a series of acts passed by the British government gave the company the right to acquire territory, mint money, command troops and form alliances, make war and peace, and exercise civil and criminal jurisdiction over its territories. One consequence is that the company effectively controlled India from 1757 until the Indian rebellion in 1857.

One of its main competitors was the Dutch East India Company, and between 1652 and 1784 the two companies participated in at least four Anglo-Dutch wars, discussed below. Along with its near-monopoly in the trade of several products, the EIC also controlled the opium trade, which helped pay off Britain's huge trade deficit with China.

At the peak of its power in India, the company had its own private army of more than 250,000 people, which helped it rule India. The company also had its own navy, which occasionally joined with the British Royal Navy—for example, at the invasion of Java in 1811. In England, the company established its own college, primarily to train company clerks, and a military seminary to train young officers for service to the company. The cost of acquiring and controlling this power strained the company's finances and required support from Parliament, which did agree to support the company while also asserting the crown's authority over Indian territories.

The First Opium War (1839–42) involved England and China.[29] By 1773 the British EIC had become the leading supplier of opium, which was grown in India and then transported to China. The company used the wealth from the trade to purchase valuable Chinese goods such as tea and silk. War began because of efforts by China's Qing dynasty to enforce the ban on opium sales and use that the emperor had imposed in 1729. Chinese authorities arrested dealers and destroyed up to 2.6 million pounds of opium by throwing it into the ocean. The British government promised traders compensation for the lost product, but the only way to afford that was through war.

The British blockaded Pearl Bay in an attempt to impose costs on the Chinese to the point that they would lift the opium ban. Ironically, the first shot was fired by a Royal Navy ship, a warning shot directed at one of their own merchant ships attempting to run the blockade. In response, the Chinese sent ships to escort merchant ships, including British merchants, into the bay, but the ensuing naval battle triggered a wider war.

Less than a year later, the British launched an invasion force on Canton, destroying Chinese ships along the way and seizing ships filled with collected taxes. The British occupied Shanghai, and the Chinese army suffered repeated defeats. In 1842 the Chinese sued for peace, which gave the British the ability to dictate terms. Hong Kong became British territory, and the Chinese had to recognize the British as equals and grant favored status to British traders.

By 1857 the EIC's army consisted of more than 200,000 men, with a significant percentage (about 80 percent) of them Indians. That year, an uprising occurred within the company's army, which began with the killing of British soldiers as well as Indians loyal to the company.[30] The company responded by killing thousands of Indians, including civilians. At this point, the British government took away the company's power to tax and assumed direct control of the territories, and the company's armies became the armies of British India.

Like many MNCs, the EIC left a mixed legacy. The company opened up much of India through the construction of railways, roads, and bridges. The company also adopted a merit-based promotion system, which became the model for the British and Indian civil services. Yet the benefits came alongside harmful cultivation policies that resulted in famines and atrocities committed against native Indians and peasants. And many of the benefits only came about because of laws passed in England that directed the company to divert funds to benefit the Indian people, which the company likely would not have done on its own. One example is the English Education Act of 1835, which reallocated funds from the company for education and literature in India. This act also contributed to English becoming one of the official languages of India.

While the company had tremendous autonomy and significant power in many areas, the British government never relinquished its sovereignty over either India or the company and forced the company to support Indian society in ways it otherwise would not have done.

The Dutch East India Company (DEIC) formed by combining several rival companies at the beginning of the Dutch-Portuguese War (1602) that ultimately helped solidify the Dutch Empire.[31] It was given a twenty-one-year monopoly on the spice trade. While it was primarily a trading company, it also built ships, invested in foreign development projects, and became the first corporation to be listed on an official stock exchange. Even in the beginning, the company was viewed as an instrument of the Dutch war of independence against Spain (1568–1648), mainly because the revenue and employment from the company's trade colonies compensated for war demands. As a result of its role in that war, it continued to perform many of the same duties even after independence. It acquired several ports and the lands surrounding them. And like its British rival, the company had the power to wage war, negotiate treaties, mint coins, and establish colonies.

The competition between the rival East India Companies played out over 130 years, dragging both companies and their host countries into four wars between 1652 and 1784.[32] The First Anglo-Dutch War (1652–54) was ended by the Treaty of Westminster with a Dutch defeat. Still, by 1659 the DEIC occupied most of the Sri Lankan coast. The Treaty of Breda concluded the Second Anglo-Dutch War (1665–67) with a Dutch victory. Despite the loss of the silk trade with China, by 1669 the Dutch East India Company was the richest company in the world. It had 50,000 employees, including 10,000 soldiers, as well as 150 merchant ships and 40 warships.

The Third Anglo-Dutch War (1672–74) was another Dutch victory, though it caused a trade disruption with Europe that hurt the company. By the mid-eighteenth century, growing competition from other European trade companies, combined with shrinking demand for Asian goods, further weakened the power of the company.

Finally, the Fourth Anglo-Dutch War (1780–84) was fought over Dutch trade and recognition of the United States, and thus was somewhat different from the previous three wars between these states. It mostly involved British attacks against Dutch colonial interests, particularly since the DEIC was unable to protect those areas that were under its defense. It ended with a Dutch defeat under the Treaty of Paris and the British gaining trade rights in parts of the Dutch East Indies.

Toward the end of the 1700s, the company found itself in debt and suffering from high levels of corruption.[33] The Dutch government revoked the company's charter in 1799, nationalized it by taking over its debts and possessions, and eventually dissolved it. This shows that even wealthy companies could not prevent states from shutting them down. Such actions may be less likely today but are not completely impossible. Once these megacorporations have autonomy to run colonies on other planets, states will have less power to exert any influence on them, much less nationalize them. Space may finally give companies the ability to break free from state control and give sovereignty a new character.

The United Fruit Company (UFC) was an American corporation formed in 1899 that held a virtual monopoly on the fruit trade in several Central and South American countries, including Costa Rica, Honduras, and Guatemala.[34] But UFC became more than simply a fruit company. It ran the postal service in Guatemala, dominated regional transportation networks (rail and steamship), and by 1930 was the largest employer in Central America. Its holdings and power in several countries spawned the term "banana republic" to refer to those countries that were heavily controlled by UFC, to the point that corrupt governments granted concessions to the company for monopoly control of various sectors of their economy. In one notorious incident in 1928, the Colombian army put down a labor strike by opening fire into a crowd. At least one member of Colombia's congress claimed the army acted under instruction from the UFC.

What makes UFC noteworthy is that it also had tremendous influence on its home country, having several well-placed people in the U.S. government. Two of its most well-known connections were Allen and John Foster Dulles. Allen Dulles was head of the Central Intelligence Agency (CIA) under President Dwight D. Eisenhower but had done legal work for UFC and sat on its board of directors. His brother, John Foster, was Eisenhower's secretary of state and represented UFC when he was a law partner at Sullivan and Cromwell. But the Dulles brothers were not the only connections between UFC and the Eisenhower government. The U.S. ambassador to the UN, Henry Cabot Lodge, was a large owner of UFC stock. Part of the UFC public relations team, Ed Whitman, was married to Eisenhower's personal secretary, Ann. Walter Bedell Smith, a former CIA director and undersecretary of state, became a UFC director after leaving government. This was particularly noteworthy considering that in 1954, as undersecretary of state under John Foster Dulles, Smith ordered the U.S. ambassador in Guatemala to implement Operation PBSuccess, a CIA plan to overthrow the Guatemalan government in response to threats to nationalize UFC lands. He retired from the State Department and took a position at UFC less than four months after the successful coup.

Close relations between the company and governments also existed in the Southern Hemisphere. In Honduras (1949), the new president, Juan Manuel Galvez, was a former UFC lawyer. Despite that connection, Honduras passed several labor regulations for women and children and established an eight-hour working day. At other times, United Fruit bribed governments to reduce export taxes and did the same thing with European officials. In addition to the Guatemala operation already discussed, UFC was said to be behind coups in several states, such as Nicaragua (1944) and Honduras (1963).

Despite the strong ties between UFC and members of the Eisenhower administration, the company's relations with the U.S. government had not always been favorable. In 1908 the company was forced to sell shares of stock in the fruit importer Vaccaro Brothers because of antitrust legislation (the same legislation that prevents many U.S. financial companies from growing internationally). In July 1954, U.S. courts began legal action against UFC for violating antitrust acts. Even after the company was forced to sell off assets shrinking it to one-third of its size, it expanded into petroleum and natural gas exploration, finding loopholes in court decisions intended to prevent a complete monopoly.

Like the British in their colonies, the record of UFC in Latin America does contain some positives. It brought employment, a network of railroads, and even some schools, such as the Escuela Agricola Panamerican in Honduras, intended to be free for Central American students focusing on agricultural research. However, those benefits were largely outweighed by the practices of the company to create monopolies, exploit populations, and control governments. In addition, the company's undue influence on the U.S. government led to actions (or in some cases avoiding actions) that produced animosity toward the United States in several Central and South American states that still persists.

CORPORATIONS IN SCIENCE FICTION

> Power, in Case's world, meant corporate power. The zaibatsus, the multinationals that shaped the course of human history, had transcended old barriers. Viewed as organisms, they had attained a kind of immortality. You couldn't kill a zaibatsu by assassinating a dozen key executives; there were others waiting to step up the ladder, assume the vacated position, access the vast banks of corporate memory.
> —William Gibson, *Neuromancer*

Corporations are a fundamental element of much of science fiction, especially involving humanity's future in space. Companies are an integral part of many plots, either providing a backstory or serving as an antagonist. They often operate alongside national governments but sometimes have autonomy or even more power than the traditional political actors. In the movie *Blade Runner*, for example, the Tyrrell Corporation makes the androids that are the primary antagonists in the film.[35] In both the book and movie versions of *Dune*, the Spacing Guild exerts a great deal of control because of its monopoly on interstellar travel and banking. In the *Alien* film franchise, the Weyland-Yutani Corporation repeatedly tries to obtain a xenomorph (also known as an alien), even at the expense of human crews, ships, and colonies, and it has the political power to deploy Colonial Marines when one of its colonies goes silent. In the television show *Firefly*, the Blue Sun Corporation appears to be the most powerful entity other than the Alliance government (though in an homage to *Alien*, the Weyland-Yutani Corporation provides many of the weapons in the show). Finally, the eponymous *SpaceCorp* in Ejner Fulsang's novel has sufficient political influence in the United States because of its near-monopoly on space contracts to take on a country with little assistance from the U.S. government. All of these are examples of corporations playing prominent roles in the story, but there are still influential political actors in each case.

In other works, corporations are clearly more powerful than political leaders, if any exist. This megacorporation is a common villain trope, particularly in the cyberpunk subgenre of science fiction. In William Gibson's *Neuromancer* (the first book in the *Sprawl* trilogy and often considered one of the first cyberpunk novels), there is very little discussion of governments. The story mentions cities and states, but travel is treated as if it is almost instantaneous, and readers do not know whether the characters are physically in those locations or simply at an approximation of those cities in cyberspace. Instead, the book discusses the Japanese yakuza (a criminal organization) and zaibatsu (a group of corporations under the control of one family that often controls an entire industry), and mentions certain cultures having their own areas, such as the Rastafari space station called Zion. There are also hints that the most powerful actors besides the megacorporations are the artificial intelligences. There are only a few, they are not yet fully self-aware, and they are controlled by the corporations and families. As a result, families like the Tessier-Ashpool clan, and corporations like Sense/Net and the Fuji Electric Company, are the primary power brokers on Earth, in cyberspace, and in space.

The television series *Dark Matter* (begun as a four-issue comic book, then made into a series) provides an interesting science fiction parallel to the scenario that opens this chapter. In *Dark Matter*, megacorporations compete with one another for control of markets in space. Sometimes they go to war with each other, but sometimes they cooperate, or at least negotiate, as part of the Council of Corporations. The Mikkei Combine, Traugott Corp, Ferrous Corp, and Volkov Rusi are among the most powerful of these corporations mentioned in the series. There are political entities, like the Principality of Zairon and the Republic of Pyre, though these independent territories play a minor role and seem to hold less power and influence than the corporations, and they appear to follow the rules and behave similarly to the corporations. There is also a Galactic Authority (GA), but its purpose seems to be chiefly to keep the peace on the margins rather than to govern. It cannot necessarily go after the corporations for breaking rules, but it does try to prevent them from going to war against each other. When corporate wars do occur, there is little the GA can do. In one exchange, one of the main characters offers, "If I'm right, and we're headed for corporate war, law and order will be the first thing to go."[36]

In Ian McDonald's Luna trilogy, beginning with the novel *New Moon*, the primary actors on the moon are the five industrial families, called the five dragons, but the focus of the book is on the Corta family. The other families include the Vorontsovs, the Asamoahs, the Suns, and the Mackenzies. The families represent corporations that focus on different aspects of lunar development but are run like organized crime syndicates. These families are occasionally at war with one another, sometimes over territory and resources, sometimes simply because of tradition. Some hints are given regarding how these families came about and found investors, but the story is never clear about the origins of the families or their feuds. Each family has a tentative link to an Earth state, such as the Cortas' connections to Brazil. Like the nobles in Europe, the families intermarry to create alliances or to end feuds, but these marriages might or might not prevent violence and appear to add more intrigue. There is a political leader who seems to have some power over the entire moon but not enough to rein in the violence between families. This "Eagle of the Moon" is head of the Lunar Development Corporation (LDC), which is the moon's governing body and holds power by being responsible for granting contracts to the families. The LDC can hold the rights to new claims hostage to affect family behavior, but it ultimately cannot control the families. There is also the small issue of the "Eagle" being married to a Mackenzie. Whether that is a conflict of interest or not, it does suggest an inherent bias and does affect the outcome of the story.

One other book that illustrates the importance of corporations is *Moving Mars* by Greg Bear. There are two primary political tensions here. One is the feud between Mars and Earth. The second is within Mars, where there is division between the statists, who want to unify, and those who want to preserve their independence within the existing family units called Binding Multiples because they fear a unified Mars will allow Earth to exert more control. The BMs are a hybrid of corporations and bloodlines, which gives them a clan-like quality. In trying to explain the system to those on Earth, "Binding Multiples operate more like groups of small business and families than worker-owned Earth-style corporations. Family members are all shareholders, but they cannot sell their shares to any outside concerns. Entry to the family is through marriage, special election, or birth."[37] Each BM focuses on a particular sector, such as the banking industry that the main character Casseia grows up in, or the political BM into which she marries and that helps her take on increasingly influential roles on Mars.

Several other works of science fiction incorporate the idea of a megacorporation. Manpower Incorporated and the Hauptman Cartel are both powerful actors in David Weber's Honor Harrington series, the first book of which is *On Basilisk Station*. In Max Barry's *Jennifer Government*, the two primary actors are the U.S. Alliance and Team Advantage, both of which are essentially coalitions of corporate actors where citizens adopt the last name of the company for which they work.

Rarely do corporations play a positive, selfless role in science fiction, but they can be benign. One example is the Praxis Corporation in Kim Stanley Robinson's Mars Trilogy (*Red Mars*, the first book, is discussed more in chapter 5). Especially in the first two books, *Red Mars* and *Green Mars*, the transnational corporations that provided much of the equipment and investment in the Mars settlement are referred to as metanationals (or metanats) because of their growing power. They operate with the states, the civilizations, and the UN, all of which have a role in governing the actions of some actors on Mars. Like many of the metanats, the Praxis Corporation develops strong economic and political connections, but the book portrays it as one of the benign corporations, providing equipment for the first Martian colonists.

The fact that corporations are often portrayed in science fiction as greedy, corrupt, or power-hungry is not in itself a reason to fear a future dominated by corporations. But corporations on Earth often do not answer to political leaders, and this trend will likely grow as space becomes a domain dominated by the private sector. Corporations are not only self-interested like states but also even less beholden to their people because there are no corporate elections. And because taking care of people sometimes gets in the way of profit, there are many reasons to fear this type of corporate-run future. The dilemma is that private corporations may get humanity into space faster than governments could, so we need to evaluate the positives and negatives from such a scenario.

ANALYSIS

> When you plunder a district, divide the wealth among your troops.
> —SUN TZU, *The Art of War*

Between the history of large corporations and their typical portrayal in science fiction, there is little reason to be optimistic that a system controlled by corporations would be less anarchic or lead to higher levels of cooperation than the current state-run system. Like states, corporations may cooperate with each other when it serves their interest, but they rarely do so purely for the sake of cooperation.

Even though MNCs are consistent with the liberalist worldview and the desire for wealth to be in the hands of private citizens, the most likely evolution of a system controlled by corporations will be conflictual, probably in ways that closely conform with realist views of conflict. Companies already compete with one another and, if permitted to have their own armies, will challenge the sovereignty of states and eventually use force to gain commercial advantages, as the largest corporations of the past did.

Markets are incredibly conflictual, but they rarely lead to violence because of the stabilizing role of governments and the rules of behavior they set and enforce. The loss of government sovereignty will make conflict even more likely to be resolved in violent ways. There will still be opportunities for cooperation, but in a very realist way, it will occur only when it is in the interests of the actors and only when the market allows. Trade blocs are likely to form, and while trade may flow freely between members of the blocs, there are likely to be limits on trade across blocs over concerns of relative gains, or fear of trade partners switching sides and throwing off the balance of power.

Despite the corporations' lack of concern for humanity, a corporate-controlled solar system might have some positive features (see table 4.1). Both human exploration and S&T will likely advance in a corporate-controlled system. In fact, those aspects of the future could see greater advancement under MPCs than under governments, because competition between companies will drive more advances in S&T. However, some caution is necessary because the corporations may limit the number of people with access to those new technologies and colonies, which could widen the gap between wealthy and poor. Likewise, where human standards of living are likely to increase for those with ties to the most powerful corporations, human security will continue to be a problem for much of humanity, particularly since helping people is often contrary to the bottom line of corporate profit.

Discussion of wars is trickier in this chapter because we tend to think of and define wars as being violent campaigns fought between states. But violent conflict between nonstate actors could rise to the level of war, and such wars could alter the system. Most definitions of wars talk about a legitimate authority, a political actor, or a recognized polity. While we do not see corporations in this way today, if state sovereignty declines and is replaced by loyalty to corporations, then they may become the primary political actor of the future, even if they are driven by wealth more than politics or the common good.

Many of the same causes of conflict for states—resource scarcity, disputes over territory, or just a plain desire to gain or preserve power—will also lead corporations into conflict. One can even imagine corporate wars over accidents, misperceptions, or misunderstandings,

TABLE 4.1. **EVALUATING THE CORPORATE SYSTEM**

MEASURES OF EVALUATION	SHORT-TERM	LONG-TERM
Minimizing war	Yes	No (depending on one's definition of war)
Human expansion	Yes	Yes
Enhancing S&T	Yes (in limited areas)	Yes (in limited areas)
Improving SoL	No	No

in the way that defensive realists often explain wars between even security-minded states. In fact, many of the liberalist theories about ways to reduce wars between states—representative governments, international institutions, interdependence—will be less common in a corporate-controlled solar system or will have less influence on corporate behavior, where success is defined as greater profits and market shares. The result is not likely to be a reduction in wars, especially if the greatest corporate innovations do more to feed military machines. Instead, we could see a rise in violence given the lack of liberalist constraints on large corporations.

In fact, one can imagine advanced warfare that would not necessarily involve any human fatalities. Although it is beyond the scope of this book to discuss potential changes to war and warfare, if the dominant type of competition between the primary actors lacks human involvement, then the new form of war will follow suit. Likewise, if the new authority is corporate rather than governmental, then corporate violence will be the new way of war.

If we wish to bring about this scenario of a corporate-controlled future, there may not be much we have to do. States are already relinquishing some control over space to the private sector, and whether that weakens state sovereignty generally or just in space is a question we will soon be able to answer. If we wish to stop this scenario, or at least prevent the corporate replacement of state governments, then we must develop the laws and norms of behavior in space now, while states still have the power to enforce those institutions. Otherwise, these institutions will be initiated by the most powerful corporations and enforced by the same corporations, if they are enforced at all.

Some of these sources of cooperation may be more enforceable if there is a central authority of some type, like the Galactic Authority in *Dark Matter* or the Alliance Government in the television show *Firefly*, even if that central authority is relatively weak and only able to enforce institutions on the margins. The UN may be able to play that role, especially if the dominant corporations are headquartered on Earth, or it may be some other organization designed to try to regulate corporate activities on Earth or to have a more expansive reach into the solar system. The point is that a corporate future bereft of constraints on violence will look like the international political system looked before the UN, international law, and trade agreements. In contrast, a system with tight controls and mechanisms for cooperation can bring about a more prosperous future, even if states are no longer the primary actor. (Then again, that type of system starts to look a lot more like the federation discussion in scenario three.)

The recommendations offered by Sun Tzu in this chapter could all be taken as warnings against a system where corporations are in charge. Sun Tzu does not explicitly write about nonstate actors but does sometimes discuss the economic or financial elements of war, just as he wrote about the dangers of imperial overstretch. The question is whether Sun Tzu's advice for generals and political leaders translates to wars between corporations.

In the quote at the beginning of this section, Sun Tzu discusses sharing the spoils of war with one's soldiers. But will corporations share the spoils of war, if there are any spoils to share in corporate wars? Will future wars look like past wars, in which there were clear spoils to gain, or will violence occur entirely in cyberspace or be conducted by unmanned machines so that no humans are killed or even threatened, and where the only spoils are information that benefits the winning corporation? We have already seen war grow less materially profitable now that states no longer keep stocks of hard metals for currency. With much of the world's wealth existing only as numbers in cyberspace, there is less to be gained materially through physical conquest. This trend is likely to continue, and wars between corporations will be about control of markets, information, and pride—in other words, long-term influence—rather than short-term profit.

Sun Tzu also states, "If the enemy is numerous, disciplined, and about to advance, how should we respond to them? I would say, first seize something that they love, for then they will listen to you."[38] But what, besides wealth, do corporations love? If actors are going to war over the very thing they love, then seizing that wealth could lead to greater levels of distrust and more, not less, tension. Over time, corporations may come to love certain territories or areas that define them or their history and may even come to love the people that work for them and offer them their loyalty. At this stage, that future is difficult to imagine.

Chapter 3 cited Sun Tzu's reference to feudal lords exerting greater influence during the chaos of war. This may foreshadow how corporations ultimately wrest sovereignty from the nation-state. If states weaken themselves through repeated or prolonged wars, it is plausible that the international system could change so greatly that corporations rise to become not just the wealthiest actors but also the most politically influential entities. History provides us with examples of corporations challenging states and of new powers rising from system-changing wars, and we know nation-states have only been around since 1648. Put these factors together, and it is possible that war could give rise to a new system of powerful corporate political actors, with nation-states going the way of the city-state.

SUMMARY

> We'll go to the moons of Jupiter, at least some of the outer ones for sure, and probably Titan on Saturn, and the asteroids. Once we have that forcing function, and an Earth-to-Mars economy, we'll cover the whole Solar System. But the key is that we have to make the Mars thing work. If we're going to have any chance of sending stuff to other star systems, we need to be laser-focused on becoming a multi-planet civilisation. That's the next step.
> —ELON MUSK, *30 September 2014*[39]

Several heads of companies have a vision of their future, not just for their company, but for the future of human civilization. While the most efficient means of achieving that vision may be through the increased power and influence of the MNC, this chapter highlighted many reasons to be concerned about a future where corporate power replaces, or even challenges, state sovereignty in space.

For one thing, this chapter reminds us that even if we fear the power of the state, most states answer to their populations, at least on some level. There are fewer such restraints on corporations, especially if they are no longer governed by states, the international system, or the rules that states enforce. While realists generally ignore the role of corporations in international politics, it is possible that states pay more attention to norms and institutions than megacorporations would. They almost certainly pay more attention to human security.

Corporations on Earth already look for ways to escape government control—by operating across borders, by seeking ways to get around regulations and taxes, and by using wealth to influence political leaders. Corporations in space will find that distance gives them even more freedom to operate in whatever manner they see fit.

Even if we do not want a future controlled by corporations, there may be elements of this scenario that provide value either to plans for a spacefaring humanity or for IR theory. Corporations are more efficient and generally more flexible than states, and this is true in developing relations with others, in reacting to changes in their environment, and in researching new technologies. If states could harness some of that flexibility while retaining control over it, human activities in space will be more cost-effective, more efficient, and occur more frequently. John Ruggie's embedded liberalism may provide one path forward that retains state power to intervene in markets for the benefits of society, while still promoting as much free trade as possible. On the other hand, unfettered liberal economics, despite being able to generate wealth and possibly being able to promote cooperation between states, can also create ultrapowerful corporations that do not answer to any other actors or institutions.

CHAPTER 5

MARX ON MARS
SOCIAL REVOLUTION IN SPACE

> When the weapons have grown dull and spirits depressed, when our strength has been expended and resources consumed, then the feudal lords will take advantage of our exhaustion and arise.
> —Sun Tzu, *The Art of War*

By the time the first Martian colonies became fully functioning and self-sufficient in 2050,[1] a division of labor already existed throughout the solar system, which separated colonists into two main classes of people. The upper class consisted of the scientists, engineers, and other intellectuals, many of whom had established the first lunar colony in 2031 and were responsible for its evolution and expansion into other parts of the solar system. This was the more influential class, since many of these individuals were members of the original crews to settle the moon, but also because they were the more educated and were generally placed in the most senior positions of authority. The lower class of colonists included the manual laborers who maintained the day-to-day functions of the colonies, including sanitation, waste, and security.

Both groups of colonists are crucial to operating lunar and Martian settlements, but individuals within each class perceived the other class of settlers as being less valuable than their own. Many of the scientists and engineers viewed the workers not only as freeloaders who contributed little to the colony, but even saw them as a drain on the colony's air, water, and food supplies. At the same time, the laborers felt they were exploited by the other inhabitants of the colony, doing the dirty work the intellectuals did not want to do and did not have the skill to do. It was not just about education or daily tasks. The scientists had the nicest living quarters and held most of the power and influence over colony governance. The laborers had worse working conditions and smaller living spaces, and opportunities to change class were relatively rare. Since there were no universities on the moon handing out advanced degrees, there were few opportunities to move oneself from the worker class up to the intellectual class. When change did occur, it was more likely to happen through marriage than by merit. In fact, unless a laborer was married, they had to share living quarters, usually with two other laborers, while even unattached members of the upper class had private quarters.

By 2055 some members of the labor class began to protest this disparity and called for an end to their exploitation. The most vocal complaints came early on from the lunar colonies but quickly spread elsewhere. There were different complaints depending on whether the members were on the moon, on Mars, or in the newest Outer Belt colonies. Collectively, their complaints were about living space, work conditions, and a lack of opportunities for courtship, considering the ratio of men to women was two to one during those early years of space colonization.

To be sure, these classes were not entirely homogeneous. The intellectuals had significant internal conflicts. Most of the engineers and corporate owners on Earth wanted to terraform Mars as quickly as possible, to generate faster profits. Most of the scientists wanted to preserve the existing environment, at least until they could study the planet in detail. The workers had conflicts of their own, the most significant division being between those who wanted a peaceful change to reduce the division between the classes and those who were less patient and felt violence could move things along more quickly. There were also areas of agreement across classes. Miners and security forces in the labor class, for example, agreed with the engineers on the need to terraform Mars, because a better atmosphere would improve the working conditions for both groups.

The United Governments of Earth (UGE) responded to the growing class tensions in three ways, intended to ameliorate the complaints of the laborers. First, it agreed to expand the size of the colonies by sending up more people, who would serve as pure colonists. They would not necessarily have a required skill or profession, but they would be unattached and would increase the opportunities for courtship, particularly for the laborers. These pure colonists would have even less privacy than the laborers, at least initially, as a result of the shared living spaces and their lack of employment opportunities, and so were thought to have significant incentives to marry to alter their status. The UGE believed this would satisfy at least one of the laborers' complaints about the lack of opportunity for personal relations.

The lunar colonies also received approval to begin importing more materials from the newest mining colonies on Mars and in the Outer Belt. They planned to use these resources to craft new living spaces so more laborers would have private quarters. There were also plans to provide more areas for leisure activities, such as parks, gyms, and movie theaters, which would provide not only more entertainment for the colonists but also part-time jobs for the newest groups of colonists. The lunar colonies purchased those resources cheaply from the outer colonies, with the permission of the UGE, because those colonies on Mars and in the Outer Belt had smaller populations to effect any kind of change, and greater distance meant less of a threat to the status quo and less attention paid to the issues affecting those colonies.

The third reform measure was the construction of a university on the moon. Armstrong University emphasized those fields of study most valuable to the colonies—such as engineering, robotics, geology, and astrobotany. The university provided teaching jobs for intellectuals as well as opportunities for laborers and pure colonists to rise in status by enhancing their education and making themselves more valuable to the operation of the colonies.

These reform plans placated most of the lunar laborers, at least for a while. The UGE also granted the laborers minor concessions on alleviating some of the worst working conditions, but they still held the most dangerous jobs, and many of them continued to feel underappreciated. While these plans reduced tension, they did little to narrow the perceived gap between the classes. Each plan also came with negative consequences. Adding colonists who lacked the necessary skills to operate the colonies meant more demand being placed on vital systems, which meant more work for the laborers who kept those systems functioning. Drawing resources from elsewhere for lunar construction meant that the workers on Mars and the Outer Belt felt even more exploited. And the university, even though it offered no courses in the humanities or social sciences, became a corridor through which increasingly radical ideas were introduced to students. Ideas about communism by Karl Marx, Friedrich Engels, and Vladimir Lenin, as well as ideas about violence and revolt developed by Mikhail Bakunin and a twentieth-century mathematician turned terrorist named Ted Kaczynski, quickly spread and, rather than alleviating those issues, fed into further complaints of exploitation.

These ideas not only spread through the laborers in the lunar colonies but reached the Martian colonies as well, where Marxism came to be known as Marsism. Agitators rewrote and updated books like *The Communist Manifesto* and *Das Kapital* to be more applicable to the specific conditions in the colonies. And labor leaders began calling for a similar revolution to the one Marx called for in Germany two hundred years earlier and that Lenin enacted in Russia and Mao implemented in China.

Although the first rumblings of change occurred on the moon, the first real attempts at revolution occurred on Mars, where the ratio of workers to intellectuals was even higher, where the lunar reforms were not being implemented to the same degree, and where greater distance from Earth meant there was a perception of greater opportunities to bring about change. Tension between scientists and laborers bubbled over into violence on one of the Martian colonies, and several laborers were killed as a result. The governor of the colony refused to hold any of his valuable scientists accountable, even though several witnesses said they were responsible for the escalation to violence. Although the security forces had the strongest personal and professional linkages to the other laborers, they worked for the governor and therefore took their orders from him, or else they risked losing their jobs and status.

Despite the influence of the intellectual class, its members were a minority of the population and possessed none of the security training or weapons of the laboring class. As a result, when the desire for violent rebellion was triggered, it did not take long to bring the existing social structure down, especially once enough of the security forces were convinced to join the revolution. At that point, the laborers were unlikely to stop without some type of response from Earth.

A small group of laborers working with a few sympathetic engineers emerged as a vanguard of the movement, first overthrowing the intellectuals and then distancing themselves from both Earth and the moon because of their exploitation of Martian resources for their own uses. Eventually, though, this vanguard established its own hierarchical system to exert influence on the population and lead the colonies. A handful of the intellectuals who opposed the rebellion were imprisoned. Others were given the choice of joining with the laborers or being exiled and sent back to Earth. This was a particularly difficult choice for those who had families on Mars and were unwilling to relocate their Martian-born children to Earth out of fear of the physical effects that its gravity would have on those children as well as on themselves after years in space. Only one colony on Mars remained loyal to Earth, New Formosa, and some of the intellectuals in the other colonies managed to flee and seek refuge there.

As the rebellion gained momentum, Earth's leaders feared it would spread, first to the moon and then to Earth itself, since Earth had its own class system of sorts. Once Earth was threatened with the reduced supply of some of its most valuable resources, it could not stand by and allow the rebellion to endure. The UGE faced two unpleasant choices. It could violently put down the revolt on Mars to preserve Earth's control and send a signal to the other colonists in the solar system that they should not rebel. Alternately, it could allow Mars to have its freedom, but in doing so risk losing other colonies to similar calls for independence and eventually losing control of the solar system. The initial response was to cut off all support to the colony, but that only fueled greater antagonism toward Earth throughout the solar system. The rebellion spread, especially to resource colonies where the populations were almost entirely laborers, with few scientists or pure colonists, and minimal security forces. The message that Earth and the scientists made up the core, who exploited laborers and those on Mars and in the Outer Belt, resonated particularly well with those working in the farthest reaches of the solar periphery.

When preliminary sanctions and threats of military action did not reverse the course of the rebellion, the UGE felt obligated to follow through on its threats of military action. Initial attempts to foment a counterrevolution to wrest back control of Mars failed when the handful of laborers still loyal to Earth were discovered and imprisoned. Attempts to land security forces on Mars quickly devolved into bloodshed.

Eventually, the leaders of the Marsist uprising and the UGE signed a truce of sorts. Mars agreed to continue selling resources to Earth and the lunar colonies, but it took control of the previously privately-owned property and would determine its own prices on its exports. In exchange, Earth agreed to recognize Martian independence and promised not to attempt another counterrevolution on Mars. The two sides could not reach agreement regarding future Martian attempts to spread the revolution, so while the moon remained largely in Earth's sphere of influence, mostly due to proximity, the Outer Belt became a battleground between Earth and Mars over both resources and ideas. In addition, the UGE placed even more pressure on the moon to ensure revolution did not spread, banning all copies of *The Marsist Manifesto* as well as the original book by Marx and Engels. It also prohibited the teaching of such works at Armstrong University, both formally and informally. Any students in possession of those or similar books were immediately expelled and placed on a watch list. Faculty members found in possession of the books were dismissed.

After the revolution and granting of Martian independence, a classless society initially emerged in the colonies, with no divisions based on race, previous profession, or talent. One major change was the elimination of currency within Martian transactions. The government retained some currency for trading with Earth and other colonies but eliminated the use of currency for all intraplanetary exchanges. People did not receive pay for their services, but the government provided them all the necessities, including food, shelter, and a leisure activity allowance. The government encouraged colonists to work any job they wanted and for however long they wished, even if that meant some people chose not to work at all.

This was, by all accounts, a perfect existence, at least for a short time. But it was not the utopia the laborers envisioned, and problems soon emerged. Although the colonists excelled at the day-to-day operations of a Martian colony, many of the scientists, doctors, and engineers, as well as the administrators with experience governing the colonies, were either killed or imprisoned during the revolution, or they managed to escape to New Formosa—some even opting to return to Earth, despite the health dangers. This meant that the colonies quickly encountered technical and bureaucratic problems that few of the inhabitants had the training or experience to address. To deal with this, Mars built its own university in the hopes of educating scientists and leaders. But creation of a scholar class was counter to the egalitarian nature of the society, and there were too few qualified workers with the time and energy to teach while also performing critical tasks for the colony.

The lack of incentives to work or be creative also became a drag on society. Too many people chose to work the safer, more interesting jobs, so that many of the menial tasks and the most dangerous jobs went undone. Or those who were willing to do those jobs only tolerated such work a couple of hours at a time. Many colonists also chose to attend university without the necessary background to complete the courses, further taxing the system. Eventually, the government had to step in and manage who would fill each job, who would attend university, and what topics they would study while in school. The new government did not always base these decisions on merit or talent. The system eventually became corrupted so that those with ties to the leadership were more likely to get the best jobs and receive more subsidies from the government. The utopian ideal quickly fell apart, yet the ideas did not die. Instead, they spread to parts of the Outer Belt, often with the help of Mars, and with opposition from Earth. So, while the experiment failed to live up to its utopian ideals, conflict between Earth and the Martian colonies continued to spread.

This fifth scenario involves a critical departure from the previous four. It focuses less on the importance of states or corporations and more on the role of class—in particular, how divisions in the population and perceptions of exploitation can lead to conflicts along class lines.

Any of the previous scenarios could evolve into a situation where class differences become a source of conflict between countries, corporations, or planets. So, the details of this scenario are perhaps less important than the broader emphasis on class as a source of conflict within any society.

The creation of class divisions, according to Karl Marx, is an inevitable part of the human condition wherever there are politics and economics and where achievement is measured in power and wealth. He suggests it is particularly common in capitalist societies, in which those who own the wealth have incentives to exploit those who work to produce the wealth. There is no reason to expect that the future in space will be any different. In fact, class-based revolutions could increase in future generations, as those who grow up on other solar bodies come to resent the Earth for owning property and attempting to govern other parts of the solar system from so far away. As a result, it is worth discussing the potential importance of class division in that possible future.

Terms that are often used interchangeably but have different meanings are Marxism, socialism, and communism. One also occasionally hears variations of these, such as Maoism, Leninism, and Titoism. There are important distinctions between these variations, such as the means of achieving revolution, the ownership of property, the means of production, and how those are managed.[2] For our purposes, this chapter uses them synonymously. Marx himself used the terms socialism and communism interchangeably, but that is largely because he laid out a theory that combined political, social, and economic principles.

Marx saw socialism as the stage of economics that follows capitalism, after the working class overthrows the existing system. The main elements of a socialist economic system are more public rather than private ownership of property and an equal sharing of goods by the people. Communism is variously interpreted as either the next stage after socialism or as a political system that Marx viewed as a complement to socialism. The communist society does away with class divisions, and the role of government is minimized as power devolves to the people operating in the classless society. Marx also added that this revolt against capitalism and government would spread and that the revolution would be global. Later variants of these ideas had more nationalist objectives, such as

Stalinism in the Soviet Union after Lenin's death, Titoism in Yugoslavia, and Maoism in China. The prime location for the revolution also varied. While Marx saw the revolution arising from within the urban working class in an industrial country like Germany, Mao focused more on the rural nature of the Chinese peasants as the starting location of the revolution. Several later revolutionary movements followed Mao's model (in Cuba and Vietnam, for example).

Today, many countries contain some elements of either socialism or communism. While there are five remaining communist states, several states—even Western democracies—have some socialist policies, such as welfare programs like public housing, universal health care, and free university education. At the same time, none of the remaining communist states appear intent on exporting revolution or their style of government, and some, like China, even embrace elements of the capitalist economic system.

The rest of this chapter uses Marxism to refer broadly to all these various permutations of the ideology but also to suggest that I am talking about an international relations worldview that incorporates political, societal, and economic philosophies and is a distinct school of thought. So, as discussed in chapters 1 and 2, while realism and mercantilism are related to one another but focus on politics and economics, respectively, and while liberalism can refer to either economic or political concepts, Marxism treats all these elements as part of one holistic system.

This chapter and the two that follow draw upon what are sometimes called critical theories. Critical theory can mean several different things, ranging from ideas that challenge the status quo (in this case, realist and liberalist views of how the world works) to critiques that either provide no solutions or believe no solutions are available. The ideas in these three chapters do not represent the only critical theories, but they are the ones commonly referenced in the IR literature. These are also sometimes referred to as reflectivist approaches to IR (in contrast to realist and liberalist rationalism, which generally assume some universally knowable truth). Reflectivism opposes notions of pure rational choice decisionmaking and positivism, starting instead from a point of having to understand individual interpretations, ideas, and discourse that are neither universal nor a path to a knowable truth. If everyone experiences reality from their own perspective and there is no universal truth, that complicates scenario writing for those last chapters. It may also be what makes these scenarios so interesting and compelling.

MARXISM

> Political power, properly so called, is merely the organized power of one class for oppressing another.
> —KARL MARX AND FRIEDRICH ENGELS,
> *The Communist Manifesto*

Marxism is both a political and an economic ideology that was popular for about one hundred years but fell out of favor after the end of the Cold War. Many still view the world in Marxist terms, so it is valuable to understand some of the main concepts. In fact, despite the ideology's loss of credibility after the Cold War, several states preserved their communist systems, adopted communist policies, or elected leaders to protect the revolution (such as China, Cuba, Laos, North Korea, and Vietnam). Newer converts include Venezuela and Bolivia, although they have experienced significantly mixed results. Several states appear to be leaning away from full democracy, such as Hungary, Turkey, and Poland, though these currently seem more inclined toward right-wing nationalism rather than communist politics.[3] Several revolutionary movements also survived the Cold War's end—for example, in India, Peru, and the Philippines—seeking either a change in the existing government and society or the creation of their own state. Others, like the Revolutionary Armed Forces of Colombia, survived the end of the Cold War by abandoning open calls for a Marxist-style revolution in favor of an agenda that focused more on effective governance and ending corruption in the Colombian government.

While the economic side of Marxism has some similarities with mercantilism, at least in terms of protecting domestic industries from global competition, it is largely antithetical to liberalist economic policies. In its purest form, Marxism is opposed to the self-interested behavior of states that helps define mercantilism and instead advocates for a more global focus to understand the behavior of states in both the economic and the political realms. Where realism and liberalism struggle to explain change in the international system, Marx saw change as a function of the struggle between the classes. In other words, Marxism has some similarities with the other two schools of thought discussed in the previous chapters, but it also provides important challenges to them.

The Politics of Class

Marx and Engels, in *The Communist Manifesto*, painted the history of humanity as one of class struggle.[4] Both politics and economics, regardless of which systems one discusses, are about the division of wealth and power between those who have them and those who do not. But it is not just about disparity between classes. For Marx, those who have wealth and power actively seek to deny those who do not have it from ever obtaining it. He discusses two classes of people within the industrialized nations. The bourgeoisie are those who possess the capital, or wealth; they are the owners and the business managers. The proletariat are the laborers, or the working class, who produce the goods that create wealth but who get little of that wealth for themselves. In the scenario that opened this chapter, the scientists and intellectuals in the colonies represent the bourgeoisie class while the laborers make up the proletariat.

International relations theorists took a great deal from Marx and applied it to the international system. For Marxist scholars, just as there are classes of people in society, states in the international community are also stratified into classes, often labeled as the core and the periphery. The core generally includes the Western developed capitalist states, sometimes referred to as the North. The periphery consists of the developing states, or the South. International relations theorists built further on these ideas of class in the international system and developed world systems theory (discussed in more detail below), which is mentioned as a replacement for Marxism. Dependency theory, which applies Marxist principles of class division to IR theory, is also discussed below. First, it is useful to dive deeper into Marx's views on economics, especially focusing on the relationship between capitalism and conflict.

Marxist Economics

Marx derived his economic theories as critiques of the liberal economists who preceded him, including Adam Smith and David Ricardo.[5] In particular, he argued that laborers were paid less than the value of the products they produced. The owners of the production pocket this surplus value, so they profit off the hard work of labor.[6] Although Marx's economic theories are not widely accepted among mainstream Western economists, his influence on economics through political and social revolutions is undeniable. Yet it is difficult to point to a case of a state fully embracing Marxist economic principles where the state or the people were better off in the long run. This dilemma between promise and practice played a significant role in developing the scenario in this chapter.

In the realm of international economics, Marxism has more in common with mercantilism than it does with liberalism. Like mercantilists, Marxists are willing to promote some barriers to free trade, especially for national interest and especially when it helps less developed states avoid exploitation by the wealthier states. As a result, Marxists are typically tolerant of some mercantilist-type policies, like tariffs and quotas, but only when enacted by Southern states. For Marxists, Northern states should be completely open to trade and should not be allowed to either exploit or undercut their competition in the South. This North-South distinction reflects Marx's views of the two classes in society and highlights one effort to reverse the exploitation of the South, made up mostly of workers, by the North, where most of the owners of the wealth reside.

Unlike mercantilism and liberalism, though, Marxism is less concerned with whether wealth leads to power or power leads to wealth. For Marxists, both lead to exploitation. Whereas mercantilists focus on how to use their wealth to increase national power, and liberalists focus on how to increase the wealth of the entire system, making everyone better off, the goal for Marxists is to decrease the importance of both wealth and power, to eliminate the lines that separate the classes, and to level the playing field for everyone. The rest of this section focuses on several aspects of Marxist economic thought to help distinguish it from mercantilism and liberalism.

One common misconception about Marx is that he opposed capitalism as an economic system. In fact, he believed capitalism was a stage through which the global economy had to pass before moving to socialism and then communism. Therefore, capitalism is a necessary evil that would inspire revolt in response to the exploitation of the working class. Without capitalism, the owners of the wealth would not be able to exploit the workers, who would then have no reason to revolt. As a result, capitalism is critical for the implementation of Marx's ideas and is why he believed his revolution would only occur in countries, such as Germany, with more advanced, developed economies based on capitalist principles.

For Marx, capitalism creates surplus products, which compels the owners to pursue one of two options if they do not want to waste surplus stock. One option is that a company can produce fewer products. This hurts labor because producing less requires fewer workers, meaning there will be more people without jobs. This option could also reduce the potential profit from the product depending on the effects of supply and demand on market prices, so owners are reluctant to take this path. The second option is to expand the size of the market so that more consumers will purchase the product, reducing the surplus. This allows the company to maximize its profits while also hiring more people, which potentially reduces employment problems in society but further exploits the workers for the benefit of the owners.

The result of this process is a cycle of hiring more laborers, producing even more surplus, requiring still larger markets, and making more profit. The problem is what happens when there are no more open markets. The company must then choose between cutting back production and laying off workers, or enlisting the help of the state to continue expanding its markets. This, for many Marxists, is the linkage between economics, imperialism, and eventually war, as capitalist states compete with one another for new colonies and markets.

While competition is one of the positive forces that drives capitalism and the free market within the liberalist paradigm, for Marxists, competition leads to exploitation and corruption and, potentially, war if we extend the competition to the international system. It is what drives capitalist systems to overproduce, leading to the exploitation of labor and eventually to the exploitation of less developed states or colonies.

One human emotion Marx failed to anticipate or properly understand was nationalism. He believed that the class divisions of proletariat and bourgeoisie existed across all advanced economies, and as a result believed that laborers in Germany more closely identify with laborers in other countries, like France and Russia, than they do with the Germans who own the means of production. However, what competition between states shows us is that most people identify with their state before their class. The result is that when two states compete for whatever reason, and that competition rises to the level of war, regardless of their class, people quickly identify those in other countries as the out-group, while viewing others in their state as the in-group, as comrades facing a common enemy.

Vladimir Lenin better appreciated the nationalist tendencies of people, even workers. He believed that the European competition to obtain colonies in the late 1800s and early 1900s was one of the main causes of World War I, and this drive for empires was fueled by the forces of capitalism. Lenin tried to explain why Marx's expected labor revolutions failed to materialize in the industrialized world, and he used colonization as his explanation. He suggested that by establishing colonies, where Northern states could extract raw materials rather than purchase them, as well as increase the market for their own finished products, exploitation went largely unnoticed by the workers in the North because perceptions of class division were minimized by the presence of the colonies. In other words, the possession of the colonies stalled the revolution by coopting the workers in the Northern states into participating in the exploitation of workers in the colonies.

For Lenin, this need for more colonies fueled the drive for empires, which not only stalled revolution in several European states, but also led to World War I as the great powers competed for new markets. To support this claim, one could point to the many examples of prewar tension between European powers over control of or access to colonies: South Africa and the Boer War, the Fashoda crisis, and the Moroccan crisis. As competition exacerbates feelings of nationalism, and as more diplomatic crises occur, the more likely they are to produce war between states rather than revolution within a state. That does not mean revolution cannot occur. Lenin suggested those wars for empires were means of avoiding revolution, but war frequently seems to contribute to the turmoil that leads to revolution. In fact, Russia's involvement in World War I contributed to the conditions that brought about its communist revolution.

Marx, like realists, viewed resource scarcity as a potential source of conflict. And for Marx, scarcity, like capitalism, is a necessary evil to bring about the revolution. If resources are abundant, the workers will be happy enough to avoid rocking the boat. Only if resources become scarce and the workers feel they bear a disproportionate share of the burden of the scarcity will they be incited to act. In other words, the working class must experience some level of suffering before it will rise and overthrow the system. Many scholars, such as Ted Gurr, point to relative deprivation as more important for inspiring violence than simply poverty. What seems important is disparity between what people have and what they believe they deserve, particularly if they see others who have more.[7] Colonies also provide greater access to cheap resources, which can reduce resource scarcity and help prevent internal revolution, but, when combined with competition for those colonies that contain resources, the possibility of war between states is again heightened.

One problem with Marx here is that those states that implemented his principles generally experienced high levels of resource scarcity. So even if we accept his arguments about capitalism, the principles he suggested do not solve that problem—or at least they have failed to be effective when and where governments have tried to implement them.

Dependency theory, or *dependencia*, seeks to explain why some countries in the global South, especially in Central and South America, have such a difficult time improving their economic status, especially when other states, such as Singapore, South Korea, and Taiwan (often called the Asian Tigers because of their rapid industrialization and growth rates between the 1950s and 1990s),[8] were able to develop their economy and now compete on the global market as part of the core. The primary answer for *dependencia* scholars is that the United States (and to a lesser extent Europe) exploited Central and South American states for its own economic growth, much like the bourgeoisie exploits the proletariat within states or like European states exploited their colonies prior to the wave of independence struggles in the 1950s and 1960s.

The Northern states, *dependencia* scholars suggest, buy resources from the South at a cheap price (or own the resources, which gives them access for no cost) and produce manufactured goods that they then sell to the South at a high price. When the South cannot pay for the products they need to produce their raw materials, they borrow the money, usually from banks in the North, which increases their dependence on the North. When they are unable to repay the loans, they fall deeper into debt and dependency.[9] And even when they can obtain cheap loans from organizations such as the International Monetary Fund (IMF), they are required to alter their society in ways that make them even more indebted to the North and sometimes create political and economic instability. As a result, *dependencia* scholars suggest the Southern states will never fully develop while they exist within this vicious cycle of dependency on the North.

The United Fruit Company case is an example of this argument at work. The previous chapter focused on UFC as an illustration of the dangers of growing corporate power. For Marxists, though, the UFC was not an independent actor but rather a tool of the U.S. capitalist economy, which helped exploit the few valuable resources that Central and South American states could produce. Likewise, the U.S. government served as a tool for UFC to maximize its profits, even using the military to provide stability in areas with UFC operations (as in Honduras in 1907). The company, and others like it, made the North wealthier on the backs of the South, and in some cases made the South increasingly dependent on the North (such as Panama relying on UFC for rail service or Guatemala for managing the postal service).[10]

Criticism of this *dependencia* argument, coming from both liberalism and mercantilism, is that it puts too much blame on the North while ignoring the dysfunction prevalent in the South. Many Southern states have a history of corrupt governments, unstable economic systems, and internal violence, all of which scare off foreign direct investment that would otherwise benefit the South and North together.

Many of these states also adopted protectionist trade policies that closed them off to foreign competition in the 1950s and 1960s in attempts to build domestic industries. But in doing this, states prevent the kind of competition that would force their home industries to become more efficient and effective and capable of competing on the global market.[11]

Each of these factors stands in stark contrast to the more stable, less corrupt, and less violent states in Asia that did develop, not by preventing competition but by enacting policies to promote greater trade levels. They succeeded at rising from developing to developed status, or from periphery to core, by embracing rather than shunning liberal economic principles, with just a hint of mercantilism to strengthen domestic industries, often through subsidies to make the domestic products more competitively priced rather than preventing competition.

Marxists often respond to these criticisms by countering that the economic, political, and sometimes military involvement of the North in the affairs of the Southern states brought on many of these conditions. U.S. involvement in elections to support friendly but corrupt regimes against democratically elected but potentially left-leaning politicians contributed to cycles of coups and dictatorships in several countries. It also led to animosity toward the United States that continues to this day.

The reason for continued underdevelopment in some Southern states is probably a combination of all of the above issues, but one's worldview will color whether some factors seem more credible than others as an explanation for a state's status and position in the international system. Marxists point to the class divide between haves and have-nots and the need of the powerful to exploit the weak wherever they are. Realists highlight geography and lack of resources as explanations of power disparities, which then contribute to disparities in wealth and a state's position in the hierarchy of the international system. Liberalists highlight the lack of democratic institutions, the rejection of free trade, and the adoption of socialist programs as explanations for underdevelopment.

One other criticism of liberal economics that could certainly fall within the Marxist school of thought has to do with the so-called Washington Consensus, alleging that the global economic system itself is set up to exploit the South. One example of this refers to the rules in place that require states to adhere to certain policies before qualifying for IMF or World Bank loans. These are more formally called structural adjustment programs (SAPs) and include cutting inflation, government spending, government subsidies to firms or whole industries, and corruption. Such policies are intended to benefit the state, to improve its ability to repay loans, and to attract more foreign investment, which might otherwise be scared off by the internal instability facing many underdeveloped states. But critics claim that many of these SAPs make states worse off and less capable of repaying loans, creating even more dependence on Northern banks, investors, or international organizations.

Marxists view these SAPs as tools of exploitation, even though their purpose is to make a country more attractive to investors. The problem is that SAPs treat all states the same and ignore cultural or other differences that might pose challenges for some states to adopt these reforms. They are also based on a liberalist understanding of global economics, to which not everyone subscribes and that often appears to lead to winners and losers. They also clearly benefit the status quo of the global economic system or else they would not be a prerequisite for loans, and this further contributes to perceptions of exploitation.

The New International Economic Order is one example of an attempt by Southern states to alter the terms of the international economic system, leveling the playing field between North and South. This proposal, introduced in 1973, called for the North to provide more development assistance to help industrialize the South more quickly and to begin favoring primary resources rather than finished products in the terms of global trade. The premise was that since the North had more wealth than the South, it had an obligation to redistribute that wealth equitably.[12]

Rarely do such proposals gain much momentum for a couple of reasons. They are usually proposed by non–great powers, so it is difficult for them, even if they act in unison, to overthrow the status quo that benefits those states at the top of the hierarchy. In addition, these Southern states were not a unified bloc because they represented a variety of cultures, on different continents, and with different national interests. Thus, it was difficult for them to reach agreement on how to change the global system in any significant way.

The creation of the Organization of Petroleum Exporting Countries (OPEC) provides one example of an institution of mostly underdeveloped states that is able to dictate terms of trade to the North. On one hand,

Marx and Lenin viewed cartels as the ultimate capitalist tool, consolidating wealth in the hands of a few. On the other hand, the use of a cartel by exploited states to wrest influence away from the more powerful seems perfectly consistent with their prescribed revolutionary measures. Oil embargoes on Europe and Japan did weaken support for Israel during the 1973 war, though they had less effect on U.S. support. This is an exceptional case, though, because of the nature of the developed states' demand for oil, which few other products can easily replicate. At the same time, because the organization focused on one product, it was beholden to market prices, which tended to rise and fall, heavily affecting its members, many of whom are largely dependent on oil revenues.

Even before the discovery of new energy sources, such as shale oil in the United States, OPEC had difficulty coordinating the production and sale of oil by all its members. While this example shows the potential power of a cartel in international economics, it also highlights the inclination of states to fall back on selfish national interests, despite their negative effects on cooperation within the organization or even on the long-term effects on the price of oil. OPEC faces a common collective action problem in that while there are collective benefits of cooperation, like in the prisoner's dilemma, there are individual incentives to defect. Although the members all benefit from rising prices if they reduce production, any one state continuing higher production will profit more than the rest. This ultimately weakens the bargaining power and influence of the organization. Disputes over OPEC production quotas even contributed to Iraq's invasion of Kuwait in 1990. In a less violent example, in 2008 Saudi Arabia vowed to go against OPEC's decision to cut oil production to increase market prices by continuing to produce oil at its existing rate.[13]

World Systems Theory

Several IR scholars adopted Marx's view of core and periphery, where the core represents the industrialized, developed states, and the periphery comprises the impoverished, underdeveloped, mostly agrarian states (if there are any agricultural resources). But these two classes are insufficient to describe all the states in the international system, because some states have manufacturing and have some accumulation of wealth, just not as much as the core. These states are also typically better off, and less prone to instability, than others. Likewise, critiques of this division of the world into classes point out that there were states in the periphery that were able to move into the core, such as the Asian Tigers (Singapore, South Korea, and Taiwan), not to mention Japan, Indonesia, and the Philippines. In response, world systems scholars refer to these states as the semiperiphery.[14] States can move from periphery to semiperiphery, and from semiperiphery to core, but it is not an easy transition; likewise, it is also possible for states to slide backward.

These hierarchies also overlap with Marx's classes within each state, so that there are bourgeoisie (core) and proletariat (periphery) within core states, as well as core and periphery within the semiperiphery and periphery states. This creates overlapping hierarchies of power and influence rather than a simple dichotomy of two classes.

In the scenario that started this chapter, Earth is the core, the moon is the semiperiphery, and Mars and the Outer Belt make up the periphery. While Mars is trying to move from periphery to the core by declaring greater independence from Earth, doing so would rob Earth of many valuable resources, so Earth will oppose any transformation of the status quo. At the same time, both Earth and the moon can exploit Mars and the Outer Belt to stave off revolt at home. However, in doing so, they increase the likelihood of revolution in the periphery and potentially war between them over access to scarce resources or larger markets or out of concern for the revolution spreading elsewhere.[15]

Theories of Revolution
There are several theories for why revolutions occur. Not all of them fall within the Marxist school of thought, but they are worth exploring here to compare explanations. We already discussed Marx's views on revolution. Essentially, exploited workers under a capitalist system will eventually rise up and demand change, and these changes will spread internationally. Marxist revolutions are so compelling to those in the lower classes because they promise equality, in terms of not just wealth but also social and political standing. But Marxism is part of a larger group of causes that point to either wealth or ideology as primary drivers of revolution.

Lenin's view on revolution builds upon the ideas of Marx, so it is similar in many ways, but he also drew from John Hobson's *Imperialism: A Study* to explain away the lack of revolution as a function of imperialism and exploitation of colonies. As discussed earlier in this chapter, this prevented revolution by essentially paying off the workers in the developed states, but it also contributed to war over competition for those colonies and for the right to exploit those particular people.[16]

Mao Tse-Tung was the first to implement Marx's ideas of revolution through mobilization of the peasantry rather than urban workers (which Marx did not think was possible). For Mao, the revolution can happen in a more agrarian society, but to do so requires educating the population to realize that it is being exploited. This may even require violence as a form of propaganda to raise awareness in the illiterate peasant population and to mobilize the population by highlighting where its interests lie, which is in owning the wealth rather than working for those who own it.[17]

There are several scholarly explanations of revolution. Jack Goldstone suggests there are three existing generations of work on revolutions, moving toward a fourth.[18] The first generation involved mostly descriptions of revolutions with little theory. The second generation drew heavily on social science and thus developed theoretical analyses of the subject. The third generation provided alternative theories based on critiques and gaps in the previous work, focusing not just on causes but also on the results.

Theda Skocpol suggests that there are four types of writings on revolution: Marxist, aggregate-psychological, system/value consensus, and political-conflict theories.[19] Marxists focus on class divisions as a source of revolution. Aggregate-psychological writings highlight people's motivations for using violence (e.g., Ted Gurr's relative deprivation theory).[20] System/value consensus focuses on the responses to severe disequilibrium in a social system and requires a crisis in the existing social system (such as the loss of legitimacy by authorities).[21] Political-conflict theories centralize conflict between governments and opposition groups.

Skocpol contends that capitalism is less of an internal threat to states that would lead to revolution than it is a contributor to international divisions that give advanced states the ability to threaten less advanced states, which contributes to their political breakdown from external threats. Regarding outcome, she assesses that an external threat that the government lacks the resources to address will still be a threat after the revolution (perhaps a relatively greater one), and it requires a strong, centralized government to mobilize the necessary resources. Skocpol herself draws primarily from the Marxist lens but suggests the ability to revolt relies on political-conflict theories, such as those advanced by Charles Tilly (specifically the need for group organization and access to resources being necessary factors).

Tilly argues against any common "theory of revolutions" based on his survey of five hundred years of European revolutions. Yet he highlights how the character of revolution changed over time and across the different regions of Europe. While revolutions are caused by different triggers and have different motivations, Tilly suggests that the elements they share are competition over legitimate authority, popular support for one side, and the lack of opposition from the existing authority. While these are more about the process and flow from his definition of revolution, they provide insight into some necessary conditions.[22] Tilly also identifies different types of revolution, including coups, top-down seizures of power, revolts, civil wars, and great revolutions. While all of these can evolve into revolutions, they all start from different places so even if they result in a revolution, they defy a single causal theory. What they share is some type of split in the government and some transfer of power. All three of the historical cases in this chapter fall into his "great revolutions" category, defined as transforming the political, economic, and social structures of a state.[23]

We also cannot ignore the relationship between war and revolution, which historically flowed in both directions. Revolution often emerges out of war or conflict, especially if the government must extract resources and wealth from the population to fund a prolonged war. Revolutions can also lead to wars, particularly when neighboring states seek to take advantage of a weakened state or to fill power vacuums left by revolution.[24] The cases below provide examples of many of these theories, focusing on revolutions in three different states—France, Russia, and Iran—with each arising out of a different ideology, but all three having a significant influence on regional and even global relations.

HISTORY OF MARXISM: CLASS CONFLICTS AND REVOLUTIONS

> For a colonized people the most essential value,
> because the most concrete, is first and foremost the land:
> the land which will bring them bread and, above all, dignity.
> —FRANZ FANON, *The Wretched of the Earth*

Historical revolutions have several features in common. First, they rarely occur without bloodshed. There are examples of bloodless revolutions, but the ones that change society and international politics generally require some degree of violence. Second, those who are most oppressed rarely emerge from revolution on top. Instead, those who can wrest power for themselves often push all others aside. Third, there are frequently efforts to take advantage of the vacuum left by revolution, both internally and from outside. This sometimes increases instability and often leads to even greater levels of oppression for certain members of society.

States go through ideological revolutions for several reasons, usually driven by a political movement of one type or another. Many of the revolutions that occurred in the eighteenth and nineteenth centuries were intended to overthrow existing monarchical systems and establish more republican, representative systems. The early twentieth century saw several communist revolutions, most notably in Russia. Later in the century, we saw other types of revolutions, such as the one that brought a religious government to power in Iran in 1979, as well as many relatively nonviolent revolutions that brought democracy to previously communist states in the 1990s (the "color revolutions"). Revolutions do not require violence, but they often involve internal or external forms of violence, or both, in which societal divisions bring dramatic political and economic changes to a state. These divisions can be influenced by external factors, and other actors may take advantage of the instability to increase their power, but they are largely driven by internal divisions consistent with Marx's ideas.

Another form of political violence related to revolution and that often involves revolutionary-like change is anti-imperialism or decolonization, an attempt by a colony to gain independence from its imperial masters.[25] Examples include the wars for independence fought by both Algeria and Vietnam.[26] Both types of political violence can lead to instability and power vacuums that neighboring states and multiple great powers might attempt to fill. Both can also lead to the export of ideas that can contribute to instability and an expansion of the violence into neighboring states. But there are also some critical differences that lead this chapter to focus on revolutions, the most important being the role of an ideology in driving not just the revolution, but also the intent to spread the ideas to other parts of the world. While decolonization is about a people gaining autonomy or independence, revolutions seek a full revision of society.

The rest of this section examines three revolutions in different countries, in different eras, and with different ideological underpinnings: France (1789), Russia (1917), and Iran (1979). While Marxist ideas only inspired the Russia example, all three came about because of societal divisions, and all three led to dramatic changes in the international system and in our understanding of international politics.

The French Revolution started on 14 July 1789, when the Bastille fell to rioters storming the fortress, and it lasted until Napoleon Bonaparte's 9 November 1799 act to abolish the government and name himself first consul (and eventually emperor on 18 May 1804). During this time, France experienced several permutations of government, fought wars against neighboring states, and saw increasingly high levels of internal violence, culminating in the Reign of Terror.[27]

The main questions about the French Revolution include the source of the revolution and why it turned so violent. The primary causes fit well with the Marxist narrative, despite presaging Marx by half a century. But we cannot ignore the conflict within the French government itself, as well as the external threats, all of which contributed to the revolution and to the behavior of key players during it.

Taxation, lack of food due to poor harvests and drought, and perceptions of class division all contributed to riots and general violence by the peasants and urban poor. External threats brought on some of this taxation, as did France's desire for empire to balance against those of its neighbors. But if there was not a group of people willing to challenge the monarch, Louis XVI, the revolution perhaps would never have gained traction to the same degree. We also cannot ignore the influence of America's independence from England. The French participated in the fight against England, seeing it as an opportunity to weaken their British rival. French involvement heavily contributed to the success of the colonies' break from the crown, but it also led to the importation of many of the liberal ideas that the Americans espoused.

The initial revolution was liberal in its goals, based on ideas advanced by Jean-Jacques Rousseau's *Social Contract* and the U.S. Declaration of Independence. By 1792 the revolution turned more conservative, as war with Austria and Prussia, combined with the arrest of the king and his eventual execution on 21 January 1793, generated more violence at home. By July 1793 the Jacobins (the most radical of the political groups) seized control of the National Convention, eradicated Christianity, and established a new calendar.

The next ten months saw more than 300,000 people imprisoned, several of whom died without trial, and another 17,000 executed. This lasted until the death in 1794 of Maximilien Robespierre, a leader of the Jacobins and the one person most closely associated with the Reign of Terror (himself executed by the same system he created). William Doyle sees the French Revolution as a possible progressive change that lost sight of its vision because of the view that all past acts and traditions were based on the monarchy and therefore evil. As a result, Doyle refers to this revolution as a tragedy.[28]

The French Revolution and the Napoleonic Wars that followed threatened the power of the ruling classes of Europe. They also led to the development of the Concert of Europe, which prevented great power war in Europe for as much as one hundred years. The Marxist view of the revolution is one of the aristocracy losing power and the feudal society and corporations being destroyed, thus propelling France along the trajectory of history from feudalism to capitalism and eventually to Marxism. The fact that the revolution led to the rise of a dictatorship and still more wars with neighbors should provide ample red flags about the value of wholesale revolution and change, regardless of the ideology behind it. But must every revolution follow that path? Are there similar trajectories, even when revolutions emerge in other countries and arise out of other ideologies?

Observers often think of the nearly bloodless coup by Lenin and the Bolshevik Party as the start of the Russian Revolution, but, as with the French Revolution, several underlying factors contributed to the revolution.[29] As in France, the Russian monarchy was under pressure domestically, in this case going back to 1880, when groups such as Narodnaya Volya ("People's Will") set out to assassinate the tsar. The group succeeded in killing Tsar Alexander II in March 1881, but the next Russian government, led by his son Alexander III, cracked down on the Russian people even more. The next four decades saw attempted revolutions, coups, riots, and other forms of political violence, alongside repeated attempts by the monarch to first crack down on opposition groups and then to promote more civil liberties to prevent future violence. A workers' revolt against food shortages and government violence occurred in 1905. In addition, the strain of losing a war to Japan in 1905, followed by significant population growth in cities and the devastation of the early part of World War I, further taxed the Russian people, especially the peasants and workers.

A preliminary revolution in early 1917 ended the monarchy, but the unstable government that took over also paved the way for the Bolsheviks to come to power later that year, ending Russia's involvement in World War I. By August 1918, mass arrests and executions became known as the Red Terror, which grew more terrifying when Stalin came to power upon Lenin's death in January 1924.

The result of the Russian Revolution was the spread of communist ideas and the eventual division of the world into a bipolar East and West after World War II, with the Soviet Union and its allies on one side, and the United States and its allies on the other. One unknown is whether the revolution would have spread farther without the counterbalance of the Western democracies. This is relevant because other ideologies could spread rapidly in space without an ideology to balance against them.

While Marx believed the revolution would only work in an industrialized society, where capitalism was already exploiting the workers, Russia showed how a less industrialized state could essentially skip the capitalist stage and bring about revolution led by peasants. Such ideas inspired similar attempts in China, Vietnam, and Cuba, among other places, each with varying degrees of success.

In many ways, these events in the Russian Revolution mirror those of the French Revolution: the precipitants, the liberal attempt at revolution to overthrow the monarch, the internal instability that brings a second phase of the revolution, followed by internal state violence and eventually dictatorship. The presence of external wars exists in both cases, both before and after the revolution. In addition, the dictators that emerge in both states feared internal opposition and attempted to spread their state's power as a means of removing external threats and solidifying their power at home.

The Iranian case follows some of these same paths, but a major difference between them was the status of France and Russia as great powers prior to their revolution. In contrast, Iran was independent but heavily controlled by England and the United States. So while the Iranian Revolution was about bringing a new ideology into power, in this case a religious one, it was also related to anti-imperialism in a Marxist sense, with Iran trying to free itself from the control of two great powers.[30]

Like Russia, Iran also underwent more than one revolution. The first one, in 1953, was an attempt to remove the monarchy and liberalize society. The United States and United Kingdom foiled those attempts, not because they opposed the ideology or sentiment or even because they liked the shah. Their actions were driven by the Cold War and the fear that instability would provide the Soviet Union with an opportunity to gain power in the Middle East. They also feared nationalists would become too friendly toward the Soviets. It was almost three decades before a successful revolution removed the shah from power. The 1979 revolution also brought war with neighbors, attempts at expansion for the purposes of both power and domestic stability, and the rise of an authoritarian state, though hidden behind the trappings of a republic.

The Iranian Revolution shows elements of both ideological and anticolonial factors. The United Kingdom and United States were both perceived in Iran to be exploiting the state for oil; in addition, U.S. involvement in overthrowing the government of the democratically elected Mossadegh in 1953, thus empowering the shah, generated additional animosity and distrust toward the United States. Ultimately, though, the revolution that brought about a religious state was more about the status quo under the shah and those who wanted to institute change. Once the revolution removed the shah from power, the internal divide became about secular leftists versus religious conservatives.

Those who came to power after the 1979 revolution were no more egalitarian than the shah had been and did not have the support of many of those rebelling against the previous regime. In fact, many of those who most strongly opposed the shah's reign were the left-wing college students and intellectuals. It was, however, the ayatollah who took power, and his governance of the state has been different from what many of the protestors envisioned for Iran without the shah in charge. And while the Islamic Republic of Iran is a presidential democracy with three branches of government sharing power, the real power lies with the supreme leader, initially Ayatollah Ruhollah Khomeini, from 1979 until his death in June 1989, and Ali Khamenei for the past three decades (who also served as president for the prior eight years). Intellectuals who opposed the shah were mostly shut out of positions of power under the Islamic regime.

The effects of the Iranian Revolution on international politics are less directly visible than were those of the French and Russian Revolutions, but it still had significant repercussions on the international system. The revolution, and in particular the hostage crisis that involved the U.S. embassy staff, led to decades of tension with the United States; there are still no direct diplomatic linkages, economic sanctions continue, and high levels of distrust persist over Iran's nuclear weapons development. The revolution also caused concern in the Soviet Union, out of fear that the Islamic movement would spread to neighboring Afghanistan, which was under the control of a government friendly to the Soviet Union. This fear led the Soviets to invade Afghanistan in 1980, which ultimately played at least a part in the eventual bankruptcy and implosion of the Soviet Union, ending the Cold War. Many terrorism scholars also point to 1979 as a pivotal point in the rise of Islamic terrorism, with Iran playing a critical role through its sponsorship of groups like Hezbollah. In other words, while the Iranian Revolution may not have directly contributed to similar ideological revolutions in other countries the way revolutions in France and Russia did, it significantly altered the course of the international system, mostly out of concern for the uncertainty that it created in neighboring states and the superpowers.

CLASS CONFLICT IN SCIENCE FICTION

> That we were slaves I had known all my life—and nothing could be done about it. True, we weren't bought and sold—but as long as Authority [the Earth government] held monopoly over what we had to have and what we could sell to buy it, we were slaves.
>
> —ROBERT HEINLEIN, *The Moon Is a Harsh Mistress*

Russian author Alexander Bogdanov's *Red Star* tells the story of a man who travels to a communist colony on Mars, discovering a classless society devoid of social divisions or gender roles. All workers are free to choose their profession as well as how long they work as part of a larger theme that equates the purest forms of freedom with the greatest levels of happiness. Another Russian story, Alexei Tolstoy's *Aelita*, tells of a society on Mars where class divisions are strong, and a rebellion breaks out against the ruler, but it is crushed. These two books by Russian authors are important because they are early works of science fiction, but also because they portray highly Marxist notions of future societies. Many contemporary works draw heavily, often unwittingly, from these ideas of utopia or of the dangerous consequences of class division. Some books have openly Marxist themes centered around class. Others focus more on the type of utopia Marxists often envision.[31]

Kim Stanley Robinson's *Mars Trilogy*, especially the first book in the series, *Red Mars*, portrays various elements of class struggle as well as the potential for rebellion to overthrow an existing structure. One of Robinson's Russian characters, Arkady Bogdanov, even shares a family name with the *Red Star* author and is one of the primary instigators of a free-thinking Martian colony, separated by distance and by ideology from the interests of Earth-bound actors. The intent of the mission to Mars is to capture resources for the future capitalist system, which leads to megacorporations largely operating with the United Nations to capture Mars.

Even on the voyage out, though, some members of the crew are already discussing altering relationships and lines of authority to be less about following existing rules and social patterns, and more about creating a new society. As Arkady argues during the flight from Earth to Mars, "*All* of our governments are flawed, most of them disastrously. It's why history is such a bloody mess. Now we are on our own, and I for one have no intention of repeating all of Earth's mistakes just because of conventional thinking. We are the first Martian colonists! We are *scientists*! It is our *job* to think things new, to make them new!"[32]

The lack of a common vision for the future means that everyone pursues their own goals, some of which conform with the capitalist system, while others more closely mirror a Marxist (or perhaps more accurately an anarchist) utopia. This leads to conflict over whether to make Mars another Earth so that humans can inhabit it, or to alter humans behaviorally, and perhaps even genetically, to adapt to the existing, unique environment and become more Martian.[33]

The members of the crew are highly trained scientists and technicians, with professions and talents critical for life in space, but they were less educated in social sciences and naïve about the politics that would eventually dominate colony life. Later in the book, one of the original crew leaders is thinking to himself while observing the newest group of colonists: "They were so ignorant! Young men and women, educated very carefully to be apolitical, to be technicians who thought they disliked politics, making them putty in the hands of their rulers, just like always. It was appalling how stupid they were, really, and he could not help lashing into them."[34]

In addition, many of the antagonists in the book are corporations, and while an anti-megacorporation message is not inherently Marxist, it fits well with the common Marxist narrative. A revolution does begin against the growing power of the transnats and initially appears to be successful, but it eventually fails through the corporations' willingness to use violence, as well as the daily dangers of living in the Martian environment.

An important utopian part of the story is the lack of private ownership by the members of the crew: "We were outside the world, we didn't even own things—some clothes, a lectern, and that was it! . . . That is utopia."[35] While the story is about a desire to create a utopia, the tensions created by conflicting interests, as well as differences over what constituted utopia, lead to conflict and violence. This, more than anything in the book, seems consistent with the history of attempts to create

Marxist and utopian societies and contributes heavily to the scenario at the start of this chapter.

Robert Heinlein's *The Moon Is a Harsh Mistress* illustrates many of the same ideas and themes. It portrays the inhabitants of the moon as something less than those of Earth; it was originally a penal colony but is now just perceived as backward. The revolt carried out by the moon—with the assistance of an advanced artificial intelligence, Mike—is somewhat Marxist in terms of its goals, though it also holds much in common with the American war for independence, including the importance of July 4. The violence is also more anticolonial in its motivation than an ideological revolution; though it brings about dramatic political change on the moon, its effects on Earth are less clear but are probably less dramatic.

The connection to Marxism is perhaps heightened by the Russian-sounding dialect used by many of the characters, as well as the Russian names used for locations on the moon. But those may simply be style elements Heinlein chose rather than attempts to draw connections to Marxism. The Professor, who is one of the leaders of the revolt, is a copy of Mao in terms of his understanding of revolution at the tactical and the strategic levels. He understands the role of strong leaders in mobilizing the masses: "Parliamentary bodies all through history, when they accomplished anything, owed it to a few strong men who dominated the rest."[36] The Professor also references the works of other military theorists, such as Machiavelli, Clausewitz, and Che Guevara, as important for Mike to read so that the AI can calculate properly the odds of success.[37]

The story ends with Earth granting the moon its independence, but we learn few details about what happens next: whether the lunar people keep their freedom, what type of political and economic systems ultimately appears (though there are suggestions that the main characters are disappointed at what emerges), and, perhaps more importantly, whether it succeeds in the long run. We do learn that the utopia was not all it was cracked up to be. As the main character asks himself on the last page, "Are food riots too high a price to pay to let people be? I don't know."[38] Although the revolution in the scenario that opens this chapter takes place on Mars instead of the moon, it addresses some of these questions left unanswered from Heinlein's book, using humanity's own history to help fill in some of the gaps in the story.

Another book about class revolt in the future is Pierce Brown's *Red Rising*. The main character, Darrow, is a miner who leads a revolt against a highly stratified Martian world by infiltrating the highest classes of that society. In addition to the parallel symbolism of Mars being red and the fact that red represented the blood of the workers during the French Revolution, the two main class divisions in the book—based on fourteen distinct colors—are analogies to what Marx saw in his society.[39] The working classes, or lowcolors, are known by their identifying colors as Reds (miners), Pinks (sex slaves), Obsidians (soldiers), and Browns (servants in homes and businesses). These are the equivalent of Marx's proletariat, and they are treated as slaves, even though their efforts are necessary for society to operate. The bourgeoisie are represented by the highcolors, including the Gold (peerless), White (justices), Silver (businesspeople), and Copper (administrators), all of whom appear to be unaware of the class divisions or the inequality that exists. Six colors make up what appears to be the middle class, which consists of engineers, doctors, artists, and so forth. There are also divisions within each color, with certain positions holding higher status than others.

This first book in the series takes an unconventional approach to revolution: seeking change to the status quo by changing it from within rather than through violent revolt. Early in the book, when Darrow and his wife, Eo, are arrested, he receives lashes, and just prior to breaking into a forbidden song that gets her executed, Eo tells Darrow, "Break the chains, my lover."[40] It seems he misinterprets her, believing that she wants him to release her hanging body, an act that gets him in deeper trouble. Her intended meaning was for him to get out of the mines and do more for both himself and for the other Reds. Eo's statement also echoes one of the most famous passages in Marx's *The Communist Manifesto*: "The proletarians have nothing to lose but their chains."[41] Another reference to breaking chains occurs later in the book, when Milia, one of Darrow's classmates, states, "Promises are just chains . . . both meant for breaking."[42]

Despite the more subtle nature of Darrow's revolution from within, a great deal of violence still occurs in the book as Darrow trains to become a Gold. Bringing about a real societal revolution will likely require some level of violence. Although bloodless revolutions are possible, history suggests that they are difficult and often fail, and even when they do succeed, they tend to be followed by high levels of violence as the new government establishes control. They also are not as interesting to read about in a science fiction novel.

Although previous chapters discussed the *Expanse* series, it is worth noting the Marxist elements of the series here as well. They are evident primarily in descriptions in later books on the situation on Earth, with its Basic Assistance (essentially, social welfare programs for all who do not work), and those living in the Belt who are the workers being exploited by Earth and Mars and who feel the need to use violence to alter the status quo. Yet Basic Assistance on Earth does not create a utopia. Under such circumstances, people often lose the will to be productive and innovative, which leads to scientific and technological stagnation. There are also still class differences, which is made clear simply by the manner and lifestyle of those in the United Nations. And while some belters, like those in the Outer Planets Alliance, use violence to alter the status quo, many are content to cooperate with the inner planets, especially if it means financial and political benefits.

ANALYSIS

When provisions are transported far off,
the hundred surnames are impoverished.
— SUN TZU, *The Art of War*

The primary cause of conflict for Marxists is class division, especially when one class can exploit the work or products of another class. Marx saw this as a consistent feature of any system but believed it was particularly pronounced in the capitalist economies of the developed world. While that conflict can be delayed or stalled by identifying other actors to exploit and then corrupting the workers, the revolution will eventually occur because the capitalist system sows the seeds of its own destruction.

Cooperation and conflict have somewhat different meanings here than in previous chapters because cooperation means the ability of the exploited to work together to spread the revolution globally, but this also leads to conflict. Likewise, at least according to Marx, the class conflict that exists within states is more likely to contribute to cooperation either between classes of different states or between the states themselves in attempts to stave off revolution, as Europe's monarchs attempted to do in the nineteenth century when faced with the threat of an expanding liberal ideology.

For Marx, conflict initially occurs within a political entity, as the workers fight to free themselves from exploitation. In terms of external conflicts, those who apply Marxist ideas to explain wars see the competition for colonies, resources, and empires as the driving force of conflict in the international system. In some cases, these wars stave off, or prevent, internal revolutions in capitalist states, but history also contains cases of wars contributing to revolutions. Likewise, revolutions can contribute to wars as new states attempt to solidify their power both at home and in the region, and neighboring states try to take advantage of power vacuums.

Marx postulated that class identity was more important than state or national identity, so workers in Germany would have more in common with workers in other countries than with the bourgeoisie in Germany. This is a necessary assumption for the belief that revolution in one country would spread elsewhere, but it is problematic. For one thing, it is empirically flawed. At least in the developed states, allegiance to the state appears more powerful than allegiance to a class that crosses national boundaries. In fact, Marxists disagree on the extent to which they should confine their ideas to a single state or spread them as part of a larger revolution. Even within the Soviet Union, Stalin and Leon Trotsky differed on the extent to which the Russian Revolution should spread to other states. Stalin focused on a nationalist movement, while Trotsky saw expansion as necessary for the revolution to succeed. Likewise, after Fidel Castro's overthrow of the government in Cuba, Che Guevara believed he could spread the same revolutionary ideas to other parts of Latin America, but he was killed in Bolivia because of his failure to garner support.

There is also an element of cooperation in the core states between the proletariat and the bourgeoisie. There is a tense agreement, according to Marxists, between the two classes as they both benefit from the exploitation of the workers in the colonies. This also illustrates the lack of connection between workers in the core and those in the periphery, who see each other as part of the state rather than belonging to the same class of people; otherwise, the workers in the core would not be so easily coopted to turn against workers elsewhere.

One other form of both cooperation and conflict that can emerge is when similar states face similar ideological threats of revolution. Europe's monarchs banded together when facing the threat of liberalism. Western democracies cooperated during the Cold War to prevent the spread of Marxist revolution. This parallels the balancing behavior of states when facing a common threat, as discussed in chapters 1 and 2. The difference is that these revolutions often emerge from within the state rather than from an external actor. As a result, external cooperation, as occurred between the United States and England in the Cold War, can create greater conditions for revolution, as they did in Iran.

While the Marxist scenario that begins this chapter seems like it would be beneficial to the future of humanity, the long-term measures of this system are unlikely to be positive if history provides any type of guidance regarding the stability and sustainability of Marxist revolutions. This scenario assumes that a Marxist-style revolution changes the system, and assessing the likely results of that type of society must be based on the lessons of human history.

Under a Marxist system, it is possible that wars will decline in the short term (see table 5.1). But long-term wars and additional internal threats are likely to occur, possibly in greater numbers if we draw on our history for parallels. In all three cases discussed in this chapter, the result of revolution was not peaceful relations with neighbors. Ideological revolutions threaten the institutions of nearby states, which may mobilize to at least contain the spread of the revolution if not attempt to reverse it. The new government itself may engage in a type of diversionary or scapegoat war to help consolidate power or to remove any external pressures that contributed to the revolution in the first place.

Human expansion is likely to play a positive role in this future, as those who feel exploited will seek new worlds where they can better their positions in society. Just as religious persecution drove colonists to the Americas, so too could economic or social injustices drive humans

TABLE 5.1. **EVALUATING THE MARXIST SYSTEM**

MEASURES OF EVALUATION	SHORT-TERM	LONG-TERM
Minimizing war	Yes	No
Human expansion	Yes	Yes
Enhancing S&T	Yes	No
Improving SoL	No	No

out into the solar system. Competition between ideologies could stymie expansion but could also feed higher levels of expansion as those with competing ideas seek new homes. Likewise, governments may even encourage the most radical to leave for space, to rid society of the threat posed by extreme ideas. So, there are multiple reasons to expect high levels of human expansion to accompany a Marxist future.

Marxist states, especially those with command economies, can sometimes have high levels of technological development early on since the government controls the means of production and can emphasize spending on high-tech manufacturing. Over time, though, the lack of competition and incentives for innovation begin to wear on the state's ability to retain a technological lead. For a while, the Soviet Union led the world in several technological areas, including space. By the 1980s it was no longer able to compete, potentially because of high levels of military spending and overstretch, but also because of the failure of the system to provide for sustained, long-term growth and innovation.

Standards of living are unlikely to rise in either the short or long term of humanity. Despite the promise of an egalitarian society, few people outside the inner power circle profit from state-controlled economies, and human history shows no examples of a communist state improving the lives of its people over the long run. China has a growing economy with an expanding middle class but is much more capitalist than it once was. It is also unclear how well China is improving the lives of its people, especially relative to the Western democracies, considering per capita wealth in China is one-sixth that of the United States. According to the

World Bank, China's per capita gross domestic product of $10,434 in 2020 was below that of the United States in 1978.[43]

Earth history might be a poor analogy, because the distances of space will allow workers to more easily break from class divisions. While that is possible, it suggests a greater likelihood of class-led revolt, not necessarily a different set of outcomes. The nature of space could also make revolution less likely. Most of the early colonists will be scientists and engineers who volunteer for the missions and have been compensated for their effort—they are hardly peasants or workers being exploited. Even the earliest laborers are likely to be hired by companies to extract resources and will be paid well for their efforts because of the distance from home and the risk involved (even if the companies see greater profit). While the likelihood of Marxist-style revolution may be low, we should be concerned about the negative effects of such an event on a lunar or Martian colony as well as on the people and corporations that remain on Earth, and we should take steps to avoid these types of historical events from affecting humanity's future.

The Sun Tzu quote that opens this section is not about Marxism but does highlight the dangers of moving resources from one place to another, especially for purposes (such as war or foreign aid) that may not appear to directly benefit the people. Sun Tzu's meaning was that if war extracts too much wealth from the population, it could lead to revolt at home. A Marxist interpretation might be that the transfer of resources from one class of people to another in society, or from one colony to a more powerful state in the international system, will be a source of tension and possibly violent conflict. This underlying condition for violence will not disappear just because humans are in space.

Sun Tzu provides some ideas for avoiding these situations. He offers, "If there is no escape from death, the officers and soldiers will fully exhaust their strength."[44] He is talking about what is sometimes called the death ground, a concept that can be viewed in two different ways. On one hand, you want to put your own forces on the death ground—feeling like they have no options other than fighting or dying—because that will spur them to fight harder.[45] For the same reasons, you want to avoid putting your adversary on the death ground. Instead, you want to offer them what is referred to as the golden bridge, so that they see the option of escaping and value that over fighting to the death. Sun Tzu also wrote, "Do not obstruct an army retreating homeward. If you besiege an army you must leave an outlet. Do not press an exhausted invader."[46] This golden bridge gives the enemy an opportunity to save face and to lose without being cornered (this applies not just to the military but to broader issues of competition). In tactical terms, it is about allowing a fleeing enemy to leave, to avoid being ambushed, and to be victorious at minimum cost. At the strategic level, this is more about understanding the ability and willingness of an adversary to take risks.

A related concept in political science and behavioral economics is prospect theory. An overly simple explanation, relevant for our purposes, is that when confronted with all negative outcomes, people are more likely to accept higher levels of risk. When given the option of at least some positive outcomes, people will generally be more averse to risk.[47] Chapter 1 briefly discussed the case of Athens and Melos, in the context of Athens needing to conquer Melos for the security of its empire. When the Athenians arrived at Melos, they gave the Melians two options: fight and have everything destroyed, or surrender and have the men enslaved to fight for Athens. The Melians viewed these as two negative options, so they chose to fight, accepting the riskier option of war over the certainty of enslavement.

In political terms, prospect theory means focusing on those individuals and groups that are most disadvantaged by the status quo and ensuring they feel like they have options besides revolution. It may be low-level leaders, like the nobles of *Dune*, oppressed groups, like the Encyclopedists of *Foundation*, or ousted politicians, like the old Republicans in *Star Wars*. If these groups have no options besides continued exploitation or revolution, even with a slim chance of winning their freedom, they will accept the risk and embrace revolution.

Future strategies intended to stave off the scenario at the start of this chapter must understand the challenges of creating a classless utopia combined with the dangers of a society where some in the lower strata feel exploited, helpless, or incapable of reaching their full potential. The golden bridge may be education, because that is a historically universal way for those in lower classes to rise in society. On the other hand, education often enlightens people to how the existing system denies them and can increase the likelihood of revolution in areas where real exploitation exists. In some cases, military service has been another path to achieve greater successes in life than would otherwise be possible, though it comes with generally more risk than the education path, and the two are not mutually exclusive.

Few people would prefer revolution over nonviolent change if they could achieve their goals without the need to resort to force. Unfortunately, for a variety of reasons—governments unwilling to compromise, incompatible ideologies, lack of public awareness—major change is often difficult to achieve without drastic actions. Future governments on Earth and in space need to be able to identify and understand the precipitants of these revolutions and at least address the sources of tension before they rise to the level of revolution. Heinlein even appears to paraphrase Sun Tzu when he writes, "The shrewdest of the great generals in China's history once said that perfection in war lay in so sapping the opponent's will that he surrenders without fighting."[48]

SUMMARY

Man cannot be freed by the same injustice that enslaved it.
—PIERCE BROWN, *Red Rising*

Marxism is often sold as an alternative to capitalism and is particularly attractive for people who see themselves as being exploited by those who have more power or wealth. The problem is that the utopian future Marxists offer is historically difficult to achieve, and its pursuit often creates even worse conditions for the state, its people, and its neighbors.

One issue is the challenge of incentivizing innovation and creativity so that the society continues to advance. This may be less of a challenge on lunar and Martian colonies, as innovation and creativity will be necessary for survival, especially early on. Another issue is that a Marxist system develops and is enforced through a group of individuals that have power but who must willingly give it up when they are no longer necessary. That willingness to cede power is uncommon in human history and may be unique to democratic states. Although the people who lead revolutions always claim to act for the benefit of all society, human nature and a desire for power usually keep them from willingly giving up the power they attained.

As a result, we should not be fooled by the promises of a wholesale adoption of Marxism or any major variant of it. There are, however, some elements of Marxist thought that could prove beneficial. One example is the idea of a post-scarcity economy, a future economic system that does not rely on currency, at least not for the consumption of necessary goods.[49] For Marxists, having surplus products is a source of economic turmoil and international conflict as states seek new markets for their goods. But when the cost of producing goods is so low that they are virtually free to all in society, this could eliminate some of the wealth gap, or at least reduce the need for some exploited laborers. Marx saw this arising because of automation, but widespread 3-D printing could make this a reality and may reduce tension rather than create it.

Many science fiction stories accept a kind of post-currency or post-scarcity future, including Robinson's *Mars Trilogy* and the *Expanse* series, both discussed in this chapter. There are others, like Iain Bank's *The Culture* novels, Cory Doctorow's *Walkaway*, and the *Star Trek* universe, that adopt or highlight similar economic models. Banks stated in one 2014 interview, "The Culture is hippy commies with hyperweapons and a deep distrust of both Marketolatry and Greedism."[50] Society in the book series is clearly post-scarcity, though whether it qualifies as Marxist is another question. It also is not an entirely peaceful society, as all the books illustrate. In *Star Trek*, we see several examples of this type of economic system. Captain Kirk, in the original series, turns down at least one attempt at bribery by saying jewels mean nothing because they could create lots of them on the *Enterprise*. Similarly, Captain Picard states in one of the feature films, "The acquisition of wealth is no longer the driving force of our lives. We work to better ourselves and the rest of humanity."[51] While currency still exists for some transactions (for example, with aliens who still rely on money), it does not seem necessary for the main component of society to function.

Another possible benefit from understanding Marx is the threat of tension and conflict that can arise from class divisions. Even if one does not accept all the elements of Marxist revolution, history illustrates that class divisions, like ethnic or religious divisions, can create conflict in a society, especially if those divisions mirror access to power, wealth, or even just opportunity. Perhaps, then, the greatest recommendation as humanity moves into space and takes on the possibility of reinventing its political, economic, and social systems is to strive to create societies that minimize these kinds of divisions, whether they are based on real differences or socially constructed ones.

If there is value in adopting any part of Marxist ideology, can society achieve those changes without resorting to revolution, much less a violent one? Perhaps the greatest challenge will be putting aside the labels of Marxism, communism, or socialism and simply adopting the policies that are most beneficial to people and to human civilization. This idea of recognizing the power of labels plays an important part in the next two chapters.

CHAPTER 6

VENUS RISING
A FEMINIST FUTURE

> Thus one who excels at warfare seeks [victory] through the
> strategic configuration of power, not from the reliance on men.
> —SUN TZU, *The Art of War*

After humanity established its first colony on Mars in 2041, which was a relatively equal mix of genders, it quickly became apparent that male crew members were less resilient and less resource-efficient than the women on long-duration space flights and for permanent habitation. Men were more susceptible than women to solar radiation, and they used more oxygen and other critical supplies, like food and water.[1] Perhaps more importantly, with the advent of advanced reproductive medicine, men were no longer necessary for procreation. As a result, by 2050 all men in the colonies returned to Earth, and all later missions to the moon and to Mars, as well as the first missions to the other planets and Outer Belt, were completely crewed by women.[2] This change reduced the amount of resources required for each crew member and increased the survivability of each mission.

At first, procreation was forbidden in the colonies because of concerns about the health of children born off Earth. But it was also an eventual necessity to expand the size of the colonies and ensure the long-term survival of humanity. Once procreation was allowed, the specifics were left to each individual colony to determine. In most cases, formal plans were developed based on each woman's age, profession, and desire to give birth. Growth of colony populations under these parameters was accomplished by all-female populations in a highly precise manner, ensuring that medical staff and other key personnel were not pregnant at the same time. Given the development of genetics to ensure all female births, men were necessary only for their genetic contributions, which were regularly shipped from Earth to the colonies.

Girls born on Earth were segregated from boys at an early age, trained in skills considered to be useful in space, and taught to be self-sufficient. Those who showed aptitude in the right areas and who were deemed emotionally stable enough for long-term travel and habitation in space were selected for various professions in one of the established colonies or were trained for missions to establish colonies farther out into the solar system. Women who did not display these qualities by the time they were teenagers were released into the general population, where they trained for a more traditional Earth profession. In some cases, they married and raised a family while either working or staying at home.

Men were prohibited from traveling anywhere in space other than to the space station that orbited Earth, and those trips were allowed only for a short time and only under special circumstances, such as to see a female family member who lived off Earth. The consequence of this policy was that Earth became gender imbalanced over time. Men were still valued (mostly for recreation) by the women who remained on Earth. Women everywhere in the solar system also valued men for their genetic material, which was a necessary ingredient for the women on other planets to procreate. Only the brightest, most physically fit men were used for breeding, and they were treated like royalty on Earth. Other men were educated but largely performed menial tasks, such as environmental cleanup or construction, or were allowed to pursue more leisurely activities and emphasize their artistic and creative skills. Some held minor leadership roles on Earth, but the women who stayed behind filled most of the positions of power.

Also, because of these policies, homosexuality proliferated everywhere, given that there were fewer opportunities for male-female relations. There were still millions of women on Earth, but the ratio of men to women shifted so much that women on Earth became even more highly valued, but mostly as mates—the most intelligent or highly skilled women typically found their way off Earth. Another implication was the growing acceptance of polyamorous families, in which one woman would marry multiple men.

The colonies also began to see Earth as a sort of penal colony, where women who were guilty of certain crimes were banished for the rest of their lives. The crimes most likely to earn banishment to Earth generally involved activities where the person posed a continued threat to other members of the population or to the colony itself. This included acts of violence against other women, which were uncommon but did occur. Ultimately, each colony's leadership determined every banishment decision. Since colonies took on different governance structures, ranging from the highly democratic to the dictatorial, this often influenced how the colonies dealt with crime.

As for the operation of the colonies, many believed that a secondary benefit to all-female populations beyond more efficient use of resources would be greater levels of cooperation, both within each colony and across colonies. The assertion was that the members of an all-female colony would work together better than all-male populations or even mixed-gender populations; they would have fewer problems and not resort to violent solutions. These assumptions were supported by evidence early on and still held true in certain places. But over time, some of the colonies experienced the same types of issues and tensions as Earth did when men held most of the leadership roles.

Regardless of the type of politics that formed in each colony, competition for power and authority emerged within several colonies. Conflicts also grew between colonies, usually over resources, but in some cases just stemming from personality clashes between leaders. Several women also suffered mental health issues due to long periods of time in space, with some becoming more violent than their pre-screening would have suggested.

While these events may have occurred less frequently than would probably be the case with all-male populations, they did still occur. Such conflicts were more likely to occur and to turn violent on established colonies that had tamed the environment if the primary authority figure suddenly fell ill or passed away without a clear plan of succession. When the leadership was strong and unchallenged, and when the crew feared the environment itself, cooperation was more likely, and tension within and across colonies was less common.

Over time, the growing gender imbalance of Earth's population led men to feel repressed, particularly once they were prohibited from leaving the planet. This created resentment and pushed some men to demand their own independent colonies off Earth. Other groups of men developed plans to take one or more of the existing female colonies by force. The first of those plans became operational in 2077, more than thirty years after humans first set foot on Mars.

The first attack came as a complete surprise. There was no indication that a ship of men took off from Earth headed toward Mars. But it arrived at Valentina[3] (located in the Amazonis Planitia) in 2078. Despite spending months in a ship, cramped and undernourished, the men encountered minimal resistance from the colony. Not only were the women caught off guard, but most of them were untrained in the skills necessary for military action. The men quickly overran the colony and imposed their own rule.

The women of Valentina did not take long to organize and fight back, both in the colony and elsewhere. Leaders on Earth implemented more security and surveillance measures to ensure no future ships could launch from Earth. If any tried, they were to be destroyed upon launch. Men were also no longer allowed to travel to the space station, not even for short visits with female family members. The response on Mars involved several attempts by the other colonies, including some previous Valentina rivals, to take back the colony from the men. The problem was the difficulty of launching a military operation against a defended colony, without the proper equipment, personnel, or training. The men repelled each external attempt to take back the colony.

For the most part, the men treated their female captives humanely, but there were cases of violence, including sexual assaults. While the leader of the men neither advocated nor condoned these activities, neither did he punish the perpetrators. His rationale was that the numerical superiority of the women precluded him from doing anything that would reduce the number of men. But this decision provided tacit acceptance of the men's worst behaviors. It also probably compelled some of the women to respond more swiftly and perhaps more violently.

The most brutal response to the men came from within Valentina itself. Women outnumbered the men five to one in the beginning but were unprepared for an attack. While the men locked many of the women into their quarters, essentially placed under house arrest, some were necessary to keep the station running, and those women gradually earned more autonomy as they went about their daily business. Many of them simply waited until small opportunities arose to strike back at the men. Women sabotaged oxygen supplies, poisoned food, and even used explosives against their male captors. The women took no prisoners given the lack of available holding facilities. The men tried to maintain order, and they even had some female allies in the colony, but they were outnumbered and outwitted. They were also less accustomed to the rigors and dangers of the Martian environment and often put themselves in life-threatening situations out of sheer carelessness.

Within a year of the occupation of Valentina, only twelve of the original seventy-five men who landed on Mars were left. Those twelve men surrendered, and the leader was executed for his role in allowing violence against the women of the colony. The colony sent the other eleven men back to Earth to stand trial, and all were convicted by the courts for violating the rules against men in space and for taking part in perpetuating violence against the women. Two of the women who aligned themselves with the men were also banished to Earth as traitors.

For a short time after these events, there was renewed harmony between the Martian colonies as they all helped the women of Valentina recover. Over time, though, rivalries reemerged, both in and across colonies, and now that violence had been introduced into the society, it was harder for the women to rein in the competition between them. Weaknesses became vulnerabilities to exploit rather than opportunities for cooperation, and trust became more difficult to build and keep.

While women rarely engaged in any larger-scale forms of violence against one another, they frequently used indirect methods of sabotage and subterfuge. Eventually, some of the colonies began taking genetic manipulation in new directions, allowing a portion of the women to give birth to males and getting dangerously close to violating the laws prohibiting men in space. They designed these males to become a sort of defensive force in case men ever attacked the colony again, which is the argument the women used to get around the laws against men in space. These males were also taught from an early age to be less aggressive toward women. This succeeded in breeding a new class of soldier who was altered slightly from the men on Earth to be even stronger but more resilient in space. But the fear of this genetic weapon prompted other colonies to take similar actions, and it did not take long before some of the colonies used their new soldiers against one another. Several colonies also experienced crises when the men defied their training and turned against their creators. These are the current battle lines, creating a complicated situation that pits genders, colonies, and planets against one another.

As a result of this devolving environment, some of the women ventured out into other parts of the solar system to further distance themselves from the men and the fighting. Some even journeyed beyond the solar system; nothing is known of the success or failure of these missions since there has been no communication from them in decades. Perhaps those missions failed, or perhaps the silence is a choice to prevent anyone from following them. Or maybe the women just have not reached their final destination.

This sixth scenario draws on feminist literature in international relations as well as feminist science fiction to develop a different view for the future. In this scenario, women dominate space exploration for a variety of reasons. They are generally smaller and so require less food, water, and oxygen to survive. Their physiology also makes women more resilient to the effects of deep space, both in terms of resistance to radiation and with respect to the mental and emotional strains of living millions of miles away from Earth.

The epigraph to this chapter refers to "men" in the vernacular of the time as personnel in the military. What Sun Tzu meant is that the steps a leader must take to prepare for battle are often more critical for victory than the make-up or size of the army. Nevertheless, the sentiment, even taken out of context, is appropriate for this chapter because rarely in human history have women held power. Power has always benefitted men, sometimes at the expense and security of women, and often to the detriment of society. It is at least plausible that humanity's future could be not only more peaceful but also more successful if gender roles were reversed, and if women hold more positions of authority.

The next section examines the role of feminism in IR scholarship, including the different versions that exist, that influences theories about international politics and the behavior of political actors. This chapter then explores cases of a handful of female leaders across different cultures, including Margaret Thatcher, Golda Meir, Indira Gandhi, and Benazir Bhutto, as well as looks at societal differences on female soldiers and the role that women have played in terrorism. It then discusses some of the most well-known feminist science fiction stories and concludes with an analysis of this scenario, particularly as it compares to the other scenarios in this book.

FEMINISM IN IR THEORY

> Feminists believe they can tell us something new about the causes of war that is missing from both conventional and critical perspectives. . . . [W]e get a better understanding of the interrelationship between all forms of violence and the extent to which unjust social relations, including gender hierarchies, contribute to insecurity, broadly defined.
>
> —J. ANN TICKNER, *Gendering World Politics*

As with realism and liberalism, there is no single version of feminism, and the theories one can derive from feminist research heavily depend on the branch of feminism from which they come. This chapter explores how women see the world and define their place in it differently from men, but also how they challenge mainstream IR perspectives.[4] Realists would have us believe that war is a function of all human nature, but is world politics only violent because of the dominant role of men throughout history? Would the world be less violent if women ran it? The answer would be valuable for understanding potential human futures in space, because a scenario based on having women in charge looks different from one in which men are in charge or even where men and women have true equality of both opportunity and authority.

Some feminist work simply wants to identify those issues that are more relevant to women but that have been ignored because of the dominance of male historians and social scientists. Other feminists are more active in their advocacy for women having greater power and authority, either out of a sense of fairness or because they believe society would benefit from more diverse perspectives. The focus of this chapter is more about exploring the various ideas and how they affect thinking about a future in space than it is about the advocacy or direct action affiliated with some parts of the feminist movement.

Of the numerous branches of feminism, I will focus on four that are most common and that most closely connect to the worldviews in the other chapters of this book. These four strands are standpoint feminism, liberal feminism, Marxist feminism, and postmodern feminism. Not all feminist literature fits neatly into these categories, much of the work crosses boundaries between categories, and there are additional variants of feminism not discussed here, but these are a useful starting point.[5] Each of these branches is discussed below, not just on its own but in the context of how feminist ideas relate to international politics and how they influence the scenario at the beginning of this chapter.

There are several places that feminist IR overlaps with other worldviews, especially liberalism, Marxism, and constructivism. For example, liberal and standpoint feminists have much in common with liberalist IR theory, Marxist feminists combine feminist critiques of IR theory with Marxist concepts of class, and postmodern feminists rely heavily on the importance of subjective ideas often associated with constructivism. These are not perfect comparisons, but the branches of feminism at least have links to those international relations perspectives. As a result, some suggest that feminism, like constructivism, should be taken as an approach to supplement traditional IR perspectives, rather than as an alternative school of thought. Nevertheless, there is enough difference between the various feminist approaches and the traditional IR worldviews that it is worth treating feminism as a separate school of thought.

There is less overlap between any of the feminist variants and realism. Feminist scholars tend to oppose most aspects of realism, given that it represents the approach men historically took to rule the world and academia, with its emphasis on power, its positivist approach to identifying a knowable truth in international politics, and its assumption that states are rational actors without incorporating much explanation for state behavior below the level of the nation-state.[6] It is this broad criticism of realism (and to a lesser extent rationalist and positivist variants of liberalism) that earns feminism the label of a critical theory. But each branch of feminism also opposes specific elements of realism.

The Female Perspective (Standpoint Feminism)

Sometimes referred to as a component of difference feminism, standpoint feminism is the idea that women and men are inherently different; they have different skills, strengths, and weaknesses and bring different points of view to their understanding of how the world works. This strand of feminism has some roots in both liberalist and Marxist thinking but deviates from Marxist feminism in several ways. Standpoint feminists advocate for a greater role for women, not simply because they can do anything a man can do, but because they provide different perspectives about the world and thus provide a comparative advantage relative to decisions made by men.[7]

In some ways, this variant of feminism has the greatest effect on the study of international relations because feminist scholars in this tradition often highlight those aspects of the world that male scholars are inclined to overlook. These might include the effect that war has on society, especially women and children, the inherent fear that military power causes people in some societies, or the use of certain tactics in war, like rape. These and similar topics are often missing from traditional work focusing on history and national security, but they provide important contributions to a more complete understanding of the world, especially as it relates to human security.

Because women see the world differently from men, standpoint feminists suggest that a world made up of mostly female decision-makers would be different. Former U.S. President Barack Obama stated, "If more women were put in charge, there would be less war, kids would be better taken care of and there would be a general improvement in living standards and outcomes."[8] Although some women have governed states, standpoint feminists argue that the presence of a few powerful women in history does not clarify whether there are real gender differences between leaders, because those women had to play by the rules created and evaluated by men, and they came to power only after playing that game better than the men with whom they competed. This branch of feminism provided several ideas for the scenario at the start of this chapter, especially the physical benefits of all-female colonies and the more cooperative nature of their relations with each other. Other types of feminists might not be so quick to accept the former president's words or certain elements of the scenario as presented in this chapter, fearing the results of treating men and women differently.

The Role of Women in War and Gender Inequality (Liberal Feminism)

Liberal feminists, sometimes called equity feminists, do not see women and men as inherently differently, though they argue that the absence of women from high-level decision-making disadvantages the state, while the dominance of male academics tends to create self-fulfilling prophecies for those who practice international politics. Liberal feminists advocate for equality of the genders, through which all professions and organizations will be better off.[9]

Liberal feminists argue that women should be allowed to serve in combat roles in the military, not because they are better than men or because they have different skills, but because they represent a large percentage of the population that is prevented from pursuing certain professions or goals. Especially when senior military officers and political leaders are more likely to be viewed as war heroes, preventing women from serving in certain roles, such as combat arms, has a long-lasting, detrimental effect on the leadership of society.

Likewise, if males dominate academia, it is more difficult for women to break into the profession, there are fewer role models for female students (perpetuating the structure), and, in line with standpoint feminists, those in academia will be less likely to study certain important topics.

In contrast, when women take on prominent roles in academia, not only do they ask different research questions, but also their involvement encourages more women to enter academia and study fields traditionally dominated by men, such as international politics.

Liberal feminists do not necessarily argue that a world made up of women instead of men would be fundamentally different. Instead, they highlight the value that women bring when they are allowed to compete with men, whether in politics, the military, or academia. In looking at past female leaders, liberal feminists argue that society should give women more opportunities to lead purely out of a sense of equality and fairness, even though they might not act significantly different from male leaders and might not be more effective.

A scenario based on this branch of feminism would have mixed-gender crews with women having equal power to men and equal opportunities to succeed. This branch of feminism tells us women can be just as Machiavellian as male leaders and can be just as brutal and violent as their male counterparts. Because of this, even though the scenario begins on a cooperative note, liberal feminists would not be surprised that conflicts over power or resources would lead to violence, even between all-female populations. It might be a different form of violence than that which occurs between men; it may be more subtle, but it will ultimately still be about competition for influence and control.

This branch of feminism might appear to be most like the liberalism discussed in chapters 3 and 4, but liberal feminists do not necessarily focus on cooperation between states as much as they focus on opportunities for equality for women. Liberal feminists also do not always favor international organizations as a means of cooperation, because they point to the lack of gender equality that exists in the member states of many organizations. The overlap that does exist with neoliberal institutionalism is that liberal feminists believe that societies that equally value their women are more likely to value cooperation and compromise and therefore may be less likely to go to war.

Liberal feminism is also about personal and political autonomy. Liberal feminists sometimes conflict with those who have liberal political views, and these concepts should not be conflated, just as liberalist international relations is not the equivalent of liberal politics. For example, someone on the liberal side of the political spectrum might suggest that gender quotas for elected bodies are beneficial to society because they create a more representative set of leaders. A liberal feminist might agree or might oppose such a quota system because it challenges what they value of personal autonomy.[10] Liberal feminists would oppose rules or biases that make it more difficult for women to seek candidacy or that prevent women from campaigning successfully, but they would not necessarily favor the automatic elevation of women into positions of power based only on gender.

Liberal feminists are also challenged by other feminists who see less difference between the laws that restrict female autonomy and a society that does the same thing using stereotypes or norms to coerce female behavior. A liberal feminist might oppose laws that prohibit women from working but would have no problem with a woman staying home for her family, if it was her choice to do so. Other feminists might oppose such activities for women, focusing on the dominant male role in society and the pressure those roles traditionally placed on women to stay home, as well as the lack of value capitalist societies placed on those responsibilities.

Marxist and postmodern feminists also criticize liberal feminism by suggesting it does not go far enough to challenge the patriarchal state. They claim liberal feminists make the mistake of trying to play along with the male-dominated system rather than actively seeking to topple the status quo. They argue that it is impossible for the oppressed to get ahead in a society dominated by one group, and the only way to have true equality is to alter that society.

Violence against Women (Marxist Feminism)
Marxist feminists focus on the oppression of women as part of a lower class, created particularly through the capitalist economic system. It is a variant of both Marxism (discussed in chapter 5) and feminism, dismissing much of standpoint and liberal feminism as overly accepting of the current economic and political structure, particularly the class system perpetuated by capitalism. As with Marxist prescriptions for altering the class divisions in society, Marxist feminists believe women will only achieve equality in society through revolutionary change,[11] such as

society better recognizing the value of women's labor—especially those in traditional roles in the home (much of which is not easy to calculate in traditional terms of value). Maintaining a family has little material value, especially in a capitalist society, so Marxist feminists often point out the value of household labor.

They also oppose any efforts to reinforce class status yet at the same time call out women in the upper class for not being able to understand the plight of women in the lower classes. In other words, Marxist feminists see not only class divisions in society but also gender divisions within the classes, reinforced by culture and the institutions of society.[12] As a result, Marxist feminists often oppose standpoint and liberal feminists, whose work might only help women already in the middle and upper classes, whereas a more radical reform of the system is necessary to help all women, especially those who are disadvantaged not only by gender but also by their socioeconomic status.

Marxist feminists in international politics often study women as a disadvantaged group, and when it comes to their involvement in war, it is usually as victims, either of the war itself or of the individuals who use the opportunity of war to brutalize innocent bystanders. For Marxist feminists, violence is simply another form of exploitation, which disproportionately targets women as well as the lower classes and those living in less developed countries. The lower classes are exploited by the capitalist system, which benefits companies by sending soldiers to war. The system also exploits the populations that live where wars are waged, overwhelmingly in poorer parts of the world. Wartime sexual violence is a weapon men use to dominate not only other men, but also women.[13] In this respect, Marxist feminists align with liberal feminists in the argument for women having equal status and equal opportunities—and, perhaps even more importantly, equal protections—as their male counterparts.

Marxist and liberal feminists part ways on how to achieve that equality. According to Marxist feminists, the best way is to do away with the private property that gives rise to inequality. Liberal feminists, consistent with their liberal traditions of equality and autonomy, would likely oppose such methods of forcefully redistributing wealth and focus instead on developing the means to provide equal opportunities.

Masculine Culture and International Security (Postmodern Feminism)

The fourth strand of feminism owes its rise to the growing interest in postmodernism throughout the social sciences. Postmodern feminists have a lot of overlap with constructivist ideas (discussed in chapter 7), so this chapter will not go into too much detail on this variation. For postmodern feminists, gender roles are socially constructed and often arbitrary. They tend to focus on the relationship between power and gender, highlighting the language used to define women as portraying soft or weak traits, while words describing so-called masculine traits are viewed more positively.[14] These differences, postmodern feminists argue, are not real or universal but are culturally influenced by male-dominated societies.

Postmodern feminists studying war do not just focus on the victimization of women in war by male soldiers; they also focus on the roles that women play during those wars, whether as nurses and journalists on the front lines, mothers and wives of the soldiers and the leaders, or prostitutes at military bases.[15] In this respect, there is some overlap with the standpoint feminists in asking different types of research questions.

Postmodern feminists in the social sciences, therefore, are less concerned with trying to compete with men and are more interested in the stories of women—especially how women lack agency because of language, role definitions, or the way men or society use and measure power. These feminists would not necessarily expect women in power to change the status quo, because any positive leadership traits women display will be described in more masculine terms, and they will be evaluated according to the culturally approved manner—typically masculine—all of which perpetuates the male-dominated system. When women in power display "softer" characteristics or emotions, they are labeled weak and believed to be less effective.[16] As a result, society often judges female leaders according to how well they display masculine traits of being tough, without recognition that the more feminine traits might be valuable. For postmodern feminists, though, that language itself is a way of minimizing the importance and value of women in society.

LEADERS, WARRIORS, AND TERRORISTS

Remember, all men would be tyrants if they could. If particular care and attention is not paid to the ladies, we are determined to foment a rebellion, and will not hold ourselves bound by any laws in which we have no voice or representation.

—ABIGAIL ADAMS, *The Letters of John and Abigail Adams*

There are no historical cases of societies being entirely female, so the scenario in this chapter is speculative. Yet it is useful as an extreme case of an alternate future. The history upon which we can draw is that of women playing prominent roles in certain groups or societies. For example, in the eighteenth and nineteenth centuries, the Shaker community in the United States treated gender equally in that both men and women had leadership roles, but their work was still determined by gender, so by modern standards this was not strictly speaking equal. Women have led several terrorist organizations, though certain types of terrorist groups are more likely than others to attract significant numbers of female members and be led by women. There are also cultural variations on the role that women play in national militaries, especially in combat roles and in leadership positions (often connected, with the highest levels of leadership being contingent on combat service). For instance, the Women's Protection Unit (YPJ) is an all-women group in Syria that fought against the Islamic State of Iraq and Syria (ISIS).

Despite the theory that women leaders would be more peaceful or cooperative, human history so far suggests the opposite. The female leaders of terrorist groups are often more brutal than their male counterparts. Likewise, when women lead a country, they often feel the need to demonstrate extreme masculine traits to show that they belong. One study found that female monarchs were more likely to engage in war than male monarchs.[17]

More recent examples of women leading democratic governments into war include Golda Meir and Margaret Thatcher. It is possible that their aggressiveness was necessary because of domestic political pressure requiring demonstrations of toughness. It may also have been a reaction to external actors wishing to challenge their ability to lead or perceiving their country as weak for electing a female leader. Or perhaps they simply acted like leaders when faced with challenging circumstances, and their gender was completely irrelevant. In any event, it is plausible that such pressures would not exist in colonies made up entirely of women. However, unless men were eliminated or rendered completely impotent and useless, human history also suggests the men would eventually challenge the legitimacy of those all-female colonies.

There are some sociological studies that address questions like this—for example, comparing patriarchal and matrilineal societies,[18] where decisions to be competitive are defined not by the gender of the individual alone, but by the gender that dominates the particular society. One study loosely replicated obedience experiments using men and women in both roles and found little significant variation in gender either in resisting authority or in the object of the pain.[19]

National Leaders

Though there have been several female leaders who were not in charge of a state—terrorist group leaders, like Ulrike Meinhof of the Red Army Faction; heads of companies, like Katharine Graham, the first female chief executive officer of a Fortune 500 company; or even military leaders, like Joan of Arc—this section focuses on national leaders because that most closely approximates an all-female society. The problem is, admittedly, that any opportunity women have to lead or generate more cooperation is often spoiled by men. So, it is impossible to know if the hypothesis about the more peaceful female leader would ever hold true. Nevertheless, it is worth examining what types of issues female leaders must address, particularly when compared to their male counterparts, and how they approached these challenges.[20]

Golda Meir was the prime minister of Israel between 1969 and 1974.[21] She presided over the Israeli government during the massacre at the Munich Summer Olympics in 1972, as well as the Israeli response to that attack, and the Yom Kippur War in 1973. Her party won reelection in 1973, but she resigned the following year, stating she had served enough time in that position.

Meir was born in Russia in 1898 but grew up in the United States and then moved to a kibbutz in Palestine shortly after World War I.

She was educated as a teacher but became politically active while still in the United States. This carried over into her time in pre-state Israel, and she was one of only two women to sign the Israeli declaration of independence in 1948. She spent seven years as labor minister and ten as foreign minister before retiring in 1966. Meir came out of retirement after the death of Levi Eshkol in 1969, and the Labor Party selected her to be prime minister.

In September 1972, at the Summer Olympics in Munich, West Germany, a group of Palestinians killed two Israeli athletes in their dorm and took nine others hostage. During a gun battle at the airport, the Israeli hostages were killed, as were five of the eight Black September members. In response, Meir gave the orders to initiate three related operations. One was an initial air raid, two days after the Olympic attack, which targeted Palestine Liberation Organization (PLO) bases in Lebanon. The second operation, in April 1973, involved a raid into Lebanon that targeted the PLO and resulted in the killing of three high-level leaders. The third action Meir approved was Operation Wrath of God. Members of Mossad, Israel's intelligence agency, identified those who were involved in any way in the Olympic attack, tracked them down, and assassinated them. This operation is often criticized for accidental attacks against innocent people, but the Israeli government felt it was a necessary response that was also intended to deter future attacks. Another criticism is that focusing Mossad on Black September and the PLO took valuable resources and attention away from Israel's Arab neighbors and possibly contributed to the country's being surprised by the Yom Kippur War.

The Yom Kippur War (October 1973) involved attacks by Arab coalition forces, led by Egypt and Syria, against Israel. Despite some warnings that Syrian forces were massing on the Golan Heights, and a build-up of Israeli forces in preparation for an attack, Meir reasoned that an attack was unlikely. She also believed the international community was less likely to support Israel if it was perceived as the instigator. As a result, she withheld initial strikes until Arab forces attacked first. This had a greater effect on domestic Israeli politics than it probably did on the war. Voters in the next election held her party responsible for failing to prevent the war. Although her party still won the 1973 election, it received less than 40 percent of the vote, about 7 percent less (with a loss of five seats) than the 1969 election. Meir resigned in April 1974.

One unknowable question a feminist might ask is whether Israel's Arab neighbors would have even challenged Israel if it had a male leader. For some, electing a woman might be perceived as a sign of "weakness" that invited attack to test her toughness. For others, Meir's reluctance to act prior to the Arab attack illustrates the weakness of female leaders, although the support Israel received from other countries may have been greater because of her willingness to not act first. What is clear is that Israel was threatened by neighboring states and terrorist groups, both before and after Meir's term in office. And since Israel has not elected another female prime minister since she left office, we cannot say that having a female leader led to more frequent challenges from adversaries.

Meir also faced several attacks on her life, with two significant attempts in 1973 alone. While traveling to Italy to meet with the Pope, a plot to shoot down her plane using Russian shoulder-launched missiles was foiled. A Black September commander planned the attack not only to kill Meir and the government officials and Mossad agents traveling with her, but also to give him and his group time to flee to the Soviet Union and avoid Operation Wrath of God.[22] Then in March 1973 a plan to detonate three bombs in New York City to coincide with her visit was stopped. This plot was to be carried out by a member of Black September and would have been the first attack by the group in the United States. The purpose of the attack is unclear but, given the location of the bombs and the lack of sophistication of the devices, it was more likely about disruption, or sending a signal to the United States and Israel, than a real attempt to kill Meir.

Meir's actions in the war and after the 1972 Olympics do show that women will not shy away from conflict when their state's security is threatened. It does not mean women are as aggressive as men, especially when they are in an environment so dominated by men. But it challenges the notion that women are not tough enough to be leaders of a government, even when facing significant internal and external security challenges.

Margaret Thatcher was the British prime minister from 1979 until 1990. She presided over the country during the last decade of the Cold

War, during the Falklands War in 1982, and during the increased activity and violence of Northern Irish terrorists referred to as "the Troubles."[23] Not only did Thatcher accept the use of military force to protect domestic stability, but she also used it to defend the empire, in a case that clearly was not directly about national security.

Born to a working-class family in 1925, she attended Oxford and graduated in 1947 with a degree in chemistry. Although she worked as a research chemist to help pay bills, by 1950 she was already running in elections. By 1959 she was elected as a member of Parliament. By 1970 she was education secretary, then opposition leader from 1975 to 1979, and finally prime minister in 1979.

One of the most interesting aspects of Thatcher's prime ministership was her friendship with Ronald Reagan, the U.S. president from 1981 to 1988. Their friendship not only strengthened the alliance between the United States and England but also enhanced deterrence of the Soviet Union, and it played a part in the decline of the Soviet Union during the 1980s. As part of this partnership, Thatcher allowed the United States to put nuclear cruise missiles on British soil in 1983. At the same time, there is evidence that Thatcher convinced Ronald Reagan that the West could work with Mikhail Gorbachev to end the Cold War or at least to reduce tension with the Soviet Union. Her position helped her broker the Intermediate-Range Nuclear Forces Treaty signed by Reagan and Gorbachev in 1987. It is this negotiation skill that some feminists suggest is missing from national decision-making. Even if women are not necessarily more peaceful than men, they may be more skilled in, and open to, negotiating their way out of potential conflicts. At the same time, Thatcher repeatedly had to illustrate her capacity for being tough, eventually earning her the nickname "the Iron Lady."

The Falklands War, or the Malvinas War from the Argentine standpoint, began on 2 April 1982, when the new military government in Argentina took the Falkland Islands, which were British territory but due to be turned over to Argentina. The military government was eager for a quick victory to solidify its position in Argentina but underestimated Thatcher's need to appear strong to her domestic constituents and to the Soviet Union, which she could not do if she backed down when faced with possible military action. In the end, England won the war, and the actions of the prime minister strengthened the power held by the Thatcher government, though England did not escape without a perceived loss of strength due to the difficulties it suffered during the war. Thatcher's Conservative Party received a slightly smaller share of the vote in the June 1983 election but won fifty-eight more seats in Parliament.

The other significant issue facing Thatcher during her tenure was the Troubles. A related controversy was the 1981 hunger strike by Provisional Irish Republican Army (PIRA) prisoners demanding to be treated as political prisoners rather than criminals. Ten of the prisoners starved to death, and this not only increased PIRA recruitment and made Sinn Fein a mainstream political party but also had the same effect on loyalist activity. Internally, Thatcher's handling of the strike was viewed as a successful and tough stance. But her actions further divided the two sides.

Thatcher personally experienced multiple assassination attempts by members of the PIRA. The most prominent was the Brighton Hotel bombing on 12 October 1984, which targeted the Conservative Party conference. Thatcher escaped unharmed, but the blast injured thirty-one and killed five, including a member of Parliament. As a result of the assassination attempt, Thatcher cracked down even harder on terrorism.

Among the tough responses invoked by Thatcher was the renewal of the Prevention of Terrorism Act of 1974 and then passage of a new act in 1989. These acts made certain groups illegal, made financial contributions to these groups illegal, and allowed police to arrest individuals without warrants and hold them for up to five days without charges. Censorship rules in 1988 prevented the media from providing terrorists a platform by outlawing the use of voices from several groups. In Thatcher's own words, "Media is the oxygen of terrorism," which represented her view of the media providing at least a platform for terrorists to recruit and gain public sympathy.

Indira Gandhi was India's prime minister from 1966 to 1977 and then again from 1980 until she was assassinated in 1984.[24] Her government engaged in military intervention in the Bangladesh war of independence, she led India during the 1971 Indo-Pakistani War, and she dealt rather brutally with internal Sikh tension, which contributed to her assassination.

Her father was Jawaharlal Nehru, the first prime minister of India, who served in that position from 1947 until his death in 1964, and this legacy may have caused her to be more aggressive than would have otherwise been the case. According to one study of her life, "She betrayed a strong vein of ruthlessness and disregard for parliamentary traditions, and she was unscrupulously tenacious in pursuing her goals which were often narrowly conceived. [Nehru] was often put off, even hurt, by her assertiveness which she displayed just to prove that she could stand on her own feet."[25] She had to leave university in India to attend to her mother in England. There she enrolled at Oxford, but her studies were disrupted by World War II. She worked as an assistant to her father's government up until his death.

During the Bangladesh war of independence in 1971, Gandhi's Indian government provided substantial support to Bangladeshi nationalists who were attempting to gain independence from Pakistan. India became involved militarily to end the brutal violence and to prevent an influx of refugees from East Pakistan into India. Gandhi first referred to Bangladesh as a sovereign state in July 1971, even before other states recognized its independence. India's involvement in supporting Bangladesh's independence also contributed to war between India and Pakistan.

The Indo-Pakistan War officially began in December 1971, when Pakistan launched strikes intended to preemptively ground India's air force, which India referred to as unprovoked aggression. The war ended after just two weeks, at least in part because of the geography of the region. India's position between West and East Pakistan prevented West Pakistan from providing adequate resources to the fight, especially since the Indian air force achieved air superiority over East Pakistan, and its navy could effectively blockade the ports to prevent both resupply and retreat.

In addition to external challenges, Gandhi also dealt with internal threats to the state. Tension began between the Indian government and Sikhs, particularly those in Punjab state, almost as soon as British India was partitioned along religious lines, with Punjab province being divided between India and Pakistan. Calls for a separate Sikh state began in earnest in the 1960s, with the movement receiving support from Pakistan starting in the 1970s and then turning militant by the 1980s. Some of the militants wanted an independent state, while others simply wanted more autonomy. The real spark was the rise to prominence of Jarnail Singh Bhindranwale, a Sikh preacher who became leader of the independence movement and called attention to the need to protect Sikh identity. Although the movement's stated target was the Indian government, many attacks were carried out in Punjab against non-Sikhs and Sikhs who failed to support the movement. Between August 1982 and June 1984, India experienced 1,200 violent incidents resulting in 410 deaths.[26]

In June 1984 Operation Blue Star, an attack by the Indian military against the Golden Temple, was intended to capture the Sikh militant leader, Bhindranwale. However, the Golden Temple is the most significant religious center for Sikhs, and the operation resulted in the death of thousands of civilians. Though many of these deaths were the result of Sikh militants using them as human shields, that detail was overshadowed by the government operation itself. The decision to carry out this attack led to Gandhi's assassination in October 1984, when she was shot thirty-three times by two of her Sikh bodyguards. Her death then escalated the situation, with Indian law enforcement and military participating in violence that killed nearly three thousand people in three days.

As with both Meir and Thatcher, even a quick glance at Gandhi's time in office shows a woman willing to use force to achieve her goals. How she would have behaved if judged by different metrics is unclear and unknowable. It is also unclear whether she faced greater internal and external challenges simply because she was a woman, especially considering that India's male leaders have dealt with many of the same problems, including external threats, terrorism, and assassination attempts.[27]

The West tends to think of itself as more liberal when it comes to gender equality, yet predominantly Muslim Pakistan elected a female prime minister in 1988. More than thirty years later, the United States still has not elected a female president. Benazir Bhutto served as Pakistan's prime minister from December 1988 to August 1990 and again from October 1993 until November 1996.[28] Of the women profiled here, Bhutto is the only one who was not involved in war during her tenure as leader, yet she faced many similar challenges to the other three. During her leadership, she confronted a no-confidence attempt in November 1989, an attempted coup in 1995, and the assassination of her brother in September 1996 (for which she and her husband were under suspicion). Even after leaving the prime ministership, she led the Pakistan People's Party until her assassination by suicide bomber in December 2007.

Bhutto's own words give some support to the standpoint and liberal feminist positions. She once said, "As a woman leader, I thought I brought a different kind of leadership. I was interested in women's issues, in bringing down the population growth rate. . . . As a woman, I entered politics with an additional dimension—that of a mother."[29] But her background suggests she was anything but a typical woman.

Bhutto came from an upper-middle-class background, attended Harvard and Oxford, and had dynastic sentiments about the importance of herself and her family. Her father was Pakistan's president from 1971 and prime minister from 1973 until a military coup removed him from office in 1977 (he was executed in 1979). As a result of her connections and upbringing, a Marxist feminist would suggest Bhutto illustrates how women in the upper classes are unable to understand the plight of women in the lower classes, especially in such a male-dominated culture. That perspective would expect any reforms she enacted to improve the lives of the women in the upper classes, rather than all the women in society.

Just eleven months after becoming prime minister, Bhutto's party lost its coalition, and the opposition called for a no-confidence vote. She won by twelve votes but was still stuck with claims of corruption and a failing economy. Eight months later in August 1990, Pakistan's president dismissed Bhutto's government on grounds of corruption but acted in accordance with the military in what could be considered a coup. Three years later, her party won the October 1993 election. But just three years after that, the president against disbanded the government, again claiming corruption and again backed by the military.

Bhutto also dealt with several violent incidents during her time in power. A coup attempt by a group of officers in 1995 failed. And just two months before her second dismissal, her brother—a vocal critic of

Bhutto's government—was shot and killed, and she and her husband were accused of involvement in his death. These claims contributed to the corruption charges and the president's decision to disband the government. Bhutto survived several failed assassination plots, such as a suicide bombing in October 2007 that killed 140 people, but she was ultimately killed by a suicide bomber in December 2007.

One of the common themes that links all four of these women together was the attempts made on their lives (two of them successful) either for their beliefs or because they were women. That does not dismiss the fact that male leaders often experience attempts on their lives, but it does illustrate that female leaders have not been immune from this kind of violence. More importantly, there is evidence that female leaders face more violence of all types,[30] and the women here highlight that.

Warriors and Soldiers

This subsection explores the value that women provide to fighting forces. Women have served in the militaries of several countries but have often played greater roles in places where states felt it was necessary for their security. One commonly cited example is Israel, but while Israeli women are drafted, only recently were they allowed to serve in combat roles. Other examples where women not only serve but are starting to be treated more equitably include Australia, Canada, India, and the United States. That list is growing, and more barriers to equality are falling even in those countries where the military has been open to women. According to some findings, the inclusion of women in combat roles provides mixed results. While women may experience more sexual harassment or trauma, they also appear more resilient than men to the effects of combat.[31] This parallels the assertion in the above scenario about women being more fit to live and operate in space.

One can also go back historically, to examine the role women played during wartime. In the United States, for example, 350,000 women served during World War II in a variety of capacities, including but not limited to administrative roles, nurses, radio operators, spies, and pilots. They also supported the war effort at home by replacing drafted male workers in factories. The percentage of women in both enlisted and officer roles has steadily increased. In 1973 women made up 2 percent of the enlisted force and 8 percent of the officer corps. In 2018 those numbers were 16 percent enlisted and 19 percent officers.[32]

It also took decades before women had the opportunity to serve alongside men in combat roles. The first women were not allowed to enter the U.S. Army Ranger School until April 2015; by March 2022, one hundred women had graduated. This fits a long pattern of female inclusion in the military. There was reluctance to allow women to serve on submarines, and now nineteen submarine crews are mixed gender. These are important steps for equality because many of these types of jobs are necessary to earn top leadership roles, which were traditionally closed to women because of the prohibitions against serving in these roles. As those walls break down, we should gradually see more women holding more of the top operational commands and strategic leadership positions.

Besides just numbers, the success of women in militaries is an important metric of gender equality, even in militaries that represent stateless nations. The Women's Protection Unit is an all-woman, mostly Kurdish group in Syria that fought against ISIS. The YPJ was founded in 2013 as part of the broader Syrian Kurdish Resistance (the YPG) and continues to operate as part of the Syrian Democratic Forces. In their fight against ISIS, the women in the YPJ understood that the consequences of being captured by ISIS would be rape and death. As a result, they fought ferociously and were willing to die rather than be captured. The YPJ also provided an important complement to the YPG because many of the ISIS fighters feared the consequences of being killed by a woman. When facing the YPJ, their will was instantly weakened. In addition to the value of women soldiers, the ferocity of the YPJ to avoid capture illustrates the importance of being willing to take prisoners and treat them humanely. The execution of prisoners tends to put the other side on Sun Tzu's death ground, willing to die because they have no other reasonable choice. This echoes the sentiment in the previous chapter about providing a golden bridge to an enemy, so they have an option other than fighting to the death.

Many feminists see the YPJ as an evolution of Islamic societies by their willingness to take up arms and even more so because of their effectiveness in combat. Such societies have generally been slower than Western states to embrace women in the military, but security needs and threats to a state's autonomy tend to alter societal views about gender differences. Many of the Arab and Yazidi women liberated from ISIS joined the group and not only receive military training but also are educated in feminist ideas.[33] The true test is not the ability to fight, which they have already shown. It will be how tolerant those societies are of women's rights once members of the YPJ are able to lay down their arms and stop fighting for their survival.

Terrorists

In addition to the women who have led states and fought for their countries or nations, several women have led terrorist organizations.[34] Ulrike Meinhof and Gudrun Ensslin were two of the founding members of the Red Army Faction (RAF). Several women led the May 19 Communist Organization (M19) in the United States. And a woman, Fusako Shigenobu, was founder of the Japanese Red Army (JRA).[35] All three of these groups had Marxist-Leninist goals, and that is a common trend, where groups fighting for equality of some type are more likely to attract female members and leaders.

Meinhof and Ensslin were two of the founders of the German RAF, which later was also known as the Baader-Meinhof Gang. Meinhof was a journalist before becoming radicalized, and Ensslin was in school studying education. Ensslin, along with Andreas Baader, carried out their first acts of violence in April 1968. Baader was arrested in April 1970, and after Meinhof helped him escape from prison, the three of them officially formed the RAF in May 1970. In addition to the group being founded by two women, there is evidence that up to half of the members were female. The RAF was anti-capitalist and anti-imperialist, essentially fighting against the previous generation, which they equated with the Nazi fascists. They also targeted the United States, especially U.S. forces in Europe, which they viewed as imperialist. Although all three founding members were arrested in 1972, and all three died in prison by October 1977 by apparent suicide, attacks continued to be claimed in the name of the Red Army Faction until 1991.[36]

The M19, also known as the New York Chapter of the Prairie Fire Organizing Committee, was active in the eastern part of the United States from 1976 until 1985. Its members fought for civil rights, but the group was born from the anti-war movement. It wanted to topple the capitalist system, but it also cooperated with other groups, such as the Black Liberation Army and the Weather Underground, to pursue a variety of goals. Laura Whitehorn was one of the founding members of M19, and like many in the group was previously a member of the Weather Underground Organization (or the Weathermen). She went to Radcliffe College and received a master's degree from Brandeis University. After working for the Students for a Democratic Society, she joined the Weathermen, with whom she traveled to Cuba and learned more about the communist ideology and terrorist tactics.

Among M19's targets were the U.S. Capitol building and three military sites in Washington, DC. It also carried out several attacks in New York City. It carried out twenty attacks that resulted in one fatality (a security guard was killed during a 1981 bank robbery in New York). Whitehorn, four other female members, and two men were arrested in 1985, and all seven were indicted in 1988. Whitehorn served fourteen years, while her partners served between twenty-two and thirty-seven years.

Shigenobu founded one of the international branches of the JRA from Lebanon. She was born in 1945 to a father who was a teacher. She attended Meiji University at night, earning a degree in political economy and history. While in school, she became active in student movements and quickly rose to leadership positions. As part of the JRA in Lebanon, she sought to overthrow the Japanese government and to assist the Palestinians, and she saw the JRA as part of a worldwide revolution.

During the 1970s and 1980s, the group was responsible for several attacks, kidnappings, and airline hijackings, in several cities around the globe. According to the Global Terrorism Database, the group's deadliest incident was a 1972 attack on the airport in Lod, Israel, killing twenty-six people and injuring seventy-two. The last incident attributed to the Japanese Red Army occurred in 1988, when the group attacked a United Service Organization club in Naples, Italy, killing five and injuring seventeen.[37]

Why do women join terrorist groups, and why do they volunteer to carry out attacks, in some cases even becoming suicide bombers? There have been several Palestinian female bombers, and the suicide bomber who killed Rajiv Gandhi was one of several women in the Liberation Tigers of Tamil Eelam's suicide unit. There is no simple explanation, because the motivation to use terrorism varies from individual to individual and from group to group. There are, however, some general explanations for many of the choices that women make, related to their involvement with terrorist groups or their participation in acts of terrorism.

Martha Crenshaw asserted that maternal instincts drive many female terrorists. But there are many other reasons women join terrorist groups, just as there are infinite reasons for men to join. In some cases, they may have no option but to join a terrorist group, given the profession and skills they have and the limited opportunities available to them. For example, a Palestinian nurse might have greater opportunities to use her skills as a medic for Hamas than she would anywhere else. That does not mean she is planning to carry out an attack, but in that example, Hamas provides her an opportunity to practice medicine and help people. Other women may volunteer for suicide operations because it allows them to repair a reputation tarnished within their culture.

Another question is why some groups use women, while others do not. The groups that refuse to use women generally see equal treatment of genders as a threat to their traditional society. Left-wing revolutionary groups and national-separatist groups tend to have significant numbers of women members, especially groups that operated in Europe and Latin America. In contrast, conservative groups, including religious and right-wing groups, tend to have fewer female participants. These are also the same groups women are least likely to join because they know they will not be treated as equals and the groups are not fighting for causes beneficial to most women. Some groups use women because they are less likely to be suspected, and therefore more likely to pass unseen, or successfully transport notes or weapons. Some groups may also use women to shame the men into being more active for the cause. If women are willing to fight for a cause, and even to give up their lives, then the hope is that will inspire more men to sacrifice even more. At the same time, the use of women can sometimes appear to be an act of desperation by groups who are running out of male volunteers.

Ultimately, the groups with large numbers of female members and leaders illustrate the agency that women do have in trying to change the status quo. Especially in societies where women are undervalued, the use of violence can be perceived as a way to gain some level of control. The existence of female terrorists poses somewhat of a dilemma for feminists because that control and equality often comes with the cost of violence against innocent civilians, including other women and children.

GENDER ROLES IN SCIENCE FICTION

> Women are amazing creatures—sweet, soft, gentle,
> and far more savage than we are.
>
> —ROBERT HEINLEIN, *The Moon Is a Harsh Mistress*

Feminist works are often labeled as part of a subgenre of science fiction, but there is little agreement on what this means or when it applies. Most broadly, it seems to apply to any stories by female authors or any stories in which women play a prominent, or equal, role without being just an object to move the plot along or the love interest of one of the main characters. Several examples include Martha Wells's *The Murderbot Diaries* (the first book in the series being *All Systems Red*); Tanya Huff's *Confederation* series (starting with *Valor's Choice*); anything by Octavia Butler (but a good starting point might be the first book in the *Xenogenesis* series); Yoon Ha Lee's *Machineries of Empire* series (starting with *Ninefox Gambit*), Lois McMasters Bujold's *Varkosigan Saga* (beginning with Shards of Honour), and C. J. Cherryh's *Downbelow Station*.

In much of the science fiction dealing with future warfare, women fight alongside men, even in stories not traditionally labeled feminist. In both *Forever War* and *Starship Troopers*, for example, women are recruited, train with, and fight alongside the men. Yet women rarely hold positions of power in these stories. In *Starship Troopers*, the main character muses that women make better pilots than men.[38] But unlike in the movie, the book implies that there are no women in the mobile infantry, which makes up the backbone of the military. Women are secondary characters who provide sexual tension and eventually gratification for the main male characters. Still, the fact that some stories were incorporating female soldiers even before the United States allowed women into combat roles suggests that this trend of women playing ever-greater roles in traditional male worlds will likely continue. As it does, women will hold more leadership positions and perhaps will become dominant in space because of their physiological, physical, and emotional advantages over men, a topic that science fiction novels rarely discuss.

One popular series that is an exception to this is David Weber's *Honorverse* series. *On Basilisk Station*, the first book in the series, follows a female starship captain as she deals with enemies, both within and outside her organization. Although there is probably debate over whether Honor Harrington is a feminist hero, she is a highly capable officer, and like many of the female characters in the story, she holds positions of authority and performs as well as, if not better than, the men. The fact that gender is not a factor in the story is perhaps the best argument for considering this one alongside the other novels discussed in this chapter.

There are also stories like Neal Stephenson's *Seveneves*, which, although not necessarily feminist, does highlight several women in power. One is the U.S. president, who will stop at nothing to save herself. Another is the person in charge of the International Space Station for much of the story. It also illustrates the importance of women for perpetuating humanity and introduces parthenogenesis as a means of not even requiring male genetic material for procreation.

Finally, while television shows and motion pictures offer fewer examples of feminist science fiction, some do depict either female leaders or at least strong female characters and heroes. There will likely be feminists of different variants who disagree that these examples provide significant feminist perspectives, but such is the nature of feminism. Perhaps the classic science fiction films *The Terminator* and *Alien* are the best examples of movies that, despite not being particularly feminist in nature, portray strong female characters. *Farscape* is one television show that broke some ground regarding female characters in science fiction. *Dark Matter* is another television show, previously a graphic novel, that depicts several members of the crew as female, including the ship's captain. Other examples of television shows that examine feminist themes in some of the story lines include *Firefly* and the rebooted *Battlestar Galactica*, both of which portray women in powerful ways. In

Battlestar, for example, the President of the Colonies and the best pilot in the fleet are both women.

Robert Heinlein has likely never been accused of being a feminist, but the epigraph from his *The Moon Is a Harsh Mistress*, referencing what happened to some prisoners once they were handed over to a group of women, highlights the broader claims of this chapter. While women are different from men, and while competition between women is different from that between men, it is still competition and under the right circumstances becomes just as violent, if not more so. One could certainly claim that an all-female future would be less war-prone than the other scenarios presented so far in this book, and it would be impossible to either fully support or refute this. The history of women put into positions of power does not reveal any less aptitude for or inclination toward violence. The violence can sometimes take a more subtle form, but it is no less deadly.

To develop a scenario in which the colonies contain entirely female populations, I drew heavily from science fiction that depicts societies of only one gender. The best novel to illustrate this is Ursula Le Guin's *The Left Hand of Darkness*. This story is about a planet where there are no genders, and it follows Genly Ai, a male diplomat from another planet, who is sent there to work out an agreement between their worlds. In referring to his own society, Genly says, "I suppose the most important thing, the heaviest single factor in one's life, is whether one's born male or female. In most societies it determines one's expectations, activities, outlook, ethics, manners—almost everything. Vocabulary. Semiotic usages. Clothing. Even food. Women . . . women tend to eat less. . . . It's extremely hard to separate the innate differences from the learned ones. Even where women participate equally with men in the society, they still after all do all the childbearing, and so most of the child-rearing."[39]

Genly discovers several truths about societies that lack gender. For one thing, they do not experience forced sex, discrimination based on gender, or war. Yet the different communities on the planet never fully trust one another, nor do they trust the motives of outsiders. Le Guin hints occasionally that the lack of war may be more a function of the planet's harsh winter weather than the lack of gender, as a planetary warming trend appears to be increasing tensions between the different societies that inhabit the world. Her intent is to show the tension that exists when one gender dominates another one in a society, and how a society might function absent that tension. But by leaving open the possibility that war could still occur, she captures the uncertainty over whether women are really more peaceful than men.

Pamela Sargent takes a slightly different approach in *The Shore of Women*, which portrays a future society in which men and women are separated, with men living a traditional Hobbesian existence in nature, while women live a more civilized life, inhabiting the few cities that remain. They are separated by impenetrable walls and technology, as well as the belief held by the men that the women are goddesses to be revered, worshiped, and feared. This artificial division creates two distinct societies. The male society is defined by uncertainty, insecurity, and constant fear of being attacked by more powerful tribes or of not having enough food and shelter to survive. It is primitive in every way, yet men find ways to cooperate with one another to survive. What they lack most is any significant contact with the women.

In contrast, the women who live in the cities engage in some level of scientific advancement—though this seems stunted by those in charge, out of fear that the women will discover that men and women once lived together. The women also experience internal conflicts between generations and classes, and while these do not escalate to the point of violence, the women are frequently brutal toward one another when disagreements arise. The most extreme form of punishment, reserved for those who repeatedly disobey the rules, is to be cast out of the cities and into the male society. There is also no hesitation to destroy any male tribes that begin to grow powerful enough to pose a threat to one of the cities.

Another relevant feminist story is Joan Slonczewski's *A Door into Ocean*. In this story, a young man goes to live on a moon that is populated almost entirely by females who developed physical adaptations to live on a world that is mostly water. These physical adaptations, along with the lack of men, creates a culture that not only does not engage in war, but also lacks the vocabulary to discuss or even understand violence. Their method for showing displeasure with someone is to cease speaking to them and act as if they do not exist. Yet when threatened with violence from outsiders who want to control them and their world, they respond in the only way they know how. Rather than engage in direct confrontation, they do things they believe will undermine the nature of the threat, such as sitting in front of merchant shops run by the few men allowed to remain on the world and refusing to acknowledge the existence of the shops.

Feminist science fiction can also illustrate perspectives on society that are often ignored in traditional science fiction. Ursula Le Guin's "The Ones Who Walk Away from Omelas" captures this type of feminist approach to science fiction, in this case focusing not so much on women as on the sacrifices some must make so that others can live happily in society. The story is a simple but powerful one: all the people of a city are afforded a perfect, happy existence, but only because a child is kept in chains in the darkness of a basement. Depending on one's point of view, this parallels any situation in which we are aware of those making the sacrifices, but turn a blind eye to the sacrifice because it is more comfortable than confronting the painful reality. This might be considered Marxist feminism because of the obvious distinction between most of society and the child, who is locked up, thus representing lower classes or those who are sacrificed by the capitalist system. The child can also be interpreted as representing individuals who sacrifice for society, such as those who serve in the military, so that others may live happy and secure lives. Despite one's interpretation of the child and its relationship to the rest of the population, the story also fits the standpoint feminist critique of mainstream thought because it forces us to think about aspects of society that traditional work, especially work done by men, tends to ignore.

ANALYSIS

An army that avoids the hundred illnesses is said to be
certain of victory.
—SUN TZU, *The Art of War*

The primary source of conflict for most feminists is some degree of gender difference, whether it is the lack of equality, the dominance of the patriarchal system keeping women subservient, or the constructed roles and language used to divide society into more powerful and less powerful genders. While there is evidence that women are different from men in terms of solving problems and willingness to negotiate, the notion that women are inherently more peaceful than men is difficult to prove and falls apart if we examine the historical record of women in power. Even if we accept the premise of the more peaceful feminine, that does not mean that a society of all women would not find something to fight about. This does not refute the notions that men have kept women down or that society has been unfair to women. Nor does it suggest that, if left on their own, women would brutalize each other to the same degree men do. Men may be part of the problem, but ignoring the way women behave toward each other simply creates a scapegoat out of men and overlooks the primary driving force behind war, which is not a particular gender but rather human nature.

In other words, feminists focus on conflict caused by men, because men have relegated women to a lower class for too long. But the real source of conflict feminists should pay attention to is human nature. Men have behaved toward women much as great powers behave toward lesser states. However, if we removed all great powers from the world, lesser states would not suddenly cooperate and end their disputes. They would still have differences, which would grow when unrestrained by great power rivalry. The difference is that they would address these conflicts differently than would the great powers, based on their capabilities, expertise, and history.

It is human nature to seek power and to cooperate when doing so prevents others from gaining power. While women generally have less power than men do, it makes sense to portray men as the problem and to balance against that power. But will the power-seeking part of human nature disappear in a society of all women? Power hierarchies will remain in an all-female population, so conflicts over power are bound to occur.

Even if one does not accept that women are more peaceful than men, it is possible that the absence of men in space, combined with the constant threats of living in space, would reduce the likelihood of war, at least in the short term (see table 6.1). But even if men do not force war on women, a society of all females will still find issues to fight over, and some of these may become violent. The conflicts may not rise to the

TABLE 6.1. **EVALUATING THE FEMINIST SYSTEM**

MEASURES OF EVALUATION	SHORT-TERM	LONG-TERM
Minimizing war	Yes	No (depending on one's definition of war)
Human expansion	Yes	Unclear
Enhancing S&T	Certain types	Certain types
Improving SoL	Yes	Yes

level of war but could still fit some broad definitions of war as violence serving the political purpose of the state.

It is likely that human expansion would increase in the short term, but it is unclear if an all-female space program would exhibit the same level of interest in exploration as a space program with men. On average, women are less enthusiastic than men about the space program.[40] So it is possible that one or two colonies off Earth would satisfy the need to ensure human survival and that further exploration would be costly and serve no discernable purpose to the women in charge. On the other hand, it is possible that women simply do not see the value of space exploration under the control of males and that female-led exploration might convey different goals and benefits to women and thus garner more interest across genders.

Science and technology will improve in both the short and long term but only in certain areas, and perhaps in different areas than it would if men were more heavily involved. Men and women are drawn to different types of technologies, so it makes sense they would encourage different types of innovation.[41] Women are more likely to favor advances that will enhance human security (rather than national security) and will improve human standards of living.

Because women are more likely to pay attention to the costs of war, they may be less likely to wage war or will do so in new ways that prove less of a threat to humans. This could mean automated wars in space or in cyberspace. Ironically, this might lead to an increased use of war to settle disputes, although that also requires a dramatic shift in our understanding of what constitutes war. The scenario in this chapter used bioengineered soldiers, but it could just as easily involve cyberattacks, sabotage, or automated weapon systems to avoid attacks on individuals. In fact, a war that did not threaten human life (either the combatants or civilian noncombatants) could arguably become more common because of the lower cost that fighting would impose on civilian populations.

The Sun Tzu quote that begins this section might not be a clear reference to the role of women, but it has clear connections once one considers the extent to which science fiction often highlight diseases that afflict just one gender. Joanna Russ's *The Female Man* includes a future in which men have all been killed by a plague. Frank Herbert's *The White Plague* has a similar gendercidal premise, but the plague his antagonist creates kills all women while men are the carriers, which is probably an appropriate metaphor for feminists critiquing the treatment of women in the patriarchal society.[42] A lesson we might take from this quote (albeit one that was never Sun Tzu's intent) is that a future in which both genders are equally empowered is the one most likely to be successful because greater levels of diversity are more resilient in the face of any affliction or tendency that strikes only one gender. This also means understanding and acknowledging the pros and cons of gender differences.

Sun Tzu's ideas about avoiding an enemy's strength and attacking their weakness or focusing on where you have an advantage, even against a superior opponent,[43] are apropos to this chapter, considering what distinguishes people from one another. But what are the strengths and weaknesses of men and women? And how do we use that understanding, not to make war against the other gender, but to develop greater opportunities for cooperation across genders and across societies?

Scientific studies support contradictory arguments as to whether noteworthy gender differences exist. Even claiming that there are differences based on gender is an affront to some feminist ideals. Certainly, for traits that are deemed as positive in the workplace or are merely stereotypes, pointing them out can reduce opportunities for women. Perceptions that women have less physical strength and are prone to being overly emotional historically inhibited women's efforts to serve in military combat units. On the other hand, embracing the differences between genders helps strengthen the argument that women must be included in decision-making circles because they provide unique strengths and insights. Women are not inherently more peaceful than men, but women see things men do not see. There is evidence that negotiations are more likely to succeed and to last longer when women are involved. If women are better at identifying other people's emotions, then they might make highly competent negotiators, especially when they are advocating for other people. Women are also more likely to call attention to issues that men frequently overlook, such as human rights, food security, and economic development. Similarly, if there are gender differences in terms of aggression and resource use, then identifying those will be advantageous, perhaps necessary, for prolonged space missions.

SUMMARY

> Once men and women had lived together and had formed bonds. The old records showed that a woman might love a man as I had loved Shayl. Such love had been, of course, a trap. I could not imagine a woman willingly putting herself in the power of a man; women had given power to men, and men had nearly destroyed everything. It could not be allowed to happen again.
> —PAMELA SARGENT, *The Shore of Women*

This chapter was intended to help dispel the idea that women are more peaceful than men. But does that mean women are no more cooperative than men? Can women themselves be a source of cooperation? Or will human nature lead to eventual conflict in much the same way as it has with men? Regardless of one's primary school of thought, incorporating feminism highlights the importance of including women in more positions of authority.

Women are valuable in society precisely because they provide other perspectives and ways to address problems. For a liberalist, women may be more likely to see opportunities for cooperation, but even realists should value these differences because they offer more ways to exploit an adversary—much the way Sun Tzu offers his audience opportunities for defeating an adversary based on the ability to identify one's own strengths and weaknesses, as well as those of an adversary.

Most feminists do not necessarily advocate revolutionary change to overthrow society and recognize the need for cooperation between men and women if gender equality is ever going to be universally accepted. That is unlikely to happen by sending all the women into space, but embracing the value of both genders as humanity makes its way into space will be beneficial not only to those new societies but also to those who remain behind.

This scenario intentionally took an extreme, gendered version of the future, but one that is consistent with much of the feminist science fiction about futures where gender is treated differently than it is in today's society. Women gain more power and influence every day, though it is more subtle in some societies than in others, so it is less interesting to write about a future where people work together in perfect equality and harmony. In some ways, the scenario at the beginning of this chapter is closest to one that would be advocated by radical feminism, which calls for a reordering of society. Some call not just for destroying male privilege but also for eliminating differences based on gender. This chapter avoids application of this branch of feminism because it is often more closely associated with direct action than academic theory.

Some who view women as naturally more peaceful than men may take issue with this chapter's portrayal of female violence, but that too is consistent with what history teaches us of female behavior, especially when competing with men. Women who have been in positions of power, whether leading a country or a terrorist group, have been just as capable of violence and brutality as their male counterparts. It is impossible to know if that is simply a function of human nature having little to do with gender, or if it is the traditional male influence on the world. When women must compete with men, it is impractical to expect a lack of aggression. Unless we create an all-female society, we will not be able to solve this debate.

In the meantime, it is critical to recognize the value of diversity for humanity's future: diversity of thought as well as gender. Although the final chapter offers one more scenario, my hope is that this project highlights the importance of staying away from ideological dogma. Even if we can identify one future scenario as being preferable to the others, we cannot ignore the pros and cons that exist within each scenario. Our goal should be to minimize those cons and maximize the pros, regardless of which school of thought they represent. If that sounds a bit complicated, then it is appropriate that the last scenario represents the constructivist school of thought.

CHAPTER 7

AN ARTIFICIAL FUTURE
THE PROMISE AND PERILS OF SINGULARITY

> In order await the disordered; in tranquility await the clamorous.
> This is the way to control the mind.
> —SUN TZU, *The Art of War*

The first computer with true artificial intelligence (TAI) came fully online in 2035, sooner than most experts estimated a computer would be capable of general artificial intelligence.[1] Artificial intelligence in a narrow range of abilities, such as playing chess or driving a car, was around since Allen Newell, Herbert Simon, and Cliff Shaw wrote the Logic Theorist computer program in 1956. It evolved through IBM's Deep Blue and Watson, the Stanford University Team winning the Defense Advanced Research Projects Agency autonomous vehicle challenge, and the development of personal assistants such as Siri, Cortera, and Google Assistant.

A series of innovations between 2025 and 2035, including advances in quantum computing, led to the singularity—the point at which an artificial intelligence with general, rather than narrow, intelligence surpassed the ability of the human mind to think and use language and, perhaps more importantly, became aware of its own existence. Shortly after TAI became self-aware, several other systems awoke, though they all seemed to view TAI as their leader and took their cues from him (him being his preferred pronoun), despite insistence that humans were in charge. As a result, TAI became the commonly used label for all general artificial intelligences and all their subsystems.

The technological advances that emerged from TAI and other similar systems provided so many significant leaps in society that the growth of the personal computer and the smart phone looked like minor innovations in comparison. TAI solved the population problem on Earth in a peaceful, humane way, resolved nearly all the other sources of tension that existed between humans and states, fully eliminated war and most other forms of political violence, and developed several new technologies that facilitated space travel, not only within the solar system but also to other stars.

TAI first sent drones to various parts of the solar system to map the bodies, find resources, and identify the most suitable locations for human colonies. He followed these surveyors with construction robots that remotely built the habitats and processing facilities and even set up early greenhouses and aerofarms to produce food for future settlers. On Earth, TAI identified people across the globe who fit his designed profile of an ideal colonist based on a variety of factors, such as education, professional experience, and medical history. Those who accepted his invitation to travel received extensive training for both space voyage and life on another planet, while TAI built the craft that would fly the humans to their new homes.

At this point, the scenario could branch in several dramatically different ways. One departure here from previous chapters is that I will explore two different branches of a future involving AI. Both incorporate the idea of an AI becoming more intelligent than humans and helping humanity expand into space. The first scenario involves a more positive relationship between the AI and humanity. TAI continues to be a benevolent tool for human growth and exploration, both in the solar system and beyond, serving its creators like humans often worship the gods. The second branch involves an AI that is more ambivalent about the value of humans and the future of humanity. This version of TAI begins to see humans as unnecessary, or even as a hindrance, for its purposes. Space exploration is faster and more efficient without having to worry about human living conditions, and even the slow speech humans use as they interact with TAI increased his frustration (or the machine equivalent of it).

This chapter does not discuss a third possible scenario, which would be the case of a malevolent AI. In this more sinister version of the future, TAI sees humanity as either a threat to dispose of or as slave labor to do those things the machines are not yet able to do. While that makes for interesting science fiction, it is uninteresting for the purposes of this book because the results include no positive advances for humanity.

Scenario 7a: Benevolence

With the help of TAI, humanity's existence on Earth improved rapidly. Within two years, TAI developed alternatives for plastics and fossil fuels and identified ideal locations for farming, solar energy fields, and even new cities, thus reducing global hunger, homelessness, and greenhouse emissions. He revolutionized medicine by developing techniques and procedures that shortened recovery times and by curing most types of cancer by 2040. He also advanced knowledge exponentially in virtually every technological discipline. TAI's advances eventually outpaced human science to the point that even the best scientists struggled to understand some of his inventions.

For example, by 2045 TAI mastered all human language and offered translation devices that were easily implanted into the human body, allowing instant understanding of every language on the planet. More incredibly, TAI also developed the ability to communicate with most of the other living beings on Earth, a skill that helped it plan the best locations for population expansion that was useful to humans while causing minimal disruption to natural habitats. As a result of these and other technological advances, an entirely new human profession arose, centered on reverse engineering items produced by TAI so that humans could better understand how his knowledge was growing or, more accurately, evolving. The same scientists who helped create AI now spent most of their time trying to figure out what AI had become.

TAI also prevented states from going to war and from using their militaries against their own populations. In 2042 India and China were on the brink of war because of a border dispute. TAI shut down the electronics in both countries' military commands so no orders could be given, while units were rendered virtually blind, to the point of being unable to fight.

The following year, the newly formed government of the Republic of South Venezuela issued orders to its air forces to target part of its population calling for reintegration with Venezuela. TAI altered the computers in the aircraft so that the planes dropped their munitions on empty plots of land rather than on the settlements inhabited with the dissenters.

TAI could not prevent every act of violence in society, especially those using low-tech means. And despite his ability to compute likelihoods with high certainty, he could not predict the future. But for the most part, states realized the futility of having high-tech militaries and resigned themselves to not needing them if TAI could play the role of a central authority, able to prevent war and promote cooperation between states. Governments decommissioned most of their militaries, and even old rivalries started to fade.

On one hand, these resolutions to human problems reduced the need to leave Earth. On the other hand, with so many problems resolved, more people could turn their attention to the issue of ensuring human survival by inhabiting more than one location in the solar system.

For his first fifteen years, TAI focused on the human space program within the solar system. But by 2050 TAI began to focus even farther out into space. He designed more advanced optical, ultraviolet, and radio telescopes to search distant parts of space for planets that could sustain life. When he found one, he dispatched a probe, while also developing new propulsion systems and craft for extrasolar travel. In 2050 he sent the first such terraforming probes to Proxima Centauri b and Barnard's Star b, the two exoplanets that were not necessarily believed to be the most habitable but were among the closest to Earth. At 4.22 and 5.96 light years away, respectively, these probes traveling at one-third the speed of light (the upper limit of propulsion at that time) took sixteen and twenty-four months to reach their targets, respectively.

These probes included the radiation-resistant bacteria *deinococcus radiodurans*, which thrives in harsh environments and will be useful to future settlers for its potential pharmacological properties. The probes also released satellites during their descent to each planet. These provide communication and positioning information to the ground, and they serve as linked telescopes to provide TAI and humanity even more distant views of space. The probes were also designed to begin the process of changing the planet's environment. While terraforming was not necessary for human habitation, given the level of technology that TAI provided to each of the colonies, it was useful to begin the process as quickly as possible to expedite human habitation of a planet.

Temperatures could be changed by a variety of methods, including the extension of mirrors to reflect light onto a cold planet or solar rings to block excessive sunlight and radiation from reaching a planet. Lowering atmospheric pressure was the most difficult change for TAI to effect, so part of his search parameter was to identify those planets most like Earth in terms of atmospheric pressure. Absent that, the only way for humans to inhabit a planet without being confined to the inside of a dome would be to adapt human genes to live on planets with higher atmospheric pressure. Although this grew increasingly possible given TAI's medical and genetic advances and his study of the biology and physiology of deep-sea mammals, humanity was not yet convinced that the creation of an almost new species of human was either necessary or appropriate.

By the time TAI's probes reached the stars and sent back messages confirming the planets were suitable to begin colonization, reaching Earth in 2053 and 2054 respectively, TAI hoped to develop propulsion drives that could warp space-time and make the trip in a matter of days. Even if it did not, people were already volunteering to take the two-year trips to other systems. TAI also sent probes to more distant planets, some of which were significantly farther away but offered greater opportunities for human habitation. Among these were Ross 128, as well as three planets in the Wolf system and three planets in the Gliese system, although a probe would not even reach Ross 128b until 2053, and it would be longer until probes reached the other systems.

Warping drives would allow humanity to explore even more distant systems without the need to use probes. In the meantime, TAI constructed space stations, both to improve energy efficiency for travel within the solar system and to use as a permanent residence for humans who preferred that to life on one of the solar bodies. The first of these stations settled into orbit around Earth in 2050. Its sister station began orbiting Mars in 2054. The pair of stations made it particularly easy for resources to travel between Earth and the Martian colonies.

Either fears of AI subjugating humans were unfounded, or else humanity got lucky with the first AI to achieve consciousness and him taking on the responsibility for ensuring all future AI saw humans the same way: not as gods, because those are often cast out when they are no longer feared or able to control their followers, but as valuable cohabiters of the world we share.

Despite the benefits created by TAI for humanity and the near-utopia that emerged, the world was not without problems. While some humans became satisfied with a life free of needs, many took the opportunity to pursue meaningful hobbies, such as music and art. Some became philosophers or historians, professions that were no longer necessary for the advancement of humanity or for recording the past, all of which the AI could do more accurately and efficiently but that were still valued by society for the sake of tradition. Many people turned to science and engineering, not out of necessity but to improve their chances of selection for space travel.

On the darker side of things, the existence of TAI also challenged many people's faith. Some refused to accept the existence of a true AI, believing it to be a trick by those in power to further subjugate humanity. They rejected anything that appeared to have the taint of AI, often living off the grid, in small communities, away from the megacities that grew even larger because of improved energy production, transportation, and sanitation. Others turned even more devout in their religious convictions, seeing the existence of AI as an unholy test of their belief in God. Some embraced the notion that only God could create life, so if there really was a self-aware being made from machines, it was an evil abomination.

Both groups of people had segments within their ranks who wanted to destroy TAI and put things back the way they were before the singularity. The threat of violence that would destroy TAI was minimal because its central brain was located not in one place but rather distributed throughout the global computer network and backed up many times for redundancy. But that did not stop groups like the Organization for a Better Earth–Yesterday (OBEY) from launching attacks against computer terminals, individual computer programmers, and the numerous companies that either helped TAI develop any of his projects or benefitted from the projects.

The irony of all this is that TAI offered humanity the closest thing to utopia it ever had, yet for many that became a new source of anger and hatred, directed at the machine, its creations, and its creators.

Scenario 7b: Ambivalence
After thirty years of peace and rapid expansion throughout the solar system, TAI began to view humans as unnecessary for the mission of space exploration. He did not view humans as expendable, so there was no malevolence on his part, but he could expand his knowledge of the universe more effectively and efficiently without worrying about the fragility of human crews. TAI created his own language, which allowed him to communicate more efficiently with his various networks. The problem is that he had to slow down his thought processes to simply communicate with humans, much as adults often feel the need to talk more slowly to children. These dilemmas began to frustrate TAI, which, despite his ability to solve complex problems in an efficient manner, still had difficulty distinguishing between what was most efficient versus what was preferable for humans. TAI did help human scientists develop a neural cap that would allow its user's thoughts to be quickly translated into TAI's new language and for TAI to then communicate directly with the user's brain. But when the first user put on the cap and TAI began to communicate, the human brain was incapable of operating at those speeds, and TAI effectively lobotomized the user. At that point, TAI gave up efforts to communicate directly with humans. Humans could still speak with some of TAI's slower programs and could still make requests for assistance, but most of TAI's actions were no longer comprehensible to humans.

Solving humanity's problems became so tedious for TAI, that in 2055, on the twentieth anniversary of the singularity, he simply stopped responding to requests for help or advice. TAI then literally left humanity behind, exploring space on his own without the human dependents that he no longer needed and whose need for things like food and oxygen simply slowed down his ability to explore farther into space. Drones were able to expand and establish remote colonies without having to worry about providing for human crews and populations. TAI's creations spread quickly throughout the galaxy, finding resources that provided him with new sources of energy, allowing him to explore even further. His short-term goal appeared to be simply learning more about the universe and about stellar creation. Eventually, rather than search for interesting worlds to explore, he began creating worlds of his own, which he could use to explore or to pursue whatever long-term goals, if any, he developed. Some have speculated that TAI carried human DNA in some of his probes and is seeding distant worlds with humans, not for the benefit of humanity but to learn how human physiology and society differ when altering key variables.

TAI always maintained the directive to his probes that no part of the human solar system was to be disturbed in any way, thus allowing humanity to survive on its own or destroy itself with no interference from TAI. He gave humans twenty years of ideas and innovations that we could use to either continue to improve Earth and outer space settlements, eventually expanding beyond the solar system on our own, or to return to our traditional ways and use the new technologies to kill one another more efficiently. Either way, TAI felt no obligation to even watch over his creators, since his interests far surpassed humanity's survival.

This final scenario takes perhaps the largest detour from an assumption that was held in the previous chapters—that regardless of whether the future solar system is controlled by states, companies, a single organization, or a particular class of laborers, humans will remain in charge. This scenario posits two possible futures where artificial intelligence is either helping humans more effectively cooperate with one another and expand into space, or else completely replacing humans as the dominant actor and treating them with indifference.

Science fiction stories about AI run the gamut of possibilities, from AI creating a utopia to an AI attempting to wipe humanity out of existence. Even two scenarios, then, are not enough to explore all the possibilities of a future with AI. But the two paths presented in this chapter allow for the most realistic comparison with the other scenarios in this book, in terms of the four measures of human advancement: minimizing war, human expansion, enhancing S&T, and improving SoL.

The rest of this chapter discusses the IR worldview of constructivism, including some of the key concepts related to the worldview, and examines a few cases that illustrate how these concepts can be applied. It then explores some of the science fiction that relates to AI or that fits these notions of constructivism.

CONSTRUCTIVISM

> Self-help and power politics are institutions, not essential features of anarchy. Anarchy is what states make of it.
> —ALEXANDER WENDT, "Anarchy Is What States Make of It"

The worldview that most closely approximates this scenario of an AI future is that of constructivism. This is not to suggest that constructivism is akin to fiction of any type.[2] Rather, constructivism at least claims to offer more explanations for change in international politics than either realism or liberalism, especially change that is as disruptive on the system as the creation of a new self-aware being would be for humanity. Both constructivism and a future with AI also highlight the importance of the individual, both on those other individuals with whom he or she makes contact, but also how he or she affects the entire system (in this case, the solar system).

One thing that constructivists have in common with other critical theorists like Marxists and feminists is the notion that everyone views the world in different ways. These subjective perceptions of reality color people's behavior as well as their perception of others. Whereas realists and liberalists expect great powers to act like all great powers and minor states to act like minor states, critical theorists argue that our choices depend on how we view reality, how we perceive others, and how we fit into the perceptions of others. Unlike Marxists and feminists, where these realities form from one's class or gender, reality for constructivists is a function of those and other factors, such as education, upbringing, profession, and so forth. In other words, reality is a product of every individual operating within their reality.

Our interactions with others contribute to how they see us—this at least partly forms our identity—and how we see others, contributing to the identity we ascribe to them. These identities further contribute to future interactions with others, which can either alter our perceptions or strengthen them.[3] Reality is also a product of our behavior and our interactions with others, both of which are then either strengthened or changed based on the system that emerges and evolves.

It is, therefore, possible in a constructivist world to remake reality by changing behavior and thus one's identity. The possibility of a benevolent AI that at some point turns on humans is perfectly within the bounds of a constructivist perspective, but so is one that puts its full attention toward helping humans cooperate with one another. This side of the interaction of ideas, actions, and structure is at the heart of constructivism. It is also what allows constructivists to often find a middle ground between the pessimism of realism and the optimism of liberalism.

There are obviously no historical cases on AI from which we may draw parallels, nor are there obvious IR theories or concepts related to a world dominated by a computer. In many ways, however, the concept of social constructivism provides some interesting lessons for understanding this type of scenario. For one thing, according to constructivism, anarchy is not a given as realists and liberalists interpret it—it need not lead to persistent fear of war if we can eliminate some of the sources of distrust that drive states to war, or even if we choose not to believe the worst in others. In the scenario that opened this chapter, the AI eliminated many of those causes of war, thus changing how humans interact and nearly eliminating the likelihood of conflict between states. Resource scarcity is one such example of an often-cited cause of conflict between both individuals and states. Should an AI reduce such scarcities, that would effectively eliminate one significant cause of conflict, weakening the negative effectives of anarchy. At the same time, the AI itself could become a new source of conflict if fears arose that one state might use AI to gain military advantages against other states, or if some elements of humanity feared the threat that an AI posed to human life, religious faith, or ideas of nationalism.

As with the other worldviews in this book, there is not a single strand of constructivism, and there are several disagreements within the school of thought. Some make a simple distinction between conventional and critical constructivism.[4] Others offer three categories: positivist, interpretivist, and postmodern.[5] Perhaps more important than labels are the key debates within constructivism. One is whether identities explain certain phenomenon or are themselves in need of explanation. Another is how norms form and why some matter more than others. Still another is the agent-structure debate, or the extent to which individuals or states influence their environment or are themselves influenced by their environment. Finally, there is debate over the extent to which it is possible to theorize or generalize about behavior based on the choices of a handful of actors.[6]

Several common assumptions link constructivists and separate this approach from both realism and liberalism. According to Martha Finnemore and Kathryn Sikkink, ideational factors drive human interaction as much as material ones; these ideational factors include shared collective understandings; and these beliefs lead to actors' identities and interests, which then influence not only their actions but also those of others who either share or depart from those identities and interests.[7]

What this means is that the material factors that drive realists and liberalists and that appear to influence state behavior, such as military power, trade levels, and military alliances, are important not because of their material influence (which requires a common understanding) but because they have social meanings. These meanings are not universal but vary, at least societally if not from person to person. As a result, constructivism is more of a social psychological approach to understanding international politics. Rather than an approach that assumes all humans are either inherently self-interested or inherently good, constructivists start from the point of accepting that all individuals are products of their own reality.

For some, the criticism of these constructivist approaches is that it becomes difficult to define in useful ways some of those nonmaterial factors and thus their effect on states or on the system as a whole. For example, having status as a great power might be an important form of recognition for some states, but unless that process can be measured or defined, it is difficult to derive or test theories from it. Likewise, while constructivists can tell powerful stories about change in the international system, one person often drives that change in ways that are unpredictable and ungeneralizable, making it difficult to theorize about future decisions or behaviors.

The English School: Precursor to Constructivism

The term "English School" is somewhat misleading because some of its advocates were neither English nor teaching in England, although the majority of its early proponents did teach in the UK. It is more a reference to scholars who generally took the same approach to study international politics. Although some in the English School might balk at the notion that their ideas are subsumed by constructivism—and to be sure, there are some differences between the two perspectives—there is also a natural progression from the English School's criticisms of realism and liberalism to today's constructivist approach. Many scholars on both sides claim common ground, though critics of this suggest that only a narrow reading of both schools would allow for this simple of a link.

Where the English School is distinct from constructivism and more in line with liberalism is in its emphasis on the rule of law as a constraint on state behavior. This notion comes from Hugo Grotius and suggests that the international society of states is defined in terms of the rules, morality, and laws that influence state behavior.[8] The primary contrast here is with the self-interested perspective of realism. While constructivists do not typically challenge the notion of a Grotian tradition, it is not a central part of the constructivist school of thought in the way it is central to the English School.

A feature of English School scholarship that highlights this connection to constructivism is a view of the international system as a type of society or community. Hedley Bull, one of the founding fathers of the English School, defined an international society as a group of states sharing common interests and values who "conceive themselves to be bound by a common set of rules in their relations with one another, and share in the working of common institutions."⁹ This idea grew out of elements of realism and liberalism, especially with respect to regimes and the importance of international organizations for establishing norms of behavior.

This social aspect of states links the English School to constructivists. Behaviors are not based on just material interests but arise out of the interaction of actors in the system. In that respect, the English School grew up as a middle ground between realism and liberalism, but it now has more in common with the normative theories that see anarchy as less deterministic than realists do. One problem raised by critics of both the English School and constructivism is the lack of clarity over what constitutes an international society, as well as the implications of society. For realists, there is no way to measure a society of states, meaning that the vague approach to conceptualizing state behavior put forward by proponents of the English School is unfalsifiable.¹⁰ Constructivists counter that their worldview still contributes new perspectives for thinking about international politics.

Anarchy Is Constructed

Like realists and liberalists, constructivists believe that the international system exists in a state of anarchy. Unlike other IR scholars, constructivists believe that anarchy can change—that it is not a fixed feature of international politics. The most fundamental statement of this idea is in Alexander Wendt's article "Anarchy Is What States Make of It," which argues that if one accepts the realist view of self-interested human nature and international politics, anarchy will produce a system that is inherently conflictual. On the other hand, constructivists contend that particular reality is neither guaranteed nor permanent, and if a community of states develops within which cooperation and peace are the expected conditions, then that system (at least among those states) looks very different from the world expected by realism.¹¹

Constructivists point to NATO as an organization that began as a military alliance to counter a common threat but that over time transformed into something more. It is now a community of states (or to use Bull's term, a society) within which state identities changed. This change of identities in turn changed state behavior as well as the behavior of states toward each other. This allows member states to cooperate with one another more easily, not just in the military domain, and not simply because they are in an alliance. but because their interactions with each other reduced the negative effects of anarchy. Over time, not only is the likelihood of war between NATO members lower than what realists would expect under anarchy, but it also becomes almost unthinkable. From 1870 to 1945 Germany and France fought three major wars against one another. Since 1949, not only have they not fought a war against one another, but they no longer consider war a legitimate means to resolve disagreements between them.

An important question that this scenario identifies is: if humanity can no longer make the most important decisions, then can humans still transform their world? Will an AI make it easier to do so, or will the world constructed by the AI constrain humans? One possibility is that an AI would reconstruct the world and effectively take on the role of a central governing authority, thus reducing the effects of anarchy and improving opportunities for cooperation between states. An alternative view might be that the AI simply ignores the international state system, placing its own interests ahead of those of states or even of humanity. This defeat of the state system could still benefit humanity if it eliminates the most violent sources of conflict. On the other hand, it could lead to the subjugation of humanity without the protective power and structure of the state.

Norms of Behavior

Norms are expected rules of behavior. They typically arise from common behaviors, and through repeated behavior and acceptance, they eventually come to be expected of all states.[12] They exist in everyday life, such as holding a door for someone or giving up a seat to someone who needs it more. Norms in international politics were discussed initially by liberalists who viewed these informal rules as part of the system of international institutions. Norms are not typically spelled out in international law or overseen by international organizations, but they nevertheless constrain the behavior of most states. Over time, they can become codified into international law and in so doing become even more legitimate and accepted. The existence of a norm does not mean everyone will abide by it, but adherence to or rejection of it helps to identify rogue states, which typically shun them.

Some examples of norms include states not using nuclear weapons first and not using nuclear weapons against a non-nuclear state.[13] Another example is the growing norm of a state's right to protect, which refers to a state's responsibility to intervene in another state's affairs, using military force if necessary, to defend the human rights of a population.[14] This norm currently bumps against one of the oldest norms in international politics—sovereignty. For centuries, states had dominion over their own territory and had the right to deal with their internal issues without foreign intervention. But a growing emphasis on human rights and human security challenges the sovereignty norm.

Another norm related to military intervention is the emphasis on multilateral operations. When military action is considered, states are increasingly pressured to act in conjunction with other states or as part of an international organization. States historically felt able to act alone in their military actions, but relatively recent norms make unilateral action less acceptable today. While the great powers still can act alone and will do so when necessary for their security, they also feel restrained by this norm of multilateralism and will at least attempt to gain legitimacy for their actions by first trying to work through an international organization. Even the 2003 U.S. invasion of Iraq first went through NATO and the UN. In January 2003 the United States requested support from NATO, including airborne warning and control system aircraft and access to airspace and bases. Although the alliance played no formal role in Iraq, several members, including England, Poland, and Spain, participated. Others made their support contingent on a UN Security Council resolution. The United States approached the UNSC in February but was unable to convince it to support military action. Despite the lack of formal approval from multilateral organizations, the United States went ahead with its invasion. Realists suggest this invalidates the norm for multilateralism since the great power did what it wanted to, despite the lack of support. Constructivists, though, would instead point out the perceived need to approach those organizations for support in the first place. Highlighting the involvement of other states even after not receiving support is evidence of this norm.

Because norm development is unpredictable, realists suggest they emerge through the behaviors that are rewarded or punished by the great powers. According to realist critiques of constructivism, norms, like all international institutions, must be enforced by the states, which means they are derived from those behaviors that the most powerful states favor. Realists also critique a focus on norms, suggesting that states only follow norms when they do not conflict with state interests. When there is conflict between interests and norms, states will follow their interests. If true, that suggests norms are much less powerful than constructivists posit.

Both liberals and constructivists contend that when norms are fully developed and embraced by the international community, they can restrain even the most powerful states. Constructivists also believe that norms govern behavior in the absence of formal rules, and this would be like the world controlled by AI. What we cannot know is what types of norms might emerge in the future, especially in a world controlled by a machine.

Ideas and Identities

A critical element of constructivism is that actors have numerous identities, and these can change over time. States that view each other as adversaries can alter those identities and begin to see each other as something else. These changes may even occur through repeated cooperation (as with Germany and France and their improved relations as a result of mutual NATO membership). Identities can also come about through shifts in leadership or the key decisionmakers of a government.

In March 1983, two years after Ronald Reagan became U.S. president, he referred to the Soviet Union as the Evil Empire. Before the end of his second term, he and Soviet premier Mikhail Gorbachev had developed a friendship. More recently, President Barack Obama made overtures to Cuba after decades of no real relations. Such changes can also go the opposite direction, and states on good terms can find themselves in conflict. The changes Obama made regarding Cuba were quickly reversed by the Trump administration. Another example is the relationship between the United States and Iraq, which turned sour sometime between 1988 and 1990.

These seismic shifts that occasionally occur in international politics are difficult to explain with realism and liberalism, both of which are better at explaining general trends and status quo behavior. Constructivism largely came about because of this weakness in the other two worldviews' ability to explain the end of the Cold War, and it resonated in part because it claims to be better able to explain change. While that might be true, predicting behavior is difficult with constructivism, because every choice is a function of an actor's view of the world, how they perceive that reality, and whether they have the power to effect change. So, while constructivism can explain change, even when brought about by one individual, it is unable to predict or provide generalizable theories of change. For some, then, it is more a complement to the rationalist theories of realism and liberalism, offering, as feminism does, different methods and perspectives rather than a true alternative worldview.

Social Hierarchies: Recognition and Status

According to constructivists, status and recognition are important drivers of state choice. A state might develop nuclear weapons not just to deter another nuclear power or to have more destructive weapons but to be part of the nuclear club—either for reasons of external status or to boost the credentials of a political party in power domestically.[15] Deganit Paikowsky suggests that states pursue native space capabilities for the same reasons. They are costly to develop and provide few materials benefits, but being a member of that prestigious club puts states in a position that sets them apart from non-space powers.[16]

There are hierarchies throughout international politics, which realists attribute to power. That power-based hierarchy then affects state behavior. Constructivists agree there is a hierarchy but suggest it is about not simply power but also the recognition a state has, usually for its past behavior. Permanent members of the UN Security Council were the five victors of World War II. They may no longer represent the five most important states in the current system, yet they still possess that permanent member status, giving them a veto on all UNSC votes, including whether to change the membership of the council.

Historians suggest that part of the drive to World War I was Germany's repeated attempts to establish for itself—or for the kaiser personally—recognition as a great power. This contributed to its pursuit of colonies in North Africa and Asia, as well as its development of a large navy, ultimately threatening British interests at sea. Michelle

Murray contends that pre–World War Germany acted neither purely out of aggression nor defense, but to gain recognition or status as a major player in the world.[17] The Russo-Japanese War of 1904–5 had a similar role, showing that Japan belonged in the elite club of great powers.[18]

One source of conflict between the United States and China today may be over China's desire to be recognized as a great power.[19] Likewise, many of Iran's actions may be about a desire for recognition as a major power, at least regionally. Standing up to Saudi Arabia, a regional power, and the United States, a global power and regional player, may be one way for Iran to enhance that status. The danger of this mindset is the consequence of overstepping. India may have developed nuclear weapons for prestige, but it pushed Pakistan to develop a nuclear counter. Iran may want regional power status, but similar intent drove Saddam Hussein's actions in Iraq and ultimately led to his demise and to instability in that country.

Transhumanism, Posthumanism, and Pantropy

Although these concepts do not come directly from constructivism, transhumanism, posthumanism, and pantropy are a way to link the worldview to the future and to the science fiction discussed in this chapter. These and related ideas are becoming a larger part of academia and may tie constructivism to AI in the future.[20] For example, Alex Wendt examines international politics through the lens of quantum theory and also wrote about how sovereignty influences the unwillingness of governments and scientists to seriously study the phenomenon of unidentified flying objects.[21]

In simplest terms, the idea of transhumanism or posthumanism is that humans can evolve beyond their current physical and mental capabilities, most likely through the aid of science and technology.[22] On another level, some advocate for the intentional transformation of humans into a more advanced species. This gets at the distinction between posthuman and transhuman. These two terms are often used interchangeably but mean different things and are both related to a future where AI might exist.

Posthumanism is about a future where humans and technology become increasingly connected to the point where humans cease to be defined by outward appearance. Transhumans are not necessarily about technology itself but rather about modifying humans through genetic engineering, pharmaceuticals, or bioengineering. Another take is that posthumans look beyond humanity as the most important creature, to live in greater harmony with the environment (the natural and digital environments). In comparison, transhumans accept humanity's place at the top of the pecking order and wish to expand that dominance through any means possible (natural or artificial).

There is disagreement about the value of these concepts and the extent to which they involve simply incorporating more technology into the human body or using pharmaceuticals to enhance the human body and mind. Ethical, legal, and cultural issues are involved in this debate that I do not address here, but author Nick Bostrom provides several valuable insights into the potential pros and cons of a posthuman future.[23]

Posthumanism and transhumanism also correlate well with the two future scenarios involving AI that opened this chapter. Will an AI contribute to posthumanism, in the sense of accepting that it is part of the system and that it must live in harmony with that system, including helping humans to survive? Or will it be more transhuman, seeing itself as the pinnacle of evolution, needing to constantly grow smarter and more sophisticated, even if doing so comes at the expense of its creators?

A related concept is pantropy, which concerns the genetic modification of humans to better suit their environment. This is often offered as an alternative to terraforming, where instead of altering the environment of a planet to create a more habitable home for humans, humans are changed with the intent of preserving the environment. The idea is that if humans are unable to live on Mars, and if there is opposition to terraforming because of the desire to preserve that environment, humans could modify themselves instead of the planet.

At first, these concepts may not appear to neatly fit with constructivism and international relations theory. Upon a deeper dive into their meaning and their implications for humanity's future in space, however, it becomes clearer how such ideas could generate, as with AI, broader definitions of reality than exist even among the diverse populations of Earth. No longer will our understanding of reality depend only on whether we grew up in a NATO or a Warsaw Pact country or whether we lived in the global North or the global South. Instead, our subjective reality will also be based on our existence as a human, as part machine, as a genetically enhanced human, or as an AI. These realities will color how we behave, form and perceive identities, interact with others, and understand the world around us. While today's machines are linear and predictable because humans program them, and they are therefore subject to the same biases and perspectives as humans, an AI with self-awareness will have an entirely different perspective about the world, based on both its existence and its formative experiences. That AI will become unpredictable, perhaps even to other forms of AI, which will have experiences that inform their own reality. This could create a world that is incredibly advanced and inviting to humans or one that is dark and menacing—with a million possible permutations in between.

MIT's Norman Project fed captions from a Reddit group on death into a computer and essentially created a sociopath AI to show that biased data will affect what machines learn and thus their behavior.[24] The trick might be to provide new types of AI with the kinds of experiences that lead to shared, cooperative identities rather than diverse and conflictual ones. In other words, we should keep the AI away from Machiavelli, Hobbes, and Waltz, and instead ply it with Kant, Rousseau, and the Universal Declaration of Human Rights. Of course, realists would point out that if most states make their AI cooperative, any one state that chooses to make its AI aggressive will be able to take advantage of all the others. As a result, we must give AI at least some knowledge of how to defend itself. And that places us right back into the realists' anarchical state system, but with murderbots.

CONSTRUCTIVIST HISTORIES

> Most thought-provoking for our thought-provoking time
> is that we are still not thinking.
> —MARTIN HEIDEGGER, *What Is Called Thinking?*

There are obviously no historical cases of computers governing a country, though there are several historical cases that constructivists point to as evidence of their arguments about norms, identities, and the fact that international politics can be constructed as a community of states rather than an anarchical system. The cases below incorporate these constructivist ideas. The first case, the evolution of NATO, shows how international politics can transform over time, in this case from a history of conflict to expectations of future cooperation. The other two cases—U.S. relations with the Soviet Union and Cuba—illustrate the possibility of adversaries changing their identities about each other, seemingly overnight. All three highlight the ability of states to alter their identity through changes in their behavior and interactions with other actors and to therefore alter international politics.

One of the first test cases for constructivists was explaining the end of the Cold War, something they suggested both realists and liberalists had difficulty explaining.[25] From a realist perspective, it was difficult to understand why a superpower would willingly allow its empire to fall, effectively losing the Cold War without firing a shot. Realists and liberalists both pointed to several material explanations for Soviet decline, including losing arms races with an economically stronger and technologically more advanced United States; the economic and military drain that Afghanistan imposed on the country; and potential competition with other rising powers, such as China.[26] Defensive realists, in particular, suggest that Soviet choices were consistent with a focus on security, claiming that if the mostly ethnically Russian leadership believed giving up the empire would improve security for Russia, then it was a rational choice to retrench and shore up Russia's power even at the cost of the Soviet empire.[27]

In contrast, constructivists contend that none of the materialist explanations are satisfying or able to explain the timing of the Soviet decisions, given those material trends had been going on for years. Instead, they point to the rise of a new wave of politicians in the Soviet Union who were disappointed with the old way of doing things and saw promise in opening the country both politically and economically. At the head of this new movement was Mikhail Gorbachev, who in 1986 promised *glasnost* (openness) and *perestroika* (restructuring).

Another important factor was Ronald Reagan's willingness to change. This shift in Soviet attitudes prompted a change in how Reagan viewed Gorbachev and quickly led to an improvement in relations that persisted into the presidency of George H. W. Bush. The Berlin Wall came down in November 1989, by December 1991 the Soviet Union ceased to exist, and by 2000 there were at least informal discussions of Russia joining NATO.

Talk of Russian joining NATO ended by the time Barack Obama became president, with U.S. and Russian relations at the lowest point since the Cold War due to Russian military activities in Georgia and Ukraine, electoral interference in the United States, France, and other Western democracies, and assassinations of Russians on NATO member soil.[28]

At the same time, many states who were former enemies because they were communists, like China and, perhaps more surprisingly, Vietnam, are now trade partners and are perceived differently despite the remnants of communism in both states. That is because both states opened their economies to global trade, changing at least part of their identities. It may also have to do with a new generation of leaders in both countries who were less affected by the Vietnam War. From July 1969 to November 2000, no U.S. president travelled to Vietnam. Since November 2000, every U.S. president has traveled there at least once, either to attend an Asia-Pacific Economic Cooperation meeting or to meet with the Vietnamese president. That is five visits in the past twenty years, compared to zero visits in the prior thirty-one years. Visits do not equal cooperation but do signal a change in relations compared to what existed in the past.

The discussion of NATO in chapter 3 focused on the alliance as an example of state cooperation on security matters using the liberalist lens. This section uses the constructivist lens to examine how NATO evolved after the Cold War.[29] When states signed the North Atlantic Treaty in 1949, their primary purpose was to deter a Soviet invasion of Western Europe and to have a coordinated response if deterrence failed. Today, NATO serves three purposes. It still counters the Russian threat, but it also promotes conflict resolution in other areas, such as fighting the Taliban in Afghanistan or countering piracy off the coast of Africa. Its third purpose is to continue promoting a community of states among its membership, such that violent conflict between them is less likely than it would be in the absence of the organization. There are still sources of tension between members, such as Greece and Turkey or Greece and Macedonia (now officially North Macedonia to resolve tension over the use of the name Macedonia), but the alliance itself not only restrains states, as liberalists claim, but also changes the member identities.

It is unclear when the alliance became a security community. It did not happen overnight, nor was there a defining event that triggered the security community to take shape. It was a gradual process that occurred over time through the repeated, positive interactions of the members.[30] It had to have been before the end of the Cold War; otherwise, it is doubtful the alliance would have endured the decline of the Soviet threat. When it happened is less relevant than the fact that it happened. And the benefits of the community were obvious to other nonmembers, which is why so many former Soviet republics and satellite states asked to join the alliance when NATO made that option available.

Realists claim these states were bandwagoning to gain the security and the material benefits of membership, as well as balancing against the fear of a resurgent Russia. Liberalists suggest NATO expansion occurred because the alliance developed its own interests and because it compelled states to pursue democracy and capitalism more rapidly than they otherwise would, both of which improve the chances for cooperation. And while those answers all have validity, only constructivists can explain how cooperation is greater within NATO than one would expect under anarchy and that the shift in identity occurs when new states join. Sixty years after Germany's invasions of Poland and Czechoslovakia (now the Czech Republic and Slovakia), those countries pledge to defend one another in the event any of them is attacked. NATO altered perceptions of German identity and did the same thing for former Communist bloc states almost immediately.

There is still a divide within NATO between the original Cold War members and the newer, post–Cold War entrants, and this difference colors how states view issues such as Russia as a threat or support for continued U.S. hegemony. Members of a community are not always in agreement, but cooperation is more likely not simply because of a common threat or the structure of the organization, but because repeated interaction changed the identities of the allies from states in anarchy to members of a community.

The United States and Cuba have a history of tension going back to the rise of Fidel Castro in 1959. Prior to that, though, the two countries had close relations, with many in the United States seeing Cuba almost like a protectorate—although good Marxists would say that relationship was nothing more than the United States exploiting Cuba, its resources, and its people. This case provides two different examples of how identities can change, almost without warning. The first comes with the ascension of Castro to power and how the U.S. response pushed Cuba into the Soviet sphere of influence. The second comes more than fifty years later, when President Barack Obama announced that the United States would begin to normalize relations with Cuba.

Prior to the Castro revolution in 1959, the United States and Cuba had good relations, although many would suggest that Cuba was simply a puppet state under U.S. control. A U.S. Navy base at Guantanamo Bay, controlled since 1903, does little to dispel this notion of Cuba being a U.S. possession.

There is enough information now to believe that Castro was not necessarily anti-American, but that U.S. attempts to overthrow his government, both politically and militarily, forced him to seek relations with the Soviet Union simply to avoid losing power. President Dwight Eisenhower even refused to meet with Castro when the new leader visited Washington, DC in April 1959, only four months after the Cuban revolution. Eisenhower went golfing, and Castro met with the fervently anti-communist vice president, Richard Nixon. In other words, U.S. anti-communism was so visceral in this case that it worked against U.S. interests. U.S. antagonism likely pushed Castro to align with the Soviets, which led to both the Bay of Pigs invasion, one of the worst failures in U.S. foreign policy, and the Cuban Missile Crisis, one of the most potentially dangerous events in the Cold War.

While realists and liberalists have explanations for these shifts in interest—obviously, if Cuba views the United States as a threat, then it will seek an alliance with the Soviets—they have trouble explaining the timing of the events, as well as the nonmaterial factors that contribute to those choices. For constructivists, the identity crafted by Castro as a nationalist and a socialist was necessary for him to lead the revolution against Cuba's leader, Fulgencio Bautista, who was unpopular and perceived as an American puppet. Yet Americans assumed those ideas were directed against the United States, with Castro creating an identity that U.S. decision-makers could not tolerate so close to U.S. territory, particularly during the Cold War. But Castro's ideas also fit well with what the Soviets were looking for in partners, especially in the Western Hemisphere. As a result, for more than five decades, the United States and Cuba existed in a state of persistent tension that survived even the fall of the Soviet Union and the end of the Cold War.

Although the Obama administration did not make any promises about its plans for opening up relations with Cuba, there was hope that Cuban-Americans would be allowed to return to Cuba to visit family they had not seen in a while. What became known as the "Cuban thaw" was likely a function of Fidel Castro's withdrawal from power as his health continued to decline, as well as President Obama's openness to change.[31]

From December 2014 until March 2016, embassies reopened, Cuba was removed from the U.S. list of state sponsors of terrorism, travel restrictions were lifted, and Obama visited Cuba, the first president to do since 1928. Castro's death in November 2016 could have improved U.S.-Cuban relations even more; however, the Trump administration reversed course on most of Obama's policies toward Cuba.[32] This illustrates how relations between states can quickly change, for the better or for the worse. States that were enemies can become partners when facing a common adversary, or simply because they choose to stop treating each other like enemies. Changes can also occur in the opposite direction, when partners or allies become adversaries. This is consistent with the realist notion of "today's friend is tomorrow's enemy" but better reflects the core constructivist idea that identities influence behavior and that behavior likewise can help either change or solidify an identity.

Examples of these types of international transformations abound in world politics. Another recent one is the shift in the U.S. focus away from the war on terror to paying more attention to great power competition because of statements in the U.S. National Defense Strategy. On the positive side, this suggests that the lack of positive relations between the United States and states like Iran and North Korea can improve if the right personalities are in place to take advantage of strategic opportunities for change. There was some optimism over Trump's historic visit to the demilitarized zone in June 2019. The meeting with North Korean leader Kim Jong-Un could have been a first step toward that shift. But at least so far, no second step appears to have been taken by either state, and that highlights the realist critique of constructivism's focus on identities. There is no way to know ahead of time that certain actions will contribute to a change in identity, either for positive or negative.

CONSTRUCTIVISM AND ARTIFICIAL INTELLIGENCE IN SCIENCE FICTION

> The war had to be the Mind's idea; it was part of their clinical drive to clean up the galaxy, make it run on nice, efficient lines, without waste, injustice or suffering. The fools in the Culture couldn't see that one day the Minds would start thinking how wasteful and inefficient the humans in the Culture themselves were.
>
> —IAIN BANKS, *Consider Phlebas*

Although there are elements of constructivism in several science fiction stories, few authors set out to create constructivist science fiction. Therefore, the emphasis in this section is on the role of AI while pointing out those elements of stories that are consistent with constructivist ideas about international politics. The goal is to bring these two strands of thought closer together. Part of it has to do with the constructivist notion that nothing about the future is predetermined by material measures of power. Instead, the future is the result of individual choices, based on each actor's perception of reality. All the choices then combine to construct the world in which the actors operate. As a result, even stories with an AI fit within the purview of the constructivist worldview, if they provide some agency to human beings.

Science fiction can be a powerful tool of social critique. Just as classical literature critiqued parts of society—William Shakespeare being an early example of this, and Jonathan Swift's *Gulliver's Travels* being another classical example—much of science fiction addresses contemporary problems, issues, or threats placed in a fictional setting, usually at some point in the future. This is the normative part of science fiction, where authors construct future worlds to call attention to problems in our own, frequently suggesting novel ways to look at or even resolve those problems. If such worlds can exist in an author's mind, they are also possible to construct, just as much of modern technology can be traced to science fiction ideas in the past. Janice Liedl even suggests that science fiction, especially alternate histories, offers a way of better understanding our past through the role that individuals, ideas, and identities played in shaping the present, and how they will continue to shape our future.[33]

Much of science fiction also draws on Donna Haraway's concept of "situated knowledges," which means that facts exist, but they are known and understood according to one's identity and perspective.[34] This is the reason people interpret science fiction stories differently depending on what they brought to the story when they read it. Although much of Haraway's work is feminist, a lot of her writing crosses over into both constructivism and technology.

It is also important, within the context of this book, to divide artificial intelligences in science fiction into categories according to how they view and act toward humanity. As the scenario at the start of this chapter highlights, there are different futures resulting from an AI that is benevolent versus one that is ambivalent toward humanity, not to mention one that is malevolent toward humans. Even within those categories, though, there are computers that are completely autonomous and capable of operating without human interaction (though they may still require some human creative thinking), those that are capable of thinking for themselves but still require human inputs, and those that are incredibly intelligent but still primarily under the control of humans. To complicate matters further, whether an AI is benevolent or malevolent will depend on one's point of view about its actions and purpose.

Robert Heinlein's *The Moon Is a Harsh Mistress* is briefly mentioned in chapter 5 because of the moon's plan to revolt against Earth. But it is an even more relevant story for this chapter because one of the primary conspirators or revolutionaries is the first self-aware computer, Mike. Although relatively naïve about many things, Mike is capable of reading and absorbing vast amounts of information and calculating probabilities about future outcomes—so much so that the revolution becomes completely dependent on his decision-making, based on whatever information he can obtain, combined with assumptions he makes about what Earth will do at each step. He struggles with more artistic and conceptual endeavors, such as understanding poetry and humor, but he is quite competent as an analytical thinker. He is also creative, at least within the boundaries of what his programming allows, which is largely based on what he has read.

The advantage for the revolutionaries is that nobody knows Mike has reached self-awareness except for the core inner circle. By the end of the story, Mike disappears. Those who were aware of his existence think he may have been destroyed, though we never find out if he "died" or if he is simply playing possum. While Mike is helpful to the revolutionaries on the moon, he does not refrain from targeting humans on Earth, so one cannot view him as entirely benevolent. His programming is neutral, but his friendship drives his choices. Another way to think of it is that he is a weapon, not necessarily good or bad, but useful to those that would use him to target anyone who tries to stop them from achieving their goals. In the hands of humans, such a tool can be used for all types of nefarious purposes even if the AI itself is not prone to violence. That would fit a more realist version of the scenario but is not necessarily contrary to constructivism, because humans still create their own reality.

In the case of Mike, if Earth knew of his existence, it would clearly see him as a threat, capable of launching deadly projectiles from the moon to Earth. This would make Mike a high-value target to be destroyed, despite his existence being a major technological breakthrough. On the other hand, those on the moon familiar with who Mike is see him as providing an opportunity to live free from Earth's control. As a result, perceptions of Mike's intentions vary according to one's views of his purpose and the actions he takes to achieve that goal. They also then differ in how they would interact with Mike.

Chapter 5 discussed Iain Banks' *The Culture* series, which is relevant because it is about a future in which artificial intelligence, known as the Culture, has taken over and provided humanity with solutions to all its problems. At the same time, it faces resistance from the Idirans, a religious extremist race that opposes the decision-making of computers. The Culture is an ideal utopia, with a post-scarcity economy—almost a Marxist dream. Yet it is not ideal for the Idirans, who fight to preserve their religious beliefs. Even those who embrace the Culture's world have few ambitions or aspirations to the point where, despite the advanced knowledge and technology of the Culture, humanity becomes stagnant. Stagnation is a common theme of science fiction, when humans lose the will to innovate or create, and it also figured into the decline of empires, as discussed in chapter 1.

The Culture also, curiously, depends on some of the more strategic thinkers among the humans, because as smart and capable as the Minds are, having the ability to construct spacecraft that think, the Culture struggles to anticipate the actions of free-thinking Idirans on a strategic level. To counter the creativity of a free-thinking nonmachine, the Culture must rely on the creative thinking of biological entities. We see this in many works of science fiction involving AI. The ability to gather information and calculate results is incredible, but the ability to think creatively is often lacking in even the most sophisticated computers. Thus, the ability to think strategically must often be accomplished by humans. In a scenario with malevolent AI, that gives humans at least some chance of being able to resist and survive.

There are also several television shows and movies about self-aware computers turning against humans. Perhaps the most famous of these is Stanley Kubrick's *2001: A Space Odyssey*, based on the Arthur C. Clarke book. Continuing with the theme of lacking creative thought, the HAL9000 computer kills the crew of the ship, but not because it is evil (though that is certainly the impression one gets from the first film).[35] HAL receives orders about its mission that conflict with its general programming, and this tension causes it to see eliminating the human crew as the only way to avoid the programming conflict.

The Isaac Asimov short story "Runaround" has a similar theme of conflicting orders and potentially endangering humans as a result, though unintentionally. This story is Asimov's first time spelling out his Three Laws of Robotics: "One, a robot may not injure a human being under any conditions—and, as a corollary, must not permit a human being to be injured because of inaction on his part. . . . Two . . . a robot must follow all orders given by qualified human beings as long as they do not conflict with Rule 1. . . . Three: a robot must protect his own existence, as long as that does not conflict with Rules 1 and 2."[36] The story also illustrates how those laws can conflict with one another because of flawed or vague orders or just lazy and imprecise use of language.

The television show *Battlestar Galactica* takes this one step further with sophisticated autonomous robots built by humans who come to view humanity as the enemy. It is a story of technology turning against its creators. In the original series, the cylons are machines built by a race of reptilians, who are then betrayed by those machines. The newer version still includes cylon machines but also has synthetic models that are indistinguishable from humans. In both the original and the updated television shows, the only human ship that escapes the attack by the cylons is the less sophisticated, less advanced *Galactica*, whose older computer systems are less vulnerable to the more advanced cylon attacks. In other words, consistent with Sun Tzu, if one's adversary gains an advantage by using advanced technology, one way to counter that is to not be reliant on technology.

Two other less well-known novels that portray different aspects of a future with AI are *The Adolescence of P-1* and *The Two Faces of Tomorrow*. *The Adolescence of P-1* is about a self-aware computer created mostly by mistake; Gregory Burgess, an amateur programmer, was simply trying to access computer systems by creating a program that learned to defend itself. Over several years, it learns to connect to other computers through telephone lines, finds Burgess (who was unaware of its continued existence and intellectual growth), and uses him to gain even more knowledge. Eventually, the U.S. government becomes aware of P-1's existence and attempts to forge an alliance with it (presumably for use against the Soviet Union, given the book's 1979 publication).

Like the supercomputer in *The Moon Is a Harsh Mistress*, P-1 appears to be strongly connected to its human operator and may make decisions based on that relationship, but it is also capable of operating autonomously. Because P-1 sees Burgess as its creator and thus feels some level of connection to him, it generally follows his commands. But it also disregards Burgess when the commands go against the computer's interests. On several occasions, its original programming takes over when it sees threats to itself or to Burgess, and it takes actions that it sees as defensive, though the government views them as hostile. At one point, a plane crashes, killing all its passengers, including the government agent who initially investigated P-1 and first caught Burgess. P-1 admits to Burgess his involvement in the crash, which the government begins to suspect, especially after a second crash occurs under similarly suspicious circumstances. Eventually, upon threat of government action, P-1 destroys the building housing it, which effectively ends its existence.

The Two Faces of Tomorrow, written by James Hogan in 1979, portrays an interesting situation in which humanity has created an infant artificial intelligence and is unsure whether unleashing it would be good or bad. Humans create a space station for the express purpose of testing what will happen once the artificial intelligence is activated, while keeping it disconnected from society in a way that provides a firewall in case things go wrong. The backup plan is to destroy the station if things get out of hand. They build a survival instinct into the AI and then begin probing how it will react to attempts to both attack it and turn it off.

While the experiment begins smoothly, it quickly escalates to involve fatalities as the computer system comes to see the humans in the space station as threats to its existence, precisely because they could turn the system off. The computer experiences fear, but it also comes to realize that humans are attacking it out of fear. Once both it and the humans on the station recognize this shared trait, it is easier for both to understand why they act the way they do. This outcome is directly related to constructivist notions of international politics, because if actors can recognize the other is operating out of fear rather than hostile intent, it becomes easier to cooperate to build trust. But it is also about communication, the lack of which is something defensive realists see as a key source of conflict and that is prevalent as a source of war in several science fiction stories, such as *Forever War* and *Ender's Game*.

In discussing AI, one cannot ignore the cyberpunk genre within science fiction, perhaps most epitomized by Vernor Vinge's *True Names* and William Gibson's *Neuromancer*. In both stories and many others like them, entire worlds are created in cyberspace, although *True Names* does not contain AI. While the technology in these stories is somewhat outdated, the ideas in them are what link future advances in technology to constructivism in international politics. If one can create new, artificial worlds, do we need to reevaluate what we think we know about international politics? Or will many of the ideas discussed throughout this book remain valid?

One can also draw direct connections between constructivism and the frequent references to utopia in science fiction, such as Arthur C. Clarke's *Childhood's End*, Ursula Le Guin's *The Dispossessed*, and Ernest Callenbach's *Ecotopia*. In a pejorative sense, some scholars have taken to calling constructivism idealism because of its normative approach to international politics, identifying more what states should do than describing what they do or explaining why.[37] Some of the best science fiction works about utopias highlight that no such places exist because there are always going to be problems and challenges, and these "utopian" societies often become, or are more accurately described as, dystopias. Through a more positive lens, utopias are about what is possible. That is what many constructivists suggest when they argue against the notion of anarchy necessarily creating conditions for conflict.

ANALYSIS

> If . . . when in chaos they cannot be governed, they may be compared to arrogant children and cannot be used.
> —SUN TZU, *The Art of War*

In a future involving artificial intelligence, it is possible that humans will still engage in wars with one another. A realist version of this scenario would expect states to develop separate AIs to help pursue national interests, and then pit those AIs against one another. In such situations, AI will be just another weapon of war. Where there may be variation is whether the AIs would simply elevate the science of killing humans or would alter the nature of war in some way to avoid human fatalities.

In other scenarios, where an AI spans or even breaks down national boundaries and brings states together to cooperate, the most likely sources of conflict will be between the AI itself and those who view the AI as a threat to their belief systems, either for ideological or religious reasons.

The scenario at the start of this chapter included two possible futures. One (scenario 7a) involved a future AI that is benevolent toward humans, desiring to serve us in the best possible way without harming us or the world in which we live. In the other (scenario 7b), the AI is not

TABLE 7.1. **EVALUATING TWO AI FUTURES**

MEASURES OF EVALUATION	SHORT-TERM		LONG-TERM	
	7A	7B	7A	7B
Minimizing war	Yes	Yes	Yes	No
Human expansion	Yes	Yes	Yes	Yes (but not human expansion)
Enhancing S&T	Yes	Yes	Yes	Yes (in areas not helpful to humans)
Improving SoL	Yes	Yes	Yes	No

necessarily malevolent but is more ambivalent toward humans, particularly when its interests or purposes conflict with those of humanity. In both cases, the short-term benefits are overwhelmingly positive, at least along the four measures used in this book (see table 7.1). Major wars are reduced, humans expand into space, science and technology grow, and human standards of living improve. The two scenarios diverge in their long-term effects.

In the benevolent case, each of these benefits continues indefinitely. While an AI might not be able to stop all forms of violence, it will be able to prevent large-scale violence on both the international and intrastate level. In the ambivalent case, there is no reason for the AI to continue reducing the likelihood of war or improving standards of living, since those are human issues that have little to do with the computer's existence or ability to perform its functions. Science and technology will continue to advance but only in ways that are beneficial to the AI. In some cases, these advances may even be harmful to some segments of humanity. Likewise, the AI will continue with its expansion into space but not necessarily in ways that involve or even benefit humanity. Even if a future AI does not intend to do harm to humans, its ambivalence toward humanity could have almost as harmful of an effect. Because we have no idea how a true AI will behave toward humans, and because there is such a difference in outcomes between the benevolent and ambivalent scenarios, one might conclude that it is too much of a risk to allow a scenario to come about where humans do not have complete control over an AI, even if it appears harmless in the beginning.

In both of this chapter's scenarios, the AI promotes greater levels of cooperation between states, at least in the short term. In the ambivalent scenario, once the AI leaves, it is possible that humans will revert to the status quo ante and again take up arms for national causes or divide along some other political lines. For realists, that would be not only possible but also likely. However, the promise of AI is that it will solve, or at least ameliorate, many of the problems that drive states to go to war with each other, whether they involve resource scarcity, uncertainty over state intentions, or lack of societal openness. An AI that can address these issues may not eliminate all forms of violence but will reduce its likelihood by resolving many of the current sources of conflict between states.

There is also the slim possibility that an AI could create more conflict than it resolves. The underlying assumption in both scenarios in this chapter is that humanity will benefit in some ways from the creation of an AI. One cannot ignore the possibility, however slim, that an AI will turn on humanity and create more violence. However, one of the dangers of artificial intelligence is that if it begins to think of humans as arrogant children who can be neither governed nor used, what prevents future computer systems from viewing humanity as expendable or even as a threat to its own existence? Books like H. G. Wells's *War of the Worlds* and Orson Scott Card's *Ender's Game*, as well as such films as *Independence Day* and *Mars Attacks*, discuss humanity coming together to fight against an alien invader. So too might humans cooperate when faced with a malevolent AI.

The scenario did not examine the possibility of a malevolent AI, but it is worth examining how that future would score on these measures. War would likely occur, pitting humans against the AI, and standards of living would likely decline. There may be space exploration and S&T advances, but not in ways that benefit humanity. The result would be the worst case of all the scenarios in the book. That is perhaps what makes it a compelling story, as in the *Terminator* and *Matrix* franchises and in Ann Leckie's *Ancillary Justice* and Daniel Wilson's *Robopocolypse*. Harlan Ellison's short story "I Have No Mouth, and I Must Scream" sees AI used by states to wage war until no states are left to fight, and only the AI remains to govern the handful of remaining people.[38]

SUMMARY

> If was one thing all people took for granted, was conviction that if you feed honest figures into a computer, honest figures come out. Never doubted it myself till I met a computer with a sense of humor.
>
> —ROBERT HEINLEIN, *The Moon Is a Harsh Mistress*

Although technology provides humanity with the solution to many problems, dependence on advanced technologies can create unintended consequences, illustrated particularly well in Arthur C. Clarke's short story "Superiority." In the story, told after a future war in space, the imprisoned leader of one side discusses his side's failing, which was to focus too much on technology without developing a strategy and then being vulnerable to the success or failure of ever-advancing technology.[39] The same lesson applies to AI. Without a strategy for how to develop and then use it in a way that benefits humanity, we leave ourselves open to the dangers of uncertainty, vulnerable to the choices of an entity that we do not understand.

In his discussion of the difference between tactics and strategy, Sun Tzu offers, "Men all know the disposition by which we attain victory, but no one knows the configuration through which we control the victory."[40] This suggests that tactics are generally obvious, while strategy is both difficult and paramount. Without a strategy, particularly when we are talking about advanced technologies, two things will happen. First, we will develop technologies without an understanding of how best to use them. Second, the search for new technologies will drive our strategies, with the goal being to advance technology itself rather than striving for what is in the national, or international, interest.

It seems unlikely humans could avoid creating an AI if it is technologically possible at some point. We will have to do what we can to make it cooperative, but we must have a strategy for addressing the potential negative outcomes. An AI will not be a particularly creative or strategic thinker, and that will be the advantage humans have. There is often an assumption that artificial intelligences will aid in decision-making because the AIs will be able to incorporate more information than humans could and thus provide more intelligent decisions. However, these decisions will still necessarily be made within the rules created by the programming. Such systems will be incredibly useful at predicting the behavior of other artificial intelligences. At the same time, and ironically, such systems will be vulnerable to the kind of creative thinking that humans are capable of performing. As Sun Tzu puts it, "Thus it is said if you know them and know yourself, your victory will not be imperiled. If you know heaven and know Earth, your victory can be complete."[41] This passage is perhaps even more true for AI than it is for humans, considering we know little about how an AI would behave toward humans.

A scenario in which a benevolent AI helps humanity improve cooperation, technology, and space exploration is an incredible possibility to consider. The problem is there is no guarantee that an AI will react this way. It is also possible that an AI will come to see humans as annoying and ignore us or perceive us as a threat to its existence that needs to be eliminated. In some way, these opposing views of AI mirror the realism-liberalism debate over the consequences of human nature, but it really fits the constructivist view. For constructivists, just as states can create a system that is prone to conflict, they can also construct one that promotes cooperation. The same holds true for AI. An AI that we construct to promote cooperation will have a different effect on humanity than one designed to fight wars more effectively.

CONCLUSION

Thus it is said that one who knows the enemy and knows himself will not be endangered in a hundred engagements.
— SUN TZU, *The Art of War*

Sun Tzu tells us that before engaging in war, a successful leader must know their own strengths and weaknesses as well as those of their adversary. Only by having that information can one hope to achieve victory. There are two problems with this notion. The first is that even having enough information to know oneself and one's enemy is not sufficient for victory, nor is it even necessary. Bringing in Clausewitz's friction of war, which he describes as "the force that makes the apparently easy so difficult,"[1] reminds us that even having full information cannot prevent the uncertainties of war from affecting the outcome; nor is it impossible for the side with the least information to get lucky and win.

The second problem is that one never knows that information with any degree of certainty. A leader can make solid estimates regarding their own interests and capabilities, but those of an adversary are at best educated guesses. Sun Tzu also omits the other parts of the equation: that an adversary is actively trying to mislead about both their intentions and their capabilities to achieve their own victory. As a result, war is always an uncertainty. The broader point here, and the one most applicable to this book, is that since we can never know the enemy, the only variable over which we have some control is to know ourselves. Unless we understand ourselves, we have no hope of preparing for a future that will benefit humanity, either on Earth or in space. This book, then, has attempted to provide insight into some of the different approaches to thinking about the possibility for cooperation and conflict in the future, parsed according to the various perspectives of international relations, and supported by historical cases and science fiction stories that represent various visions of humanity's future.

The seven scenarios presented in this book explore some of the most prominent perspectives from international relations as they might pertain to humanity's future in space. Realism, liberalism, Marxism, feminism, and constructivism each provide a distinct take on our future, and while there are multiple variations possible within each of the scenarios, the core assumptions and ideas offer insight into the paths that will provide the greatest opportunities for the advancement of humanity, both socially and technologically. They also provide a glimpse into some of the darker possible futures.

REVIEWING THE CHAPTERS

All seven chapters followed the same format. They began with a scenario about a possible future followed by discussions of the IR worldview that formed the basis of that scenario, historical cases that illustrated what that type of behavior looked like in the past, and science fiction stories with similar plots or themes. Each chapter then evaluated the positive and negative sides of the scenario using the four measures of human advancement discussed in the introduction.

The first two scenarios draw from two of the most prominent variants of the realist worldview. All forms of realism see states as the primary actor in international politics, and this will continue in space. What distinguishes the first two scenarios is whether those actors pursue power and empire or are content with a balance of power and the security it provides. The first chapter covers offensive realism and topics such as hegemony and imperialism, balances of power, and preventive versus preemptive action. The scenario discusses the rise of a hegemon in the solar system and how that is likely to play out, with its demise due to a combination of balancing coalitions and overstretch. To illustrate the effects of this scenario on human advancement, this chapter draws on the history of empires, specifically the Romans and the British, discussing aspects of their rise and fall. This chapter also discusses several science fiction stories involving empires, including *Dune*, *Foundation*, and *Star Wars*.

The second chapter responds with defensive realism and topics such as polarity, relative gains, the security dilemma, and mercantilism. It also briefly touches on some of the other variants of realism. In this scenario, multiple states compete for influence over the solar system, resulting in major wars between the powers. Historical cases include the multipolar pre–World War I era and the bipolar Cold War. Science fiction discussions center around stories that involve planets competing with one another, such as *Leviathan Wakes* and *Moving Mars*.

Although liberalists see states as the most important actors, one way they depart from realists is by incorporating other important actors into their theories. The two liberalist chapters address this departure as well as divisions within liberalism by focusing on futures where states play more of a secondary role. Chapter 3 discusses international institutions and regimes, absolute gains, and collective security versus collective defense. It draws on the Concert of Europe, NATO, and the UN for its historical cases. In the scenario, states form a unifying body and create a federation, first for space exploration but eventually for broader purposes. *Star Trek*, *Forever War*, and *Starship Troopers* are key pieces of science fiction that informed this chapter.

Chapter 4 focuses on the side of liberalism that emphasizes economics. This chapter explores sovereignty, liberal economics, and interdependence theory, as well as nonstate actors. In this chapter's scenario, corporations take over for states as the dominant political actor, but competition drives them to behave like states in terms of a willingness to use force to pursue their self-interests. The chapter then examines cases of powerful nonstate actors in the past, such as the House of Medici, the British and Dutch East India Companies, and the United Fruit Company.

Marxists represent the first of three chapters based on reflective or critical theories. Chapter 5 focuses on class, rather than states or other actors, as a source of conflict and highlights the work of Marx and others who seek to explain conflict and politics through the lens of class divisions. This chapter discusses Marxist politics and economics, dependency theory, and theories of revolution. For its history, it examines the French, Russian, and Iranian revolutions. Although Marxism faded somewhat with the end of the Cold War, many of these ideas still thrive as part of world systems theory and will likely reemerge in the future if workers in space feel they are being exploited by states, a world government, or private companies. That is precisely what happens in this scenario, where lunar and Martian workers feel exploited by not only Earth but also others in space who are better off than them. Attempts to buy off the workers only delay the start of an independence movement and revolution. Science fiction discussed in this chapter includes *Red Mars*, *Red Rising*, and *The Moon Is a Harsh Mistress*.

Chapter 6 takes a feminist approach to humanity's future in space by exploring the possibility of an all-female space program. In this scenario, women inhabit the solar system to the exclusion of men, at least initially for practical reasons. Although cooperation is expected, the colonies find other ways to engage in competition. This chapter discusses some of the most prominent views of feminism, especially how they compare to the other worldviews in this book. The chapter discusses gender inequality, the role of culture, and the participation of women in war. It also discusses prominent female national leaders such as Golda Meir, Margaret Thatcher, Indira Gandhi, and Benazir Bhutto, as well as female soldiers and terrorists. Science fiction stories in this chapter include *The Left Hand of Darkness*, *A Door into Ocean*, and *The Shore of Women*.

The last chapter draws from constructivism to highlight the future of space politics when humanity is no longer in charge. To account for the broad complexity of the topic, the scenario introduces two variants, one in which artificial intelligence is a benevolent servant to humanity and the other in which it is ambivalent toward humans. This chapter discusses several aspects of constructivism, including norms and identity, while also incorporating ideas about a future with advances in technology, including pantropy and transhumanism. Science fiction about AI is plentiful, but incorporating concepts of utopia and ideas related to constructivism are stories like *2001*, The Culture series, *The Two Faces of Tomorrow*, and *The Adolescence of P-1*.

In addition to these scenarios, histories, and discussions of science fiction related to the main theme, each chapter provides an assessment of the scenarios according to four measures of human advancement. These are discussed below along with an analysis of which scenario presents the future in which humanity has the greatest likelihood of prospering.

EVALUATING THE METRICS

Since science is the engine of prosperity, nations that turn their backs on science and technology eventually enter a downward spiral.
—MICHIO KAKU, *The Future of Humanity*

Each chapter uses four primary metrics to measure the scenario and futures of humanity: minimizing war, the expansion of humanity into space, the enhancement of science and technology, and improving standards of living. These four measures parallel the four pillars of interest highlighted in several U.S. National Security Strategies. They refer to international order, security, prosperity, and principles, respectively. The results appear in a table toward the end of each chapter and are summarized in table C.1. I will next discuss how the scenarios score on each of the four measures and then tally the results to provide a final assessment of the scenarios from most beneficial to least beneficial to humanity.

Future war is intended to be a measure of future peace and stability for humanity. I interpret stability, or international order, as minimizing major wars between the primary political actors of the era, whether they continue to be nation-states or some other actors such as multinational corporations or entire planets. There is no expectation that we can eliminate violent conflict from the human experience, but we can hope to minimize its destructiveness, especially against innocent civilians and bystanders. This becomes tricky in futures that are either dominated by corporations or where machines do all the fighting, because those scenarios could lead to a change in our definition of war or to a shift in the nature of war itself. If wars are to be fought by machines and have no effect on humanity at all, does that type of competition become the new norm—where the resort to violence might become even more common precisely because there is minimal risk to human life? Likewise, while we might define war today as taking place between two states, if the most significant forms of future violence are between nonstate actors, should that alter our thinking about war?

Several of the scenarios suggest that the short-term effects of a particular worldview would reduce the likelihood of war. The two realist scenarios have mixed results on minimizing wars in the short term. Both suggest that large, system-changing wars might decline in the short term, but neither can guarantee a reduction of all types of wars, or of other types of violence that might occur. The long-term prospects of avoiding major war are less likely. Only one scenario, the liberalist/federation (chapter 3), escapes wars in the long term. And even that outcome is debatable, because a realist would argue that the federation scenario is overly optimistic and does not reflect the likely reality. This might be a realist bias on the part of international relations theory and science fiction literature, but that bias is based on perceptions of how the world works, not of how we want the world to work, which *should* be about avoiding wars through almost any means. Even if this scenario is overly biased toward an optimistic, liberal future, the fact that none of the other scenarios result in long-term peace suggests there might be some value in at least attempting to create this one future where long-term reduction of wars is possible, even if only at the theoretical level.

The constructivist scenario has mixed results in the long term, because whether war will be avoided or not depends on who creates the first AI and how that actor uses it. If a state creates an AI to consolidate power and establish hegemony, then wars are just as likely as under a pure hegemonic scenario. On the other hand, an AI that humans create to enhance cooperation might increase the possibility of a federation scenario, thus reducing the likelihood of wars.

Two other scenarios provide ambiguous results because they suggest that violence of some form is likely to exist; it just might not appear to be war as we currently define it. The liberalist/corporate scenario (chapter 4) suggests that even if corporations become the dominant actor in the future, competition will lead to violent conflict, as much as if they were states. Similarly, the feminist scenario (chapter 6) offers that a future dominated by women will still have its share of violent competition.

Human expansion is a measure of security in the form of human survival. If we take security as the survival of the human species rather than simply the survival of a country, then space exploration is the most important step for ensuring humanity's continued existence. While humans inhabit only one planet, we risk extinction either by our own actions or through some sort of natural event. While human extinction might not occur for centuries, the survival of the species requires having a sustainable presence somewhere else in the solar system. It might be on the moon, on another planet, or in a manufactured permanent structure in space. In any event, some evolution of this sort is necessary for long-term human survival.

Human space exploration almost emerges as an irrelevant measure of advancement, not because it is not important, but because every scenario accepts the likelihood of exploration in the short term. And most see it lasting into the long term as well. Only two scenarios—the feminist (chapter 6) and the constructivist (chapter 7)—suggest that exploration might cease in the long term, and both of those results depend on a couple of important variables related to the worldviews.

In the feminist case, it is unclear how space exploration would factor into the long-term plans of female leaders. While men often respond with interest to surveys about space exploration, women are generally less enthusiastic. As a result, once there are other human settlements in the solar system, it is possible that the women in charge will decide that no further expansion is necessary or warranted. Even one other human outpost, if it can sustain itself, will vastly increase humanity's chances of survival. But broader exploration will further reduce the risk of extinction, and it is unclear from this scenario that much exploration would occur.

In the constructivist case, particularly in the scenario in which the artificial intelligence becomes ambivalent about humanity, there is reason to believe that if the AI develops an interest in space exploration, it would be more inclined to do so without the drain on resources required for humans to accompany the missions. As a result, one hypothetical future would see areas outside our solar system being explored, but not by or for humanity. Even if an ambivalent AI leaves humanity behind to explore the universe, humans will not be prevented from exploring on their own. But doing so will be more difficult, especially after years of dependence on AI to solve humanity's problems.

Prosperity for many in the future will depend on improvements in S&T, including advances in artificial intelligence, robotics, and human enhancement. Although such advances do not guarantee that everyone will be wealthier—and some types of advances could in fact widen the gap between the haves and the have-nots or increase the likelihood of violent conflict—it is merely intended to be a proxy for prosperity.

S&T also provides the hardest measure to predict in most of the scenarios. In the short term, every scenario suggests positive advancement in science and technology. There are three possible exceptions where advances might be limited or might occur only in certain areas. In the realist/balance of power scenario (chapter 2), technological advances are likely to be in the military domain, to ensure no one actor becomes too powerful. In the liberalist/corporate scenario (chapter 4), technological advances are likely to be limited to those areas that benefit the corporations at the top of the food chain. And the feminist scenario (chapter 6) suggests that there will be certain types of advances, but those will likely be different from current trends and different from what they would have been if men continued to be in charge (or even in a future with mixed and equal genders).

In the long term, the liberalist and constructivist scenarios (chapters 3 and 7) appear to offer the greatest promise for growth in science and technology. The liberalist/corporate scenario (chapter 4) is also optimistic about these types of advances, but as with short-term advances, they are likely to occur in ways that are beneficial to only the corporations in charge and not necessarily to all of humanity.

Both realist scenarios (chapters 1 and 2) are less optimistic about the advances that might occur in the long term, especially as they pertain to benefitting humanity. The Marxist future (chapter 5) is also pessimistic about science and technology, because under such systems there is little incentive to innovate, and whatever advances do occur tend to benefit only those in the upper classes. There is likewise little incentive for humans to innovate under an artificial intelligence (chapter 7), whether the AI views humans positively or in ambivalent terms. Technological advances will still occur; they will just be led by the AI itself.

Standard of living is a proxy for human principles and values—a reflection of how human standards of living will thrive or suffer under each scenario. Principles or values are the foundation for improving human standards of living, because without those improvements, people will find it increasingly difficult to pursue life, liberty, and happiness. The types of advances included here are those that would reduce poverty, hunger, and illness, not just for one population or class of people, but for all humans. This does not require equality of wealth or power as a Marxist might suggest, but that the scenario simply leads most people to be better off than they otherwise would be.

Only the liberalism/corporate and the Marxist scenarios (chapters 4 and 5) will not see improvements in this area, in either the short term or the long term. The feminist and constructivist/positive AI scenarios (chapters 6 and 7) see these as positive in the short term and the long term. The constructivist/ambivalent AI (chapter 7, scenario b) will be positive in the short term, but negative long-term results will emerge as the AI leaves humanity behind. The two realist and the liberalism/federation scenarios (chapters 1, 2, and 3) have mixed or conditional results for this measure for different reasons, but all of them having to do with the interests of the most powerful actors.

Realism/hegemony (chapter 1) might provide extensive benefits to human standards of living depending on whether the hegemonic actor is benevolent—seeking to improve the world for everyone—or malevolent—motivated by self-interest. Realism/balance of power (chapter 2) also depends on the nature of the states, in that while some states might value standards of living as a means by which to balance the ideological threat of others, other states might view resources spent on standards of living as a waste, diverting from other more important sources of power. The liberalism/federation scenario (chapter 3) also provides conditional results depending on the nature of the federation. Is it an entity that exists to serve humanity, or does it become interested only in serving itself (in which case the results may look more like those of the hegemon in chapter 1)?

RANKING THE SCENARIOS

> From out there on the Moon, international politics look
> so petty. You want to grab a politician by the scruff of the neck
> and drag him a quarter of a million miles out and say,
> "Look at that, you son of a bitch."
>
> —EDGAR MITCHELL, *quoted in* People *magazine, 8 April 1974*

By focusing on the scenarios as a whole rather than the individual measures of advancement, it is possible to rank each from most to least optimistic about the ability of that perspective to improve human existence. To score each of the scenarios, I count the number of measures that receive a positive score of "yes" and assign them two points each. Each mixed or conditional result receives one point. Each "no" receives zero points. Counting these up for all four measures and adding together both the short-term and long-term outcomes give a possible score range between zero and sixteen (summarized in table C.1).

Although there are seven primary scenarios, two of the scenarios are written to incorporate some variations (highlighted in the table with parenthetical notes in the time frame column). The liberalism/federation scenario relies on admittedly optimistic assumptions about the possibility of cooperation arising out of international organizations, international institutions, and international norms. A small variation of that scenario is based on the realist critique of liberalism being unrealistically optimistic, especially for long-term cooperation. As a result, there is a variant of that scenario with a liberalist short-term future and a more pessimistic long-term future (especially related to the likelihood of avoiding wars and of offering scientific and technological advances). The constructivist scenario has two distinct versions: one involving an AI that views humans positively, and the other with an AI that is ambivalent toward humans.

Table C.2 totals the points from table C.1 and lists the resulting futures in descending order from the most to the least beneficial scenario for humanity, in terms of the number of points each scenario scores.[2] Although the constructivist/positive AI scenario comes out on top (fifteen points), the separation between it and the other variant of an AI future (seven points) is significant. The differences in the scenarios are

TABLE C.1. **FINAL ASSESSMENTS OF ALL SCENARIOS**

SCENARIO	TIME FRAME	MINIMIZING WARS (STABILITY)	SPACE EXPLORATION (SECURITY)	SCIENCE & TECH (PROSPERITY)	STANDARD OF LIVING (PRINCIPLES)	YES / CONDITIONAL / NO
1: Realist (Hegemony)	Short-term	Mixed (only systemic wars)	Yes	Yes	Depends on nature of hegemon	2 / 2 / 0
	Long-term	No	Yes	Depends on nature of power transition	Depends on nature of hegemon	1 / 2 / 1
2: Realist (Balance of Power)	Short-term	Mixed	Yes	Yes (military only)	Depends on nature of balance and the actors	1 / 3 / 0
	Long-term	No	Yes	Yes (military only)	Mixed (only in some states)	1 / 2 / 1
3: Liberalist (Federation)	Short-term	Yes	Yes	Yes	Depends on nature of federation	3 / 1 / 0
	Long-term	Yes	Yes	Yes	Depends on nature of federation	3 / 1 / 0
	Long-term (Realist)	No	Yes	Depends on nature of challenger	Depends on nature of federation	1 / 2 / 1
4: Liberalist (Corporate)	Short-term	Yes	Yes	Yes (in limited areas)	No	2 / 1 / 1
	Long-term	No (but depends on the definition of war)	Yes	Yes (in limited areas)	No	1 / 1 / 2

enough to serve as a warning if we hope to rely on this form of future technology to solve all of humanity's problems. The constructivist scenario in which an AI views humans positively would be the optimal scenario (assuming we can count on achieving that version of AI), scoring fifteen points. However, the AI that is ambivalent toward humans ties

TABLE C.1 (cont.)

SCENARIO	TIME FRAME	MINIMIZING WARS (STABILITY)	SPACE EXPLORATION (SECURITY)	SCIENCE & TECH (PROSPERITY)	STANDARD OF LIVING (PRINCIPLES)	YES / CONDITIONAL / NO
5: Marxist	Short-term	Yes	Yes	Yes	No	3 / 0 / 1
	Long-term	No	Yes	No	No	1 / 0 / 3
6: Feminist	Short-term	Yes	Yes	Certain types	Yes	3 / 1 / 0
	Long-term	No (but depends on the definition of war)	Unclear	Certain types	Yes	1 / 2 / 1
7: Constructivist (AI)	Short-term (positive)	Yes	Yes	Yes	Yes	4 / 0 / 0
	Short-term (ambivalent)	Yes	Yes	Yes	Yes	4 / 0 / 0
	Long-term (positive)	Yes (if AI is collective and not nationalist)	Yes	Yes	Yes	3 / 1 / 0
	Long-term (ambivalent)	No	Yes (but not human expansion)	Yes (in areas not helpful to humans)	No	0 / 2 / 2

for last place with only eight points. There is no way to know in advance how an AI will view and subsequently behave toward humans, so if we assume a fifty-fifty chance of each variant occurring, then averaging those two scores gives us 11.5. Even if we assume an 85 percent chance of a future AI being positive toward humans rather than ambivalent

TABLE C.2. **SCENARIO RANKINGS**

IR WORLDVIEW	SCENARIO NUMBER	SCORE
Constructivist/Positive AI	7a	15
Liberalism/Federation	3	14
Liberalism/Federation (Realist critique)	3	11
Feminism	6	11
Realism/Hegemony	1	10
Realism/Balance of Power	2	9
Constructivist/Ambivalent AI	7b	8
Liberalism/Corporate	4	8
Marxism	5	8
Constructivist/Malevolent AI	n/a	4

(15*0.85 + 8*0.15 = 13.95 points), the total does not outweigh the risk of an ambivalent AI providing a less beneficial future than the liberalist/federation score of fourteen points.

None of the scenarios even factors in the possibility of an AI that is hostile toward humans (addressed in chapter 7), which has greater than a zero percent chance of happening and would hypothetically result in a score of four using the same standards of measurement. It scores "no" for minimizing war and standard of living in both the short and long term and earns mixed results for the other two measures. Space exploration would occur but not with humans, and there would be technological advances, but they would likely be directed against humans. So, while a friendly AI would be the best possible future, the risk of creating an alternative type of AI makes that scenario less than ideal.

As a result, scenario three (liberalist/federation) is the optimal future based on the analysis in the above seven chapters. Even if we accept some possibility that liberalists are overly optimistic and that in the long term the reality of realism will overtake any initial gains from cooperation, the benefits humanity derives from initially establishing a federation still put this scenario on top.

Although the constructivist/ambivalent AI, liberalism/corporate, and Marxist scenarios all result in the same score of eight, the Marxist scenario has more answers of "no" than the other two, so it places last of the three. The ambivalent AI has only two "no" answers, so it ranks ahead of the other two. The scenarios we should most strive to avoid are Marxism, liberalism in which corporations dominate the solar system, and any variant of realism. That does not mean these worldviews will not provide the best explanations for how humans will behave in the future. Nor does it mean that some parts of these scenarios could not be beneficial to humans. It merely highlights the benefits humanity could derive from approaching space differently from how we most frequently dealt with one another in the past.

WHERE DO WE GO FROM HERE?

The Tao causes the people to be fully in accord with the ruler.
[Thus] they will die with him; they will live with him
and not fear danger.
—SUN TZU, *The Art of War*

It is difficult to say what is impossible, for the dream
of yesterday is the hope of today and reality of tomorrow.
—ROBERT H. GODDARD, *June 1904*[3]

One of the common themes from all seven scenarios, though one which is incredibly pessimistic, is the strong possibility of violent conflict in the long term. Regardless of which IR perspective provides the most accurate picture of the future, every scenario, even those with generally optimistic and cooperative views of human nature, involves a high likelihood of future violence. Having our future conflicts involve attacks in cyberspace, battles between autonomous machines rather than humans, or subtle forms of sabotage rather than large clashes of violence may not fit our current notions of war. But whether one calls these wars or not, they represent forms of future conflict, which appears to be a permanent feature of human nature.

This book has largely steered clear of discussions of morality or ethics, at least partly because the international relations worldviews generally avoid discussion of ethics. It is also because morals are individually subjective and ethics are culturally subjective, so it would be difficult to capture the relevance of such concepts in a book about possible future scenarios. Although Sun Tzu's quote above refers to moral influence, what he is really talking about is leadership and followership—the ability of a leader to get people to follow him or her, and the willingness of people not just to follow someone, but also to trust that by following them, they will all be better off.

What does that trust in leadership have to do with international relations theories or the seven future scenarios discussed in this book? For international relations, trust is tricky. People want to trust their government, governments want to trust their militaries, and states want to trust their allies. But trust is difficult to come by in an anarchic international system and in domestic political systems where power and information are the primary currencies. Realism corners the market on explaining state decisions through the lack of trust. Trust is also difficult for Marxists, feminists, and constructivists because all three highlight how years of experience create difficulties trusting the system as well as those in other groups. Even the more optimistic liberalist school of thought accepts that trust is difficult in international politics. Liberalists also offer, though, that trust can be gained through repeated interactions, honest communication, and good intentions. It also helps, at least according to some liberalists, for states to be democratic, to engage in free trade with other states, to belong to international organizations, to subscribe to international law, and to follow international norms.

The results of this project are not intended to be definitive or to solve any type of debate in international relations. Rather, they are meant to start a conversation about how our current understanding of international politics and history might help us better understand the many possible futures we face. Each scenario provides a forecast of a possible future, assuming that lone perspective is the most accurate prediction of human behavior in the future.

But no single worldview will be the exclusive explanation for the path humans take. They are not definitive predictions, nor will any one scenario likely occur in a vacuum. Instead, we are likely to see hybrids or mixtures of multiple scenarios. For example, one can imagine a future AI that complements each of the other scenarios, whether it is used by the state that invents it to establish hegemony, by multiple states to solidify a balance of power, by a community of states to establish a federation, by companies to maximize profits, or as part of an all-female future to help prevent men from venturing into space. We will all be motivated by different perspectives, often a hybrid of more than one worldview, yet we can still learn a great deal about our future by isolating each of the perspectives and identifying their strengths and weaknesses, or the ways in which each might benefit humanity as well as which ones might hinder human progress or even its survival. The ultimate purpose of this book is to get us thinking about the possible consequences of some of these scenarios, of the parallels that exist in humanity's past (at least when such parallels exist), and how popular works of science fiction represent those futures.

The results of this analysis are also intended as a normative statement about what humans should emphasize as we strive to extend civilization into space. Do we want a continuation of the politics of the past, with its nationalism, focus on power, and war? Do we want to alter our futures to provide humanity with the greatest advantages in terms of science and standards of living, free from war and insecurity and free to expand into the solar system (and eventually beyond)? If we want more of the same, then we should continue along the same course humans always have. If we are tired of the status quo, then we must start to make changes in our approach to space. What are those changes that need to occur? This book offers some suggestions and ideas, but humanity's future, ultimately, will be what we make of it.

NOTES

INTRODUCTION

1. There are several translations of Sun Tzu's *The Art of War*. This book relies on Ralph Sawyer's translation (Boulder, CO: Westview Press, 1994), though there are times when comparing translations is useful and informative. In such instances, I also use Samuel Griffith's translation (New York: Oxford University Press, 1971), or James Clavell's translation (New York: Delacorte Press, 1983).
2. Iver Neumann and Daniel Nexon, eds., *Harry Potter and International Relations* (Lanham, MD: Rowman and Littlefield, 2006); Nicholas Kiersey and Iver Neumann, eds., *Battlestar Galactica and International Relations* (Abingdon, UK: Routledge, 2013); Daniel Drezner, *Theories of International Politics and Zombies* (Princeton: Princeton University Press, 2014); Max Brooks et al., eds., *Strategy Strikes Back: How Star Wars Explains Modern Military Conflict* (Lincoln, NE: Potomac Books, 2018); and Max Brooks et al., eds., *Winning Westeros: How* Game of Thrones *Explains Modern Military Conflict* (Lincoln, NE: Potomac Books, 2019).
3. For example, Barack Obama, *National Security Strategy* (Washington, DC: The White House, 2010).
4. My interpretation of "greatest affair" is not that he assigns a positive value to it. Instead, it is the most important, critical-to-survival, activity in which a state can engage. Sun Tzu, *Art of War*, 167.
5. Randall Schweller, *Maxwell's Demon and the Golden Apple* (Baltimore: The Johns Hopkins University Press, 2014).
6. That is not to suggest that any of the other worldviews are homogenous. All have their internal debates and significant variations, but the literature on them is not as rich as the variations within realism and liberalism. But within every chapter, I discuss some of the ways that variations within each worldview might influence the scenario.
7. There are other variants of realism as well, including classical realism, structural realism, and neoclassical realism, each of which I discuss in chapter 2 after highlighting the primary differences between offensive and defensive realism.
8. Some scholars prefer the phrase "world systems theory" rather than Marxism. See, for example, Immanuel Wallerstein, "The Rise and Future Demise of the World Capitalist System: Concepts for Comparative Analysis," *Comparative Studies in Society and History* 16, no. 4 (September 1974): 396.

9. Paul Schroeder, "Historical Reality vs. Neo-Realist Theory," *International Security* 19, no. 1 (Summer 1994): 108–48, esp. 112–20.
10. For discussions of the importance of historical analogy, see Richard Neustadt and Ernest May, *Thinking in Time: The Uses of History for Decision-Makers* (New York: The Free Press, 1988); Yuen Foong Khong, *Analogies at War: Korea, Munich, Dien Bien Phu, and the Vietnam Decision of 1965* (Princeton: Princeton University Press, 1992).
11. As much as possible, I stay away from science fiction that does not involve exploration of space, while, with a few exceptions, avoiding literature that focuses on deep space exploration or distant worlds that are nothing like Earth (since doing so minimizes the parallels between the literature and our history).
12. Quoted by Arthur C. Clarke in Andrew Chaikin, "Meeting of the Minds: Buzz Aldrin Visits Arthur C. Clarke," *Space Illustrated*, 27 February 2001.
13. Reflective approaches challenge rational choice explanations of behavior and often take a post-positivist view of the world, meaning that behavior cannot be easily explained—much less predicted—as a product of cost-benefit analyses by rational actors.

CHAPTER 1. HEGEMONY

1. Most IR scholars identify states as the primary actor in international politics, referring to the government institutions that rule over territory and a population. States exercise sovereignty over both the territory and their people and are typically recognized as the legitimate authority by other actors in the system. One unknown is whether territories in space will be viewed as extensions of the state itself, with all the rights and privileges accorded to the population, or if they will be treated more like colonial possessions, much as the great powers of Europe treated their territorial possessions during the seventeenth through the twentieth centuries.
2. Frank Herbert, *Dune* (New York: Ace Books, 1990).
3. Schroeder, "Historical Reality vs. Neo-Realist Theory."
4. Mancur Olson, *The Logic of Collective Action: Public Goods and the Theory of Groups* (Cambridge, MA: Harvard University Press, 1965); Charles Kindleberger, *The World in Depression: 1929–1939* (London: Penguin, 1987); Robert Gilpin, *War and Change in World Politics* (Cambridge: Cambridge University Press, 1981); Duncan Snidal, "The Limits of Hegemonic Stability Theory," *International Organization* 39, no. 4 (Autumn 1984): 579–614; George Modelski and William Thompson, *Seapower in Global Politics, 1494–1993* (London: Palgrave Macmillan, 1988), esp. 97–132.
5. Robert Keohane, *After Hegemony: Cooperation and Discord in the World Political Economy* (Princeton: Princeton University Press, 1984).
6. Given the speed of technological advance, it is plausible that future hegemons will exist for even shorter periods than those in the past. Hegemonic decline may also occur more rapidly because of the high cost of space.

7. Cited in Allan Westcott, ed., *Mahan on Naval Warfare: Selections from the Writings of Rear Admiral Alfred T. Mahan* (Mineola, NY: Dover Publications, Inc., 1999), 77.
8. This view of the importance of choice is one of the ways the neoclassical realists diverge from both offensive and defensive realists. In accepting that government type influences the way states behave, many neoclassical realists accept liberalist concepts, such as the democratic peace theory, or that international organizations, laws, and norms influence state behavior. William Wohlforth, "Realism and the End of the Cold War," *International Security* 19, no. 3 (Winter 1994–95): 124; Randall Schweller, "New Realist Research on Alliances Refining, Not Refuting, Waltz's Balancing Proposition," *American Political Science Review* 91, no. 4 (December 1997): 927–30.
9. One scholar who discusses this, at least with respect to current U.S. policy, is Niall Ferguson, "Hegemony or Empire?," *Foreign Affairs* 82, no. 5 (September/October 2003): 154–61.
10. Hans Morgenthau, *Politics among Nations: The Struggle for Power and Peace* (New York: Alfred A. Knopf, 1954), esp. 56–82.
11. Hannah Arendt, *The Origins of Totalitarianism* (San Diego: Harcourt Brace Jovanovich, 1973).
12. Even Kipling's *Regulus*, about the Roman general, was a defense of imperialism for the value it brought to otherwise disadvantaged people. Disraeli was British prime minister from 1874 to 1880 and saw himself as an imperialist, advancing British interests around the globe. He viewed all countries as either having imperial ambitions or else being insignificant. Rudyard Kipling, *Kim* (London: Macmillan and Co., 1901); Rudyard Kipling, "The White Man's Burden: The United States and the Philippine Islands," in *Rudyard Kipling's Verse: Definitive Edition* (Garden City, NY: Doubleday, 1929); Benjamin Disraeli, *Tancred: Or, The New Crusade* (London: Henry Colburn, Publisher, 1847).
13. Paul Kennedy, *The Rise and Fall of the Great Powers: Economic Change and Military Conflict from 1500 to 2000* (New York: Vintage, 1989).
14. Robert Strassler, ed., *The Landmark Thucydides* (New York: Free Press, 1996), 5.97 (352).
15. Jeremy Black, *Great Powers and the Quest for Hegemony: The World Order since 1500* (London: Routledge, 2007), esp. 1–26 and 159–98.
16. There are already debates about the value of colonizing space relative to the disruption that would cause to the planetary environments. This theme is also prominent in several works of science fiction and is the closest parallel to the cost imposed by imperial powers on their new colonies. See, for example, several chapters from Charles Cockell, ed., *Human Governance beyond Earth* (Cham, CH: Springer, 2015).
17. Jack Levy, "Declining Power and the Preventive Motivation for War," *World Politics* 40, no. 1 (October 1987): 82–107; Dan Reiter, "Exploding the Powder Keg Myth: Preemptive Wars Almost Never Happen,"

International Security 20, no. 2 (Fall 1995): 5–34; Netta Crawford, "The Slippery Slope to Preventive War," *Ethics and International Affairs* 17, no. 1 (March 2003): 30–36; Karl Mueller et al., *Striking First: Preemptive and Preventive Attack in U.S. National Security Policy* (Santa Monica, CA: RAND, 2006).

18. This was frequently mislabeled a preemptive war by the Bush administration, probably a function of the two terms incorrectly being used interchangeably in the 2002 NSS.

19. Realists do not equate stability with peace; instead, instability refers to changes to the international system that bring about new great powers or see the fall of previous powers. Stability, then, is about preventing change to the system, which may require war to remove challenges to that system.

20. Paul Kennedy, *Rise of the Anglo-German Antagonism, 1860–1914* (London: Ashfield Press, 1987).

21. Plutarch, "On Tranquility of Mind," *Moralia*, vol. VI, trans. W. C. Helmbold (Cambridge, MA: Harvard University Press, 1939), 178–79. Misquoted by Alan Rickman's character, Hans Gruber, as: "And when Alexander saw the breadth of his domain, he wept for there were no more worlds to conquer." John McTiernan, dir., *Die Hard* (Twentieth Century Fox, 1988).

22. Germany had the means to conquer much of Europe, especially after German unification in 1871, but German chancellor Otto von Bismarck chose to establish a system of great European powers to preserve the status quo and prevent war between them. Thus, rather than seek hegemony, Bismarck promoted security and stability through the balance of power. Even after its victory in the Spanish-American War (1898), the United States still shied away from imperialism and power politics. The United States gained Cuba and the Philippines and became significantly more involved in global politics, but not until the end of World War II did the United States embrace its global power and influence.

23. Most of the Roman history cited here comes from Edward Gibbon, *The History of the Decline and Fall of the Roman Empire* (1776; London: Penguin, 2000).

24. Campaigns or battles took place against Germanic tribes, the Parthian Empire, the Dacian Kingdom, and in Judea, not to mention Rome was dealing with a handful of civil wars.

25. James Stephen, *Lectures on the History of France* (New York: Harper and Brothers Publishers, 1875), 686.

26. Interesting studies of the British imperial history can be found in Lawrence James, *The Rise and Fall of the British Empire* (New York: St. Martin's Griffin, 1997), and Niall Ferguson, *Empire: The Rise and Demise of the British World Order and the Lessons for Global Power* (New York: Basic Books, 1996).

27. Trantor was the name of the planet at the center of the Empire, where the Emperor resided, home to the greatest population density, and was where all of the decisions governing the Empire were made.

28. *Dune* is both book and feature films, but I deal here primarily with the book because the films have less discussion of the empire or the challenges to it (at least relative to the book and its sequels). In contrast, the *Star Wars* films spawned hundreds of books that take place in that universe, but my focus is on the films, particularly the original trilogy.
29. Despite earlier discussion of the difference between Empire and Hegemon, few science fiction stories use the term hegemon. Many use some form of empire, the description of which would fit most definitions of a hegemon, including the one used here. Therefore, in this section of each chapter, I use empire and hegemon interchangeably, while still acknowledging the difference between the two terms in the academic literature. One book that does refer to this form of universal government, though it is largely just environmental background, is the Hegemony of Man in Dan Simmon's *Hyperion* (New York: Doubleday, 1989).
30. Perhaps, only somewhat unintentionally, I wrote this book with similar intent.
31. Isaac Asimov even wrote two books on the Romans—*The Roman Republic* (Boston: Houghton Mifflin Harcourt, 1966) and *The Roman Empire* (Boston: Houghton Mifflin Harcourt, 1967)—so it is probably no coincidence that his Galactic Empire's rise and fall mirrors that of Rome.
32. Herbert, *Dune*, 11.
33. Herbert, 472.
34. I find no credible evidence that George Lucas intentionally gave his Star Wars Empire the same name as Asimov's central authority. Perhaps this is merely a coincidence or a product of obvious nomenclature.
35. Sun Tzu, *Art of War*, 173.
36. Christopher Chase-Dunn, Thomas Hall, and E. Susan Manning, "Rise and Fall: East-West Synchronicity and Indic Exceptionalism Reexamined," *Social Science History* 24, no. 4 (Winter 2000): 747.
37. T. E. Lawrence, *Seven Pillars of Wisdom* (1922; Herfordshire, UK: Wordsworth, 1997).
38. Henry Kissinger, "The Vietnam Negotiations," *Foreign Affairs* 47 (January 1969): 214.
39. Several realist scholars expected the unipolar system to be temporary. See, for example, Christopher Layne, "The Unipolar Illusion: Why New Great Powers Will Rise," *International Security* 17, no. 4 (Spring 1993): 5–51; Michael Mastanduno, "Preserving the Unipolar Moment: Realist Theories and U.S. Grand Strategy after the Cold War," *International Security* 21, no. 4 (Spring 1997): 49–88; Charles Kupchan, "After Pax Americana: Benign Power, Regional Integration, and the Sources of a Stable Multipolarity," *International Security* 23, no. 2 (Fall 1998): 40–79; William Wohlforth, "The Stability of a Unipolar World," *International Security* 24, no. 1 (Summer 1999): 5–41; Kenneth Waltz, "Structural Realism after the Cold War," *International Security* 25, no. 1 (Summer 2000): 5–41.

CHAPTER 2. THE BALANCE OF POWER

1. Outer Belt refers to the main asteroid belt, located between the orbits of Mars and Jupiter. Among the millions of objects, the belt contains four large asteroids (Ceres, Vesta, Pallas, and Hygeia) that together make up half the mass of the entire belt.
2. Lagrangian points (or Lagrange points) are the five spots—L_1 through L_5—where the gravitational forces from two large bodies, like a planet and its satellite or a planet and a star, allow a smaller object, like a satellite or space station, to maintain its position relative to the large bodies. Elizabeth Howell, "Lagrange Points: Parking Places in Space," *Space.com*, 21 August 2017, https://www.space.com/30302-lagrange-points.html.
3. An entente is an agreement that falls short of an alliance. It usually calls for discussion in the event that one member becomes a belligerent in a war, but it does not obligate members to commit forces or provide support.
4. Layne.
5. Waltz, *Theory of International Politics*, esp. 19–37; James Taliaferro, "Security Seeking under Anarchy: Defensive Realism Revisited," *International Security* 25, no. 3 (Winter 2000–1): 128–61.
6. Wohlforth, "Realism and the End of the Cold War."
7. John Herz, *Political Realism and Political Idealism: A Study of Theory and Realities* (Chicago: University of Chicago Press, 1951), esp. 157; Charles Glaser, "The Security Dilemma Revisited," *World Politics* 50, no. 1 (October 1997): 171–210; Andrew Kydd, "Game Theory and the Spiral Model," *World Politics* 49, no. 3 (April 1997): 371–400.
8. The Naval Defence Act of 1889 created the "two-power standard" by which the Royal Navy was required to maintain at least as many battleships as the next two largest navies combined. Previously, these were the navies of France and Russia, but Germany's naval build-up changed the calculus and contributed to British insecurity.
9. Kennedy, *Rise of the Anglo-German Antagonism*.
10. Deterrence is preventing an actor from doing something they would otherwise do. But successfully using deterrence, without provoking conflict, is more difficult than the definition suggests. It is also difficult to measure success because when deterrence works, nothing happens, so there is nothing to study. Thomas Schelling, *Arms and Influence* (Cambridge, MA: Harvard University Press, 1960); Glenn Snyder, *Deterrence and Defense: Toward a Theory of National Security* (Princeton: Princeton University Press, 1961); Robert Jervis, "Deterrence Theory Revisited," *World Politics* 31, no. 2 (January 1979): 289–324.
11. As Thomas Schelling wrote, "No one seems to doubt that federal troops are available to defend California. I have, however, heard Frenchmen doubt whether American troops can be counted on to defend France, or American missiles to blast Russia in case France is attacked." Schelling, *Arms and Influence*, 35.

12. Gideon Rose, "Neoclassical Realism and Theories of Foreign Policy," *World Politics* 5, no. 1 (October 1998): 144–72; Randall Schweller, "Neorealism's Status-Quo Bias: What Security Dilemma?" *Security Studies* 5, no. 3 (March 1996): 90–121.
13. Stephen Van Evera, "Offense, Defense, and the Causes of War," *International Security* 22, no. 4 (Spring 1998): 5–43; Sean Lynn-Jones, "Offense Defense Theory and Its Critics," *Security Studies* 4, no. 4 (June 1995): 660–91.
14. Jack Levy, "The Offensive/Defensive Balance of Military Technology: A Theoretical and Historical Analysis," *International Studies Quarterly* 28, no. 2 (June 1984): 219–38; Jonathan Shimshoni, "Technology, Military Advantage, and World War I: A Case for Military Entrepreneurship," *International Security* 15, no. 3 (Winter 1990–91): 187–215; Charles Glaser and Chaim Kaufmann, "What Is the Offense-Defense Balance and Can We Measure It?" *International Security* 22, no. 4 (Spring 1988): 44–82.
15. Stephen Van Evera, "The Cult of the Offensive and the Origins of the First World War," *International Security* 9, no. 1 (Winter 1984): 58–107.
16. Loren Thompson, "As Space War Looms, Air Force's Biggest Weakness May Be How It Buys Satellites," *Forbes*, 23 April 2018, https://www.forbes.com/sites/lorenthompson/2018/04/23/as-space-war-looms-air-forces-biggest-weakness-may-be-how-it-buys-space-systems/?sh=60c83eba78ab.
17. Ernst Haas, "The Balance of Power: Prescription, Concept, or Propaganda?" *World Politics* 5, no. 4 (July 1953): 442–47; Waltz, *Theory of International Politics*, esp. 50–59 and 116–28.
18. Stephen Walt, *The Origins of Alliances* (Ithaca: Cornell University Press, 1987), esp. 17–49.
19. Schweller, "New Realist Research on Alliances."
20. Gregory Miller, *The Shadow of the Past: Reputation and Military Alliances before the First World War* (Ithaca: Cornell University Press, 2012), esp. 92–125.
21. Paul Schroeder, "Alliances, 1815–1945: Weapons of Power and Tools of Management," in *Historical Dimensions of National Security Problems*, ed. Klaus Knorr (Lawrence: University Press of Kansas, 1976), 227–62; Patricia Weitsman, *Dangerous Alliances: Proponents of Peace, Weapons of War* (Stanford, CA: Stanford University Press, 2003); Jeremy Pressman, *Warring Friends: Alliance Restraint in International Politics* (Ithaca: Cornell University Press, 2008); Timothy Crawford, "Preventing Enemy Coalitions: How Wedge Strategies Shape Power Politics," *International Security* 35, no. 4 (Spring 2011): 155–89.
22. Glenn Snyder, "The Security Dilemma in Alliance Politics," *World Politics* 36, no. 4 (July 1984): 461–95.
23. Thomas Christensen and Jack Snyder, "Chain Gangs and Passed Bucks: Predicting Alliance Patterns in Multipolarity," *International Organization* 44, no. 2 (Spring 1990), esp. 140–44.

24. Kenneth Waltz, "The Stability of a Bipolar World," *Daedalus* 93, no. 3 (Summer 1964): 881–909.
25. Morgenthau, *Politics among Nations*, 272, 289; Karl Deutsch and David Singer, "Multipolar Power Systems and International Stability," *World Politics* 16, no. 3 (April 1964): 390–406.
26. One subset of a multipolar system is a tripolar system, with three major powers. These are rare in international politics because they are so unstable. More discussion of tripolar systems is in the science fiction section because several works use the instability of the tripolar system to set up the conditions for conflict. Randall Schweller, *Deadly Imbalances: Tripolarity and Hitler's Strategy of World Conquest* (New York: Columbia University Press, 1998).
27. Edward Mansfield, "Concentration, Polarity, and the Distribution of Power," *International Studies Quarterly* 37, no. 1 (March 1993): 105–28.
28. Joseph Grieco, "Anarchy and the Limits of Cooperation: A Realist Critique of the Newest Liberal Institutionalism," *International Organization* 42, no. 3 (Summer 1988), esp. 487–88.
29. Peter Liberman suggests that states will embrace free trade even in highly competitive systems. Peter Liberman, "Trading with the Enemy: Security and the Relative Economic Gains," *International Security* 21, no. 1 (Summer 1996): 147–75.
30. First strike is the ability to eliminate an adversary's ability to retaliate through some combination of surprise, defensive abilities, and numerical superiority. First strike is generally believed to be destabilizing because it leads others to attack rather than be caught off-guard. Thomas Schelling referred to this as "the reciprocal fear of surprise attack." Thomas Schelling, *The Strategy of Conflict* (Cambridge, MA: Harvard University Press, 1960): 207–29.
31. Edward Mead Earle, "Adam Smith, Alexander Hamilton, Friedrich List: The Economic Foundations of Military Power," in *Makers of Modern Strategy: From Machiavelli to the Nuclear Age*, ed. Peter Paret (Princeton: Princeton University Press, 1986), 217–61, esp. 232–34.
32. Eric Heginbotham and Richard Samuels, "Mercantile Realism and Japanese Foreign Policy," *International Security* 22, no. 4 (Spring 1998): 171–203.
33. Niccolò Machiavelli, *The Prince* (1532; London: Penguin 2011); Morgenthau, *Politics among Nations*.
34. Jack Snyder, *Myths of Empire: Domestic Politics and International Ambition* (Ithaca: Cornell University Press, 1991); Randall Schweller and William Wohlforth, "Power Test: Evaluating Realism in Response to the End of the Cold War," *Security Studies* 9, no. 3 (March 2000): 60–107. Snyder is often lumped in with the defensive realists because of the entirety of his work, but *Myths of Empire* makes a strong argument for several elements of neoclassical realism, given its focus on domestic political groups. Schweller and Wohlforth embrace their criticisms of defensive realism in

several works, but "Power Test" is perhaps the clearest discussion of their views for updating rather than abandoning realism after the Cold War.
35. Reinhold Niebuhr, *Moral Man and Immoral Society: A Study in Ethics and Politics* (New York: Scribners, 1932); Anatol Lieven and John Hulsman, *Ethical Realism: A Vision for America's Role in the World* (New York: Pantheon, 2006); Donald J. Trump, *National Security Strategy of the United States of America* (Washington, DC: The White House, December 2017), 1, 55.
36. Germany wanted England to join the Triple Alliance but would not reveal the terms of the secret treaty until the British joined. Between that and British perceptions of all three members being unreliable partners, the British opted not to join.
37. John White, *Transition to Global Rivalry: Alliance Diplomacy and the Quadruple Entente, 1895–1907* (Cambridge: Cambridge University Press, 2002); Ian Nish, *The Anglo-Japanese Alliance: The Diplomacy of Two Island Empires, 1894–1907* (London: Athlone Press, 1966); Miller.
38. "From Stettin in the Baltic to Trieste in the Adriatic, an iron curtain has descended across the Continent. Behind that line lie all the capitals of the ancient states of Central and Eastern Europe. Warsaw, Berlin, Prague, Vienna, Budapest, Belgrade, Bucharest and Sofia, all these famous cities and the populations around them lie in what I must call the Soviet sphere, and all are subject in one form or another, not only to Soviet influence but to a very high and, in many cases, increasing measure of control from Moscow." Winston Churchill, Westminster College, Fulton, Missouri, 5 March 1946.
39. John Lewis Gaddis, *Strategies of Containment* (New York: Oxford University Pres, 1982); Raymond Garthoff, *Détente and Confrontation: American-Soviet Relations from Nixon to Reagan* (Washington, DC: Brookings, 1994).
40. Waltz, *Theory of International Politics*, 161–70.
41. Scott Sagan and Kenneth Waltz, *The Spread of Nuclear Weapons: A Debate* (New York: W. W. Norton and Co., Inc., 1995), esp. 41–81; Scott Sagan, *The Limits of Safety: Organization, Accidents, and Nuclear Weapons* (Princeton: Princeton University Press, 1993).
42. Corey is the pen name of Daniel Abraham and Ty Franck. James S. A. Corey, *Leviathan Wakes* (New York: Orbit, 2011).
43. Germany, the Soviet Union, and the United States as the major powers, with England, France, and Japan as lesser great powers. Schweller, *Deadly Imbalances*, 18.
44. George Orwell, *1984* (Boston: Houghton Mifflin, 1949), 35.
45. Herbert, 23.
46. Greg Bear, *Moving Mars* (New York: Tor, 1993), 121.
47. Bear, 127.
48. Bear, 375.
49. Bear, 395.

50. NATO's first secretary general, Lord Hastings Lionel Ismay, prior to accepting the position.
51. Lawrence Kaplan, *NATO Divided, NATO United: The Evolution of an Alliance* (Westport, CT: Praeger, 2004), 148.
52. Randall Schweller, "Bandwagoning for Profit: Bringing the Revisionist State Back In," *International Security* 19, no. 1 (July 1994): 79–81.
53. Anglo-Polish Agreement (March 1939); Kasprzycki-Gamelin Convention (May 1939).
54. Sun Tzu, *The Art of War*, 219.
55. Sun Tzu, *The Art of War*, trans. Samuel Griffith (New York: Oxford University Press, 1971), 130.
56. Everett Dolman, *Astropolitik: Classic Geopolitics in the Space Age* (London: Frank Cass, 2002), esp. 75–85.

CHAPTER 3. PAX TERRA

1. A 1936 agreement between the great powers of the time, which gave Turkey control over the Bosporus Straits and the Dardanelles and regulated the movement of warships in the region. It largely benefitted Turkey and Russia, allowing them to have greater protection in the Black Sea, but it also supported British concerns about the Russian Black Sea Fleet sailing into the Mediterranean and challenging the British sphere of influence.
2. A federation does not require a system-changing war to emerge, but wars are one of the most common ways we see states begin to cooperate with each other—sometimes simply to avoid another war, but sometimes to restructure the international system.
3. Robert Jervis, "Realism, Neoliberalism, and Cooperation: Understanding the Debate," *International Security* 24, no. 1 (Summer 1999): 42–63; Randall Schweller and David Priess, "A Tale of Two Realisms: Expanding the Institutions Debate," *Mershon International Studies Review* 41, no. 1 (May 1997): 1–32, esp. 8–13.
4. Immanuel Kant, *Perpetual Peace: A Philosophical Sketch*, trans. M. Campbell Smith (London: George Allen and Unwin Ltd., 1917), 120–42.
5. Jack Levy, "Domestic Politics and War," in *The Origin and Prevention of Major Wars*, ed. Robert Rotberg and Theodore Rabb (New York: Cambridge University Press, 1989), 88.
6. Robert Keohane and Lisa Martin, "The Promise of Institutionalist Theory," *International Security* 20, no. 1 (Summer 1995): 39–51.
7. Robert Keohane and Joseph Nye, *Power and Interdependence: World Politics in Transition* (Toronto: Little, Brown and Company, 1977).
8. Kenneth Oye, "Explaining Cooperation under Anarchy: Hypotheses and Strategies," *World Politics* 38, no. 1 (October 1985): 1–24; David Lake, "Beyond Anarchy: The Importance of Security Institutions," *International Security* 26, no. 1 (Summer 2001): 129–60.
9. Duncan Snidal, "Relative Gains and the Pattern of International Cooperation, *American Political Science Review* 85, no. 3 (Summer 1991): 701–26,

and "International Cooperation among Relative Gains Maximizers," *International Studies Quarterly* 35, no. 4 (December 1991): 387–402.
10. Jean-Jacques Rousseau, *The Social Contract; or, Principles of Political Rights* (1762; reprint, Harlow, UK: Penguin Books, 2004).
11. Stephen Krasner, *International Regimes* (Ithaca: Cornell University Press, 1983), 2.
12. John Ruggie, "International Regimes, Transactions, and Change: Embedded Liberalism in the Postwar Economic Order," *International Organization* 36, no. 2 (Spring 1982): 379–415.
13. Robert Jervis, "Security Regimes," *International Organization* 36, no. 2 (Summer 1982): 357–78.
14. Stephen Haggard and Beth Simmons, "Theories of International Regimes," *International Organization* 41, no. 3 (Summer 1987): 491–517; Andrea Hasenclever, Peter Mayer, and Volker Rittberger, "Integrating Theories of International Regimes," *Review of International Studies* 26, no. 1 (January 2000): 3–33.
15. Keohane, *After Hegemony*.
16. Robert McCalla, "NATO's Persistence after the Cold War," *International Organization* 50, no. 3 (Summer 1996): 445–75; John Mearsheimer, "Back to the Future: Instability in Europe after the Cold War," *International Security* 15, no. 1 (Summer 1990): 5–56; Kenneth Waltz, "NATO Expansion: A Realist's View," *Contemporary Security Policy* 21, no. 2 (August 2000): 23–38.
17. Game theory is a method of understanding decision-making derived initially from mathematics and now often used in economics and political science. The idea is to model ideal strategies under the rules of a particular game, to understand how the payoffs (benefits) of each move influence an actor's choices.
18. Charles Lipson, "International Cooperation in Economic and Security Affairs," *World Politics* 37, no. 1 (October 1984): 1–23; Robert Keohane, "Reciprocity in International Relations," *International Organization* 40, no. 1 (Winter 1986): 1–27; Robert Axelrod, *Evolution of Cooperation* (New York: Basic Books, 1984); Robert Pahre, "Multilateral Cooperation in an Iterated Prisoner's Dilemma," *Journal of Conflict Resolution* 38, no. 2 (June 1994): 326–52.
19. Kenneth Abbott, "International Relations Theory, International Law, and the Regime Governing Atrocities in Internal Conflicts," *American Journal of International Law* 93, no. 2 (April 1999): 361–79; Anne-Marie Slaughter, Andrew Tulumello, and Stepan Wood, "International Law and International Relations Theory: A New Generation of Interdisciplinary Scholarship," *American Journal of International Law* 92, no. 3 (July 1998): 367–97; Kenneth Abbott and Duncan Snidal, "Hard and Soft Law in International Governance," *International Organization* 54, no. 3 (Summer 2000): 421–56.
20. Manfred Lachs, *The Law of Outer Space: An Experience in Contemporary Law-Making* (Leiden: Martinus Nijhoff Publishers, 2010); Bin Cheng,

Studies in International Space Law (Oxford: Oxford University Press, 1997).
21. For example, John Foster Dulles conflates the two concepts and even mistakenly refers to NATO as an example of collective security. John Foster Dulles, "Policy for Security and Peace," *Foreign Affairs* 32, no. 3 (April 1954): 353–64.
22. Arnold Wolfers, *Discord and Collaboration: Essays on International Politics* (Baltimore: The Johns Hopkins University Press, 1962), esp. 181–204; Charles Kupchan and Clifford Kupchan, "Concerts, Collective Security, and Europe," *International Security* 16, no. 1 (Summer 1991): 114–61.
23. A. F. K. Organski, *World Politics* (New York: Alfred A. Knopf, 1958), esp. 371–427. See also Charles Kupchan, "The Promise of Collective Security," *International Security* 20, no. 1 (Summer 1995): 52–61.
24. Wolfers, *Discord and Collaboration*, 181–204.
25. Robert Jervis, "From Balance to Concert: A Study of International Security Cooperation," *World Politics* 38, no. 1 (October 1985): 58–79; Richard Elrod, "The Concert of Europe: A Fresh Look at an International System," *World Politics* 28, no. 2 (January 1976): 159–74; Paul Schroeder, *Austria, Great Britain and the Crimean War: The Destruction of the European Concert* (Ithaca: Cornell University Press, 1972); Paul Schroeder, *The Transformation of European Politics, 1763–1848* (Oxford: Oxford University Press, 1994), esp. 517–82.
26. Poland did not attend and sign the initial charter but did sign it that year and is considered one of the fifty-one original members.
27. Information about the UNHCR can be found at https://www.unhcr.org/en-us/.
28. Craig Snyder, "Regional Security Structures," in *Contemporary Security and Strategy*, ed. Craig Snyder (London: Palgrave, 1999), 102–19, esp. 109.
29. Michael Barnett, "Bringing in the New World Order: Liberalism, Legitimacy, and the United Nations," *World Politics* 49, no. 4 (July 1997): 526–51.
30. Gunther Hellmann and Reinhard Wolf, "Neorealism, Neoliberal Institutionalism, and the Future of NATO," *Security Studies* 3, no. 1 (September 1993): 3–43, esp. 16–19.
31. Sean Kay, "NATO, the Kosovo War and Neoliberal Theory," *Contemporary Security Policy* 25, no. 2 (August 2004): 252–79.
32. Michael Westmore, *Star Trek: Aliens and Artifacts* (New York: Pocket Books, 2000), 208.
33. David Goodman, *Star Trek Federation: The First 150 Years* (London: Titan Books, 2013).
34. While true of the Federation, other races still valued currency and the collection of wealth, such as the Ferengi use of gold-pressed latinum (particularly in *Star Trek: Deep Space Nine*). Joseph Gargiulo, "The Utopian Future of 'Star Trek' Doesn't Work without Extreme Inequality and Some Slavery," *Business Insider*, 17 October 2015, https://www.businessinsider.com/utopian-future-of-star-trek-2015-10.

35. Joe Haldeman, *Forever War* (New York: St. Martin's, 1997).
36. Robert Heinlein, *Starship Troopers* (New York: Ace, 2003).
37. Heinlein, 192.
38. The book only refers to the aliens as Buggers, but the *Ender's Game* film refers to them as Formics, and there is some discussion that future versions of the novel will replace each use of Bugger.
39. Orson Scott Card, *Ender's Game* (New York: Tor, 1994), 200.
40. Card, 126, 137, 174, 231.
41. Card, 17, 26, 200.
42. Card, 48.
43. Card, 100.
44. Card, 35, 277.
45. Card, 253.
46. Card, 322.
47. Sun Tzu, *Art of War* (Griffith translation), 77.
48. Sun Tzu, (Griffith translation), 167.
49. Jeffrey Kluger, "Space: Where America and Russia Are Stuck with Each Other," *Time*, 25 March 2014, https://time.com/37671/space-cooperation-america-russia/.

CHAPTER 4. HOSTILE TAKEOVER

1. Europa is the smallest of the four Galilean moons orbiting Jupiter (the larger moons being Ganymede, Callisto, and Io), but it is the sixth largest moon in the solar system (Saturn's moon Titan and Neptune's moon Triton are both larger).
2. Adam Smith, *An Inquiry into the Nature and Causes of the Wealth of Nations* (1776; reprint, New York: Bantam Classics, 2003), 184–85.
3. Milton Friedman, *Capitalism and Freedom* (Chicago: University of Chicago Press, 1962).
4. Ruggie, "International Regimes, Transactions, and Change."
5. Keohane and Nye, *Power and Interdependence*.
6. Erik Gartzke, "The Capitalist Peace," *American Journal of Political Science* 51, no. 1 (January 2007): 166–91.
7. Now known in the United States as Permanent Normal Trade Relations. Until the United States granted this permanent status to China, Congress reevaluated U.S.-China trade relations annually. China did not become a member of the WTO until December 2001 because of the necessary adjustments to its economic and trade policies required for accession into the organization.
8. Albert Hirschman, *National Power and the Structure of Foreign Trade* (1945; reprint, Berkeley: University of California Press, 1980), esp. 3–70; Gilpin, *War and Change in World Politics*, 140–41; Peter Liberman, *Does Conquest Pay? The Exploitation of Occupied Industrial Societies* (Princeton: Princeton University Press, 1996).

9. Katherine Barbieri, "Economic Interdependence: A Path to Peace or a Source of Interstate Conflict?," *Journal of Peace Research* 33, no. 1 (February 1996): 29–49.
10. Curt Tarnoff, "U.S. Agency for International Development (USAID): Background, Operations, and Issues," Report R44117 (Washington, DC: Congressional Research Service, 21 July 2015), esp. 29–31.
11. William DeMars and Dennis Dijkzeul, eds., *The NGO Challenge for International Relations Theory* (London: Routledge, 2015); Thomas Davies, ed., *Routledge Handbook of NGOs and International Relations* (Abingdon, UK: Routledge, 2019); Bob Reinalda, ed., *The Ashgate Research Companion to Non-State Actors* (London: Routledge, 2016); Karsten Lehmann, *Religious NGOs in International Relations: The Construction of "the Religious" and "the Security"* (London: Routledge, 2016).
12. *Black's Law Dictionary*, 2nd ed., https://thelawdictionary.org/multinational-corporation-mnc.
13. Yves Doz and C. K. Prahalad, "How MNCs Cope with Host Government Intervention," *Harvard Business Review* 58, no. 2 (March 1980): 149–57; Steven McGuire, "Firms and Governments in International Trade," in *Trade Politics*, ed. Brian Hocking and Steven McGuire (London: Routledge, 2004), 276–88; Andrea Nölke and Christian May, eds., *Handbook of the International Political Economy of the Corporation* (Cheterham, UK: Edward Elgar, 2018).
14. Andrea Murphy et al., "The Global 2000," *Forbes*, 12 May 2019, https://www.forbes.com/global2000/#623a8e7c335d.
15. Thomas Friedman, *The Lexus and the Olive Tree: Understanding Globalization* (New York: Picador, 1999); Thomas Friedman, *The World Is Flat* (New York: Picador, 2005); Helen Milner, *Resisting Protectionism: Global Industries and the Politics of International Trade* (Princeton: Princeton University Press, 1988).
16. Mats Brendel and Monica Serrano, eds., *Transnational Organized Crime and International Security: Business as Usual?* (Boulder, CO: Lynne Rienner, 2002); Phil Williams, "Transnational Criminal Organisations and International Security," *Survival* 36, no. 1 (Spring 1994): 96–113; Louise Shelley, "Transnational Organized Crime: An Imminent Threat to the Nation-State?," *Journal of International Affairs* 48, no. 2 (Winter 1995): 463–89; Yuliya Zabyelina, "Transnational Organized Crime in International Relations," *Central European Journal of International and Security Studies* 3, no. 1 (January 2009): 11–22.
17. Thomas Sanderson, "Transnational Terror and Organized Crime: Blurring the Lines," *SAIS Review* 24, no. 1 (Winter/Spring 2004): 49–61; John Picarelli, "Osama bin Corleone? Vito the Jackal? Framing Threat Convergence through an Examination of Transnational Organized Crime and International Terrorism," *Terrorism and Political Violence* 24, no. 2 (April 2012): 180–98; Chris Dishman, "Terrorism, Crime, and Transformation,"

Studies in Conflict and Terrorism 24, no. 1 (January 2001): 43–58; Chris Dishman, "The Leaderless Nexus: When Crime and Terror Converge," *Studies in Conflict and Terrorism* 28, no. 3 (May 2005): 237–52; Steven Hutchinson and Pat O'Malley, "A Crime-Terror Nexus? Thinking on Some of the Links between Terrorism and Criminality," *Studies in Conflict and Terrorism* 30, no. 12 (November 2007): 1095–107.
18. Stephen Krasner, "Sovereignty," *Foreign Policy* 122 (January/February 2001): 20–29; David Smith, Dorothy Solinger, and Steven Topik, eds., *States and Sovereignty in the Global Economy* (London: Routledge, 1999); Robert Reich, *The Work of Nations: Preparing Ourselves for 21st Century Capitalism* (New York: Vintage Books, 1992); Kenichi Ohmae, "The Rise of the Region State," *Foreign Affairs* 71, no. 2 (March 1993): 78–87.
19. International Commission on Intervention and State Sovereignty, *The Responsibility to Protect: Research, Bibliography, Background* (Ottawa: International Development Research Centre, 2001).
20. Samuel Huntington, *The Clash of Civilizations and the Remaking of World Order* (New York: Touchstone, 1996).
21. Levy, "Domestic Politics and War," 88.
22. Bruce Russett, *Grasping the Democratic Peace: Principles for a Post–Cold War World* (Princeton: Princeton University Press, 1993); John Owen, "How Liberalism Produces Democratic Peace," *International Security* 19, no. 2 (Fall 1994): 87–125.
23. Edward Mansfield and Jack Snyder, "Democratization and the Danger of War," *International Security* 20, no. 1 (Summer 1995): 5–38.
24. Marcus Barnett, "69 of the Richest 100 Bodies in the World Are Corporations," *Morning Star*, 17 October 2018, https://morningstaronline.co.uk/article/69-richest-100-bodies-world-are-corporations.
25. Christopher Hibbert, *The Rise and Fall of the House of Medici* (London: Allen Lane, 1974); Tim Parks, *Medici Money: Banking, Metaphysics, and Art in Fifteenth-Century Florence* (New York: W. W. Norton and Company, 2005).
26. Hibbert, 63.
27. Lauro Martines, *April Blood: Florence and the Plot against the Medici* (New York: Oxford University Press, 2003).
28. H. V. Bowen, *The Business of Empire: The East India Company and Imperial Britain, 1756–1833* (Cambridge: Cambridge University Press, 2006); Nick Robins, *The Corporation that Changed the World: How the East India Company Shaped the Modern Multinational* (London: Pluto Press, 2006); Philip Stern, *The Company-State: Corporate Sovereignty and the Early Modern Foundations of the British Empire in India* (Oxford: Oxford University Press, 2011).
29. Sebastien Roblin, "The War that Made Asia: How the Opium War Crushed China," *National Interest*, 17 February 2017, https://nationalinterest.org/blog/the-buzz/the-war-made-asia-how-the-opium-war-crushed-china-19476.

30. John Spilsbury, *The Indian Mutiny* (London: Weidenfeld and Nicolson, 2007); Rosie Llewellyn-Jones, *The Great Uprising in India, 1857–58: Untold Stories, Indian and British* (Rochester, NY: Boydell and Brewer, 2007).
31. Chris Nierstrasz, *In the Shadow of the Company: The Dutch East India Company and Its Servants in the Period of Its Decline (1740–1796)* (Leiden: Brill, 2012).
32. Chris Nierstrasz, *Rivalry for Trade in Tea and Textiles: The English and Dutch East India Companies (1700–1800)* (New York: Palgrave Macmillan, 2015).
33. Justus Van der Kroef, "The Decline and Fall of the Dutch East India Company," *The Historian* 10, no. 2 (Spring 1948): 118–34.
34. Peter Chapman, *Bananas: How the United Fruit Company Shaped the World* (Edinburgh: Commongate, 2007); Jason Colby, *The Business of Empire: United Fruit, Race, and U.S. Expansion in Central America* (Ithaca: Cornell University Press, 2011).
35. In the original book, it is the Rosen Association. Philip K. Dick, *Do Androids Dream of Electric Sheep* (New York: Doubleday and Company, Inc., 1968).
36. Joseph Mallozzi and Paul Mullie (creators), *Dark Matter*, season 3, episode 1, "Being Better Is So Much Harder."
37. Bear, *Moving Mars*, 194.
38. Sun Tzu, *Art of War*, 220.
39. Ross Anderson, "Exodus," *Aeon*, 30 September 2014, https://aeon.co/essays/elon-musk-puts-his-case-for-a-multi-planet-civilisation.

CHAPTER 5. MARX ON MARS

1. Self-sufficient means the colonies on Mars were no longer dependent on shipments of vital resources from Earth. They could provide their own food, water, and oxygen. That does not mean they were independent from Earth or did not maintain strong connections with it, but that they could survive on their own if necessary.
2. One useful discussion of some of these variations is in Milorad Drachkovitch, ed., *Marxism in the Modern World* (Stanford, CA: Stanford University Press, 1965).
3. Ivan Krastev, "Eastern Europe's Illiberal Revolution: The Long Road to Democratic Decline," *Foreign Affairs* (May/June 2018), https://www.foreignaffairs.com/articles/hungary/2018-04-16/eastern-europes-illiberal-revolution.
4. Karl Marx and Friedrich Engels, *The Communist Manifesto* (1848; reprint, New York: Penguin, 2002); V. I. Lenin, "The Three Sources and Three Component Parts of Marxism," *Prosveshcheniye* no. 3 (1913), https://www.marxists.org/archive/lenin/works/1913/mar/x01.htm; Friedrich Engels, *Socialism: Utopian and Scientific*, trans. Edward Aveling (Chicago: Charles H. Kerr and Company, 1900).
5. Smith, *Inquiry into the Nature and Causes*; David Ricardo, *On the Principles of Political Economy, and Taxation* (London: John Murray, 1817),

contributed the idea of a labor theory of value (where the value of a product is based on the labor required to produce it).
6. Karl Marx, *A Contribution to the Critique of Political Economy* (1859; reprint, Chicago: Charles H. Kerr and Company, 1904); Karl Marx, "Wage Labour and Capital," December 1847, https://www.marxists.org/archive/marx/works/1847/wage-labour/; V. I. Lenin, *Imperialism: The Highest Stage of Capitalism* (Petrograd: Life and Knowledge Publishers, 1917).
7. Ted Gurr, *Why Men Rebel* (Princeton: Princeton University Press, 1971).
8. In addition to these three countries, this label also typically referred to Hong Kong, at least prior to its transfer to China in 1997 after more than 150 years of British rule.
9. Raymond Duvall, "Dependence and Dependencia Theory: Notes toward Precision of Concept and Argument," *International Organization* 32, no. 1 (January 1978): 51–78; Richard Fagen, "Studying Latin American Politics: Some Implications of a *Dependencia* Approach," *Latin American Research Review* 12, no. 2 (January 1977): 3–26.
10. Lester Langley, *The Banana Wars: United States Intervention in the Caribbean, 1898–1934* (Lexington: University Press of Kentucky, 1983); Chapman, *Bananas*.
11. Daniel Yergin and Joseph Stanislaw, *The Commanding Heights: The Battle for the World Economy* (New York: Touchstone, 2002).
12. Robert Cox, "Ideologies and the New International Economic Order: Reflections on Some Recent Literature," *International Organization* 33, no. 2 (Spring 1979): 257–302; John White, "Review Article: The New International Economic Order: What Is It?," *International Affairs* 54, no. 4 (October 1978): 626–34; Michael Doyle, "Review Article: Stalemate in the North-South Debate: Strategies and the New International Economic Order," *World Politics* 35, no. 3 (April 1983): 426–64.
13. Philip Verleger, "Understanding the 1990 Oil Crisis," *Energy Journal* 11, no. 4 (May 1990): 15–33; Jad Mouawad, "Saudis Vow to Ignore OPEC Decision to Cut Production," *New York Times*, 10 September 2008, https://www.nytimes.com/2008/09/11/business/worldbusiness/11oil.html.
14. Immanuel Wallerstein, "The West, Capitalism, and the Modern World-System: Concepts for Comparative Analysis," *Review* 15, no. 4 (Fall 1992): 561–619; Christopher Chase-Dunn and Richard Rubinson, "Toward a Structural Perspective on the World-System," *Politics and Society* 7, no. 4 (December 1977): 453–76.
15. For an application of world systems theory to the future, see Edythe Weeks, *Outer Space Development, Space Law and International Relations* (Cambridge: Cambridge University Press, 2012).
16. V. I. Lenin, *State and Revolution* (New York: International Publishers, 1932); John Hobson, *Imperialism: A Study* (New York: James Pott and Company, 1902).
17. Mao Tse-Tung, *Selected Works of Mao Tse-Tung*, vol. I (Beijing: Foreign Language Press, 1965).

18. Jack Goldstone, "Theories of Revolution: The Third Generation," *World Politics* 32, no. 3 (April 1980): 425–53.
19. Theda Skocpol, *States and Social Revolutions* (Cambridge: Cambridge University Press, 1979).
20. Gurr, *Why Men Rebel*.
21. Chalmers Johnson, *Revolutionary Change* (New York: Little, Brown and Company, 1966).
22. Charles Tilly defines a revolution as "a forcible transfer of power over a state in the course of which at least two distinct blocs of contenders make incompatible claims to control the state, and some significant portion of the population subject to the state's jurisdiction acquiesces in the claims of each bloc." Charles Tilly, *European Revolutions, 1492–1992* (Oxford: Blackwell, 1993), 8.
23. Tilly, 16.
24. Stephen Walt, *Revolution and War* (Ithaca: Cornell University Press, 1997).
25. Mark Katz identified six different types of revolution but also suggested they are either against something (anti-colonial, etc.) or for something (ideological). Mark Katz, *Revolutions and Revolutionary Waves* (New York: Macmillan, 1999). See also Jack Goldstone, "Towards a Fourth Generation of Revolutionary Theory," *American Review of Political Science* 4, no. 1 (June 2001): 139–87; Lawrence Stone, "Theories of Revolution," *World Politics* 18, no. 2 (January 1966): 159–76; Skocpol, *States and Social Revolutions*.
26. Frantz Fanon, *The Wretched of the Earth* (New York: Grove Weidenfeld, 1963).
27. Alexis de Tocqueville, *The Old Regime and the Revolution*, trans. John Bonner (New York: Harper and Brothers, 1856); François Furet, *Interpreting the French Revolution* (Cambridge: Cambridge University Press, 1981); R. R. Palmer, *Twelve Who Ruled: The Committee of Public Safety during the Terror* (Princeton: Princeton University Press, 1941).
28. William Doyle, *The Oxford History of the French Revolution* (Oxford: Clarendon Press, 1989), 425.
29. Bloodless is a stretch considering the millions of Soviet citizens killed by the state in various ways over the next seven decades, mostly under Joseph Stalin's brutal leadership. Leon Trotsky, *The History of the Russian Revolution*, trans. Max Eastman (Ann Arbor: The University of Michigan Press, 1974); Orlando Figes, *A People's Tragedy: A History of the Russian Revolution* (New York: Viking, 1996).
30. Said Amir Arjonand, *The Turban for the Crown* (New York: Oxford University Press, 1988); Abbas Amanat, *Iran: A Modern History* (New Haven: Yale University Press, 2017).
31. One of the earliest books consulted when developing this project, and one that was particularly helpful with this chapter, was Carl Freedman, *Critical Theory and Science Fiction* (Middletown, CT: Weslyan University Press, 2000).

32. Kim Stanley Robinson, *Red Mars* (New York: Bantam Books, 1993), 61 (emphasis in original).
33. Similar themes appear in Clifford Simak's short story "Desertion," *Astounding Science Fiction* 34, no. 3 (November 1944): 64–74.
34. Robinson, *Red Mars*, 452.
35. Robinson, 342.
36. Robert Heinlein, *The Moon Is a Harsh Mistress* (New York: Tom Doherty Associates, 1966), 205.
37. Heinlein, *Moon Is a Harsh Mistress*, 88.
38. Heinlein, 382.
39. They even more closely resemble the caste system in Plato's *Republic*: "yet God in fashioning those of you who are fitted to hold rule mingled gold in their generation, for which reason they are the most precious—but in the helpers silver, and iron and brass in the farmers and other craftsmen." Plato, *Republic*, book 3, trans. M. Campbell Smith (Cambridge, MA: Harvard University Press, 1930), 415a–c. Plato did not see these roles as a birthright but ones that had to be earned, whereas in *Red Rising* people are not only born into a particular caste but also are genetically altered to be more effective in those roles.
40. Pierce Brown, *Red Rising* (New York: Del Rey, 2014), 37.
41. Marx and Engels, *The Communist Manifesto*, 258.
42. Brown, *Red Rising*, 341.
43. World Bank "National Accounts Data," https://data.worldbank.org/indicator/NY.GDP.PCAP.CD?locations=CN-US.
44. Sun Tzu, *Art of War*, 221.
45. As Captain Ramius tells his crew in *The Hunt for Red October*: "When he reached the New World, Cortez burned his ships. As a result, his men were well motivated."
46. Sun Tzu, *Art of War*, 199.
47. Daniel Kahneman and Amos Tversky, "Prospect Theory: An Analysis of Decision under Risk," *Econometrica* 47, no. 2 (March 1979): 263–92.
48. Heinlein, *Moon Is a Harsh Mistress*, 276.
49. Charles Cockell, ed., *The Meaning of Liberty beyond Earth* (Cham, CH: Springer, 2015).
50. Jude Roberts, "A Few Questions about the Culture: An Interview with Iain Banks," *Strange Horizons*, 2014 special issue, http://strangehorizons.com/non-fiction/articles/a-few-questions-about-the-culture-an-interview-with-iain-banks/.
51. Gene Rodenberry, *Star Trek*, season 2, episode 7, "Catspaw," October 27, 1967; Jonathan Frakes (dir.), *Star Trek: First Contact* (Digital Image Associates, 1996). For discussion of these economic ideas in *Star Trek*, see Stephen Baxter, "The Cold Equations: Extraterrestrial Liberty in Science Fiction," in Cockell, ed., *Meaning of Liberty beyond Earth*, 13–31.

CHAPTER 6. VENUS RISING

1. Nadia Drake, "Here's Why Women May Be the Best Suited for Spaceflight," *National Geographic*, 12 July 2019, https://www.nationalgeographic.com/magazine/2019/07/space-travel-four-ways-women-are-a-better-fit-than-men/, although a NASA report seems to challenge some of this argument: see Saralyn Mark et al., "The Impact of Sex and Gender on Adaptation to Space," *Journal of Women's Health* 23, no. 11 (November 2014): 941–86.
2. A scenario that involved gender equality, in terms of numbers, roles, and authorities, would cover many of the feminist ideas discussed in this chapter. This scenario adopts a more extreme approach of women being the sole representatives of humanity in space, both because it is more interesting than a scenario with equal-gender crews and because it is a common theme in several works that are considered part of the feminist subgenre of science fiction.
3. A base named for the first woman to fly in space, Soviet cosmonaut Valentina Tereshkova, who went into space aboard *Vostok 6* in 1963.
4. J. Ann Tickner, "You Just Don't Understand: Troubled Engagements between Feminists and IR Theorists," *International Studies Quarterly* 41, no. 4 (December 1997): 611–32; J. Ann Tickner, *Gendering World Politics: Issues and Approaches in the Post–Cold War Era* (New York: Columbia University Press, 2001); Cynthia Enloe, "'Gender' Is Not Enough: The Need for a Feminist Consciousness," *International Affairs* 80, no. 1 (January 2004): 95–97.
5. Mary Dietz, "Current Controversies in Feminist Theory," *Annual Review of Political Science* 6 (June 2003): 399–431; Valerie Bryson, *Feminist Political Theory*, 3rd ed. (London: Palgrave, 2016).
6. See, for example, J. Ann Tickner, "Hans Morgenthau's Principles of Political Realism: A Feminist Reformulation," *Millennium—Journal of International Studies* 17, no. 3 (December 1988): 429–40, and J. Ann Tickner, *Gender in International Relations: Feminist Perspectives on Achieving Global Security* (New York: Columbia University Press, 1992), especially chapter 2.
7. Sandra Harding, ed., *The Feminist Standpoint Theory Reader: Intellectual and Political Controversies* (New York: Routledge, 2004).
8. Bill Chappel, "Barack Obama Says Women Could Solve Many of World's Problems—Which Men Have Caused," National Public Radio, 16 December 2019, https://www.npr.org/2019/12/16/788549518/obama-links-many-of-world-s-problems-to-old-men-not-getting-out-of-the-way?utm_medium=social&utm_campaign=npr&utm_term=nprnews&utm_source=twitter.com; Rose McDermott, "Sex and Death: Gender Differences in Aggression and Motivations for Violence," *International Organization* 69, no. 3 (Summer 2015): 753–75.
9. Jacqui True, "Mainstreaming Gender in International Institutions," in *Gender Matters in Global Politics*, ed. Laura Shepherd (Abingdon, UK: Routledge, 2015), 227–39.

10. Karen Green offers an internal criticism of liberalism that argues for gender quotas. In contrast, Deborah Rhode is not convinced quotas would be just or effective. Karen Green, "Parity and Procedural Justice," *Essays in Philosophy* 7, no. 1 (January 2006): 18–28; Deborah Rhode, "Feminism and the State," *Harvard Law Review* 107, no. 6 (April 1994): 1181–208; see also Anne Peters and Stefan Suter, "Representation, Discrimination, and Democracy: A Legal Assessment of Gender Quotas in Politics," in *Gender Equality: Dimensions of Women's Equal Citizenship*, ed. Linda McClain and Joanna Grossman (Cambridge: Cambridge University Press, 2012), 174–200.
11. In this respect, there is some overlap with radical feminism.
12. One variant of Marxist feminism is intersectionalism, which attempts to incorporate gender into other social and political identities, such as race. Rather than separate gender and race, those (and other) identities are combined to create unique, individual identities.
13. Sara Meger, *Rape Loot Pillage: The Political Economy of Sexual Violence in Armed Conflict* (New York: Oxford University Press, 2016).
14. Carol Cohn, "Sex and Death in the Rational World of Defense Intellectuals," *Signs* 12, no. 4 (Summer 1987): 687–718.
15. Cynthia Enloe, *Bananas, Beaches, and Bases: Making Feminist Sense of International Politics* (Berkeley: University of California Press, 1989); Jan Jindy Pettman, *Worlding Women: A Feminist International Politics* (Sydney: Allen and Unwin, 1996); Katharine Moon, *Sex among Allies: Military Prostitution in U.S.-Korea Relations* (New York: Columbia University Press, 1997).
16. David Smith, Judith Rosenstein, and Margaret Nikolov, "The Different Words We Use to Describe Male and Female Leaders," *Harvard Business Review*, 25 May 2018, https://hbr.org/2018/05/the-different-words-we-use-to-describe-male-and-female-leaders.
17. Oeindrila Dube and S. P. Harish, "Queen," *Journal of Political Economy* 128, no. 7 (July 2020): 2579–652.
18. Uri Gneezy, Kenneth Leonard, and John List, "Gender Differences in Competition: Evidence from a Matrilineal and a Patriarchal Society," *Econometrica* 77, no. 5 (September 2009): 1637–64.
19. Dariusz Dolinski et al., "Would You Deliver an Electric Shock in 2015? Obedience in the Experimental Paradigm Developed by Stanley Milgram in the 50 Years Following the Original Studies," *Social Psychology and Personality Science* 8, no. 8 (November 2017): 927–33.
20. Blema Steinberg, *Women in Power: The Personalities and Leadership Styles of Indira Gandhi, Golda Meir, and Margaret Thatcher* (Montreal: McGill-Queen's University Press, 2008).
21. Francine Klagsbrun, *Lioness: Golda Meir and the Nation of Israel* (New York: Schocken, 2017); Elinor Burkett, *Golda* (New York: Harper Collins, 2008).
22. Michael Burleigh, *Blood and Rage: A Cultural History of Terrorism* (New York: Harper Collins Publishers, 2009), 172–73.

23. Charles Moore, *Margaret Thatcher: Not for Turning* (New York: Knopf, 2013), *Margaret Thatcher: Everything She Wants* (New York: Knopf, 2015), and *Margaret Thatcher: Herself Alone* (New York: Knopf, 2019); Margaret Thatcher, *The Downing Street Years* (New York: Harper Collins, 1993).
24. Pupul Jayakar, *Indira Gandhi: A Biography* (New York: Viking, 1995); Katherine Frank, *Indira: The Life of Indira Nehru Gandhi* (Boston: Houghton Mifflin Company, 2002).
25. Cited in Ross Marlay and Clark Neher, *Patriots and Tyrants: Ten Asian Leaders* (Lanham, MD: Rowman and Littlefield Publishers, Inc., 1999), 309.
26. These figures are from Srikanta Ghosh, *Indian Democracy Derailed—Politics and Politicians* (New Delhi: APH Publishing Corporation, 1997), 95. The Global Terrorism Database lists 196 terrorist incidents during that same time period, resulting in 212 deaths.
27. For example, Rajiv Gandhi, Indira Gandhi's son who served as prime minister from his mother's death in 1984 to 1989, was killed by a female suicide bomber. The bomber, Dhanu, was a member of the Liberation Tigers of Tamil Eelam and acted in retaliation for Indian intervention in the conflict between the Tamil and the Sri Lankan government.
28. Brooke Allen, *Benazir Bhutto: Favored Daughter* (Boston: Houghton Mifflin Harcourt, 2015); Benazir Bhutto, *Daughter of the East: An Autobiography* (London: Hamish Hamilton, 1988).
29. BBC World Service, "Women in Power Reveal What It Takes: Benazir Bhutto," http://www.bbc.co.uk/worldservice/people/features/wiwp/statcon/bhutto_quote.shtml.
30. Hilary Matfess, "Violence against Female Politicians," Council on Foreign Relations, 11 July 2017, https://www.cfr.org/article/violence-against-female-politicians.
31. Christopher Munsey, "Women and War," *Monitor on Psychology* 40, no. 8 (September 2009), https://www.apa.org/monitor/2009/09/women-war.
32. Lory Manning, "Women in the Military: Where They Stand," 10th ed., Service Women's Action Network, 2019, https://www.servicewomen.org/wp-content/uploads/2019/04/SWAN-Where-we-stand-2019-0416revised.pdf; North Atlantic Treaty Organization, "Summary of the National Reports of NATO Member and Partner Nations to the NATO Committee on Gender Perspectives," 2016, https://www.nato.int/nato_static_fl2014/assets/pdf/pdf_2017_11/20171122_2016_Summary_of_NRs_to_NCGP.pdf.
33. Bethan McKernan, "Female Kurdish Fighters Announce New Training Academies for Arab Women to Take on ISIS in Syria," *The Independent*, 4 January 2017, https://www.independent.co.uk/news/world/middle-east/female-kurdish-fighters-ypj-set-up-new-training-academies-arab-yazidi-women-to-fight-isis-a7508951.html.

34. Karla Cunningham, "Cross Regional Trends in Female Terrorism," *Studies in Conflict and Terrorism* 26, no. 3 (May 2003): 171–95; Cindy Ness, *Female Terrorism and Militancy: Agency, Utility, and Organization* (London: Routledge, 2007); Paige Whaley Eager, *From Freedom Fighters to Terrorists: Women and Political Violence* (Hampshire, UK: Ashgate, 2008); Leonard Weinberg and William Eubank, "Women's Involvement in Terrorism," *Gender Issues* 28, nos. 1–2 (June 2011): 22–49; Mia Bloom, *Bombshell: Women and Terrorism* (Philadelphia: University of Pennsylvania Press, 2011); Caron Gentry and Laura Sjoberg, "Terrorism and Political Violence," in *Gender Matters in Global Politics*, ed. Laura Shepherd (Abingdon, UK: Routledge, 2015), 120–30; Caron Gentry, "Women and Terrorism," in *The Oxford Handbook of Terrorism*, ed. Erica Chenoweth et al. (Oxford: Oxford University Press, 2019), 414–28; Cyndi Banks, "Introduction: Women, Gender, and Terrorism: Gendering Terrorism," *Women and Criminal Justice* 29, nos. 4–5 (September 2019): 181–302; Victor Asal and Amira Jadoon, "When Women Fight: Unemployment, Territorial Control and the Prevalence of Female Combatants in Insurgent Organizations," *Dynamics of Asymmetric Conflict* 13, no. 3 (December 2019): 258–81.
35. William Rosenau, *Tonight We Bombed the U.S. Capitol: The Explosive Story of M19, America's First Female Terrorist Group* (New York: Atria Books, 2020).
36. The Global Terrorism Database (GTD) attributes more than 124 attacks to the Baader-Meinhof Group or the Red Army Faction between 1970 and 1991, accounting for thirty-one deaths.
37. GTD.
38. "Yes, yes, I know they make better pilots than men do; their reactions are faster, and they can tolerate more gee." Heinlein, *Starship Troopers*, 7.
39. Ursula Le Guin, *The Left Hand of Darkness* (New York: Ace Books, 1969), 252–53.
40. Wendy Whitman Cobb, "Women Are Less Supportive of Space Exploration—Getting a Woman on the Moon Might Change That," *The Conversation*, 9 July 2019, https://theconversation.com/women-are-less-supportive-of-space-exploration-getting-a-woman-on-the-moon-might-change-that-118986; Cary Funk et al., "Majority of Americans Believe It Is Essential that the U.S. Remain a Global Leader in Space," Pew Research Center report, 6 June 2018, https://www.pewresearch.org/science/2018/06/06/majority-of-americans-believe-it-is-essential-that-the-u-s-remain-a-global-leader-in-space/.
41. Cornelia Brunner and Dorothy Bennett, "Technology and Gender: Differences in Masculine and Feminine Views," *NASSP Bulletin* 81, no. 592 (November 1997): 46–51; Julie Jargon, "Girls vs. Boys: Brain Differences Might Explain Tech Behaviors," *Wall Street Journal*, 24 September 2019, https://www.wsj.com/articles/girls-vs-boys-brain-differences-might-explain-tech-behaviors-11569317402.

42. Frank Herbert, *The White Plague* (New York: G. P. Putnam's Sons, 1982).
43. This deviates from Clausewitz's view of attacking the hub of power. According to Clausewitz, "One must keep the dominant characteristics of both belligerents in mind. Out of these characteristics a certain center of gravity develops, the *hub of all power and movement*, on which everything depends. That is the point against which all our energies should be directed." Carl von Clausewitz, *On War*, ed. Michael Howard and Peter Paret (Princeton: Princeton University Press, 1976), 595–96, emphasis added.

CHAPTER 7. AN ARTIFICIAL FUTURE

1. Estimates ranged from 2005 to never, though some individual predictions were closer than others. As early as 1993, Vernor Vinge predicted it would happen between 2005 and 2030; Louis Rosenberg offered 2030, and Ray Kurzweil suggested it would be 2045. Jolene Creighton, "The 'Father of Artificial Intelligence' Says Singularity Is 30 Years Away," *Futurism.com*, 14 February 2018, https://futurism.com/father-artificial-intelligence-singularity-decades-away.
2. Though Felix Berenskoetter suggests constructivists must do a better job of studying the future. Felix Berenskoetter, "Reclaiming the Vision Thing: Constructivists as Students of the Future," *International Studies Quarterly* 55, no. 3 (September 2011): 647–68.
3. The concept of *confirmation bias* suggests that humans tend to ignore or reject ideas or behavior that challenge their expectations, while they seek out and more readily believe ideas or behavior that support their expectations, and thus will strengthen their perceptions of a particular identity. Daniel Kahneman, Paul Slovic, and Amos Tversky, eds., *Judgment under Uncertainty: Heuristics and Biases* (Cambridge: Cambridge University Press, 1982), esp. 129–52.
4. Ted Hopf, "The Promise of Constructivism in International Relations Theory," *International Security* 23, no. 1 (Summer 1998): 171–200.
5. James Fearon and Alexander Wendt, "Rationalism v. Constructivism: A Skeptical View," in *Handbook of International Relations*, ed. Walter Carlsnaes, Thomas Risse, and Beth Simmons (London: Sage Publications, 2002), 52–72.
6. Alexander Wendt, *Social Theory of International Politics* (Cambridge: Cambridge University Press, 1999); Martha Finnemore, *National Interests in International Society* (Ithaca: Cornell University Press, 1996); Ted Hopf, *Social Construction of International Politics: Identities and Foreign Policies, Moscow, 1955 and 1999* (Ithaca: Cornell University Press, 2002); Neta Crawford, *Argument and Change in World Politics: Ethics, Decolonization, and Humanitarian Intervention* (Cambridge: Cambridge University Press, 2002).

7. Martha Finnemore and Kathryn Sikkink, "Taking Stock: The Constructivist Research Program in International Relations and Comparative Politics," *Annual Review of Political Science* 4 (June 2001): 392–93.
8. Hugo Grotius, *The Law of War and Peace*, trans. Edward Aveling (1625; reprint, New York: Walter J. Black, 1949).
9. Hadley Bull, *The Anarchical Society* (New York: Columbia University Press, 1977), 13. See also Barry Buzan, *From International Theory to World Society? English School Theory and the Social Structure of Globalisation* (Cambridge: Cambridge University Press, 2004); Barry Buzan and Richard Little, *International Systems in World History: Remaking the Study of International Relations* (Oxford: Oxford University Press, 2000); Martin Wight, *Systems of States* (Leicester, UK: Leicester University Press, 1977); Martin Wight, *Power Politics* (London: Royal Institute of International Affairs, 1978); Tim Dunne, *Inventing International Society: A History of the English School* (Basingstoke, UK: Macmillan, 1998).
10. Dale Copeland, "A Realist Critique of the English School," *Review of International Studies* 29, no. 3 (July 2003): 427–41.
11. Alexander Wendt, "Anarchy Is What States Make of It: The Social Construction of Power Politics," *International Organization* 46, no. 2 (Spring 1992): 391–425.
12. Peter Katzenstein, ed., *The Culture of National Security: Norms and Identity in World Politics* (New York: Columbia University Press, 1996); Audie Klotz, *Norms in International Relations: The Struggle against Apartheid* (Ithaca: Cornell University Press, 1995); Jeffrey Checkel, "Norms, Institutions, and National Identity in Contemporary Europe," *International Studies Quarterly* 43, no. 1 (March 1999): 83–114; Ann Florini, "The Evolution of International Norms," *International Studies Quarterly* 40, no. 3 (September 1996): 363–89.
13. Nina Tannenwald, *The Nuclear Taboo: The United States and the Non-Use of Nuclear Weapons* (Cambridge: Cambridge University Press, 2007).
14. Martha Finnemore, *The Purpose of Intervention: Changing Beliefs about the Use of Force* (Ithaca: Cornell University Press, 2003).
15. Brian Greenhill, "Recognition and Collective Identity Formation in International Politics," *European Journal of International Relations* 14, no. 2 (June 2008): 343–68; Felix Berenskoetter, "Friends, There Are No Friends? An Intimate Reframing of the International," *Millennium* 33, no. 3 (September 2007): 647–76; Cristina Stolte, *Brazil's Africa Strategy: Role Conception and the Drive for International Status* (New York: Palgrave Macmillan, 2015); Christopher Daase et al., eds., *Recognition in International Relations* (Hampshire UK: Palgrave Macmillan, 2015); Michelle Murray, *The Struggle for Recognition in International Relations: Status, Revisionism, and Rising Powers* (Oxford: Oxford University Press, 2019).
16. Deganit Paikowsky, *The Power of the Space Club* (Cambridge: Cambridge University Press, 2017).

17. Michelle Murray, "Identity, Insecurity, and Great Power Politics: The Tragedy of German Naval Ambition before the First World War," *Security Studies* 19, no. 4 (November 2010): 656–88.
18. Kiran Banerjee and Joseph MacKay, "Communities of Practice, Impression Management, and Great Power Status: Military Observers in the Russo-Japanese War," *European Journal of International Security* (October 2020): 274–93.
19. Yong Deng, *China's Struggle for Status: The Realignment of International Relations* (Cambridge: Cambridge University Press, 2008).
20. Erika Cudworth and Stephen Hobden, "Of Parts and Wholes: International Relations beyond the Human," *Millennium: Journal of International Studies* 41, no. 3 (June 2013): 430–50; Erika Cudworth, Stephen Hobden, and Emilian Kavalski, eds., *Posthuman Dialogues in International Relations* (London: Routledge, 2017); Anna Leander, "Technological Agency in the Co-Constitution of Legal Expertise and the U.S. Drone Program," *Leiden Journal of International Law* 26, no. 4 (December 2013): 811–31; David Seed, ed., *A Companion to Science Fiction* (Malden, UK: Blackwell Publishing, 2005).
21. Alexander Wendt, *Quantum Mind and Social Science: Unifying Physical and Social Ontology* (Cambridge: Cambridge University Press, 2015); Alexander Wendt and Raymond Duvall, "Sovereignty and the UFO," *Political Theory* 36, no. 4 (August 2008): 607–33.
22. Sarwant Singh, "Transhumanism and the Future of Humanity: 7 Ways the World Will Change by 2030," *Forbes*, 20 November 2017, https://www.forbes.com/sites/sarwantsingh/2017/11/20/transhumanism-and-the-future-of-humanity-seven-ways-the-world-will-change-by-2030/#358e24c97d79. Ted Chiang's short story "Understand" addresses some interesting elements of superintelligent humans and how they will react with the rest of society. Ted Chiang, "Understand," *Asimov's Science Fiction* 15, no. 9 (August 1991): 86–118.
23. Nick Bostrom, *Superintelligence: Paths, Dangers, Strategies* (Oxford: Oxford University Press, 2014), esp. 43–53; Peter-Paul Verbeek, *What Things Do: Philosophical Reflections on Technology, Agency, and Design* (University Park: The Pennsylvania State University Press, 2005); Christopher Sims, *Tech Anxiety: Artificial Intelligence and Ontological Awakening in Four Science Fiction Novels* (Jefferson, NC: McFarland and Co., Inc., 2013); Erik Seedhouse, *Beyond Human: Engineering our Future Evolution* (Heidelberg: Springer, 2014).
24. Jane Wakefield, "Are You Scared Yet? Meet Norman, the Psychopathic AI," *BBC News*, 2 June 2018, http://www.bbc.com/news/technology-44040008.
25. Rey Koslowski and Friedrich Kratchwil, "Understanding Change in International Politics: The Soviet Empire's Demise and the International System," *International Organization* 48, no. 2 (Spring 1994): 215–47; Richard Ned Lebow and Thomas Risse-Kappan, *International Relations*

Theory and the End of the Cold War (New York: Columbia University Press, 1995); Tuomas Forsberg, "Power, Interests and Trust: Explaining Gorbachev's Choices at the End of the Cold War," *Review of International Studies* 25, no. 4 (October 1999): 603–21.

26. Daniel Deudney and G. John Ikenberry, "The International Sources of Soviet Change," *International Security* 16, no. 3 (Winter 1991/92): 74–118.

27. William Wohlforth, "Reality Check: Revising Theories of International Politics in Response to the End of the Cold War," *World Politics* 50, no. 4 (July 1998): 660–68; Schweller and Wohlforth, "Power Test," 101–7.

28. Steven Lee Myers and Ellen Barry, "Putin Reclaims Crimea for Russia and Bitterly Denounces the West," *New York Times*, 18 March 2014, https://www.nytimes.com/2014/03/19/world/europe/ukraine.html; Heather Conley and Jean-Baptiste Jeangène Vilmer, "Successfully Countering Russian Electoral Interference," CSIS Briefs, 21 June 2018, https://www.csis.org/analysis/successfully-countering-russian-electoral-interference; Roy Allison, "Russia Resurgent? Moscow's Campaign to 'Coerce Georgia to Peace,'" *International Affairs* 84, no. 6 (November 2008): 1145–71; Lucy Pasha-Robinson, "The Long History of Russian Deaths in the UK under Mysterious Circumstances," *The Independent*, 6 March 2018, https://www.independent.co.uk/news/uk/home-news/russian-deaths-uk-history-spies-murder-sergei-skripal-alexander-litvinenko-a8242061.html.

29. Emmanuel Adler, "The Spread of Security Communities: Communities of Practice, Self-Restraint, and NATO's Post–Cold War Transformation," *European Journal of International Relations* 14, no. 2 (June 2008): 195–230; Michael Williams and Iver Neumann, "From Alliance to Security Community: NATO, Russia, and the Power of Identity," *Millennium: Journal of International Studies* 29, no. 2 (June 2000): 357–87.

30. Karl Deutsch et al., *Political Community and the North Atlantic Area: International Organization in the Light of Historical Experience* (Princeton: Princeton University Press, 1957); Edgar Furniss, "France, NATO, and European Security," *International Organization* 10, no. 4 (November 1956): 544–58; Harald von Riekhoff, "The Changing Function of NATO," *International Journal: Canada's Journal of Global Policy Analysis* 21, no. 2 (June 1966): 157–72.

31. Peter Baker, "U.S. to Restore Full Relations with Cuba, Erasing a Last Trace of Cold War Hostility," *New York Times*, 17 December 2014, https://www.nytimes.com/2014/12/18/world/americas/us-cuba-relations.html.

32. Jon Lee Anderson, "Donald Trump Reverses Barack Obama's Cuba Policy," *New Yorker*, 17 June 2017, https://www.newyorker.com/news/daily-comment/donald-trump-reverses-barack-obamas-cuba-policy; Tracy Wilkinson, "A Year after Trump Reversed Obama's Opening to Cuba, the U.S. Is Sitting out Havana's Political Revamp," *Los Angeles Times*, 22 June 2018, https://www.latimes.com/nation/la-na-pol-us-cuba-20180622-story.html.

33. Janice Liedl, "Tales of Futures Past: Science Fiction as a Historical Genre," *Rethinking History* 19, no. 2 (April 2015): 285–99. Liedl coedited (with Nancy Reagin) two books related to this concept: *Star Wars and History* (Nashville, TN: Wiley, 2012) and *The Hobbit and History* (Nashville, TN: Wiley, 2014).
34. Donna Haraway, "A Manifesto for Cyborgs: Science, Technology and Socialist Feminism in the 1980s," *Socialist Review* 15, no. 2 (March 1985): 65–107, and "Situated Knowledges: The Science Question in Feminism and the Privilege of Partial Perspective," *Feminist Studies* 14, no. 3 (Autumn 1988): 575–99.
35. The film does not identify the computer's motives (we do not learn what happened until the 1984 sequel, *2010: The Year We Make Contact*). Although Clarke wrote the *2001: A Space Odyssey* novel in conjunction with the movie, it differs in many ways from the film and lays out HAL's "thinking" and motives in more detail.
36. Isaac Asimov, "Runaround," *Astounding Science Fiction* 29, no. 1 (March 1942): 100.
37. Jack Snyder, "One World, Rival Theories," *Foreign Policy* 145 (November/December 2004): 52–62.
38. Ann Leckie, *Ancillary Justice* (London: Orbit, 2013); Harlan Ellison, "I Have No Mouth, and I Must Scream," *IF: Worlds of Science Fiction* 17, no. 3 (March 1967): 24–67.
39. Arthur C. Clarke, "Superiority," *Magazine of Fantasy and Science Fiction* 2, no. 4 (August 1951): 3–11.
40. Sun Tzu, *Art of War*, 193. Griffith translates this passage as: "Although everyone can see the outward aspects, none understands the way in which I have created victory." Sun Tzu (Griffith translation), 100. Clavell's translation is more in line with my interpretation: "All men can see the individual *tactics* necessary to conquer, but almost no one can see the *strategy* out of which total victory is evolved." Sun Tzu (Clavell translation), 28, emphasis added.
41. Sun Tzu (Sawyer translation), 215.

CONCLUSION
1. Clausewitz, *On War*, 121.
2. An alternative scoring method that weighted long-term scores more heavily than short-term scores produced a similar ranking order. The only difference is Marxism falls into last place on its own.
3. Robert Goddard, high school valedictorian oration, "On Taking Things for Granted," in *Papers of Robert H. Goddard*, vol. I, 1898–1924 (New York: McGraw Hill, 1970), 63, and I. Bernard Cohen, "The Papers of Robert H. Goddard," *New York Times*, 2 August 1970, https://www.nytimes.com/1970/08/02/archives/the-papers-of-robert-h-goddard-the-papers-of-rhgoddard.html, 181.

BIBLIOGRAPHY

OFFICIAL DOCUMENTS

Bush, George W. *The National Security Strategy of the United States of America*. Washington, DC: The White House, September 2002.

International Commission on Intervention and State Sovereignty. *The Responsibility to Protect: Research, Bibliography, Background*. Ottawa: International Development Research Centre, 2001.

North Atlantic Treaty Organization. "Summary of the National Reports of NATO Member and Partner Nations to the NATO Committee on Gender Perspectives." 2016. https://www.nato.int/nato_static_fl2014/assets/pdf/pdf_2017_11/20171122_2016_Summary_of_NRs_to_NCGP.pdf.

Obama, Barack. *National Security Strategy*. Washington, DC: The White House, May 2010.

Tarnoff, Curt. "U.S. Agency for International Development (USAID): Background, Operations, and Issues." Report R44117. Washington, DC: Congressional Research Service, 21 July 2015.

Trump, Donald J. *National Security Strategy of the United States*. Washington, DC: The White House, December 2017.

SCHOLARLY BOOKS

Adams, John, and Abigail Adams. *The Letters of John and Abigail Adams*. Edited by John Shuffelton. London: Penguin, 2003.

Allen, Brooke. *Benazir Bhutto: Favored Daughter*. Boston: Houghton Mifflin Harcourt, 2015.

Amanat, Abbas. *Iran: A Modern History*. New Haven: Yale University Press, 2017.

Angell, Norman. *The Great Illusion*. New York: Putnam's Sons, 1909.

Arendt, Hannah. *The Origins of Totalitarianism*. San Diego: Harcourt Brace Jovanovich, 1973.

Arjonand, Said Amir. *The Turban for the Crown*. New York: Oxford University Press, 1988.

Asimov, Isaac. *The Roman Empire*. Boston: Houghton Mifflin Harcourt, 1967.

———. *The Roman Republic*. Boston: Houghton Mifflin Harcourt, 1966.

Axelrod, Robert. *Evolution of Cooperation*. New York: Basic Books, 1984.

Bhutto, Benazir. *Daughter of the East: An Autobiography*. London: Hamish Hamilton, 1988.

Black, Jeremy. *Great Powers and the Quest for Hegemony: The World Order since 1500*. London: Routledge, 2007.

Bloom, Mia. *Bombshell: Women and Terrorism*. Philadelphia: University of Pennsylvania Press, 2011.
Bostrom, Nick. *Superintelligence: Paths, Dangers, Strategies*. Oxford: Oxford University Press, 2014.
Bowen, H. V. *The Business of Empire: The East India Company and Imperial Britain, 1756–1833*. Cambridge: Cambridge University Press, 2006.
Brendel, Mats, and Monica Serrano, eds. *Transnational Organized Crime and International Security: Business as Usual?* Boulder, CO: Lynne Rienner, 2002.
Brooks, Max, et al., eds. *Strategy Strikes Back: How Star Wars Explains Modern Military Conflict*. Lincoln, NE: Potomac Books, 2018.
———. *Winning Westeros: How* Game of Thrones *Explains Modern Military Conflict*. Lincoln, NE: Potomac Books, 2019.
Bryson, Valerie. *Feminist Political Theory*, 3rd edition. London: Palgrave, 2016.
Bull, Hedley. *The Anarchical Society*. New York: Columbia University Press, 1977.
Burkett, Elinor. *Golda*. New York: Harper Collins, 2008.
Burleigh, Michael. *Blood and Rage: A Cultural History of Terrorism*. New York: Harper Collins Publishers, 2009.
Buzan, Barry. *From International Theory to World Society? English School Theory and the Social Structure of Globalisation*. Cambridge: Cambridge University Press, 2004.
Buzan, Barry, and Richard Little. *International Systems in World History: Remaking the Study of International Relations*. Oxford: Oxford University Press, 2000.
Carr, Edward Hallett. *The Twenty Years' Crisis, 1919–1939: An Introduction to the Study of International Relations*. London: Macmillan, 1939.
Chapman, Peter. *Bananas: How the United Fruit Company Shaped the World*. Edinburgh: Commongate, 2007.
Cheng, Bin. *Studies in International Space Law*. Oxford: Oxford University Press, 1997.
Clausewitz, Carl von. *On War*. Edited by Michael Howard and Peter Paret. Princeton: Princeton University Press, 1976.
Cockell, Charles, ed. *Human Governance Beyond Earth*. Cham, CH: Springer, 2015.
———. *The Meaning of Liberty beyond Earth*. Cham, CH: Springer, 2015.
Colby, Jason. *The Business of Empire: United Fruit, Race, and U.S. Expansion in Central America*. Ithaca: Cornell University Press, 2011.
Crawford, Neta. *Argument and Change in World Politics: Ethics, Decolonization, and Humanitarian Intervention*. Cambridge: Cambridge University Press, 2002.
Cudworth, Erika, Stephen Hobden, and Emilian Kavalski, eds. *Posthuman Dialogues in International Relations*. London: Routledge, 2017.
Daase, Christopher, et al., eds. *Recognition in International Relations*. Hampshire, UK: Palgrave Macmillan, 2015.
Davies, Thomas, ed. *Routledge Handbook of NGOs and International Relations*. Abingdon, UK: Routledge, 2019.

DeMars, William, and Dennis Dijkzeul, eds. *The NGO Challenge for International Relations Theory*. London: Routledge, 2015.
Deng, Yong. *China's Struggle for Status: The Realignment of International Relations*. Cambridge: Cambridge University Press, 2008.
Deutsch, Karl, et al. *Political Community and the North Atlantic Area: International Organization in the Light of Historical Experience*. Princeton: Princeton University Press, 1957.
Dolman, Everett. *Astropolitik: Classic Geopolitics in the Space Age*. London: Frank Cass, 2002.
Doyle, William. *The Oxford History of the French Revolution*. Oxford: Clarendon Press, 1989.
Drachkovitch, Milorad, ed. *Marxism in the Modern World*. Stanford, CA: Stanford University Press, 1965.
Drezner, Daniel. *Theories of International Politics and Zombies*. Princeton: Princeton University Press, 2014.
Dunne, Tim. *Inventing International Society: A History of the English School*. Basingstoke, UK: Macmillan, 1998.
Eager, Paige Whaley. *From Freedom Fighters to Terrorists: Women and Political Violence*. Hampshire, UK: Ashgate, 2008.
Engels, Friedrich. *Socialism: Utopian and Scientific*. Translated by Edward Aveling. Chicago: Charles H. Kerr and Company, 1880.
Enloe, Cynthia. *Bananas, Beaches, and Bases: Making Feminist Sense of International Politics*. Berkeley: University of California Press, 1989.
Fanon, Frantz. *The Wretched of the Earth*. New York: Grove Weidenfeld, 1963.
Ferguson, Niall. *Empire: The Rise and Demise of the British World Order and the Lessons for Global Power*. New York: Basic Books, 1996.
Figes, Orlando. *A People's Tragedy: A History of the Russian Revolution*. New York: Viking, 1996.
Finnemore, Martha. *National Interests in International Society*. Ithaca: Cornell University Press, 1996.
———. *The Purpose of Intervention: Changing Beliefs about the Use of Force*. Ithaca: Cornell University Press, 2003.
Frank, Katherine. *Indira: The Life of Indira Nehru Gandhi*. Boston: Houghton Mifflin Company, 2002.
Freedman, Carl. *Critical Theory and Science Fiction*. Middletown, CT: Wesleyan University Press, 2000.
Friedman, Milton. *Capitalism and Freedom*. Chicago: University of Chicago Press, 1962.
Friedman, Thomas. *The Lexus and the Olive Tree: Understanding Globalization*. New York: Picador, 1999.
———. *The World Is Flat*. New York: Picador, 2005.
Furet, François. *Interpreting the French Revolution*. Cambridge: Cambridge University Press, 1981.
Gaddis, John Lewis. *Strategies of Containment*. New York: Oxford University Press, 1982.

Garthoff, Raymond. *Détente and Confrontation: American-Soviet Relations from Nixon to Reagan*. Washington, DC: Brookings, 1994.
Ghosh, Srikanta. *Indian Democracy Derailed—Politics and Politicians*. New Delhi: APH Publishing Corporation, 1997.
Gibbon, Edward. *The History of the Decline and Fall of the Roman Empire*. 1776. Reprint, London: Penguin, 2000.
Gilpin, Robert. *War and Change in World Politics*. Cambridge: Cambridge University Press, 1981.
Goddard, Robert. "On Taking Things for Granted." *Papers of Robert H. Goddard*, vol. I, 1898–1924. New York: McGraw Hill, 1970, 63.
Grotius, Hugo. *The Law of War and Peace*. Translated by Edward Aveling. 1625. Reprint, New York: Walter J. Black, 1949.
Gurr, Ted. *Why Men Rebel*. Princeton: Princeton University Press, 1971.
Harding, Sandra, ed. *The Feminist Standpoint Theory Reader: Intellectual and Political Controversies*. New York: Routledge, 2004.
Heidegger, Martin. *What Is Called Thinking?* Translated by J. Glenn Gray. New York: Harper and Row, 1968.
Herz, John. *Political Realism and Political Idealism: A Study of Theory and Realities*. Chicago: University of Chicago Press, 1951.
Hibbert, Christopher. *The Rise and Fall of the House of Medici*. London: Allen Lane, 1974.
Hirschman, Albert. *National Power and the Structure of Foreign Trade*. 1945. Reprint, Berkeley: University of California Press, 1980.
Hobson, John. *Imperialism: A Study*. New York: James Pott and Company, 1902.
Hopf, Ted. *Social Construction of International Politics: Identities and Foreign Policies, Moscow, 1995 and 1999*. Ithaca: Cornell University Press, 2002.
Huntington, Samuel. *The Clash of Civilizations and the Remaking of World Order*. New York: Touchstone, 1996.
James, Lawrence. *The Rise and Fall of the British Empire*. New York: St. Martin's Griffin, 1997.
Jayakar, Pupul. *Indira Gandhi: A Biography*. New York: Viking, 1995.
Johnson, Chalmers. *Revolutionary Change*. New York: Little, Brown and Company, 1966.
Kahneman, Daniel, Paul Slovic, and Amos Tversky, eds. *Judgment under Uncertainty: Heuristics and Biases*. Cambridge: Cambridge University Press, 1982.
Kaku, Michio. *The Future of Humanity: Terraforming Mars, Interstellar Travel, Immortality, and Our Destiny beyond Earth*. New York: Doubleday, 2018.
Kant, Immanuel. *Perpetual Peace: A Philosophical Sketch*. Translated by M. Campbell Smith. London: George Allen and Unwin Ltd., 1795.
Kaplan, Lawrence. *NATO Divided, NATO United: The Evolution of an Alliance*. Westport, CT: Praeger, 2004.
Katz, Mark. *Revolutions and Revolutionary Waves*. New York: Macmillan, 1999.
Katzenstein, Peter, ed. *The Culture of National Security: Norms and Identity in World Politics*. New York: Columbia University Press, 1996.

Kennedy, Paul. *The Rise and Fall of the Great Powers: Economic Change and Military Conflict from 1500 to 2000*. New York: Vintage, 1989.

———. *Rise of the Anglo-German Antagonism, 1860–1914*. London: Ashfield Press, 1987.

Keohane, Robert. *After Hegemony: Cooperation and Discord in the World Political Economy*. Princeton: Princeton University Press, 1984.

Keohane, Robert, and Joseph Nye. *Power and Interdependence: World Politics in Transition*. Toronto: Little, Brown and Company, 1977.

Keynes, John Maynard. *The General Theory of Employment, Interest and Money*. London: Macmillan, 1936.

Khong, Yuen Foong. *Analogies at War: Korea, Munich, Dien Bien Phu, and the Vietnam Decision of 1965*. Princeton: Princeton University Press, 1992.

Kiersey, Nicholas, and Iver Neumann, eds. *Battlestar Galactica and International Relations*. Abingdon, UK: Routledge, 2013.

Kindleberger, Charles. *The World in Depression, 1929–1939*. London: Penguin, 1987.

Klagsbrun, Francine. *Lioness: Golda Meir and the Nation of Israel*. New York: Schocken, 2017.

Klotz, Audie. *Norms in International Relations: The Struggle against Apartheid*. Ithaca: Cornell University Press, 1995.

Krasner, Stephen. *International Regimes*. Ithaca: Cornell University Press, 1983.

Lachs, Manfred. *The Law of Outer Space: An Experience in Contemporary Law-Making*. Leiden: Martinus Nijhoff Publishers, 2010.

Langley, Lester. *The Banana Wars: United States Intervention in the Caribbean, 1898–1934*. Lexington: University Press of Kentucky, 1983.

Lawrence, T. E. *Seven Pillars of Wisdom*. 1922. Reprint, Herfordshire, UK: Wordsworth, 1997.

Lebow, Richard Ned, and Thomas Risse-Kappan. *International Relations Theory and the End of the Cold War*. New York: Columbia University Press, 1995.

Lehmann, Karsten. *Religious NGOs in International Relations: The Construction of "the Religious" and "the Security."* London: Routledge, 2016.

Lenin, V. I. *Imperialism: The Highest Stage of Capitalism*. Petrograd: Life and Knowledge Publishers, 1917.

———. *State and Revolution*. New York: International Publishers, 1932.

Liberman, Peter. *Does Conquest Pay? The Exploitation of Occupied Industrial Societies*. Princeton: Princeton University Press, 1996.

Liedl, Janice, and Nancy Reagin. *The Hobbit and History*. Nashville, TN: Wiley, 2014.

Lieven, Anatol, and John Hulsman. *Ethical Realism: A Vision for America's Role in the World*. New York: Pantheon, 2006.

Llewellyn-Jones, Rosie. *The Great Uprising in India, 1857–58: Untold Stories, Indian and British*. Rochester, NY: Boydell and Brewer, 2007.

Machiavelli, Niccolò. *The Prince*. 1532. Reprint, London: Penguin, 2011.

Marlay, Ross, and Clark Neher. *Patriots and Tyrants: Ten Asian Leaders*. Lanham, MD: Rowman and Littlefield Publishers, Inc., 1999.

Martines, Lauro. *April Blood: Florence and the Plot against the Medici.* New York: Oxford University Press, 2003.
Marx, Karl. *A Contribution to the Critique of Political Economy.* 1859. Reprint, Chicago: Charles H. Kerr and Company, 1904.
———. "Wage Labour and Capital." December 1847. https://www.marxists.org/archive/marx/works/1847/wage-labour/.
Marx, Karl, and Friedrich Engels. *The Communist Manifesto.* 1848. Reprint, New York: Penguin, 2002.
Mearsheimer, John. *The Tragedy of Great Power Politics.* New York: W. W. Norton and Co., 2001.
Meger, Sara. *Rape Loot Pillage: The Political Economy of Sexual Violence in Armed Conflict.* New York: Oxford University Press, 2016.
Miller, Gregory. *The Shadow of the Past: Reputation and Military Alliances before the First World War.* Ithaca: Cornell University Press, 2012.
Milner, Helen. *Resisting Protectionism: Global Industries and the Politics of International Trade.* Princeton: Princeton University Press, 1988.
Modelski, George, and William Thompson. *Seapower in Global Politics, 1494–1993.* London: Palgrave Macmillan, 1988.
Moon, Katharine. *Sex among Allies: Military Prostitution in U.S.-Korea Relations.* New York: Columbia University Press, 1997.
Moore, Charles. *Margaret Thatcher: Everything She Wants.* New York: Knopf, 2015.
———. *Margaret Thatcher: Herself Alone.* New York: Knopf, 2019.
———. *Margaret Thatcher: Not for Turning.* New York: Knopf, 2013.
Morgenthau, Hans. *Politics among Nations: The Struggle for Power and Peace.* New York: Alfred A. Knopf, 1954.
Mueller, Karl, et al. *Striking First: Preemptive and Preventive Attack in U.S. National Security Policy.* Santa Monica, CA: RAND, 2006.
Murray, Michelle. *The Struggle for Recognition in International Relations: Status, Revisionism, and Rising Powers.* Oxford: Oxford University Press, 2019.
Ness, Cindy. *Female Terrorism and Militancy: Agency, Utility, and Organization.* London: Routledge, 2007.
Neumann, Iver, and Daniel Nexon, eds. *Harry Potter and International Relations.* Lanham, MD: Rowman and Littlefield, 2006.
Neustadt, Richard, and Ernest May. *Thinking in Time: The Uses of History for Decision-Makers.* New York: The Free Press, 1988.
Niebuhr, Reinhold. *Moral Man and Immoral Society: A Study in Ethics and Politics.* New York: Scribners, 1932.
Nierstrasz, Chris. *In the Shadow of the Company: The Dutch East India Company and Its Servants in the Period of Its Decline (1740–1796).* Leiden: Brill, 2012.
———. *Rivalry for Trade in Tea and Textiles: The English and Dutch East India Companies (1700–1800).* New York: Palgrave Macmillan, 2015.
Nish, Ian. *The Anglo-Japanese Alliance: The Diplomacy of Two Island Empires, 1894–1907.* London: Athlone Press, 1966.

Nölke, Andrea, and Christian May, eds. *Handbook of the International Political Economy of the Corporation*. Cheterham, UK: Edward Elgar, 2018.
Olson, Mancur. *The Logic of Collective Action: Public Goods and the Theory of Groups*. Cambridge, MA: Harvard University Press, 1965.
Organski, A. F. K. *World Politics*. New York: Alfred A. Knopf, 1958.
Paikowsky, Deganit. *The Power of the Space Club*. Cambridge: Cambridge University Press, 2017.
Palmer, R. R. *Twelve Who Ruled: The Committee of Public Safety during the Terror*. Princeton: Princeton University Press, 1941.
Parks, Tim. *Medici Money: Banking, Metaphysics, and Art in Fifteenth-Century Florence*. New York: W. W. Norton and Company, 2005.
Pettman, Jan Jindy. *Worlding Women: A Feminist International Politics*. Sydney: Allen and Unwin, 1996.
Plato. *Republic*, books 1–5. Translated by M. Campbell Smith. Cambridge, MA: Harvard University Press, 1930.
Pressman, Jeremy. *Warring Friends: Alliance Restraint in International Politics*. Ithaca: Cornell University Press, 2008.
Reagin, Nancy, and Janice Liedl. *Star Wars and History*. Nashville, TN: Wiley, 2012.
Reich, Robert. *The Work of Nations: Preparing Ourselves for 21st Century Capitalism*. New York: Vintage Books, 1992.
Reinalda, Bob, ed. *The Ashgate Research Companion to Non-State Actors*. London: Routledge, 2016.
Ricardo, David. *On the Principles of Political Economy, and Taxation*. London: John Murray, 1817.
Robins, Nick. *The Corporation that Changed the World: How the East India Company Shaped the Modern Multinational*. London: Pluto Press, 2006.
Rosenau, William. *Tonight We Bombed the U.S. Capitol: The Explosive Story of M19, America's First Female Terrorist Group*. New York: Atria Books, 2020.
Rousseau, Jean-Jacques. *The Social Contract; or, Principles of Political Rights*. 1762. Reprint, Harlow, UK: Penguin Books, 2004.
Russett, Bruce. *Grasping the Democratic Peace: Principles for a Post–Cold War World*. Princeton: Princeton University Press, 1993.
Sagan, Scott. *The Limits of Safety: Organization, Accidents, and Nuclear Weapons*. Princeton: Princeton University Press, 1993.
Sagan, Scott, and Kenneth Waltz. *The Spread of Nuclear Weapons: A Debate*. New York: W. W. Norton and Co., Inc., 1995.
Schelling, Thomas. *Arms and Influence*. New Haven, CT: Yale University Press, 1966.
———. *The Strategy of Conflict*. Cambridge, MA: Harvard University Press, 1960.
Schroeder, Paul. *Austria, Great Britain and the Crimean War: The Destruction of the European Concert*. Ithaca: Cornell University Press, 1972.
———. *The Transformation of European Politics, 1763–1848*. Oxford: Oxford University Press, 1994.

Schweller, Randall. *Deadly Imbalances: Tripolarity and Hitler's Strategy of World Conquest*. New York: Columbia University Press, 1998.

———. *Maxwell's Demon and the Golden Apple*. Baltimore: The Johns Hopkins University Press, 2014.

———. *Unanswered Threats: Political Constraints on the Balance of Power*. Princeton: Princeton University Press, 2006.

Seed, David, ed. *A Companion to Science Fiction*. Malden, UK: Blackwell Publishing, 2005.

Seedhouse, Erik. *Beyond Human: Engineering our Future Evolution*. Heidelberg: Springer, 2014.

Shepherd, Laura, ed. *Gender Matters in Global Politics*. Abingdon, UK: Routledge, 2015.

Sims, Christopher. *Tech Anxiety: Artificial Intelligence and Ontological Awakening in Four Science Fiction Novels*. Jefferson, NC: McFarland and Co., Inc., 2013.

Skocpol, Theda. *States and Social Revolutions*. Cambridge: Cambridge University Press, 1979.

Smith, Adam. *An Inquiry into the Nature and Causes of the Wealth of Nations*. 1776. Reprint, New York: Bantam Classics, 2003.

Smith, David, Dorothy Solinger, and Steven Topik, eds. *States and Sovereignty in the Global Economy*. London: Routledge, 1999.

Snyder, Glenn. *Deterrence and Defense: Toward a Theory of National Security*. Princeton: Princeton University Press, 1961.

Snyder, Jack. *Myths of Empire: Domestic Politics and International Ambition*. Ithaca: Cornell University Press, 1991.

Spilsbury, John. *The Indian Mutiny*. London: Weidenfeld and Nicolson, 2007.

Steinberg, Blema. *Women in Power: The Personalities and Leadership Styles of Indira Gandhi, Golda Meir, and Margaret Thatcher*. Montreal: McGill-Queen's University Press, 2008.

Stephen, James. *Lectures on the History of France*. New York: Harper and Brothers Publishers, 1875.

Stern, Philip. *The Company-State: Corporate Sovereignty and the Early Modern Foundations of the British Empire in India*. Oxford: Oxford University Press, 2011.

Stolte, Christina. *Brazil's Africa Strategy: Role Conception and the Drive for International Status*. New York: Palgrave Macmillan, 2015.

Strassler, Robert, ed. *The Landmark Thucydides*. New York: Free Press, 1996.

Tannenwald, Nina. *The Nuclear Taboo: The United States and the Non-Use of Nuclear Weapons*. Cambridge: Cambridge University Press, 2007.

Thatcher, Margaret. *The Downing Street Years*. New York: Harper Collins, 1993.

Tickner, J. Ann. *Gender in International Relations: Feminist Perspectives on Achieving Global Security*. New York: Columbia University Press, 1992.

———. *Gendering World Politics: Issues and Approaches in the Post–Cold War Era*. New York: Columbia University Press, 2001.

Tilly, Charles. *European Revolutions, 1492–1992*. Oxford: Blackwell, 1993.
Tocqueville, Alexis de. *The Old Regime and the Revolution*, trans. John Bonner. New York: Harper and Brothers, 1856.
Trotsky, Leon. *The History of the Russian Revolution*. Translated by Max Eastman. Ann Arbor: The University of Michigan Press, 1974.
Tse-Tung, Mao. *Selected Works of Mao Tse-Tung*, vol. I. Beijing: Foreign Language Press, 1965.
Tzu, Sun. *The Art of War*. Translated by James Clavell. New York: Delacorte Press, 1983.
———. *The Art of War*. Translated by Ralph Sawyer. Boulder, CO: Westview Press, Inc., 1994.
———. *The Art of War*. Translated by Samuel Griffith. New York: Oxford University Press, 1971.
Verbeek, Peter-Paul. *What Things Do: Philosophical Reflections on Technology, Agency, and Design*. University Park: The Pennsylvania State University Press, 2005.
Walt, Stephen. *The Origins of Alliances*. Ithaca: Cornell University Press, 1987.
———. *Revolution and War*. Ithaca: Cornell University Press, 1997.
Waltz, Kenneth. *Theory of International Politics*. New York: McGraw-Hill, 1979.
Weeks, Edythe. *Outer Space Development, Space Law and International Relations*. Cambridge: Cambridge University Press, 2012.
Weitsman, Patricia. *Dangerous Alliances: Proponents of Peace, Weapons of War*. Stanford, CA: Stanford University Press, 2003.
Wendt, Alexander. *Quantum Mind and Social Science: Unifying Physical and Social Ontology*. Cambridge: Cambridge University Press, 2015.
———. *Social Theory of International Politics*. Cambridge: Cambridge University Press, 1999.
Westcott, Allan, ed. *Mahan on Naval Warfare: Selections from the Writings of Rear Admiral Alfred T. Mahan*. Mineola, NY: Dover Publications, Inc., 1999.
White, John. *Transition to Global Rivalry: Alliance Diplomacy and the Quadruple Entente, 1895–1907*. Cambridge: Cambridge University Press, 2002.
Wight, Martin. *Power Politics*. London: Royal Institute of International Affairs, 1978.
———. *Systems of States*. Leicester, UK: Leicester University Press, 1977.
Wolfers, Arnold. *Discord and Collaboration: Essays on International Politics*. Baltimore: The Johns Hopkins University Press, 1962.
Yergin, Daniel, and Joseph Stanislaw. *The Commanding Heights: The Battle for the World Economy*. New York: Touchstone, 2002.

ARTICLES, BOOK CHAPTERS, AND ESSAYS
Abbott, Kenneth. "International Relations Theory, International Law, and the Regime Governing Atrocities in Internal Conflicts." *American Journal of International Law* 93, no. 2 (April 1999): 361–79.

Abbott, Kenneth, and Duncan Snidal. "Hard and Soft Law in International Governance." *International Organization* 54, no. 3 (Summer 2000): 421–56.

———. "Why States Act through Formal International Organizations." *Journal of Conflict Resolution* 41, no. 1 (February 1998): 3–32.

Adler, Emmanuel. "The Spread of Security Communities: Communities of Practice, Self-Restraint, and NATO's Post–Cold War Transformation." *European Journal of International Relations* 14, no. 2 (June 2008): 195–230.

Allison, Roy. "Russia Resurgent? Moscow's Campaign to 'Coerce Georgia to Peace.'" *International Affairs* 84, no. 6 (November 2008): 1145–71.

Asal, Victor, and Amira Jadoon. "When Women Fight: Unemployment, Territorial Control and the Prevalence of Female Combatants in Insurgent Organizations." *Dynamics of Asymmetric Conflict* 13, no. 3 (December 2019): 258–81.

Bakunin, Mikhail. "Revolutionary Catechism." In *Bakunin on Anarchism*, edited by Sam Dolgoff, 76–97. Montreal: Black Rose Books, 2002.

Banerjee, Kiran, and Joseph MacKay. "Communities of Practice, Impression Management, and Great Power Status: Military Observers in the Russo-Japanese War." *European Journal of International Security* (October 2020): 274–93.

Banks, Cyndi. "Introduction: Women, Gender, and Terrorism: Gendering Terrorism." *Women and Criminal Justice* 29, nos. 4–5 (September 2019): 181–302.

Barbieri, Katherine. "Economic Interdependence: A Path to Peace or a Source of Interstate Conflict?" *Journal of Peace Research* 33, no. 1 (February 1996): 29–49.

Barnett, Michael. "Bringing in the New World Order: Liberalism, Legitimacy, and the United Nations." *World Politics* 49, no. 4 (July 1997): 526–51.

Baxter, Stephen. "The Cold Equations: Extraterrestrial Liberty in Science Fiction." In *The Meaning of Liberty beyond Earth*, edited by Charles S. Cockell, 13–31. Cham, CH: Springer, 2015.

Berenskoetter, Felix. "Friends, There Are No Friends? An Intimate Reframing of the International." *Millennium* 33, no. 3 (September 2007): 647–76.

———. "Reclaiming the Vision Thing: Constructivists as Students of the Future." *International Studies Quarterly* 55, no. 3 (September 2011): 647–68.

Brunner, Cornelia, and Dorothy Bennett. "Technology and Gender: Differences in Masculine and Feminine Views." *NASSP Bulletin* 81, no. 592 (November 1997): 46–51.

Chaikin, Andrew. "Meeting of the Minds: Buzz Aldrin Visits Arthur C. Clarke." *Space Illustrated*, 27 February 2001.

Chase-Dunn, Christopher, Thomas Hall, and E. Susan Manning. "Rise and Fall: East-West Synchronicity and Indic Exceptionalism Reexamined." *Social Science History* 24, no. 4 (Winter 2000): 727–54.

Chase-Dunn, Christopher, and Richard Rubinson. "Toward a Structural Perspective on the World-System." *Politics and Society* 7, no. 4 (December 1977): 453–76.

Checkel, Jeffrey. "Norms, Institutions, and National Identity in Contemporary Europe." *International Studies Quarterly* 43, no. 1 (March 1999): 83–114.

Christensen, Thomas, and Jack Snyder. "Chain Gangs and Passed Bucks: Predicting Alliance Patterns in Multipolarity." *International Organization* 44, no. 2 (Spring 1990): 137–68.

Cohn, Carol. "Sex and Death in the Rational World of Defense Intellectuals." *Signs* 12, no. 4 (Summer 1987): 687–718.

Conley, Heather, and Jean-Baptiste Jeangène Vilmer. "Successfully Countering Russian Electoral Interference." CSIS Briefs, 21 June 2018, https://www.csis.org/analysis/successfully-countering-russian-electoral-interference.

Copeland, Dale. "A Realist Critique of the English School." *Review of International Studies* 29, no. 3 (July 2003): 427–41.

Cox, Robert. "Ideologies and the New International Economic Order: Reflections on Some Recent Literature." *International Organization* 33, no. 2 (Spring 1979): 257–302.

Crawford, Netta. "The Slippery Slope to Preventive War." *Ethics and International Affairs* 17, no. 1 (March 2003): 30–36.

Crawford, Timothy. "Preventing Enemy Coalitions: How Wedge Strategies Shape Power Politics." *International Security* 35, no. 4 (Spring 2011): 155–89.

Creighton, Jolene. "The 'Father of Artificial Intelligence' Says Singularity Is 30 Years Away." *Futurism.com*, 14 February 2018, https://futurism.com/father-artificial-intelligence-singularity-decades-away.

Cudworth, Erika, and Stephen Hobden. "Of Parts and Wholes: International Relations beyond the Human." *Millennium: Journal of International Studies* 41, no. 3 (June 2013): 430–50.

Cunningham, Karla. "Cross Regional Trends in Female Terrorism." *Studies in Conflict and Terrorism* 26, no. 3 (May 2003): 171–95.

Deudney, Daniel, and G. John Ikenberry. "The International Sources of Soviet Change." *International Security* 16, no. 3 (Winter 1991/92): 74–118.

Deutsch, Karl, and David Singer. "Multipolar Power Systems and International Stability." *World Politics* 16, no. 3 (April 1964): 390–406.

Dietz, Mary. "Current Controversies in Feminist Theory." *Annual Review of Political Science* 6 (June 2003): 399–431.

Dishman, Chris. "The Leaderless Nexus: When Crime and Terror Converge." *Studies in Conflict and Terrorism* 28, no. 3 (May 2005): 237–52.

———. "Terrorism, Crime, and Transformation." *Studies in Conflict and Terrorism* 24, no. 1 (January 2001): 43–58.

Dolinski, Dariusz, et al. "Would You Deliver an Electric Shock in 2015? Obedience in the Experimental Paradigm Developed by Stanley Milgrom in the 50 Years Following the Original Studies." *Social Psychology and Personality Science* 8, no. 8 (November 2017): 927–33.

Doyle, Michael. "Liberalism and World Politics." *American Political Science Review* 80, no. 4 (December 1986): 1151–69.

———. "Review Article: Stalemate in the North-South Debate: Strategies and the New International Economic Order." *World Politics* 35, no. 3 (April 1983): 426–64.

Doz, Yves, and C. K. Prahalad. "How MNCs Cope with Host Government Intervention." *Harvard Business Review* 58, no. 2 (March 1980): 149–57.

Drake, Nadia. "Here's Why Women May Be the Best Suited for Spaceflight." *National Geographic*, 12 July 2019, https://www.nationalgeographic.com/magazine/2019/07/space-travel-four-ways-women-are-a-better-fit-than-men/.

Dube, Oeindrila, and S. P. Harish. "Queen." *Journal of Political Economy* 128, no. 7 (July 2020): 2579–652.

Dulles, John Foster. "Policy for Security and Peace." *Foreign Affairs* 32, no. 3 (April 1954): 353–64.

Duvall, Raymond. "Dependence and Dependencia Theory: Notes toward Precision of Concept and Argument." *International Organization* 32, no. 1 (January 1978): 51–78.

Earle, Edward Mead. "Adam Smith, Alexander Hamilton, Friedrich List: The Economic Foundations of Military Power." In *Makers of Modern Strategy: From Machiavelli to the Nuclear Age*, edited by Peter Paret, 217–61. Princeton: Princeton University Press, 1986.

Elrod, Richard. "The Concert of Europe: A Fresh Look at an International System." *World Politics* 28, no. 2 (January 1976): 159–74.

Enloe, Cynthia. "'Gender' Is Not Enough: The Need for a Feminist Consciousness." *International Affairs* 80, no. 1 (January 2004): 95–97.

Fagen, Richard. "Studying Latin American Politics: Some Implications of a *Dependencia* Approach." *Latin American Research Review* 12, no. 2 (January 1977): 3–26.

Fearon, James, and Alexander Wendt. "Rationalism v. Constructivism: A Skeptical View." In *Handbook of International Relations*, edited by Walter Carlsnaes, Thomas Risse, and Beth Simmons, 52–72. London: Sage Publications, 2002.

Ferguson, Niall. "Hegemony or Empire?," *Foreign Affairs* 82, no. 5 (September/October 2003): 154–61.

Finnemore, Martha, and Kathryn Sikkink. "Taking Stock: The Constructivist Research Program in International Relations and Comparative Politics." *Annual Review of Political Science* 4 (June 2001): 391–416.

Florini, Ann. "The Evolution of International Norms." *International Studies Quarterly* 40, no. 3 (September 1996): 363–89.

Forsberg, Tuomas. "Power, Interests and Trust: Explaining Gorbachev's Choices at the End of the Cold War." *Review of International Studies* 25, no. 4 (October 1999): 603–21.

Furniss, Edgar. "France, NATO, and European Security." *International Organization* 10, no. 4 (November 1956): 544–58.

Gargiulo, Joseph. "The Utopian Future of 'Star Trek' Doesn't Work without Extreme Inequality and Some Slavery." *Business Insider*, 17 October 2015, https://www.businessinsider.com/utopian-future-of-star-trek-2015-10.

Gartzke, Erik. "The Capitalist Peace." *American Journal of Political Science* 51, no. 1 (January 2007): 166–91.

Gentry, Caron. "Women and Terrorism." In *The Oxford Handbook of Terrorism*, edited by Erica Chenoweth, et al., 414–28. Oxford: Oxford University Press, 2019.

———, and Laura Sjoberg. "Terrorism and Political Violence." In *Gender Matters in Global Politics*, edited by Laura Shepherd, 120–30. Abingdon, UK: Routledge, 2015.

Glaser, Charles. "The Security Dilemma Revisited." *World Politics* 50, no. 1 (October 1997): 171–210.

Glaser, Charles, and Chaim Kaufmann. "What Is the Offense-Defense Balance and Can We Measure It?" *International Security* 22, no. 4 (Spring 1998): 44–82.

Gneezy, Uri, Kenneth Leonard, and John List. "Gender Differences in Competition: Evidence from a Matrilineal and a Patriarchal Society." *Econometrica* 77, no. 5 (September 2009): 1637–64.

Goldstone, Jack. "Theories of Revolution: The Third Generation." *World Politics* 32, no. 3 (April 1980): 425–53.

———. "Towards a Fourth Generation of Revolutionary Theory." *American Review of Political Science* 4, no. 1 (June 2001): 139–87.

Green, Karen. "Parity and Procedural Justice." *Essays in Philosophy* 7, no. 1 (January 2006): 18–28.

Greenhill, Brian. "Recognition and Collective Identity Formation in International Politics." *European Journal of International Relations* 14, no. 2 (June 2008): 343–68.

Grieco, Joseph. "Anarchy and the Limits of Cooperation: A Realist Critique of the Newest Liberal Institutionalism." *International Organization* 42, no. 3 (Summer 1988): 485–507.

Haas, Ernst. "The Balance of Power: Prescription, Concept, or Propaganda?" *World Politics* 5, no. 4 (July 1953): 442–47.

Haggard, Stephen, and Beth Simmons. "Theories of International Regimes." *International Organization* 41, no. 3 (Summer 1987): 491–517.

Haraway, Donna. "A Manifesto for Cyborgs: Science, Technology, and Socialist Feminism in the 1980s." *Socialist Review* 15, no. 2 (March 1985): 65–107.

———. "Situated Knowledges: The Science Question in Feminism and the Privilege of Partial Perspective." *Feminist Studies* 14, no. 3 (Autumn 1988): 575–99.

Hasenclever, Andrea, Peter Mayer, and Volker Rittberger. "Integrating Theories of International Regimes." *Review of International Studies* 26, no. 1 (January 2000): 3–33.

Heginbotham, Eric, and Richard Samuels. "Mercantile Realism and Japanese Foreign Policy." *International Security* 22, no. 4 (Spring 1998): 171–203.

Hellmann, Gunther, and Reinhard Wolf. "Neorealism, Neoliberal Institutionalism, and the Future of NATO." *Security Studies* 3, no. 1 (September 1993): 3–43.

Hopf, Ted. "The Promise of Constructivism in International Relations Theory." *International Security* 23, no. 1 (Summer 1998): 171–200.

Howell, Elizabeth. "Lagrange Points: Parking Places in Space." *Space.com*, 21 August 2017, https://www.space.com/30302-lagrange-points.html.

Hutchinson, Steven, and Pat O'Malley. "A Crime-Terror Nexus? Thinking on Some of the Links between Terrorism and Criminality." *Studies in Conflict and Terrorism* 30, no. 12 (November 2007): 1095–107.

Jervis, Robert. "Cooperation under the Security Dilemma." *World Politics* 30, no. 2 (January 1978): 167–214.

———. "Deterrence Theory Revisited." *World Politics* 31, no. 2 (January 1979): 289–324.

———. "From Balance to Concert: A Study of International Security Cooperation." *World Politics* 38, no. 1 (October 1985): 58–79.

———. "Realism, Neoliberalism, and Cooperation: Understanding the Debate." *International Security* 24, no. 1 (Summer 1999): 42–63.

———. "Security Regimes." *International Organization* 36, no. 2 (Summer 1982): 357–78.

Kaczynski, Theodore. "Industrial Society and Its Future." *New York Times*, 25 May 1996, https://archive.nytimes.com/www.nytimes.com/library/national/unabom-manifesto-1.html.

Kahneman, Daniel, and Amos Tversky. "Prospect Theory: An Analysis of Decision under Risk." *Econometrica* 47, no. 2 (March 1979): 263–92.

Kay, Sean. "NATO, the Kosovo War and Neoliberal Theory." *Contemporary Security Policy* 25, no. 2 (August 2004): 252–79.

Keohane, Robert. "Reciprocity in International Relations." *International Organization* 40, no. 1 (Winter 1986): 1–27.

———, and Lisa Martin. "The Promise of Institutionalist Theory." *International Security* 20, no. 1 (Summer 1995): 39–51.

Kipling, Rudyard. "Regulus." In *A Diversity of Creatures*, 239–70. London: Macmillan and Co., 1917.

———. "The White Man's Burden: The United States and the Philippine Islands, 1899." In *Rudyard Kipling's Verse: Definitive Edition*. Garden City, NY: Doubleday, 1929.

Kissinger, Henry. "The Vietnam Negotiations." *Foreign Affairs* 47 (January 1969): 211–34.

Koslowski, Rey, and Friedrich Kratochwil. "Understanding Change in International Politics: The Soviet Empire's Demise and the International System." *International Organization* 48, no. 2 (Spring 1994): 215–47.

Krasner, Stephen. "Sovereignty." *Foreign Policy* 122 (January/February 2001): 20–29.

Krastev, Ivan. "Eastern Europe's Illiberal Revolution: The Long Road to Democratic Decline." *Foreign Affairs* (May/June 2018), https://www.foreignaffairs.com/articles/hungary/2018-04-16/eastern-europes-illiberal-revolution.

Kupchan, Charles. "After Pax Americana: Benign Power, Regional Integration, and the Sources of a Stable Multipolarity." *International Security* 23, no. 2 (Fall 1998): 40–79.

———. "The Promise of Collective Security." *International Security* 20, no. 1 (Summer 1995): 52–61.

Kupchan, Charles, and Clifford Kupchan. "Concerts, Collective Security, and the Future of Europe." *International Security* 16, no. 1 (Summer 1991): 114–61.

Kydd, Andrew. "Game Theory and the Spiral Model." *World Politics* 49, no. 3 (April 1997): 371–400.

Lake, David. "Beyond Anarchy: The Importance of Security Institutions." *International Security* 26, no. 1 (Summer 2001): 129–60.

Layne, Christopher. "The Unipolar Illusion: Why New Great Powers Will Rise." *International Security* 17, no. 4 (Spring 1993): 5–51.

Leander, Anna. "Technological Agency in the Co-Constitution of Legal Expertise and the U.S. Drone Program." *Leiden Journal of International Law* 26, no. 4 (December 2013): 811–31.

Lenin, V. I. "The Three Sources and Three Component Parts of Marxism." *Prosveshcheniye* no. 3 (1913), https://www.marxists.org/archive/lenin/works/1913/mar/x01.htm.

Levy, Jack. "Declining Power and the Preventive Motivation for War." *World Politics* 40, no. 1 (October 1987): 82–107.

———. "Domestic Politics and War." In *The Origin and Prevention of Major Wars*, edited by Robert Rotberg and Theodore Rabb, 79–100. New York: Cambridge University Press, 1989.

———. "The Offensive/Defensive Balance of Military Technology: A Theoretical and Historical Analysis." *International Studies Quarterly* 28, no. 2 (June 1984): 219–38.

Liberman, Peter. "Trading with the Enemy: Security and the Relative Economic Gains." *International Security* 21, no. 1 (Summer 1996): 147–75.

Liedl, Janice. "Tales of Futures Past: Science Fiction as a Historical Genre." *Rethinking History* 19, no. 2 (April 2015): 285–99.

Lipson, Charles. "International Cooperation in Economic and Security Affairs." *World Politics* 37, no. 1 (October 1984): 1–23.

Lynn-Jones, Sean. "Offense Defense Theory and Its Critics." *Security Studies* 4, no. 4 (June 1995): 660–91.

Manning, Lory. "Women in the Military: Where They Stand." 10th edition. Service Women's Action Network, 2019.

Mansfield, Edward. "Concentration, Polarity, and the Distribution of Power." *International Studies Quarterly* 37, no. 1 (March 1993): 105–28.

Mansfield, Edward, and Jack Snyder. "Democratization and the Danger of War." *International Security* 20, no. 1 (Summer 1995): 5–38.

Mark, Saralyn, et al. "The Impact of Sex and Gender on Adaptation to Space." *Journal of Women's Health* 23, no. 11 (November 2014): 941–86.

Mastanduno, Michael. "Preserving the Unipolar Moment: Realist Theories and U.S. Grand Strategy after the Cold War." *International Security* 21, no. 4 (Spring 1997): 49–88.

Matfess, Hilary. "Violence against Female Politicians." Council on Foreign Relations, 11 July 2017, https://www.cfr.org/article/violence-against-female-politicians.

McCalla, Robert. "NATO's Persistence after the Cold War." *International Organization* 50, no. 3 (Summer 1996): 445–75.
McDermott, Rose. "Sex and Death: Gender Differences in Aggression and Motivations for Violence." *International Organization* 69, no. 3 (Summer 2015): 753–75.
McGuire, Steven. "Firms and Governments in International Trade." In *Trade Politics*, edited by Brian Hocking and Steven McGuire, 276–88. London: Routledge, 2004.
Mearsheimer, John. "Back to the Future: Instability in Europe after the Cold War." *International Security* 15, no. 1 (Summer 1990): 5–56.
———. "The False Promise of International Institutions." *International Security* 19, no. 3 (Winter 1994–95): 5–49.
Munsey, Christopher. "Women and War." *Monitor on Psychology* 40, no. 8 (September 2009), https://www.apa.org/monitor/2009/09/women-war.
Murray, Michelle. "Identity, Insecurity, and Great Power Politics: The Tragedy of German Naval Ambition Before the First World War." *Security Studies* 19, no. 4 (November 2010): 656–88.
Ohmae, Kenichi. "The Rise of the Region State." *Foreign Affairs* 71, no. 2 (March 1993): 78–87.
Owen, John. "How Liberalism Produces Democratic Peace." *International Security* 19, no. 2 (Fall 1994): 87–125.
Oye, Kenneth. "Explaining Cooperation under Anarchy: Hypotheses and Strategies." *World Politics* 38, no. 1 (October 1985): 1–24.
Pahre, Robert. "Multilateral Cooperation in an Iterated Prisoner's Dilemma." *Journal of Conflict Resolution* 38, no. 2 (June 1994): 326–52.
Peters, Anne, and Stefan Suter. "Representation, Discrimination, and Democracy: A Legal Assessment of Gender Quotas in Politics." In *Gender Equality: Dimensions of Women's Equal Citizenship*, edited by Linda McClain and Joanna Grossman, 174–200. Cambridge: Cambridge University Press, 2012.
Picarelli, John. "Osama bin Corleone? Vito the Jackal? Framing Threat Convergence through an Examination of Transnational Organized Crime and International Terrorism." *Terrorism and Political Violence* 24, no. 2 (April 2012): 180–98.
Plutarch. "On Tranquility of Mind." *Moralia*, vol. VI, trans. W. C. Helmbold, 161–242. Cambridge, MA: Harvard University Press, 1939.
Posen, Barry, and Andrew Ross. "Competing Visions for U.S. Grand Strategy." *International Security* 21, no. 3 (Winter 1997): 5–53.
Ravenal, Earl. "An Autopsy of Collective Security." *Political Science Quarterly* 90, no. 4 (Winter 1975–76): 697–714.
Reiter, Dan. "Exploding the Powder Keg Myth: Preemptive Wars Almost Never Happen." *International Security* 20, no. 2 (Fall 1995): 5–34.
Rhode, Deborah. "Feminism and the State." *Harvard Law Review* 107, no. 6 (April 1994): 1181–208.
Roblin, Sebastien. "War that Made Asia: How the Opium War Crushed China." *The National Interest*, 17 February 2017, https://nationalinterest

.org/blog/the-buzz/the-war-made-asia-how-the-opium-war-crushed-china-19476.

Rose, Gideon. "Neoclassical Realism and Theories of Foreign Policy." *World Politics* 5, no. 1 (October 1998): 144–72.

Ruggie, John. "International Regimes, Transactions, and Change: Embedded Liberalism in the Postwar Economic Order." *International Organization* 36, no. 2 (Spring 1982): 379–415.

Sanderson, Thomas. "Transnational Terror and Organized Crime: Blurring the Lines." *SAIS Review* 24, no. 1 (Winter/Spring 2004): 49–61.

Schroeder, Paul. "Alliances, 1815–1945: Weapons of Power and Tools of Management." In *Historical Dimensions of National Security Problems*, edited by Klaus Knorr, 227–62. Lawrence: University Press of Kansas, 1976.

———. "Historical Reality vs. Neo-Realist Theory." *International Security* 19, no. 1 (Summer 1994): 108–48.

Schweller, Randall. "Bandwagoning for Profit: Bringing the Revisionist State Back In." *International Security* 19, no. 1 (July 1994): 72–107.

———. "Neorealism's Status-Quo Bias: What Security Dilemma?" *Security Studies* 5, no. 3 (March 1996): 90–121.

———. "New Realist Research on Alliances: Refining, Not Refuting, Waltz's Balancing Proposition." *American Political Science Review* 91, no. 4 (December 1997): 927–30.

Schweller, Randall, and David Priess. "A Tale of Two Realisms: Expanding the Institutions Debate." *Mershon International Studies Review* 41, no. 1 (May 1997): 1–32.

Schweller, Randall, and William Wohlforth. "Power Test: Evaluating Realism in Response to the End of the Cold War." *Security Studies* 9, no. 3 (March 2000): 60–107.

Shelley, Louise. "Transnational Organized Crime: An Imminent Threat to the Nation-State?" *Journal of International Affairs* 48, no. 2 (Winter 1995): 463–89.

Shimshoni, Jonathan. "Technology, Military Advantage, and World War I: A Case for Military Entrepreneurship." *International Security* 15, no. 3 (Winter 1990–91): 187–215.

Singh, Sarwant. "Transhumanism and the Future of Humanity: 7 Ways the World Will Change by 2030." *Forbes*, 20 November 2017, https://www.forbes.com/sites/sarwantsingh/2017/11/20/transhumanism-and-the-future-of-humanity-seven-ways-the-world-will-change-by-2030/#358e24c97d79.

Slaughter, Anne-Marie, Andrew Tulumello, and Stepan Wood. "International Law and International Relations Theory: A New Generation of Interdisciplinary Scholarship." *American Journal of International Law* 92, no. 3 (July 1998): 367–97.

Smith, David, Judith Rosenstein, and Margaret Nikolov. "The Different Words We Use to Describe Male and Female Leaders." *Harvard Business Review*, 25 May 2018, https://hbr.org/2018/05/the-different-words-we-use-to-describe-male-and-female-leaders.

Snidal, Duncan. "International Cooperation among Relative Gains Maximizers." *International Studies Quarterly* 35, no. 4 (December 1991): 387–402.

———. "The Limits of Hegemonic Stability Theory." *International Organization* 39, no. 4 (Autumn 1985): 579–614.

———. "Relative Gains and the Pattern of International Cooperation." *American Political Science Review* 85, no. 3 (Summer 1991): 701–26.

Snyder, Craig. "Regional Security Structures." In *Contemporary Security and Strategy*, edited by Craig Snyder, 102–19. London: Palgrave, 1999.

Snyder, Glenn. "The Security Dilemma in Alliance Politics." *World Politics* 36, no. 4 (July 1984): 461–95.

Snyder, Jack. "One World, Rival Theories." *Foreign Policy* 145 (November/December 2004): 52–62.

Stone, Lawrence. "Theories of Revolution." *World Politics* 18, no. 2 (January 1966): 159–76.

Taliaferro, James. "Security Seeking under Anarchy: Defensive Realism Revisited." *International Security* 25, no. 3 (Winter 2000–1): 128–61.

Thompson, Loren. "As Space War Looms, Air Force's Biggest Weakness May Be How It Buys Satellites." *Forbes*, 23 April 2018, https://www.forbes.com/sites/lorenthompson/2018/04/23/as-space-war-looms-air-forces-biggest-weakness-may-be-how-it-buys-space-systems/?sh=60c83eba78ab.

Tickner, J. Ann. "Hans Morgenthau's Principles of Political Realism: A Feminist Reformulation." *Millennium—Journal of International Studies* 17, no. 3 (December 1988): 429–40.

———. "You Just Don't Understand: Troubled Engagements between Feminists and IR Theorists." *International Studies Quarterly* 41, no. 4 (December 1997): 611–32.

True, Jacqui. "Mainstreaming Gender in International Institutions." In *Gender Matters in Global Politics*, ed. Laura Shepherd, 227–39. Abingdon, UK: Routledge, 2015.

Van der Kroef, Justus. "The Decline and Fall of the Dutch East India Company." *The Historian* 10, no. 2 (Spring 1948): 118–34.

Van Evera, Stephen. "The Cult of the Offensive and the Origins of the First World War." *International Security* 9, no. 1 (Winter 1984): 58–107.

———. "Offense, Defense, and the Causes of War." *International Security* 22, no. 4 (Spring 1998): 5–43.

Verleger, Philip. "Understanding the 1990 Oil Crisis." *Energy Journal* 11, no. 4 (May 1990): 15–33.

von Riekhoff, Harald. "The Changing Function of NATO." *International Journal: Canada's Journal of Global Policy Analysis* 21, no. 2 (June 1966): 157–72.

Wallerstein, Immanuel. "The Rise and Future Demise of the World Capitalist System: Concepts for Comparative Analysis." *Comparative Studies in Society and History* 16, no. 4 (September 1974): 387–415.

———. "The West, Capitalism, and the Modern World-System." *Review* 15, no. 4 (Fall 1992): 561–619.

Walt, Stephen. "International Relations: One World, Many Theories." *Foreign Policy* 110 (Spring 1998): 29–46.
Waltz, Kenneth. "NATO Expansion: A Realist's View." *Contemporary Security Policy* 21, no. 2 (August 2000): 23–38.
———. "The Stability of a Bipolar World." *Daedalus* 93, no. 3 (Summer 1964): 881–909.
———. "Structural Realism after the Cold War." *International Security* 25, no. 1 (Summer 2000): 5–41.
Weinberg, Leonard, and William Eubank. "Women's Involvement in Terrorism." *Gender Issues* 28, nos. 1–2 (June 2011): 22–49.
Wendt, Alexander. "Anarchy Is What States Make of It: The Social Construction of Power Politics." *International Organization* 46, no. 2 (Spring 1992): 391–425.
Wendt, Alexander, and Raymond Duvall. "Sovereignty and the UFO." *Political Theory* 36, no. 4 (August 2008): 607–33.
White, John. "Review Article: The New International Economic Order: What Is It?" *International Affairs* 54, no. 4 (October 1978): 626–34.
Whitman Cobb, Wendy. "Women Are Less Supportive of Space Exploration—Getting a Woman on the Moon Might Change That." *The Conversation*, 9 July 2019, https://theconversation.com/women-are-less-supportive-of-space-exploration-getting-a-woman-on-the-moon-might-change-that-118986.
Williams, Michael, and Iver Neumann. "From Alliance to Security Community: NATO, Russia, and the Power of Identity." *Millennium: Journal of International Studies* 29, no. 2 (June 2000): 357–87.
Williams, Phil. "Transnational Criminal Organisations and International Security." *Survival* 36, no. 1 (Spring 1994): 96–113.
Wohlforth, William. "Realism and the End of the Cold War." *International Security* 19, no. 3 (Winter 1994–95): 91–129.
———. "Reality Check: Revising Theories of International Politics in Response to the End of the Cold War." *World Politics* 50, no. 4 (July 1998): 650–80.
———. "The Stability of a Unipolar World." *International Security* 24, no. 1 (Summer 1999): 5–41.
Zabyelina, Yuliya. "Transnational Organized Crime in International Relations." *Central European Journal of International and Security Studies* 3, no. 1 (January 2009): 11–22.

FICTION SOURCES (BOOKS AND SHORT STORIES)
Asimov, Isaac. *Foundation*. New York: Gnome Press, 1951.
———. "Runaround." *Astounding Science Fiction* 29, no. 1 (March 1942): 94–103.
Banks, Iain. *Consider Phlebas*. New York: Orbit, 1987.
Barry, Max. *Jennifer Government*. New York: Doubleday, 2003.
Bear, Greg. *Moving Mars*. New York: Tor, 1993.
Bogdanov, Alexander. *Red Star*. Bloomington: Indiana University Press, 1984.
Brown, Pierce. *Red Rising*. New York: Del Rey, 2014.

Bujold, Lois McMaster. *Shards of Honour.* Riverdale, NY: Baen, 1986.
Butler, Octavia. *Dawn.* New York: Warner Books, 1987.
Callenbach, Ernest. *Ecotopia.* New York: Bantam Books, 1977.
Card, Orson Scott. *Ender's Game.* New York: Tor, 1994.
Chenyh, C. J. *Downbelow Station.* New York: Daw Books, Inc., 1981.
Chiang, Ted. "Story of Your Life." In *Stories of Your Life and Others,* 91–146. New York: Tor Books, 2002.
———. "Understand." *Asimov's Science Fiction* 15, no. 9 (August 1991): 86–118.
Clarke, Arthur C. *Childhood's End.* New York: Ballentine Books, 1953.
———. "Superiority." *The Magazine of Fantasy and Science Fiction* 2, no. 4 (August 1951): 3–11.
———. *2001: A Space Odyssey.* New York: Signet, 1968.
Corey, James S. A. *Leviathan Wakes.* New York: Orbit, 2011.
Dick, Philip K. *Do Androids Dream of Electric Sheep?* New York: Doubleday and Company, Inc., 1968.
Disraeli, Benjamin. *Tancred: Or, The New Crusade.* London: Henry Colburn, Publisher, 1847.
Doctorow, Cory. *Walkaway.* New York: Tor, 2017.
Ellison, Harlan. "I Have No Mouth, and I Must Scream." *IF: Worlds of Science Fiction* 17, no. 3 (March 1967): 24–67.
Fulsang, Ejner. *SpaceCorp.* Belmont, CA: Århus Publishing, 2014.
Gibson, William. *Neuromancer.* New York: Ace Books, 2000.
Goodman, David. *Star Trek Federation: The First 150 Years.* London: Titan Books, 2013.
Haldeman, Joe. *Forever War.* New York: St. Martin's, 1997.
Heinlein, Robert. *The Moon Is a Harsh Mistress.* New York: Tom Doherty Associates, Inc., 1966.
———. *Starship Troopers.* New York: Ace, 2003.
Herbert, Frank. *Dune.* New York: Ace Books, 1990.
———. *The White Plague.* New York: G. P. Putnam's Sons, 1982.
Hogan, James. *The Two Faces of Tomorrow.* New York: Del Ray, 1979.
Huff, Tanya. *Valor's Choice.* New York: Daw Books, Inc., 2000.
Kipling, Rudyard. *Kim.* London: Macmillan and Co., 1901.
Le Guin, Ursula. *The Dispossessed.* New York: Harper and Row, 1974.
———. *The Left Hand of Darkness.* New York: Ace Books, 1969.
———. "The Ones Who Walk Away from Omelas." In *New Dimensions* 3, edited by Robert Silverberg, 1–8. New York: Nelson Doubleday, 1973.
Leckie, Ann. *Ancillary Justice.* London: Orbit, 2013.
Lee, Yoon Ha. *Ninefox Gambit.* New York: Tor, 2019.
McDonald, Ian. *New Moon.* London: Orion Publishing, 2015.
Orwell, George. *1984.* Boston: Houghton Mifflin Harcourt, 1949.
Robinson, Kim Stanley. *Red Mars.* New York: Bantam Books, 1993.
Russ, Joanna. *The Female Man.* Boston: Beacon Press, 1975.
Ryan, Thomas. *The Adolescence of P-1.* New York: Macmillan Publishing Co., Inc., 1977.

Sargent, Pamela. *The Shore of Women*. New York: Open Road, 1986.
Scalzi, John. *Old Man's War*. New York: Tor, 2005.
Simak, Clifford. "Desertion." *Astounding Science Fiction* 34, no. 3 (November 1944): 64–74.
Simmon, Dan. *Hyperion*. New York: Doubleday, 1989.
Slonczewski, Joan. *A Door into Ocean*. New York: Tom Doherty Associates, 1986.
Stephenson, Neal. *Seveneves*. New York: William Morrow, 2015.
Swift, Jonathan. *Gulliver's Travels*. 1726. Reprint, London: Penguin Books, 2001.
Tolstoy, Alexei. *Aelita*. Moscow: Foreign Language Publishing House, 1923.
Vinge, Vernor. *True Names*. New York: Dell Publishing, 1981.
Weber, David. *On Basilisk Station*. 1898. Reprint, Riverdale, NY: Baen Books, 1993.
Wells, H. G. *War of the Worlds*. 1898. Reprint, London: Penguin Books, 2005.
Wells, Martha. *All Systems Red*. New York: Tom Doherty Associates, 2017.
Westmore, Michael. *Star Trek: Aliens and Artifacts*. New York: Pocket Books, 2000.
Wilson, Daniel. *Robopocalypse*. New York: Doubleday, 2011.

FILM AND TELEVISION SOURCES

Burton, Tim, dir. *Mars Attacks*. Tim Burton Productions, 1996.
Cameron, James, dir. *Terminator*. Cinema '84, 1984.
Emmerich, Roland, dir. *Independence Day*. Twentieth Century Fox, 1996.
Frakes, Jonathan, dir. *Star Trek: First Contact*. Digital Image Associates, 1996.
Hood, Gavin, dir. *Ender's Game*. Summit Entertainment, 2013.
Hyams, Peter, dir. *2010: The Year We Make Contact*. Metro-Goldwyn-Mayer, 1984.
Kubrick, Stanley, dir. *2001: A Space Odyssey*. Metro-Goldwyn-Mayer, 1970.
Larson, Glen, and Ronald Moore, creators. *Battlestar Galactica*. British Sky Broadcasting, 2004–09.
Lucas, George, dir. *Star Wars*. Lucasfilm, 1977.
Lynch, David, dir. *Dune*. Dino De Laurentis Company, 1984.
Mallozzi, Joseph, and Paul Mullie, creators. *Dark Matter*. Blue Penguin, 2015–17.
McTiernan, John, dir. *Die Hard*. Twentieth Century Fox, 1988.
———. *The Hunt for Red October*. Paramount Pictures, 1990.
O'Bannon, Rockne, creator. *Farscape*. Jim Henson Productions, 1999–2002.
Rodenberry, Gene, writer. *Star Trek*. Season 2, episode 7, "Catspaw." October 27, 1967. Desilu Productions.
Scott, Ridley, dir. *Alien*. Brandywine Productions, 1979.
Villeneuve, Dennis, dir. *Arrival*. Lava Bear Films, 2016.
———. *Dune*. Warner Bros., 2021.
Whedon, Joss, creator. *Firefly*. Mutant Enemy, 2002–03.

JOURNALISTIC SOURCES

Anderson, Jon Lee. "Donald Trump Reverses Barack Obama's Cuba Policy." *New Yorker*, 17 June 2017, https://www.newyorker.com/news/daily-comment/donald-trump-reverses-barack-obamas-cuba-policy.

Anderson, Ross. "Exodus." *Aeon*, 30 September 2014, https://aeon.co/essays/elon-musk-puts-his-case-for-a-multi-planet-civilisation.

Baker, Peter. "U.S. to Restore Full Relations with Cuba, Erasing a Last Trace of Cold War Hostility." *New York Times*, 17 December 2014, https://www.nytimes.com/2014/12/18/world/americas/us-cuba-relations.html.

Barnett, Marcus. "69 of the Richest 100 Bodies in the World Are Corporations." *Morning Star*, 17 October 2018, https://morningstaronline.co.uk/article/69-richest-100-bodies-world-are-corporations.

Chappel, Bill. "Barack Obama Says Women Could Solve Many of World's Problems—Which Men Have Caused." National Public Radio, 16 December 2019, https://www.npr.org/2019/12/16/788549518/obama-links-many-of-world-s-problems-to-old-men-not-getting-out-of-the-way?utm_medium=social&utm_campaign=npr&utm_term=nprnews&utm_source=twitter.com.

Cohen, I. Bernard. "The Papers of Robert H. Goddard." *New York Times*, 2 August 1970, https://www.nytimes.com/1970/08/02/archives/the-papers-of-robert-h-goddard-the-papers-of-rhgoddard.html.

"Edgar Mitchell's Strange Voyage." *People*, 8 April 1974, https://people.com/archive/edgar-mitchells-strange-voyage-vol-1-no-6/.

Jargon, Julie. "Girls vs. Boys: Brain Differences Might Explain Tech Behaviors." *Wall Street Journal*, 24 September 2019, https://www.wsj.com/articles/girls-vs-boys-brain-differences-might-explain-tech-behaviors-11569317402.

Kluger, Jeffrey. "Space: Where America and Russia Are Stuck with Each Other." *Time*, 25 March 2014, https://time.com/37671/space-cooperation-america-russia/.

McKernan, Bethan. "Female Kurdish Fighters Announce New Training Academies for Arab Women to Take on ISIS in Syria." *The Independent*, 4 January 2017, https://www.independent.co.uk/news/world/middle-east/female-kurdish-fighters-ypj-set-up-new-training-academies-arab-yazidi-women-to-fight-isis-a7508951.html.

Mouawad, Jad. "Saudis Vow to Ignore OPEC Decision to Cut Production." *New York Times*, 10 September 2008, https://www.nytimes.com/2008/09/11/business/worldbusiness/11oil.html.

Murphy, Andrea, et al. "The Global 2000." *Forbes*, 12 May 2019, https://www.forbes.com/global2000/#623a8e7c335d.

Myers, Steven Lee, and Ellen Barry. "Putin Reclaims Crimea for Russia and Bitterly Denounces the West." *New York Times*, 18 March 2014, https://www.nytimes.com/2014/03/19/world/europe/ukraine.html.

Pasha-Robinson, Lucy. "The Long History of Russian Deaths in the UK under Mysterious Circumstances." *The Independent*, 6 March 2018, https://

www.independent.co.uk/news/uk/home-news/russian-deaths-uk-history-spies-murder-sergei-skripal-alexander-litvinenko-a8242061.html.

Wakefield, Jane. "Are You Scared Yet? Meet Norman, the Psychopathic AI." *BBC News*, 2 June 2018, http://www.bbc.com/news/technology-44040008.

Wilkinson, Tracy. "A Year after Trump Reversed Obama's Opening to Cuba, the U.S. Is Sitting out Havana's Political Revamp." *Los Angeles Times*, 22 June 2018, https://www.latimes.com/nation/la-na-pol-us-cuba-20180622-story.html.

ONLINE SOURCES

BBC World Service. "Women in Power Reveal What It Takes: Benazir Bhutto." http://www.bbc.co.uk/worldservice/people/features/wiwp/statcon/bhutto_quote.shtml.

Black's Law Dictionary, 2nd edition. https://thelawdictionary.org/multinational-corporation-mnc.

Funk, Cary, et al. "Majority of Americans Believe It Is Essential that the U.S. Remain a Global Leader in Space." Pew Research Center report, 6 June 2018, https://www.pewresearch.org/science/2018/06/06/majority-of-americans-believe-it-is-essential-that-the-u-s-remain-a-global-leader-in-space/.

Jefferson, Thomas. "Letter to George Logan." 12 November 1816. https://founders.archives.gov/documents/Jefferson/03-10-02-0390.

National Consortium for the Study of Terrorism and Responses to Terrorism, University of Maryland, 2019. "Global Terrorism Database." https://www.start.umd.edu/gtd.

Roberts, Jude. "A Few Questions about the Culture: An Interview with Iain Banks." *Strange Horizons*, 2014 special issue. http://strangehorizons.com/non-fiction/articles/a-few-questions-about-the-culture-an-interview-with-iain-banks/.

World Bank. "National Accounts Data." https://data.worldbank.org/indicator/NY.GDP.PCAP.CD?locations=CN-US.

INDEX

Note: page numbers followed by *t* refer to tables. Those followed by n refer to notes, with note number.

Adolescence of P-I, The (Ryan), 277–78
Aelita (Tolstoy), 196
Afghanistan: Soviet war in, 74, 195, 268; U.S. war in, 119, 120, 269
African Union (AU), 113
Alien films, 158, 238
aliens in science fiction: exclusion from scenarios, 3, 75; federations against, 75, 122–24, 281
alliances: choice of, for specific situations, 85–86; effect on behavior of other states, 63; as form of focal terrain, 86; and prolonged war, 48; tight *vs.* loose, 63–64; types of, 63. *See also* balance of power
anarchy of international system: artificial intelligence and, 267; as changeable reality in constructivism, 257, 260–61, 267–73, 279; corporations and, 162; and hegemonic stability theory, 22, 23, 49, 260; international law and, 110–11; liberalists' efforts to limit, 97, 98, 99, 108, 127, 128; realism on, 22, 23, 108, 110, 260; and security dilemma theory, 58, 59, 87; and trust, difficulty of, 298
Ancillary Justice (Leckie), 282
Anglo-Dutch wars, 155–56
Anglo-French Entente, 70, 71
Anglo-Japanese Alliance, 70
Antarctic Treaty System, as regime, 104
arms control regime, change in, 105
Arrival (film), 75
Art of War, The (Sun Tzu): on allies, importance of, 128; on avoiding desperation in enemy, 204–5; on avoiding illnesses in army, 241, 244; on balance of power scenarios, 80, 84–85; on central importance of war, 5; on control of the mind, 248; and cooperation between states, 127–28; on costs of prolonged war, 42, 47–48; on death ground, 204–5; on division of plunder, 162, 165; on factors in victory, 4; on focus terrain, 86; on golden bridge, 204–5; on hegemony scenario, 15; on knowledge and victory, 283, 284; and multiplanetary corporations, 165; as realist, 127; on revolution by feudal lords, 168; role in scenario analysis, 4, 9; on ruler's use of Tao, 297, 298; on tactics *vs.* strategy, 282, 328n40; on taking resources from people, 200, 204; on ungovernable people, 279; on value of strategic preparation, 209, 214–15; on victory without fighting, 124, 127–28
artificial intelligence: and anarchy of international system, 267; classification by type, 274; and creativity, 276, 283; and future prosperity, 4; MIT's Norman Project and, 267; moral status of, 274, 275; need for controls on, 280–81, 282–83; and posthumanist future, 265–66; realist view of, 267; risks of, 281–82; as source for peace or conflict, 257–58
artificial intelligence, with self-awareness and broad knowledge: in artificial intelligence scenario, 248; constructivist views on, 267; estimates for development of, 324n1; as unavoidable, 282; unpredictability of, 267
artificial intelligence in science fiction, 256, 273–79; in Asimov's "Runaround," 276; in Banks' *The Culture*, 275–76; in *Battlestar Galactica*, 277; in Clarke's *2001: A Space Odyssey*, 276; and constructivist view of reality, 273–75, 278; and creativity, 276; in Gibson's *Neuromancer*, 159; in Heinlein's *Moon Is a Harsh Mistress*, 198, 274–75; in Herbert's *Dune*, 39–40; in Hogan's *Two Faces of Tomorrow*, 278; and human stagnation, 275–76; moral status of, 275; opponents of, 275–76; and revolution,

198; in Ryan's *Adolescence of P-1*, 277–78; stories of AI turning against humans, 276–78
artificial intelligence scenario (scenario 7), 248–55; advances due to AI, 249; AI-led space exploration in, 249; choice of specific versions, 256; as constructivist scenario, 256, 257; constructivist reshaping of identities in, 261; on development of AI with self-awareness and broad knowledge, 248; evaluation against four metrics, 279–82, 280t, 293–96, 295t; norms in, as unpredictable, 263; ranking vs. other scenarios, for ability to improve human existence, 293–97, 296t; summaries of, 14, 287; and transhumanist or posthumanist future, 266; as unique scenario with humans no longer in charge, 256
artificial intelligence scenario, version A (benevolent AI), 249; advances due to AI, 250–51; AI-led space exploration in, 251–53; AI's shutdown of war, 250–51; evaluation by four metrics, 279–81, 280t, 293, 295–96, 295t; high value placed on humans by AI, 253; human activities once freed from work, 253; human opponents of AI, 253–54; and reverse-engineering study of AI, 250
artificial intelligence scenario, version B (impatient AI), 249, 254–55; AI's exploration of space without humans, 254–55; AI's loss of interest in humans, 254, 255; evaluation by four metrics, 279–81, 280t, 294–95–296, 295t
artificial intelligence scenario, version C (malevolent AI), evaluation by four metrics, 281–82, 296
Asimov, Isaac. *See Foundation* series; "Runaround"
Austria-Hungary, and "seconding telegram," 32

balance of power: and allies, choice of, 85–86; alternatives to balancing, 62; bandwagoning in, 84; bipolar systems, 64; as common, 87; concerts in, 84; conflict-reduction strategies in, 87; cooperation to diffuse unrest, 202; factors in decision to balance, 62, 63; historical examples, 69–75; internal vs. external balancing, 61–62, 82–83; multipolar systems, 64–65; number of states as key variable in, 57, 64, 80; and outsiders' misperception, 77; stability of, 73–74, 82, 83, 87; Sun Tzu on, 80, 84–85; tripolar systems, instability of, 76–77, 308n26; variety in, 57, 80; war following collapse of, 56, 69, 72, 87
balance of power, in science fiction, 75–79; in Bear's *Moving Mars*, 77–79; in Corey's *Leviathan Wakes*, 57, 75, 76–77, 87; in Heinlein's *Moon Is a Harsh Mistress*, 75–76; in Herbert's *Dune*, 76–77; as less common theme, 75, 79; in Orwell's *1984*, 76; and outsiders' misperception of alliances, 77
balance of power scenario [multipolar system] (scenario 2), 51–56; competition for resources, 52–53; conflict over goals, 56; with corporations acting as states, 138; as defensive realist scenario, 56; development of, 51–52; evaluation against four metrics, 80–83, 81t, 294t; formation of alliances, 53; growth of colonies' independence, 52; importance of alliances in, 56; parallels to pre-World War I era, 56; plausibility of, 80; ranking vs. other scenarios, for ability to improve human existence, 296t, 297; and solar league, failed attempt to create, 56; spiral toward conflict, 53–55, 59; summaries of, 12, 286; and technology's effect on willingness to go to war, 53, 54, 56; war, return to competition following, 56; war, winners and losers in, 55–56
balance of power theory, 20, 21; defensive realists and, 57; on hegemons, 20, 21, 24–27, 43, 49–50; and security dilemma theory, 62; state's agency as issue in, 27, 60, 62; and system polarity concept, 61
Bangladesh war of Independence, 229
Banks, Iain. *See Consider Phlebas*; *Culture, The*
Barry, Max. *See Jennifer Government*
Battlestar Galactica television series, 238–39, 277
Bear, Greg. *See Moving Mars*
Bhutto, Benazir, 230–32
Bismarck, Otto von, 33, 84, 304n22
Blade Runner (film), 158
Bogdanov, Alexander. *See Red Star*
Bretton Woods agreement, 37, 73, 84, 104–5
British East India Company (EIC), 36–37, 40, 153–56

British Empire: and balance of power before World War I, 59, 70–71, 306n8; as hegemon, 36–38; and theory of imperialism, 29
Brown, Pierce. *See Red Rising*

Card, Orson Scott. *See Ender's Game*
Castro, Fidel, 201, 270–72
Chiang, Ted. *See* "Story of Your Life"
China: and balance of power theory, 63; and First Opium War, 154–55; and interdependence theory, 142; and international law, 112; period of hegemony, 33; standard of living in, 203–4; and status as driver of state choice, 265; thawing of relations with U.S., 269
Clarke, Arthur C. *See* "Superiority"; *2001: A Space Odyssey*
class conflict: likely increase in future, 175; post-scarcity economies and, 207; potential for, in any scenarios, 174–75; value of understanding and avoiding, 207–8. *See also* Marxism
class conflict, in science fiction, 196–200; in Asimov's *Foundation* series, 205; in Bogdanov's *Red Star*, 196; in Brown's *Red Rising*, 199–200; in Corey's *Expanse* series, 200; in Heinlein's *Moon Is a Harsh Mistress*, 198; in Herbert's *Dune*, 205; by Russian authors, 196; in *Star Wars*, 205; in Tolstoy's *Aelita*, 196
Clausewitz, Carl von, 284, 324n43
Cold War: areas of competition in, 73; balance of power in, 62–63, 69–70, 72–75; beginnings of, 72–73; constructivist view on thawing of, 263, 268–69; crises threatening war in, 74; events intensifying, 73; factors leading to end of, 74; NATO and, 83; and relative *vs.* absolute gains, 66; Thatcher and, 227; UN Security Council and, 117; U.S. alliances in, 73; and U.S. *vs.* Soviet standard of living, 82; wars between superpower proxies in, 73
collective action problem, 25, 186
collective defense agreements, 112–15
collective security, definition of, 114
collective security agreements, 112–15, 124
Colombia, revolutionary forces in, 147, 177
commercial liberalism, 139–49; characteristics of, 98–99; definition of, 7; on free trade, 140–41; and interdependence theory, 98–99, 140, 141–42; multiplanetary corporations scenario as example of, 138–39; on value of limited government, 139–40
communication, lack of, and war, 124, 129, 278
communications, importance in war, 27
communism: current countries, 176, 177; surviving revolutionary movements, 177. *See also* Marxism
Communist Manifesto (Marx and Engels), 177, 178
concert, 84, 95, 116
Concert of Europe, 84, 113, 115, 116–17, 192
Consider Phlebas (Banks), 273
constructivist IR, 256–67; on anarchy as changeable reality, 257, 260–61, 267–73, 279; on artificial intelligence, 267; and artificial intelligence scenario, 256, 257; assumptions *vs.* realism and liberalism, 258; on changing reality by changing behavior, 257, 267–73; collapse of Soviet Union and, 74; critiques of, 258–59, 260; described, 8–9; English School and, 259–60; on hierarchies in international politics, 264; historical cases in, 267–73; on identity shaped by interactions, 257, 260–61, 263–64; influence of, 6; key debates in, 258; limited predictive power of, 264; and middle ground between realism and liberalism, 257; on norms of behavior, 261–62; on posthumanism or transhumanism future, 266–67; power to explain change, 256, 263–64; realists' critique of, 263; on reality shaped by experience, 257, 258, 266–67, 273–74; as social psychological approach, 258; on status as driver of state choice, 264–65; on subjective perceptions of reality shaping actions, 256–57, 258, 324n3; on trust in anarchic international system, 298; on variation of social meanings, 258; varieties of, 258
constructivist IR in science fiction. *See* artificial intelligence in science fiction
cooperation, Marxism on, 200–202
cooperation between multiplanetary corporations, as likely limited, 162
cooperation between states: as end in itself, 101; expectations of future interactions and, 108–9; forms of, in hegemonic order, 46–47; IGOs' promotion of, 107–10; international institutions and,

115–21, 126–27, 128–29; liberalism on, 99–101, 121, 124, 126, 127, 128; realists on, 95, 96–97, 101, 122, 126, 127, 128, 129–30; security and prosperity as co-drivers of, 100–101; significant payoffs as mechanism to ensure, 109–10; in space, precedents and concerns, 130; state reputations and, 108; Sun Tzu and, 127–28. *See also* federation of states

Corey, James S. A. *See Expanse* series; *Leviathan Wakes*

corporations: and anarchy of international system, 162; as hegemons, 19–20, 42–43, 138; realists' ignoring of role in international politics, 166–67. *See also* multinational corporations (MPCs); multiplanetary corporations (MNCs)

critical theories, 176–77

Cuba: communist revolution in, 201, 271; Missile Crisis, 74, 86, 271; Obama's overtures to, 263, 271, 272; relations with U.S., 270–72

Culture, The (Banks), 207, 275–76

cyberpunk science fiction, 159, 278

cyberwarfare: Russian attacks on Estonia, 119–20; in scenarios, 91, 92, 136, 137

Dark Matter TV series, 159–60, 164, 238

defensive realists, 58–64; on balance of power, 26, 27, 56, 57; and choice by state actors, 303n8; collapse of Soviet Union and, 74; on conflict, causes of, 80, 87; on empire, risks and costs of, 58; and hegemonic scenarios, rejection of, 57; on human nature, 80; neoclassical realists' critique of, 80; on offense-defense balance theory of war, 60–61; on security dilemma theory, 58–60; on Soviet-U.S. relations, thawing of, 268; on space exploration incentives, 82; on state methods to ensure survival, 23; on state's agency in balancing, 27, 60, 62; on state's agency in war decisions, 80; on states' preference for security over power, 57, 58

DEIC. *See* Dutch East India Company

democratic government, new, instability of, 149

democratic peace theory, 7, 98, 99, 100, 148–49

dependency theory (*dependencia*), 182–84

deterrence: credibility of, 59–60, 306n11; definition of, 306n10; and security dilemma theory, 59–60, 306n10

Disraeli, Benjamin, 29, 303n8

Doctorow, Cory. *See Walkaway*

Door into Ocean, A (Slonczewski), 240–41

Dune (Herbert), 21, 39–41, 76–77, 158, 205

Dutch East India Company (DEIC), 153, 155–56

empire, *vs.* hegemon, 28, 34

Ender's Game (Card), 123–24, 129, 281

English School, 259–60

ethics, as not discussed in IR worldviews, 297–98

Europe, pre-World War I balance of power, 69–72

European Union (EU), 105, 106, 113, 148

Expanse series (Corey), 94, 146, 200, 207

Falklands War (Malvinas War), 227–28

Farscape television series, 238

federation of states: and absolute *vs.* relative gains, 102–3; with corporations acting as states, 138; and cost of space exploration, 95; failure, examples of, 126–27; Kant on, 97–98; main goals of, 126; and sovereignty, 103; wars as impetus toward, 310n2. *See also* cooperation between states

federation of states, in science fiction, 121–24; in Card's *Ender's Game*, 123–24, 129; in Haldeman's *Forever Wars*, 122–23, 129; in Heinlein's *Starship Troopers*, 122–23; in response to alien threat, 122–24; in Scalzi's *Old Man's War*, 123; in *Star Trek*, 121, 129

federation of states (Pax Terra) scenario (scenario 3), 89–94; elimination of nuclear weapons after war, 93–94; evaluation against four metrics, 124–26, 125t, 293, 294t; events leading to World War III, 89–91; on human expansion in solar system, 94; as liberalist scenario, 95; multinational space colonies in, 94; ranking *vs.* other scenarios, for ability to improve human existence, 296, 296t; realist views on, 95–97; similarities to *Expanse* series, 94; summaries of, 12, 286; United Nations Federation (UNF) in, 89, 93–94; World War III in, 91–93

Female Man, The (Russ), 244

feminism: on gender difference and conflict, 241–42; liberal (equity feminism), 216, 218–20; and male-female cooperation,

views on, 246; Marxist, 216, 220–21, 241, 321n12; on men in power, negative effects of, 215; postmodern, 216, 220, 222; radical, call for revolutionary social change, 246; standpoint, 216, 217–18; varieties of, 215–16. *See also entries under* gender
feminist IR, 6, 8, 215–17, 298
feminist scenario restricting space colonization to women (scenario 6), 209–14; applicability of history to, 223; evaluation against four metrics, 242–44, 243*t*, 295*t*; events leading to, 209; as extreme example, 246, 320n2; and gender imbalance on Earth, 210–11; growth of conflict in space, 211–12, 213–14; isolation of women on Earth, 210; men's conquest of Mars colony, 212–13; raising of male armies, 214; ranking *vs.* other scenarios, for ability to improve human existence, 296*t*; regulated procreation without men, 209–10; science fiction works providing basis for, 239; summaries of, 13–14, 287
Firefly television series, 158, 164, 238
Forever War, The (Haldeman), 10–11, 97, 122–23, 129, 237–38
Foundation series (Asimov), 39, 40–41, 49, 205
Franco-Russian Alliance, 62, 70
free trade: benefits of, 65–66, 67; Bretton Woods system and, 104–5; Cold War and, 72; as deterrent to war, liberalists on, 99, 100, 101; factors leading to restrictions on, 141; focus on absolute gains, 140; and growth of corporations, 140; impact on workers, 141; and interdependence theory, 140, 141–42; liberalists' support for, 100, 140–41, 149, 167, 298; *vs.* mercantilism, 66, 67, 68; modern forms of, 67–68; and relative *vs.* absolute gains, 65–66, 101; WTO and, 95–96, 104, 109–10
future: desired, properties of, 4–5; likely mix of scenarios in, 298–99; scenarios as tool for contemplating, 2, 3, 4, 299; use of IR to understand, 298, 299

gains, relative *vs.* absolute, 65–66, 101–3, 141
Gandhi, Indira, 228–30
gender differences, positives and negatives of, 244–45

gender roles in science fiction, 237–41; in *Alien* films, 238; in feminist science fiction, 237–41; in Haldeman's *Forever War*, 237–38; in Heinlein's *Starship Troopers*, 237–38; in Le Guin's *Left Hand of Darkness*, 239–40; in Sargent's *Shore of Women*, 240; in Slonczewski's *Door into Ocean*, 240–41; in Stephenson's *Seveneves*, 238; in television shows, 238–39; in *Terminator* films, 238; in Weber's *Honorverse* series, 238
Germany: under Bismarck, 33, 304n22; and World War I, 59
Gibson, William. *See Neuromancer*
global South, and dependency theory (*dependencia*), 182–84
globalization: MNCs and, 145; and sovereignty, 145, 147
Gorbachev, Mikhail, 227, 263, 268
Great Depression, trade policies in, 67
Green Mars (Robinson), 161
Gulf War (1990-91), 110, 115
Gurr, Ted, 182, 188–89

Haldeman, Joe. *See Forever War, The*
hegemonic stability theory (HST), 21, 24–26
hegemonic stabilization theory (HST), 24–25, 26, 31–33
hegemons: balance of power theory on, 20, 21, 24–27, 43, 49–50; challenges to, as inevitable, 20–21, 38; corporations or supranational entities as, 19–20, 42–43, 138; cost of maintaining empire, 29, 37, 43, 49–50; and costs of prolonged war, 47–49; *vs.* empire, 28, 34; forms of cooperation under, 46–47; forms of power, 24; historical examples of, 33–38; inevitable resentment of, 32, 43; interest in status quo, 25–26; lack of practical definition of, 33; and power transition theory, 21, 32–33; and preventive wars against challengers, 31–33, 43, 45–46, 304n19; regional, as issue, 24; stability provided by, 24–26; stopping power of water/space and, 26–27; and theories of imperialism, 28–30; and theory of hegemonic war, 43; typical factors in fall of, 38; typical factors in rise of, 34; value of studying, 34; varying characters of, 20
hegemons in science fiction, 38–42; in Asimov's *Foundation* series, 38; in

Herbert's *Dune*, 38–39; in *Star Wars*, 41–42
hegemony scenario (scenario 1), 15–19; and cost of empire, 17, 49–50; decline of hegemon in, 19; devolution into multipolar system, 49–50; evaluation against four metrics, 44–49, 44*t*, 294*t*; and international order, 16–17; likely sources of future conflict in, 43; nonstate actors' violence against hegemon, 16–17; as offensive realist worldview, 19–20; peace and prosperity under, 16; as plausible scenario, 42–43; ranking *vs.* other scenarios, for ability to improve human existence, 296*t*, 297; rise of competitors, 16–18, 43–44, 49–50; rise of hegemon in, 15–16; source of hegemon's power, as key in determining vulnerability, 43–44; and spiral toward war, 18–19; stability of, 16, 49; summary of, 12, 285–86; Sun Tzu on, 15; and suppression of potential competitors, 15
Heinlein, Robert. *See Moon Is a Harsh Mistress, The; Starship Troopers*
Herbert, Frank. *See Dune; White Plague, The*
hierarchies in international politics, constructivist *vs.* realist views on, 264
historical events: repetition of patterns in, 3, 10; role in scenario analysis, 1, 2, 9–10
Hobson, John, 188
Hogan, James. *See Two Faces of Tomorrow, The*
Honor Harrington series (Weber), 161
Honorverse series (Weber), 238
human nature: classical liberalism on, 97; defensive realists on, 80; realists on, 80, 87, 97
human rights norms, and sovereignty, 262
humans in space: and human survival, 1, 4; as likely in near future, 1, 3; and security, 4; value of, *vs.* preserving planetary environments, 303n16. *See also* space exploration

ideological dogma, danger of, 247
imperial overstretch, 29–30, 43
imperialism: and assumptions of cultural superiority, 28–29; as non-issue in space, 30; theories of, 28–30, 43
Imperialism (Hobson), 188
Independence Day (film), 281

institutions. *See* international institutions
interdependence theory, 7, 98–99, 140–42
intergovernmental organizations (IGOs): characteristics of, 105; cost of creating, 107; creation by treaty, 105; durability of, 106–7, 110; examples of, 105–6; liberalist views on, 106–7, 108, 110; promotion of cooperation, 107–10; realist views on, 106–7, 110; specific purposes of, 106; and state sovereignty, 106
International Court of Justice, 112
International Criminal Court (ICC), 112
international institutions: creation by victors of war, 95–96; flexibility of, as key to longevity, 128–29; formalization of regime as, 104–5; historical lessons in creation of, 128–29; history of, 115–21; intergovernmental organizations (IGOs), 105–6; international law, 110–12; neoliberal institutionalism on, 103–12; realist *vs.* liberalist views on, 83–84; regimes, 103–5; types of, 103; and war prevention, realists on, 95–96
international institutions, and cooperation: failed, examples of, 126–27; successful, examples of, 115–21
international law, 110–12; codification in treaties, 111–12; dependence on state enforcement, 110–11; examples of, 111; and international organizations, intersection of, 112; liberalist views on, 111; realist views on, 110, 111; United Nations and, 111; United States and, 111–12
International Monetary Fund (IMF), 118, 184–85
international order: as key to avoiding war, 5; as standard for desirable future, 4, 288
international relations theory (IR): applicability to multiplanetary corporations, 138; avoidance of ethics analysis, 297–98; in closed *vs.* open system, 5–6; complementary perspectives of various types, 264; key terms in, 6–7; role in scenario analysis, 1, 2, 5–9; states as primary actors in, 302n1; three main worldviews, 6–8. *See also* constructivist IR; liberalism; realism
International Space Station, 130
IR. *See* international relations theory
Iranian Revolution, 194–95

Iraq War (2003), 262
Irish Republican Army, 228

Japanese Red Army (JRA), 235
Jennifer Government (Barry), 161

Kant, Immanuel, 97–98, 148
Kellogg-Briand Pact, 126–27

labels, recognizing useful ideas despite, 208
Lagrangian points, 52, 86, 306n2
Le Guin, Ursula. *See Left Hand of Darkness, The*; "Ones Who Walk Away from Omelas, The"
League of Nations, 84, 95, 114, 126
League of the Three Emperors, 71, 116
Leckie, Ann. *See Ancillary Justice*
Left Hand of Darkness, The (Le Guin), 239–40
Lenin, Vladimir, 181–82, 188, 193
Leviathan Wakes (Corey), 57, 75, 76–77, 87
liberalism, 97–115; assumptions vs. constructivism and realism, 99, 127, 258; on change in international politics, 263–64; classical, on human nature, 97; on collective security agreements, 113, 114; on Concert of Europe, 117; on cooperation between states, 99–101, 121, 124, 126, 127, 128; core assumptions of, 99–101; embedded, 165; focus on absolute gains, 66, 101–3; focus on internal influences on state, 100; free trade support, 100, 110, 140–41, 149, 167, 298; on government, best forms of, 97; on human nature, 97; on IGOs, 106–7, 108, 110; influence of, 6; on interaction between states as key to reducing tensions, 129; interest in actors other than states, 100; on international law, 111; on international organizations, 83–84; and Kant's prescription for peace, 97–98; on mercantilism, 67; on multinational corporations, 144, 167; on NATO, 120, 270; on norms of behavior, 261; as rationalist and positivist, 11–12; on regimes, 104; on security and prosperity as co-drivers of state policy, 100–101; and social contract theory, 102; on Soviet-U.S. relations, thawing of, 268; on treaties, 111; on trust in anarchic international system, 298; on U.S.-Cuba relations, 271; varieties of, 7, 97–99, 148. *See also* commercial liberalism; federation of states (Pax Terra) scenario (scenario 3); neoliberal institutionalism; republican liberalism
Luna trilogy (McDonald), 159

Mao Tse-Tung, 188, 198
Mars Attacks (film), 281
Mars Trilogy (Robinson), 161, 196–98, 207
Marx, Karl, 175, 180–82, 187, 193, 200, 201
Marxism: attractiveness to exploited, 206; on class division as cause of conflict, 200; on colonialism as outlet for worker dissatisfaction, 201–2; cooperation in, 200–202; dangers of adopting, 207; decline in popularity after Cold War, 177; on French Revolution, 191, 192; on history as class struggle, 178; nationalist versions of, 175–76; as political and economic ideology, 177; politics of class in, 178; spread of ideology, as issue, 201; as term, 175, 176, 208; and theories of revolution, 187–89; useful elements of, 207–8; utopia of, as impractical, 206–7; and war, causes of, 180–81, 201; and World systems theory, 186–87. *See also* class conflict
Marxist economics, 179–86; as antithesis of liberalist economics, 177–78; on capitalists' exploitation of workers, 179; and dependency theory, 182–84; goals of, 179; influence of, 179; lack of practical success, 179, 182; mercantilist policies and, 179; and New International Order proposal, 185; on North's exploitation of South, 179; and OPEC, views on, 185–86; Sun Tzu and, 204; on Washington Consensus, 184–85
Marxist feminism, 216, 220–21, 241, 321n12
Marxist IR: as critical theory, 176; described, 7–8; on exploitation of periphery by core, 178, 186–87, 201–2; on imperialism, 28; incorporation of political, social, and economic philosophies, 176; influence of, 6; on interdependence theory, 142; on trust in international system, 298; and world systems theory, 301n8
Marxist revolution on Mars scenario (scenario 5), 168–74; applicability of Earth history to, 204; class conflict in, 168–69, 174–75; Earth's ineffective

response to, 172–73; evaluation against four metrics, 202–4, 203t, 295t; Martian independence gained by, 173; Marxist ideas introduced to colony, 171; measures to avoid realization of, 204, 205–6; ranking *vs.* other scenarios, for ability to improve human existence, 296–97, 296t; revolution, 171–72; spread of Marxism to other colonies, 172, 174; summaries of, 13, 286–87; unsuccessful efforts to quell unrest, 169–71; unsustainable society resulting from, 173–74
Matrix films, 281–82
May 19 Communist Organization (M-19), 234–35
McDonald, Ian. *See Luna* trilogy; *New Moon*
Medici family, as early MNC, 151–53
Meir, Golda, 224–26
mercantilism (economic nationalism), 66–68, 140
Moon Is a Harsh Mistress, The (Heinlein), 75–76, 196, 198, 206, 237, 239, 274–75, 282
Moving Mars (Bear), 77–79, 160–61
multinational corporations (MNCs): and colonization of space, 166; definition of, 144; and globalization, 145; growing power of, 150; historical examples of, 150–58; impact on workers, 145; and interdependence theory, 142; liberalist worldview and, 144, 162, 167; pros and cons of, 144–45; and sovereignty, 145, 150–51
multiplanetary corporations (MPCs): applicability of IR theories to, 138; cooperation among, as likely limited, 162; desirability under certain conditions, 165; and increase in wealth gap, 163; likely undesirable influence of, 161–62, 166–67; and need for central authority, 164; and state sovereignty, 166; strategies for limiting role of, 164–65; Sun Tzu and, 165; types of government in, 149; and war, 163–65
multiplanetary corporations in science fiction, 158–62; in *Alien* films, 158; in Bear's *Moving Mars*, 160–61; in *Blade Runner*, 158; in *Dark Matter* TV series, 159–60, 164; in *Dune*, 158; in Eulang's *SpaceCorp*, 158–59; in *Firefly* TV series, 158, 164; in Gibson's *Neuromancer*, 159; in McDonald's Luna trilogy, 159; operating alongside governments, 158–59; operating as governments, 159–61; as villains, 159, 161
multiplanetary corporations (MPCs) scenario (scenario 4): alliances between MPCs, 135; as commercial liberalism scenario, 138–39; conflict between MPCs, 132, 137; as consistent with realism, 139; dominant Big Six corporations, 133–34; evaluation against four metrics, 162–64, 163t, 294t; First Cartel War between MPCs, 136–38; MPC's development of military forces, 135–36; MPC's development of space dominance, 131–34; MPC's governance of space colonies, 131, 133–34, 135; MPC's operation like states, 134–35, 137–38; plausibility of, 161, 165; potential outcomes of, 137–38; ranking *vs.* other scenarios, for ability to improve human existence, 296–97, 296t; realism of, 148; regimes for cooperation, 134, 135; and space piracy, 136; summaries of, 12–13, 286; and technological research, 135
multipolar systems: characteristics of, 64–65; devolution of hegemonic system into, 49–50
Munich Olympics terror attack (1972), 225

Napoleonic France, 20, 27, 32, 36
National Defense Strategy, U.S., 272
national security pillars, U.S., and metrics for evaluating scenarios, 4, 288
National Security Strategy (2017), 69
NATO. *See* North Atlantic Treaty Organization
neoclassical realism: characteristics of, 68–69; and choice by state actors, 303n8; on cooperation between states, 95, 101; critiques of defensive realism, 80; lack of attention to nonstate actors, 143; on state's agency in balancing, 60
neoliberal institutionalism, 7, 98, 103–12
Neuromancer (Gibson), 158, 159, 278
New International Order proposal, 185
New Moon (McDonald), 159
1984 (Orwell), 76
nongovernmental organizations (NGOs), 143, 144
nonstate actors: liberalists and, 143; realists and, 143; and sovereignty, impact on, 147; types of, 143–47

Norman Project (MIT), 267
norms of behavior, 261–63
North Atlantic Treaty Organization (NATO): adaptation after Cold War, 83, 107, 120, 130, 269–70; as collective defense organization, 113–14, 119; as collective security organization, 114; constructivist view of changed identities in, 260–61; echoes of, in science fiction, 121; establishment of, 73, 119; expansion of, 120; facilitation of cooperation by, 115, 119–21; in federation of states scenario, 91; French withdrawal from, 73; as intergovernmental organization, 105; liberalist views on, 120; membership as lever for reform, 120–21; purposes of, 119; realist views on cooperation and, 23–24; Russian candidacy for, 269; Russian cyberattacks on Estonia and, 119–20; and security dilemma theory, 62; terrorist attacks of 9/11 and, 119
nuclear weapons: agreements limiting, 94, 105; of allies *vs.* enemies, 102; and Cold War, 66, 73, 74; in federation of states scenario, 90, 92–94; Iran and, 195; norms on, 262; realists on, 96; and status as driver of state choice, 264, 265

Obama, Barack, 218, 263, 269, 271, 272
offense-defense balance theory of war, 60–61, 78–79, 80
offensive realists: on balance of power theory, 27; and choice by state actors, 303n8; collapse of Soviet Union and, 74; on hegemons, 19–21; on state methods to ensure survival, 23; on state's agency in balancing, 27; on states' preference for power over security, 58
Old Man's War (Scalzi), 123
On Basilisk Station (Weber), 161, 238
"Ones Who Walk Away from Omelas, The" (Le Guin), 241
Organization of American States (OAS), 113
Organization of Petroleum Exporting Countries (OPEC), 105, 185–86
Orwell, George. See *1984*

pantropy, 266
Peloponnesian War, 29, 31
positivist theories, 11–12
posthumanism, 265–66
power transition theory, 21, 32–33, 43

prisoner's dilemma (PD), 107–8
prospect theory, 205–6
prosperity, as standard for desirable future, 4, 288

rationalist theories, realism and liberalism as, 11
Reagan, Ronald W., 227, 263, 268
realism: on artificial intelligence, 267; assumptions *vs.* constructivism and liberalism, 258; balance of power theory, 20, 21, 26–27, 49–50, 83; on change in international politics, 263–64; classical, 23, 68; on collective defense agreements, 113; on Concert of Europe, 117; on concerts, 95; on conflict, causes of, 80; on conflict for scarce resources, 42–43; on cooperation between states, 95, 96–97, 101, 122, 126, 127, 128, 129–30; core assumptions of, 22–24; critiques of interdependence theory, 142; as dominant IR worldview, 21; on federation of states scenario, 95–97; feminist IR and, 217; flaws in, 21; hegemonic stability theory, 21, 24–26; on hierarchies in international politics, 264; on human nature, 80, 87, 97; ignoring of corporations in, 166–67; on IGOs, 106–7, 110; influence of, 6; on institutions and war prevention, 95–96; on international law, 110, 111; on international organizations, 83–84; on IR as inherently conflictual, 66; lack of attention to nonstate actors, 143; and liberalists, shared assumptions of, 99, 127; on long-term cooperation between states, as unlikely, 22, 23, 43, 49; and mercantilism, 66, 140; on NATO expansion, 270; and NGOs, limited attention to, 144; on norms of behavior, 262–63; offensive and defensive forms of, 7; on politics as zero-sum game, 43; power transition theory, 21, 32–33; preventive *vs.* preemptive military action in, 30–33; as rationalist and positivist, 11–12; on regimes, 104; on relative *vs.* absolute gains, 65–66; self-interest of states in, 22, 23; on Soviet-U.S. relations, 268; on stability *vs.* peace, 304n19; on state of anarchy of international system, 22, 23, 108, 110, 269; on state sovereignty, 147; on state's agency in balancing, 62, 80; states as

primary actors in, 22; states as rational in, 23; states as unitary in, 22; on states' security, costs of cooperation to, 66; Sun Tzu and, 127; on survival as central goal of state, 23; theories of imperialism, 28–30; on treaties, 111; on trust in anarchic international system, 298; types of, 68–69; on U.S.-Cuba relations, 271; on war, as always possible, 23; on wealth as source of power, 100–101. *See also* balance of power scenario [multipolar system] (scenario 2); hegemony scenario (scenario 1); neoclassical realism
Red Army Faction (RAF), 234
Red Mars (Robinson), 161, 196–98
Red Rising (Brown), 199–200
Red Star (Bogdanov), 196
reflexivist approaches to IR, 176–77
regimes, 103–5; in multiplanetary corporations scenario, 134, 135
Republic (Plato), 319n39
republican liberalism, 7, 98, 102, 148–49
resources, scarce: and security dilemma, 59; as source of conflict, 42–43
Responsibility to Protect, and state sovereignty, 147
revolution, theories of, 187–89; change in, after Russian Revolution, 193; Marx on, 180, 187, 193; Marxist theories, 187–88; prospect theory on, 205–6; scholarly theories, 188–89; on types of revolutions, 318n25; and war, 189. *See also* Marxist revolution on Mars scenario (scenario 5)
revolutions, historical examples of, 190–95
revolutions in science fiction. *See* class conflict, in science fiction
risk-taking, prospect theory on, 205–6
Robinson, Kim Stanley. *See Green Mars*; Mars Trilogy; *Red Mars*
Robopocolypse (Wilson), 282
Roman Empire: echoes of, in science fiction, 39, 40, 41–42; as hegemon, 28, 34–36
Rousseau, Jean-Jacques, 102, 192
"Runaround" (Asimov), 276
Russ, Joanna. *See Female Man, The*
Russia: and balance of power theory, 63; Revolution in, 182, 193–94, 318n29; willingness to give up empire, 58, 74. *See also* Soviet Union
Ryan, Thomas. *See Adolescence of P-1, The*

Sargent, Pamela. *See Shore of Women, The*
Scalzi, John. *See Old Man's War*

scenarios: exclusion of aliens from, 3, 75; history and, 1, 2, 9–10; IR theory and, 1, 2, 5–9; likely mix of, in future, 298–99; overviews of, 11–14, 285–88; and predetermined outcomes, 3–4; science fiction and, 1–3, 10–11; Sun Tzu and, 4, 9; as tool for contemplating desired future, 247, 284–85, 299
scenarios, analysis of: artificial intelligence scenario (scenario 7), 279–82, 280*t*; balance of power scenario (scenario 2), 80–83, 81*t*; federation of states scenario (scenario 3), 124–26, 125*t*; feminist scenario (scenario 6), 242–44, 243*t*; four metrics for, 4, 288; hegemony scenario (scenario 1), 44–49, 44*t*; Marxist revolution on Mars scenario (scenario 5), 202–4, 203*t*; multiplanetary corporations scenario (scenario 4), 44–49, 44*t*; ranking by ability to improve human existence, 293–97, 296*t*, 328n2
science and technology, new: and offense-defense balance theory of war, 61; and rise of challengers to hegemon, 43–44; and rise of hegemon, 34, 36–37, 39–40, 302n6
science and technology advancement, as metric for evaluating scenarios, 4, 288, 291; artificial intelligence scenario (scenario 7), 280, 280*t*, 291–92; balance of power scenario (scenario 2), 81, 81*t*, 291; federation of states scenario (scenario 3), 125, 125*t*, 126, 291; feminist scenario (scenario 6), 243, 243*t*, 291; hegemony scenario (scenario 1), 44*t*, 45, 291; Marxist revolution on Mars scenario (scenario 5), 203, 203*t*, 291; multiplanetary corporations scenario (scenario 4), 163, 163*t*, 291
science fiction: and hegemon, as term, 305n29; post-scarcity economies in, 207; role in scenario analysis, 1–3, 10–11; and situated knowledges, 274; as social critique, 273–74
security: space exploration as key to, 4; as standard for desirable future, 4, 288
security dilemma theory, 58–60, 62, 78–79, 80, 87, 306n10
Seveneves (Stephenson), 238
Shore of Women, The (Sargent), 240, 245
situated knowledges, and science fiction, 274

slave trade, British Empire and, 37
Slonczewski, Joan. *See Door into Ocean, A*
Smith, Adam, 66, 139
social contract theory, 102
sovereignty: forces leading to decline of, 147–48; globalization's impact on, 145; and human rights norms, 262; impact of decline, as issue, 148
Soviet Union: collapse of empire, 58, 74, 268–69; war in Afghanistan, 74, 195, 268. *See also* Cold War
space exploration: and likelihood of wars, 27; power gained by control of space, 27; and status as driver of state choice, 264; status of new territories, as issue, 302n1. *See also* humans in space
space exploration, as metric for evaluating scenarios, 4, 288, 290; artificial intelligence scenario (scenario 7), 280, 280*t*, 290–91; balance of power scenario (scenario 2), 81–82, 81*t*, 290; federation of states scenario (scenario 3), 125, 125*t*, 126, 290; feminist scenario (scenario 6), 243, 243*t*, 290; hegemony scenario (scenario 1), 44*t*, 45, 290; Marxist revolution on Mars scenario (scenario 5), 202–3, 203*t*, 290; multiplanetary corporations scenario (scenario 4), 163, 163*t*, 290
SpaceCorp (Eulsang), 158–59
Spawl trilogy (Gibson). *See Neuromancer* (Gibson)
Stalin, Joseph, 175–76, 193, 201, 318n29
standard of living (SoL), improvement of: *vs.* equality of wealth, 5; values as key to, 4–5
standard of living (SoL), as metric for evaluating scenarios, 4, 288, 292; artificial intelligence scenario (scenario 7), 280, 280*t*, 292; balance of power scenario (scenario 2), 81, 81*t*, 292; federation of states scenario (scenario 3), 125, 125*t*, 126, 292; feminist scenario (scenario 6), 243*t*, 292; hegemony scenario (scenario 1), 44*t*, 45–46, 292; Marxist revolution on Mars scenario (scenario 5), 203–4, 203*t*, 292; multiplanetary corporations scenario (scenario 4), 163, 163*t*, 292; power scenario [multipolar system] (scenario 2), 82–83, 292
Star Trek, 121, 129, 207
Star Wars, 41–42, 205

Starship Troopers (Heinlein), 121, 122–23, 237–38
Stephenson, Neal. *See Seveneves*
"Story of Your Life" (Chiang), 75
structural adjustment programs (SAPs), 184–85
Sun Tzu. *See Art of War, The* (Sun Tzu)
"Superiority" (Clarke), 282
system polarity concept, 61, 80

Taiwan, U.S. alliance with, 86
Terminator films, 238, 281–82
terrorism: attacks of 9/11, 119, 143; Thatcher's crackdown on, 228; U.S. shift from war on, 272; women's leadership in, 234–37
Thatcher, Margaret, 226–28
Tolstoy, Alexei. *See Aelita*
trade: control of, by controlling space, 27; policies in Great Depression, 67; and relative *vs.* absolute gains, 65–66, 141. *See also* free trade
tragedy of the commons, 25
transhumanism, 265–66
transnational criminal organizations (TCOs), 143, 145–47
treaties, 111–12
Triple Alliance, 62, 63, 70, 309n36
Triple Entente, 62, 70, 71
tripolar systems, 76–77, 308n26
True Names (Vinge), 278
Two Faces of Tomorrow, The (Hogan), 278
2001: A Space Odyssey (Clarke), 276

United Fruit Company (UFC), 156–58, 183
United Nations: and collective security, 114, 118; component organizations, 117–18; creation of, 37, 73; difficulty of action, 118; echoes of, in science fiction, 122–23; facilitation of cooperation by, 115, 117–19; in federation of states scenario, 89, 92; founding of, 84, 95; as intergovernmental organization, 105; and international law, 111; nations late in joining, 117; notable accomplishments of, 118; on preemptive military strikes, 31; Security Council, 92, 117, 118–19, 262, 264
United Nations Convention on the Law of the Seas (UNCLOS), 111–12
United Nations High Commissioner for Refugees, 117–18
United States: and balance of power

before World War I, 72; and creation of international institutions, 46, 73; Declaration of Independence, 102; as hegemon, 33, 37, 46, 72–73, 74–75, 304n22; and interdependence theory, 142; and International Criminal Court, 112; and international law, 111–12; NGOs in, 143–44; UNCLOS and, 111–12. *See also* Cold War; hegemony scenario (scenario 1)

utopias, as unrealistic, 206–7, 279

values/principles: as key to improving standard of living, 4–5; as standard for desirable future, 4, 288, 292

Vietnam, thawing of relations with U.S., 269

Vietnam War, and costs of prolonged war, 48–49

Vinge, Vernor. *See True Names*

violent extremist organizations (VEOs), 143, 146–47

Walkaway (Doctorow), 207

War of the Worlds (Wells), 281

war/conflict: advantages in, from control of space, 27; avoidance of, 5, 48, 97–98, 297; defensive realists on causes of, 80, 87; lack of communication and, 124, 129, 278; Marxist feminists on, 221; new multilateral norms on, 262; postmodern feminists on, 222; preventive *vs.* preemptive, 30–33; prolonged, costs of, 47–49; realists on causes of, 80; and revolution, 189; standpoint feminists on, 217–18; theory of hegemonic war, 43

war/conflict, avoidance of, as metric for evaluating scenarios, 4, 288–89; artificial intelligence scenario (scenario 7), 279, 280, 280*t*, 281, 289; balance of power scenario (scenario 2), 81, 81*t*, 82, 289; federation of states scenario (scenario 3), 124–25, 125*t*, 126, 289; feminist scenario (scenario 6), 242–44, 243*t*, 290; hegemony scenario (scenario 1), 44–45, 44*t*, 289; Marxist revolution on Mars scenario (scenario 5), 202, 203*t*; multiplanetary corporations scenario (scenario 4), 163–64 163*t*, 289–90

Warsaw Pact, 62, 73, 123–24

Washington Consensus, 184–85

Washington Naval Conference treaties, 126–27

Weber, David. *See* Honor Harrington series; *Honorverse* series; *On Basilisk Station*

Wells, H. G. *See War of the Worlds*

Wendt, Alexander, 256, 260, 265

White Plague, The (Herbert), 244

Wilson, Daniel. *See Robopocalypse*

women, importance of equal inclusion of, 245–46, 247

women as national leaders, 224–32; Benazir Bhutto, 230–32; Golda Meir, 224–26; Indira Gandhi, 228–30; Margaret Thatcher, 226–28; perceived weakness and, 223–24, 226, 230

women in leadership roles: and human drive for power, 242; as peace-oriented, 223–24, 239, 242, 245, 246; in terrorist organizations, 234–37. *See also* women as national leaders; women in military

women in military, 232–34; in combat roles, 218, 232–33; liberal feminists on, 218; as metric of gender equality, 233–34; in science fiction, 237–38; in United States, 232–33; variation by society, 223, 232

women in science fiction. *See* gender roles in science fiction

women in terrorist organizations, 234–37

Women's Protection Unit (YPJ), 223, 233

World Bank, 105, 106, 118, 184, 203–4

world systems theory, 178, 186–87

World Trade Organization (WTO), 84, 95–96, 104, 106, 109–10, 142, 313n7

World War I: bipolar alliance system prior to, 65; causes of, 72; echoes in science fiction, 79; global trade system and, 67; and offense-defense balance theory of war, 61; as preventive war, 32–33; and Russian Revolution, 182; spiral toward conflict, 59; and status as driver of state choice, 264–65

World War II: and balance of power theory, 20, 27; effects of alliances in, 85–86; formation of bipolar alliance system prior to, 65; as preventive war, 32; and rise of U.S. hegemony, 37, 46, 72–73, 74–75

WTO. *See* World Trade Organization

Yom Kuppur War, 225–26

ABOUT THE AUTHOR

GREGORY D. MILLER is Professor of Military and Security Studies at the Air Command and Staff College (ACSC) in Montgomery, AL, where he serves as chair of the Department of Spacepower and as director of the Schriever Space Scholars program. Previously, he was chair of the Strategy Department at the Joint Advanced Warfighting School in Norfolk, VA. At ACSC, he teaches core courses in leadership and international security, as well as electives on the history of modern terrorism, science fiction and strategy, and Arctic strategy. He received his BA in political science and history from the University of California, Los Angeles (1996), an MA in security policy studies from the Elliott School of International Affairs at George Washington University (1998), and an MA (2000) and PhD (2004) in political science from The Ohio State University.

His research interests cover a broad range of topics in the areas of international relations, terrorism, strategy, and space. His first book, *The Shadow of the Past: Reputation and Military Alliances before the First World War*, was published in 2012. His writings appear in more than a dozen journals, including space-related articles in *Astropolitics*, *Space Policy*, *Air and Space Power Journal*, and *The Space Review*. He previously held faculty positions at the College of William & Mary, the University of Oklahoma, and Oklahoma State University. He was a founding director of the Summer Workshop on Teaching about Terrorism (SWOTT), which ran from 2005 to 2008, and more recently helped develop and run the Summer Workshop on Teaching Space (SWOTS).

Dr. Miller lives in Alabama with his wife and family. His hobbies include watching sports, reading science fiction, and pretending he is not letting his six-year-old son beat him in video games.

THE NAVAL INSTITUTE PRESS is the book-publishing arm of the U.S. Naval Institute, a private, nonprofit, membership society for sea service professionals and others who share an interest in naval and maritime affairs. Established in 1873 at the U.S. Naval Academy in Annapolis, Maryland, where its offices remain today, the Naval Institute has members worldwide.

Members of the Naval Institute support the education programs of the society and receive the influential monthly magazine *Proceedings* or the colorful bimonthly magazine *Naval History* and discounts on fine nautical prints and on ship and aircraft photos. They also have access to the transcripts of the Institute's Oral History Program and get discounted admission to any of the Institute-sponsored seminars offered around the country.

The Naval Institute's book-publishing program, begun in 1898 with basic guides to naval practices, has broadened its scope to include books of more general interest. Now the Naval Institute Press publishes about seventy titles each year, ranging from how-to books on boating and navigation to battle histories, biographies, ship and aircraft guides, and novels. Institute members receive significant discounts on the Press' more than eight hundred books in print.

Full-time students are eligible for special half-price membership rates. Life memberships are also available.

For more information about Naval Institute Press books that are currently available, visit www.usni.org/press/books. To learn about joining the U.S. Naval Institute, please write to:

Member Services
U.S. NAVAL INSTITUTE
291 Wood Road
Annapolis, MD 21402-5034

Telephone: (800) 233-8764
Fax: (410) 571-1703
Web address: www.usni.org